## DATE DUE

| JUN 2 5 2015 | |
|---|---|
| | |
| | |
| | |
| | |
| | |
| | |
| | |
| | |
| | |
| | |
| | |
| | |
| | |
| | |
| | |

BRODART, CO.  Cat. No. 23-221

D1087418

# Black Victory

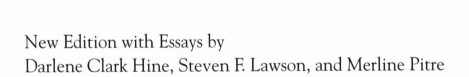

New Edition with Essays by
Darlene Clark Hine, Steven F. Lawson, and Merline Pitre

# Black Victory

## The Rise and Fall of the White Primary in Texas

Darlene Clark Hine

University of Missouri Press
Columbia and London

Copyright © 1979, 2003 by
The Curators of the University of Missouri
University of Missouri Press, Columbia, Missouri 65201
Printed and bound in the United States of America
All rights reserved
5 4 3 2 1   07 06 05 04 03

Library of Congress Cataloging-in-Publication Data

Hine, Darlene Clark.
    Black victory : the rise and fall of the white primary in
Texas / Darlene Clark Hine.—New ed. / with essays by
Darlene Clark Hine, Steven F. Lawson, and Merline Pitre.
            p. cm.
    Includes bibliographical references and index.
    ISBN 0-8262-1462-2 (alk. paper)
    1. African-Americans—Suffrage—Texas—History.
2. Primaries—Texas—Case studies.   I. Lawson, Steven
F., 1945–   II. Pitre, Merline, 1943–   III. Title.

KFT1620.85.S9H56 2003
324.6'2'08996073076409041—dc21

                                    2003042641

⊗™ This paper meets the requirements of the
American National Standard for Permanence of Paper
for Printed Library Materials, Z39.48, 1984.

Designer: Jennifer Cropp
Typesetter: The Composing Room of Michigan, Inc.
Printer and binder: Thomson-Shore, Inc.
Typefaces: Minion, Matura

# Dedicated to
Robbie Davine

# Contents

# Acknowledgments
## to the 2003 Edition

Without the University of Missouri Press's Director Beverly Jarrett's enthusiasm and encouragement, this new edition of *Black Victory* would not exist. I am especially pleased that the Press was able to release this new edition to coincide with my presidency of the Southern Historical Association (2002–2003). Moreover, Beverly Jarrett and the University of Missouri Press have remained unflagging in their support of the Southern Association of Women Historians. The press has published all of the Southern Association of Women Historians' superb conference anthologies, which include substantial articles in black women's history. Thus, for a multiplicity of reasons, I am enormously grateful to Beverly Jarrett and to her splendid colleagues at the University of Missouri Press.

I count high among the many blessings of my life and career the friendship and scholarship of Steven F. Lawson and Merline Pitre. They were willing to set aside innumerable administrative, professional, and teaching obligations to collaborate on the preparation of this edition. Their insightful reflections on *Black Victory* helped to launch the magnificent kinds of conversations that we all need in order to grow intellectually and politically. I am grateful for their inspiration and sacrifice.

I owe a special debt to my graduate assistant, Marshanda Smith, for scanning *Black Victory* and making copies available to the press and outside reviewers. Similarly, my assistant, Theresa Marquez, typed my essay and oversaw the final preparation of the book. I treasure her many contributions to this project. My family—sisters Barbara and Alma, and daughter, Robbie—remain essential to my life and work. William C. Hine believes *Black Victory* to be the best thing I have produced. I appreciate his faith and wisdom.

Finally, I thank Michigan State University for supporting my work in southern history, comparative black history, and my presidency of the Southern Historical Association. My MSU colleagues Harold Marcus, David Robinson,

Daina Ramey-Berry, Richard Thomas, David Bailey, William Hixson, and Gordon Stewart, and graduate students Jacqueline McLeod, Felix Armfield, Randal Jelks, Matthew Whitaker, and Carmen Harris, are deeply appreciated. I am grateful for the intellectual stimulation and for the good times we have shared.

# Black Victory

# Collaboration and Conversations

## Revisioning *Black Victory*

### Darlene Clark Hine

In November 1973, I interviewed Judge William H. Hastie, in his chambers in the Third Circuit Court of Appeals in Philadelphia, about the National Association for the Advancement of Colored People's (NAACP) campaign to end white disfranchisement of black southerners. After I turned off the tape recorder and prepared to leave I told the judge that I was pleased with, yet perplexed by, the warm and welcoming reception I had consistently received from remarkably forthcoming Texans who had been active in the campaign to overthrow the white primary. I confided that he, too, seemed to have been truly delighted to talk to me. I wondered aloud, "Why?" As I waited for his response, a smile lit up his handsome and dignified face. He said, simply, "We are happy to see and to talk to you, Ms. Hine, because we did it all for you." I thanked him, confident that I would never fully comprehend the full import of his words or act on the implicit challenge conveyed.

I did understand the heart of Hastie's succinct review of the white primary campaign. White Texans, ever mindful of the potential of the black electorate to hold the balance of power when white people divided, were determined to eliminate black ballots. Absent the vote, black Americans remain vulnerable to the negative consequences of the concentration of enormous political, social, and economic power in the hands of white adversaries. For decades Afro-Texans waged a relentless struggle to end their exclusion from membership in the Democratic party and to claim the right to participate in the party's primary elections.

It has taken me longer, however, fully to appreciate what Judge Hastie, Thurgood Marshall, and an array of activist black Texans that included James Nabrit, Carter Wesley, L. A. Nixon, Lonnie Smith, Richard Randolph Grovey, Julius and Lulu White, and others did, not only for me, but for the nation, in their successful struggle for black ballots. I wrote the dissertation under the direction of August Meier and published it, with assistance from Harold Hyman and Harold Woodman, as *Black Victory: The Rise and Fall of the White Primary in Texas* (1979). After receiving tenure and promotion at Purdue University, I became involved in various projects concerning the history of black women and the history of African Americans in medicine, nursing, and law and moved away from the study of black political history in the South.[1] Although my intellectual pursuits shifted from political issues and the white primary, Judge Hastie's words reverberated in my mind. What more was I supposed to do or say about the history of disfranchisement and the significance of the black struggle to retrieve the right to vote lost after the collapse of the first Reconstruction? How could I acknowledge the gift and honor the debt? The process of revisiting *Black Victory* has helped to answer both questions.

This is a propitious juncture in which to release a new edition of a study of black resistance to disfranchisement first published a quarter of a century ago. Many historical studies have examined the spectrum of ingenious and simplistic disfranchisement schemes that included the poll tax, literacy tests, and grandfather clauses. Black southerners and the legal staff of the NAACP demonstrated unwavering commitment to fight every infringement on their right to vote. It took decades for the NAACP attorneys to win the United States Supreme Court *Smith* v. *Allwright* decision outlawing the "white primary." In 1944 the Supreme Court repudiated the claims of the Democratic party to be a private organization open only to white members who were therefore eligible to vote in its primary elections. In Texas (as in Virginia, Florida, and Arkansas), the only election that truly mattered was the primary.

To be denied the right to vote or to have the ballot tossed is an egregious assault on the democratic claims of our society. Judge Hastie's words echoed as I watched the debacle of the 2000 presidential election and listened to the chilling stories of black disfranchisement and attendant allegations of voting irregularities in Florida. In this context, the history of the black struggle against the white primary harbors lessons worth revisiting. Since the passage of the 1965 Voting Rights Act, I, like many Americans, assumed that the disfranchisement of black people was a thing of the past. The victorious U.S. Supreme Court decision in *Smith* v. *Allwright,* in 1944, and the passage of the Voting Rights Act of 1965 invited sanguinity. The 2000 election, however, reminded us all that revolutions can and sometimes do go backward. I became more de-

1. Darlene Clark Hine, *Black Women in White: Racial Conflict and Cooperation in the Nursing Profession, 1890–1950* (Bloomington: Indiana University Press, 1989).

termined to release a new edition of *Black Victory* in the wake of the ill-fated 2000 presidential election.[2] I reasoned that perhaps this account of an earlier black struggle to retrieve the vote may help to thwart alienation, cynicism, or inclination to disengage from the political process. The disfranchisement of any group in the American polity is a cause for alarm and warrants sustained scrutiny.

Although there were documented irregularities in other states during the 2000 elections, the Florida disputes captured the country's attention as it engaged the nation's judiciary in political affairs to an unprecedented degree. George Bush received the Florida electoral college votes and assumed the presidency of the United States despite having lost the popular election to Vice President Albert Gore.[3] Ensuing national events, most notably the terrorist attack of September 11, 2001, and, to a lesser extent, the implosion of several giant corporations such as Enron and Global Crossing that threw the economy into a downward spiral, forced the 2000 election controversy to the back burner, and muted public discourse. The disquiet that percolates beneath the surface, however, still rankles those of us who remain sensitive to issues of social justice and concerned about racial inequality. It is imperative that conversations about the sanctity of the ballot continue.

At the center of *Black Victory* is the African American community in Texas, most especially the professional, entrepreneurial, and political vanguard. The black lawyers, business professionals, newspaper editors, and medical practitioners provided essential local leadership. These men and women improvised strategies, defined objectives, inspired and mobilized fellow citizens, raised money, and bridged the chasm between the local and state NAACP and national headquarters. A professional cadre of black lawyers and white allies mobilized support, raised funds, and prepared arguments in the early cases. To be sure, internal tensions in black Texas often frustrated the NAACP attorneys in New York, especially Thurgood Marshall, as the campaign unfolded in the 1930s and 1940s. In *Black Victory,* I sought to understand the culture of black struggle and the mechanisms of black mobilization at the state and local levels.

2. For a discussion of the election of 2000 from diverse historical perspectives, see Joanne Meyerowitz, ed., "Elections, Conflict, and Democracy: A Round Table," *Journal of American History* 88, no. 2 (September 2001): 407–54.

3. Michael J. Klarman, "*Bush* v. *Gore,* through the Lens of Constitutional History," *California Law Review* 89, no. 6 (December 2001): 1721–65; Mary Frances Berry, "Diluting the Vote: The Irony of *Bush* v. *Gore,*" *Journal of American History* 88, no. 2 (September 2001): 436–43.

One of the truisms that emerged from the classic Civil Rights movement of the 1950s and 1960s was the often repeated admonition that "Freedom is a constant struggle." The cause of freedom and the sustaining of hope and vigilance are fortified by an appreciation of past struggles waged by unsung and often obscure local people, many of whom are women. When I was interviewing black Texans and NAACP attorneys for *Black Victory,* I had little understanding or appreciation of the value of black women's contributions to the development of the whole legal campaign to overthrow the white primary and of their work to transform the NAACP into one of the most successful civil rights organizations in twentieth-century America. Thanks to historian Merline Pitre's biography of Lulu White and the work of other scholars in black women's studies, a gendered analysis of the Texas white primary campaign and of southern black politics is now within reach.[4] There is still much more to do. Similarly, thanks to the civil rights studies by historian Steven F. Lawson and several pivotal works of other scholars, a more sophisticated and nuanced analysis of the processes and politics of protest within state and local communities is available.[5] Historians are devoting more attention to microstudies of small communities and individuals whose multiclass and interracial movements affect the macropolitics of social change.

4. See Rosalyn Terborg-Penn, *African American Women in the Struggle for the Vote, 1850– 1920* (Bloomington: Indiana University Press, 1998); Deborah Gray White, *Too Heavy a Load: Black Women in Defense of Themselves* (New York: Norton, 1999); Margo Perkins, *Autobiography of Activism: Three Black Women of the Sixties* (Jackson: University Press of Mississippi, 2000); Cynthia Griggs Fleming, *Soon We Will Not Cry: The Liberation of Ruby Doris Robinson* (Lanham, Md.: Rowman and Littlefield, 1998); China Kai Lee, *For Freedom's Sake: The Life of Fannie Lou Hamer* (Urbana: University of Illinois Press, 1999); JoAnn Grant, *Ella Baker, Freedom Bound* (New York: John Wiley and Sons, 1998); Kay Mills, *This Little Light of Mine: The Life of Fannie Lou Hamer* (New York: Penguin, 1993); JoAnn Gibson Robinson, *The Montgomery Bus Boycott and the Women Who Started It: The Memoir of JoAnn Gibson Robinson* (Knoxville: University of Tennessee Press, 1987); Septima Clark, *Ready from Within: Septima Clark and the Civil Rights Movement* (Navarro, Calif.: Wild Tree Press, 1986); Belinda Robnett, *How Long? How Long? African-American Women in the Struggle for Civil Rights* (New York: Oxford University Press, 1997); and Lorraine N. Spritzer and Jean B. Bergmark, *Grace Townes Hamilton and the Politics of Southern Change* (Athens: University of Georgia Press, 1997).

5. See Aldon D. Morris, *The Origins of the Civil Rights Movement: Black Communities Organizing for Change* (New York: Free Press, 1984); John Dittmer, *Local People: The Struggle for Civil Rights in Mississippi* (Urbana: University of Illinois Press, 1994); Charles M. Payne, *I've Got the Light of Freedom: The Organizing Tradition and the Mississippi Freedom Struggle* (Berkeley: University of California Press, 1991); Jack M. Bloom, *Class, Race, and the Civil Rights Movement* (Bloomington: Indiana University Press, 1987); and Adam Fairclough, *Race and Democracy: The Civil Rights Struggle in Louisiana, 1915–1972* (Athens: University of Georgia Press, 1995).

This edition of *Black Victory* avoids the "old wine in a new bottle" trap thanks to the addition of Lawson's and Pitre's contributions of new spirits. To say that I am grateful to Steven F. Lawson, of Rutgers University, and Merline Pitre, of Texas Southern University, for their reflections and retrospection is to understate the case. These friends and fellow southern historians enthusiastically collaborated in launching a new conversation about *Black Victory*. Lawson and Pitre prepared illuminating essays about larger historiographical issues and various themes in southern political history. They raised questions about the intersection of race, gender, and class and the connections between the local and the national. Steven Lawson and Merline Pitre, in sharing their reflections, extend the shelf life of *Black Victory*. Together, our collaboration and ongoing conversation underscores the importance of understanding how micromobilization generated macrotransformation in the nation's politics. The essays, including my own, also indicate the different historiographical lineages and contexts in which it is possible to situate *Black Victory*.

Lawson calls for a closing of the gap between the nation's democratic promise and its racist reality. For most of the twentieth century, African Americans struggled to reconstruct each state in the South in order to expand economic and political democracy in the region. An interconnected approach to the history of the Civil Rights movement links local struggles with national consequences. Black Americans inextricably associated suffrage with improvement in education, access to decent housing, and protection from abuse. The ballot was the centerpiece of a multifaceted campaign to end white supremacy. As Lawson observed, "Having fought hard and sacrificed much to obtain the right to vote, southern blacks did not regard it lightly as a weapon for liberation."[6]

Lawson comments subtly on one of the core emphases in *Black Victory*. He chides me and other historians to reject notions that locate power to effect racial change only in the social group of professional, entrepreneurial, and political elites. Rather, it is important to give more prominence to the unsung efforts and contributions of local communities, of civic and social organizations, and of indigenous citizens who used an array of tactics to end white supremacists' hydra-headed constriction of the black electorate. Significantly, Lawson reminds us that *Smith* v. *Allwright* (1944) did not end the violent intimidations and quasi-legal subterfuges that shackled black Americans to

---

6. Steven F. Lawson, *In Pursuit of Power: Southern Blacks and Electoral Politics, 1965–1982* (New York: Columbia University Press, 1985), 295; see also Lawson's *Black Ballots: Voting Rights in the South, 1944–1969* (New York: Columbia University Press, 1976).

second-class citizenship. Rather, it was one of the many precursors to the achievements of the classic Civil Rights movement, notably, the passage of the Voting Rights Act of 1965, which within four years raised the enrollment of southern black registered voters from 58 percent to 83 percent. Throughout the body of his impressive and voluminous scholarship, Lawson has admirably explored how African Americans with persistence, creativity, and courage peeled off the many layers of restrictions that white southerners constructed to keep black ballots at bay.

As Steven Lawson notes in his reflections on *Black Victory,* until recently, only a small number of scholars have subjected the NAACP to extensive treatment. Indeed, with few exceptions, most of us have virtually ignored the nation's oldest continuing civil rights group.[7] The neglect of the NAACP may be a thing of the past. The 1990s registered many new studies of the NAACP and of its various leaders. Law professors, journalists, and biographers published several insightful volumes on select NAACP legal campaigns. The careers of black lawyers, especially ones active in the 1930s through 1950s, have attracted the most attention. There is room for more work in this area. I can envision graduate seminars, symposia, and anthologies on the history of the NAACP. The accessible microfilm versions of the NAACP papers, edited by August Meier and John Bracey, eases the research difficulties.

The current scholarship on the NAACP falls into three categories: articles published in law journals, biographies of famous lawyers, and studies of specific campaigns. Law professor Michael J. Klarman has conducted exhaustive research in the NAACP papers and has published an illuminating account of white resistance to the U.S. Supreme Court's decision in *Smith* v. *Allwright.* Similarly, law professor Susan D. Carle has focused on the early litigation campaigns of the Legal Redress Committee of the NAACP.[8] Historians have published several noteworthy studies of the NAACP, including Robert L. Zangrando's *The NAACP Crusade against Lynching, 1909–1950* (1980); Richard C. Cortner's *A Mob Intent on Death: The NAACP and the Arkansas Riot Case* (1988); Kenneth W. Going's *The NAACP Comes of Age: The Defeat of Judge John*

---

7. A past president of the SHA, August Meier, however, made the NAACP the topic of his presidential address.

8. Michael J. Klarman, "The White Primary Rulings: A Case Study in the Consequences of Supreme Court Decisionmaking," *Florida State University Law Review* 29, no. 1 (fall 2001): 55–109; Susan D. Carle, "Race, Class, and Legal Ethics in the Early NAACP, 1910–1920," *Race and History Review* 20 (spring 2002): 97–151; Susan D. Carle, "From *Buchanan* to *Button:* Legal Ethics and the NAACP (Part II)," *University of Chicago Law School Roundtable* 8 (2001): 281–311.

*J. Parker* (1990), and Christopher Robert Reed's *The Chicago NAACP and the Rise of Black Professional Leadership, 1910–1966* (1997).[9]

Biographies of leading NAACP lawyers have enriched our understanding of the development of specific legal challenges to white supremacy, while illuminating the personal costs extracted. Shortly after *Black Victory* was published, Genna Rae McNeil's *Groundwork: Charles Hamilton Houston and the Struggle for Civil Rights* (1983) and Gilbert Ware's *William Hastie: Grace under Pressure* (1984) appeared. In 1994 Mark V. Tushnet followed his study of the NAACP's campaign against segregated education with a study of Thurgood Marshall's career during his years at the helm of the Legal Defense and Education Fund of the NAACP.[10] Three additional biographies of Thurgood Marshall were published by the end of the 1990s: Roger Godman with David Galler, *Thurgood Marshall: Justice for All* (1992); Michael Davis and Hunter Clark, *Thurgood Marshall: Warrior at the Bar, Rebel on the Bench* (1992); and Juan Williams, *Thurgood Marshall: American Revolutionary* (1998). Important new works underscore the need for more critical analyses of the NAACP's treatment of its branches and its dealings with local leaders who challenged its ideological hegemony. A provocative reassessment of the NAACP is advanced in Timothy B. Tyson's *Radio Free Dixie: Robert F. Williams and the Roots of Black Power* (1999). Finally, there exists considerable need, and opportunity, for a full-scale investigation of the participation of black women in the NAACP's state and local branches and in its national headquarters.

Merline Pitre's retrospective examination of *Black Victory* calls for equal consideration of the complex role of black women in the challenge to white supremacist politics at the state and national levels.[11] Pitre rescued Lulu White from her undeserved obscurity in *Black Victory* and persuasively demonstrated the importance of White's leadership in the white primary campaign. Pitre's expert scholarship and her reflections on both the shortcomings and strengths

9. For detailed information on hundreds of black lawyers, see J. Clay Smith, *Emancipation: The Making of the Black Lawyer: 1844–1944* (Philadelphia: University of Pennsylvania Press, 1993).

10. Mark V. Tushnet, *Making Civil Rights Law: Thurgood Marshall and the Supreme Court, 1936–1961* (New York: Oxford University Press, 1994); see also Mark V. Tushnet, *The NAACP's Legal Strategy against Segregated Education, 1925–1950* (Chapel Hill: University of North Carolina Press, 1987).

11. See Merline Pitre, *In Struggle against Jim Crow: Lulu B. White and the NAACP, 1900–1957* (College Station: Texas A&M University Press, 1999). In the preface of her book, Pitre declares "to be black was 'to struggle to struggle'—to struggle to salvage the 'self,' to struggle against racial and gender stereotypes in order to struggle against prejudice, injustice, and hatred. Lulu White's life story is reflective of this collective memory of Jim Crow" (xi).

of *Black Victory* suggest the value of a gendered analysis of leadership, community mobilization, and organizational development.

The gendered responses of black men and women to disfranchisement reflect a shared commitment to regaining the ballot, but for different reasons. We need to probe the connections between black men's relentless struggle for the vote and their definition of manhood. To be a man equaled the ability to exercise all the rights and privileges of citizenship, most especially the vote. Black women often equated the ballot with security and justice and with access to better schools and economic opportunity. It bears reiteration that the black community has never been monolithic, yet virtually every member of it has experienced some manifestation of racism and the attendant unequal distribution of power and resources. Black men and women collaborated in the campaign to overthrow the white primary, but this should not blind us to the different ways in which they contributed.

Pitre reminds us that the internal class structure and the gender dynamics of the black community helped to shape and to complicate the culture of struggle against white supremacy ideology, institutions, and violence. Internal conflicts and external forces combined to disrupt community coherence and to make effective struggle more difficult. Black women were instrumental, as Pitre and others have proven, in deploying their skills to build and to use coalitions for any given cause. Black women counterparts to Lulu White in every southern state orchestrated fund-raising drives, devised strategies, defined objectives, and attended to the daily operational demands of wide-ranging local, state, and national organizations such as the NAACP.

The time is ripe for what we might term a "Third Reconstruction" and a fully mobilized registered national black electorate. Meanwhile, revisiting *Black Victory* will help us to envision a future course of action that preserves black ballots and safeguards the democratic process. A generation ago, in an insightful assessment, a political organizer in Mississippi, Lawrence Guyet, declared that "the number of victories isn't as important as the fact that they symbolize a bit of black authority, a gradual return to respect for those accustomed to having their lives manipulated by white hands."[12] A Third Reconstruction that ends white political manipulation and devises strategies effectively to meet the economic and political needs of diverse African Americans in the twenty-first century is what we must do for those yet to come.

---

12. Quoted in Lawson, *Pursuit of Power,* 303.

# Reflection on Darlene Clark Hine's *Black Victory*

## Steven F. Lawson

The publication of *Black Victory* in 1979 marked an important crossroads in the study of the Civil Rights movement and black politics. Looking back, it is easier to see this now than it was at the time. Until the mid-1970s, less than a decade after the civil rights struggle had reached its peak, most of the books written about the movement had focused on legislative battles in Congress, famous national leaders such as Martin Luther King, Jr., the role of the presidency in shaping the freedom agenda, and the adjudication of the Supreme Court in resolving disputes in education and housing.[1] Perhaps because much of the story was contemporary and had barely concluded, historians for the most part left the writing to political scientists and journalists. Darlene Clark Hine's volume reflected a move then underway by historians to become more seriously engaged in chronicling and evaluating the origins, development, successes, and shortcomings of the greatest reform effort of the twentieth century: the campaign to achieve racial equality and overthrow white supremacy.

---

1. For example, J. W. Anderson, *Eisenhower, Brownell, and the Congress: The Tangled Origins of the Civil Rights Bill of 1956–1957* (University, Ala.: University of Alabama Press, 1964); Daniel M. Berman, *A Bill Becomes a Law* (New York: MacMillan, 1966); Anthony Lewis, *Portrait of a Decade* (New York: Random House, 1966); David L. Lewis, *King: A Critical Biography* (New York: Praeger, 1970); Richard P. Longaker, *The Presidency and Individual Liberties* (Ithaca: Cornell University Press, 1961); Benjamin Muse, *Ten Years of Prelude: The Story of Integration since the Supreme Court's 1954 Decision* (New York: Viking Press, 1964); Victor Navasky, *Kennedy Justice* (New York: Atheneum, 1971); L. D. Reddick, *Crusader without Violence: A Biography of Martin Luther King, Jr.* (New York: Harper, 1959); and James L. Sundquist, *Politics and Policy: The Eisenhower, Kennedy, and Johnson Years* (Washington, D.C.: Brookings Institute, 1968).

## The Origins of *Black Victory*

Not all of the early books looked at the problems facing African Americans and their efforts to challenge them solely from the perspective of the national arena. Perhaps the earliest comprehensive study of discrimination against African Americans was Gunnar Myrdal's *An American Dilemma*. Sponsored by the Carnegie Corporation, the Swedish economist employed a team of researchers, including prominent black scholars, such as the political scientist Ralph Bunche and the sociologist E. Franklin Frazier, to investigate the so-called Negro problem. Started in 1938 and completed in 1944, *An American Dilemma* laid the blame for racial inequality on the nation's failure to live up to its own democratic creed and moral conscience. Myrdal's researchers conducted in-depth probes of black communities in the North and South, and Bunche produced an insightful report that explored black suffrage in the South and found some hopeful signs for expanding it. The book recommended the abolition of the poll tax and the enfranchisement of black southerners, the use of the courts to enforce the Fourteenth Amendment, and expanded efforts by the federal government to provide economic assistance in employment and pave the way for desegregation in housing. Despite his call for increased governmental programs and his awareness of the World War II–era rise in black militancy, Myrdal relied mainly upon white Americans to see the error of their racial ways, soothe their guilty consciences, and close the gap between the nation's democratic promise and its racist reality.[2]

Five years later, the political scientist V. O. Key's magisterial *Southern Politics in State and Nation* meticulously reviewed the political systems of the eleven former states of the Confederacy. Each preserved one-party Democratic domination by excluding southern blacks and a substantial portion of the poor-white population from electoral participation. Key's hefty volume combined the microscopic study of state and local politics with ample discussion of the impact that southern white lawmakers in Congress had in shaping national affairs and stifling reform efforts to expand economic and political democracy in the region. Key carefully cataloged the various electoral barriers

2. Gunnar Myrdal, *An American Dilemma: The Negro Problem and Modern Democracy* (New York: Harper and Brothers, 1944); Walter A. Jackson, *Gunnar Myrdal and America's Conscience: Social Engineering and Racial Liberalism, 1938–1987* (Chapel Hill: University of North Carolina Press, 1990), 230; David W. Southern, *Gunnar Myrdal and Black-White Relations: The Use and Abuse of an American Dilemma, 1944–1969* (Baton Rouge: Louisiana State University Press, 1987), 69; Ralph Bunche, Jr., *Political Status of the Negro in the Age of FDR*, ed. Dewey W. Grantham (Chicago: University of Chicago Press, 1973).

that prevented some 95 percent of adult African Americans living in the South from exercising the ballot. Literacy tests, understanding clauses, the Democratic white primary, and outright intimidation had devastating effects in disfranchising black citizens, while poll taxes impeded the poor of both races. For all of his astute observations and analyses, Key, like Myrdal, did not foresee the rise of the Civil Rights movement as the chief means of eradicating racial inequality. Indeed, he did not envision African Americans as the centerpiece of the rejuvenation of southern politics. "[T]he Negro is not in the normal course in the forefront of the debate," he concluded. "Rather the presence of the Negro has created conditions under which the political process operates."[3] Key did not envision the Civil Rights movement or federal intervention rehabilitating the South; instead, he predicted that urbanization, industrialization, and the decline of the black population through outmigration to the North and West would usher in progressive change to Dixie. Nevertheless, Key's book provided a model for a succeeding generation of scholars, who did recognize the centrality of the African American liberation struggle in reconstructing the South, to explore both the national and local scenes.

One of the early examples of this interconnective approach was Clement E. Vose's *Caucasians Only: The Supreme Court, the NAACP, and the Restrictive Covenant Cases,* published in 1959. A political scientist, Vose focused on the single issue of housing discrimination, specifically racial covenants. Written into homeowners' deeds, these restrictive clauses prevented sellers from transferring their property to members of designated racial and religious minorities in perpetuity. The courts had upheld these arrangements as private negotiations between individuals and held that they did not violate the Fourteenth Amendment's prohibition against racial discrimination by state agencies. Vose detailed the efforts of the NAACP and local black lawyers to convince the Supreme Court to reverse itself, which it did in 1948, ruling that such covenants contravened the Fourteenth Amendment because municipal and state courts enforced them. The book traced the initiation of the lawsuit from St. Louis, Missouri, to its settlement in Washington, D.C., where the Supreme Court decided in favor of the black plaintiffs in *Shelley* v. *Kraemer.* In connecting events at the local level with those at the national, this volume also spotlighted the effort of the Truman administration in filing an *amicus curiae* brief with the Supreme Court. By throwing the White House's considerable weight behind African Americans, President Harry S. Truman was signaling a

---

3. V. O. Key, Jr., *Southern Politics in State and Nation* (1949; new ed., Knoxville: University of Tennessee Press, 1984), 671.

break from his predecessors in placing the national government on the side of racial equality. Indeed, in 1947, the President's Committee on Civil Rights had issued its landmark report, *To Secure These Rights,* recommending the elimination of restrictive covenants.[4]

Vose broke new ground by concentrating on black litigants at the local level while linking their cause to national institutions; however, he was not primarily interested in exploring the Civil Rights movement. As a political scientist and a scholar of judicial decision making, the author was more concerned with "the role of interest groups in the judicial process." To this end, he sought "to investigate the interplay of historical forces in recent constitutional development."[5] The civil rights issue of racial covenants became the focus of this case study, but the overarching goal was to demonstrate that the Supreme Court was a political as well as a legal institution, and organized groups greatly affected its behavior. To a large extent, *Caucasians Only* provided a model for the construction of *Black Victory;* yet the appearance of the latter work would represent a shift in emphasis from studying political and legal structures to investigating the black freedom movement itself.

As mentioned above, civil rights studies published contemporaneously with and shortly after the heyday of the movement tended to highlight national organizations and leaders. Three excellent books by historians among the outpouring of works in the 1960s and 1970s underscore this point. William C. Berman (1970) and Donald R. McCoy and Richard T. Reutten (1973) published studies of the Truman administration and civil rights. Berman's work was far more critical of Truman's performance than was McCoy and Reutten's, but both volumes highlighted the importance of federal action in launching the movement. In 1977, Carl M. Brauer wrote a favorable account of the Kennedy administration's approach to civil rights during a period when the freedom struggle accelerated into high gear.[6] Overall, these monographs reinforced the impression that the power to effect racial change was exercised from the top down by pluralistic elites in the nation's capital, albeit responding to increasingly unsettling black demands. More than the scholarship of political

---

4. Clement E. Vose, *Caucasians Only: The Supreme Court, the NAACP, and the Restrictive Covenant Cases* (Berkeley: University of California Press, 1959).

5. Ibid., ix.

6. William C. Berman, *The Politics of Civil Rights in the Truman Administration* (Columbus: Ohio State University Press, 1970); Donald R. McCoy and Richard T. Reutten, *Quest and Response: Minority Rights and the Truman Administration* (Lawrence: University Press of Kansas, 1973); and Carl M. Brauer, *John F. Kennedy and the Second Reconstruction* (New York: Columbia University Press, 1977).

and social scientists in the 1940s and 1950s, these historical assessments acknowledged the significance of African American protest. However, in examining this history through the lens of presidential administrations, they did not sufficiently capture political and social developments in southern black communities that gave the Civil Rights movement the strength to force intervention from the traditionally complacent federal government. To do this, writers had to expand both their temporal and geographic sights, ranging back over time and readjusting the balance between national and grassroots coverage.

Several contributions in the mid-1970s aided this attempt. The journalist Howell Raines compiled oral history interviews with proponents, opponents, and observers of the Civil Rights movement from 1955 to 1968 in his book *My Soul Is Rested*.[7] Although following what had become the traditional chronology of the liberation struggle, Raines published conversations with many people who, unlike Martin Luther King, Jr., had not become household names. He demonstrated that oral history could reveal stories from people who were as responsible as Dr. King for advancing the battle against white supremacy but who were far less heralded. In so doing, Raines helped popularize the value of oral history, which many scholars were using as a means of investigating the social and political history of so-called ordinary people.

Another journalist, Richard Kluger, in his splendid book *Simple Justice*, effectively exhibited the use of oral history to uncover hidden stories in grassroots communities and connect them to critical events at the national level.[8] This 1975 tome explored the five cases that constituted the monumental decision in *Brown* v. *Board of Education* (1954). Not just an examination of the years surrounding the case, *Simple Justice* was a tour de force based on archival records, government documents, and oral interviews that charted the two-hundred-year freedom struggle central to African American history. Lawyers, plaintiffs, witnesses, students, teachers, common laborers, preachers, men, and women—the backbone of black communities—came to life in the pages of this book to illuminate the indigenous sources of power that propelled the Civil Rights movement into life. In no-less-exhaustive fashion, Kluger paid equal attention to the operation of the federal judiciary in responding to black lawsuits for educational equality. To a much greater extent than did Vose, he

7. Howell Raines, *My Soul Is Rested: Movement Days in the Deep South Remembered* (New York: G. P. Putnam's Sons, 1977).

8. Richard Kluger, *Simple Justice: The History of* Brown *v.* Board of Education *and Black America's Struggle for Equality* (New York: Knopf, 1975).

brought the inner workings of the Supreme Court to light and penetrated the politics and principles of the sitting justices. The book remains unmatched as a portrait of a complex civil rights history that juxtaposes the national with the local, the social with the political and legal, and the prominent with the unsung leaders.

By concentrating on the issue of education, Kluger could more easily track the evolution of black attempts to break down racial inequality over a long period of time. Vose too had employed the single-issue approach, though his focus on civil rights was admittedly narrower. The strategy of accentuating one aspect of the civil rights struggle to provide an in-depth account of change and continuity over time was taken up in my *Black Ballots: Voting Rights in the South, 1944–1969.*[9] Published a year after *Simple Justice,* this volume traces the disfranchisement of black citizens in the decades following Reconstruction and the slow, episodic efforts from the 1940s through the 1960s to restore the ballot to African American men and women. In the tradition of Key and Vose, I attempted to show how the executive, legislative, and judicial branches of the national government both responded to and shaped demands for first-class citizenship. Yet my aim was not exclusively to dissect and analyze the functioning of the political and legal systems or develop theories about interest-group behavior. I came to the project with the Civil Rights movement as my main concern. From the elimination of the white primary to the passage of the 1965 Voting Rights Act, the book details the multifaceted ways in which African Americans and their liberal white allies, whether in Washington, D.C., Greenwood, Mississippi, or Selma, Alabama, devised strategies and tactics to peel off the many layers of restrictions that white southerners had constructed to keep qualified blacks from exercising suffrage. Persistence, creativity, and solidarity allowed civil rights forces to sustain protest, to push the federal government to their side, and to keep up sufficient pressure to ensure that Washington did not retreat in the face of southern white intransigence.

Although a large portion of the book focused on the hammering out of legislative and legal remedies, it never lost track of the campaigns throughout the South to gain political tools for black communities to liberate themselves from white supremacy. In looking at black southerners as forceful agents of social change, *Black Ballots* stressed the importance of the vote to local people. African Americans derived meanings from the franchise that went beyond the formalistic process of turning out at the polls and performing their civic duty.

---

9. Steven F. Lawson, *Black Ballots: Voting Rights in the South, 1944–1969* (New York: Columbia University Press, 1976).

Suffrage meant not only acquisition of traditional citizenship but also mobilization for electoral participation to improve communities economically, educationally, residentially, and politically. I argued that exercising the right to vote unencumbered by racial discrimination, as first promised by the Fifteenth Amendment, was not a matter, as Kluger put it, of "simple justice." Otherwise, it would not have taken so long to achieve and resulted in so many deaths, reprisals, and confrontations.

In retrospect, one can see that *Black Victory* forms a triad with *Simple Justice* and *Black Ballots*. Published in 1979, Darlene Clark Hine's book, like the other two, deals with a single issue: obtaining the right to vote through the destruction of the white primary in Texas.[10] By looking at one state, Hine had an even greater opportunity to link the study of local communities with the national arena. She meticulously follows the twenty-year legal battle from the mid-1920s to the mid-1940s, which resulted in the eradication of the lily-white election in the contest that mattered most in the South of that period— the Democratic primary. Afro-Texans were absolutely correct in pursuing the ballot as a key element in their emancipation from the vestiges of slavery and Jim Crow. All they had to do was look at how hard white Texans tried to keep them away from the ballot boxes. Each time the Supreme Court struck down the Democrats' exclusionary rule, Lone Star politicos found a new way to evade the decision. That is until *Smith* v. *Allwright* in 1944, when the high tribunal shattered the last prop sustaining the white primary.

Had Hine's work merely discussed the nature of judicial decision making, it would not have gained the significance it deserves within the field of civil rights studies. The chief importance of the book derives from its attention to the efforts of black communities within Texas, especially Houston and El Paso, to mobilize their internal resources against systematic disfranchisement. As Hine writes, the "constant reminder of their political impotence goaded Texas blacks into developing community-based political organizations through which they persisted in attempts to gain entry into the political process."[11] In these pages, Lawrence A. Nixon, Richard R. Grovey, and Lonnie Smith become more than the names of plaintiffs on the Supreme Court docket; they emerge as palpable representatives of political and civic groups in black Texas. The notion of local and statewide communities as the core ingredient in the black liberation struggle finds expression in this volume. As one book reviewer com-

10. Darlene Clark Hine, *Black Victory: The Rise and Fall of the White Primary in Texas* (Millwood, N.Y.: KTO Press, 1979).
    11. Ibid., 155.

mented: "*Black Victory* demonstrates how the rise of black political awareness foreshadowed the civil rights movement and changed the political map in the 1950s and 1960s."[12]

Although Hine emphasizes the concept of community solidarity, she does not fall into the trap of presenting blacks as a monolithic group. She describes the conflicts between national NAACP attorneys and black Texas lawyers over who should handle the cases and how they should be developed. This problem did not simply arise from a bureaucratic turf war, but reflected the growing racial consciousness and political maturity of local black leaders and professionals. Indeed, Hine points out the irony that the exclusionary primary was originally conceived as "a basis for white solidarity, but the process of fighting to overturn it led to the unity of blacks."[13] Furthermore, her detailed investigation of the NAACP, both locally and nationally, paid welcome attention to the nation's oldest continuing civil rights group, an organization that over the past three decades most scholars have taken for granted and virtually ignored, with the exception of studies of school desegregation.

*Black Victory*, along with its immediate predecessors, outlined the intricate ways in which local struggles for racial advancement were intertwined with and mutually dependent on national leaders and institutions for their development and success.[14] However, much work remained undone. Certainly one of the areas that deserved much greater research was the role played by women. Ironically, Hine, who would emerge as one of the premier scholars of African American women, made no special reference to how local women helped mobilize community resources against the white primary, especially after 1920 when the Nineteenth Amendment conferred upon them the right to vote. In part women did not show up in these studies because they did not practice law or hold formal political and judicial leadership positions nationally or locally. Yet, as later inquiries into the Civil Rights movement revealed, women provided the backbone of the black liberation struggle through their familial, religious, and civic networks.[15]

Subsequently, with a greater orientation toward social than political or le-

12. Barry Crouch, review of *Black Victory*, in *Journal of American History* 68 (June 1981): 176.

13. Hine, *Black Victory*, 236.

14. I have argued this point at greater length in Steven F. Lawson and Charles Payne, *Debating the Civil Rights Movement, 1945–1968* (Lanham, Md.: Rowman and Littlefield, 1998), 3–42.

15. For example, see Belinda Robnett, *How Long? How Long? African-American Women in the Struggle for Civil Rights* (New York: Oxford University Press, 1997).

gal investigations, historians produced an ever-growing body of work focusing on community institutions and the uncelebrated people who pressured them to challenge white supremacy in the first place. Greensboro, North Carolina; Tuskegee, Alabama; St. Augustine and Tallahassee, Florida; Montgomery and Birmingham Alabama; the state of Mississippi and its Delta; and the state of Louisiana received attention not because they fit in with a larger national narrative of the Civil Rights movement, but because they had histories of their own that unfolded independently of events in Washington, D.C.[16] Over time, however, these works moved away from linking local with national experiences, creating as distorted a picture as those that give inadequate coverage to the grassroots story. Future scholars will be justifiably rewarded by building upon the interconnected approach to the history of the Civil Rights movement sketched out in *Black Victory.*

## The Legacy of *Smith* v. *Allwright*

According to Darlene Clark Hine, the victory in *Smith* v. *Allwright* "signaled the beginning of the so-called Second Reconstruction and the modern Civil Rights movement." As the saying goes, "victory finds a hundred fathers, but defeat is an orphan," and this applies to the Civil Rights movement.[17] Historians have credited a variety of "parents" for giving birth to the black freedom struggle. Besides those who toppled the white primary, the ancestors include Franklin Roosevelt's New Deal, A. Philip Randolph's March on Washington

16. William H. Chafe, *Civilities and Civil Rights: Greensboro, North Carolina, and the Struggle for Black Freedom* (New York: Oxford University Press, 1981); Robert J. Norrell, *Reaping the Whirlwind: The Civil Rights Movement in Tuskegee* (New York: Vintage, 1985); Charles Payne, *I've Got the Light of Freedom: The Organizing Tradition and the Mississippi Freedom Struggle* (Berkeley: University of California Press, 1995); John Dittmer, *Local People: The Struggle for Civil Rights in Mississippi* (Urbana: University of Illinois Press, 1994); David R. Colburn, *Racial Change and Community Crisis: St. Augustine, Florida, 1877–1980* (New York: Columbia University Press, 1985); Adam Fairclough, *Race and Democracy: The Civil Rights Struggle in Louisiana, 1915–1972* (Athens: University of Georgia Press, 1995); Glenda Alice Rabby, *The Pain and the Promise: The Struggle for Civil Rights in Tallahassee, Florida* (Athens: University of Georgia Press, 1999); Glen Eskew, *But for Birmingham: The Local and National Movements in the Civil Rights Struggle* (Chapel Hill: University of North Carolina Press, 1997).

17. Hine, *Black Victory,* 233. The saying is attributed to Count Galeazzo Ciano, September 9, 1942, and was quoted by President John F. Kennedy on April 21, 1961. See John Bartlett, *Familiar Quotations,* ed. Emily Morison Beck (Boston: Little, Brown, 1980), 857.

Movement, *Brown* v. *Board of Education,* and the Montgomery bus boycott.[18] A necessary part of the historical enterprise is finding origins of major events, but as in all such efforts, the Civil Rights movement's DNA comprises a multiplicity of causative markers. The movement for racial equality did not arise spontaneously but slowly gained momentum over the first half of the twentieth century. *Smith* v. *Allwright* provided an important boost in tearing down a major barrier impeding African Americans in the South from participating in the electoral process. Along with a series of other court victories obtained by the NAACP, it demonstrated the power of black communities working together with national organizations to swing the power of the federal government behind their goal of first-class citizenship. Without this Second Reconstruction, one that had much more staying power than its post–Civil War antecedent, the Civil Rights movement would have been stillborn.

The destruction of the white primary produced immediate, measurable improvement. Before the ruling, approximately 3 percent of eligible black southerners had managed to register to vote. In 1947, the figure had jumped to 12 percent, and by the end of the 1950s, about 29 percent had signed up to cast their ballots.[19] The Texas decision did not account for the entire increase, as voter registration drives, the removal of poll tax regulations in other states (Georgia, South Carolina, and Tennessee), and passage of the 1957 Civil Rights Act also had important effects.

The black victory, which Hine chronicles so well, turned out to be a necessary but insufficient step toward African American enfranchisement. *Smith* v. *Allwright* did not prove after all to be a second emancipation for the two-thirds of southern blacks who, by 1960, still could not vote. The ruling exposed the flaw of counting on the judiciary to tear down the great wall of white supremacy that spanned the South. However, the fault did not rest with the plaintiffs and their lawyers, who correctly understood that they could not achieve racial advancement without first reshaping the legal doctrines that sustained segregation and voting restrictions. The problem resulted from institutional and political considerations that retarded enforcement of poten-

18. See Harvard Sitkoff, *A New Deal for Blacks: The Emergence of Civil Rights as a National Issue: The Depression Decade* (New York: Oxford University Press, 1978); Patricia Sullivan, *Days of Hope: Race and Democracy in the New Deal Era* (Chapel Hill: University of North Carolina Press, 1996); Richard M. Dalfiume, "The 'Forgotten Years' of the Negro Revolution," *Journal of American History* 55 (June 1968): 90–106; Richard Kluger, *Simple Justice* (New York: Knopf, 1976); and Taylor Branch, *Parting the Waters: America in the King Years, 1954–63* (New York: Simon and Schuster, 1988).

19. Steven F. Lawson, *Running for Freedom: Civil Rights and Black Politics in America since 1941,* 2d ed. (New York: McGraw-Hill, 1997), 81.

tially liberating judicial decisions. The existence of a federal system of government meant that the Supreme Court deferred to federal district judges in the South, most of whom shared the prejudices of the white communities in which they lived. In a similar vein, presidential administrations yielded to state and local authorities in carrying out law enforcement and punishing crimes against civil rights activists, notwithstanding the fact that local authorities aided and abetted the troublemakers and lawbreakers. Democratic chief executives, including Harry S. Truman and John F. Kennedy, shied away from vigorously pressing their legislative civil rights agendas because they hesitated to alienate their party's southern representatives who wielded extraordinary power in Congress. Until the federal government enacted landmark legislation but also enforced it, the promises of judicial victories painfully won by African Americans remained unfulfilled.

Not until passage of the Voting Rights Act in 1965 did Washington affirm its commitment to waging the Second Reconstruction. Rather than relying on the judiciary, lawmakers singled out the seven southern states where the greatest problems existed, swept away the chief barriers—poll taxes and literacy tests—to electoral participation, and provided the Justice Department with extraordinary authority to monitor compliance, challenge new discriminatory procedures that might arise, and dispatch federal registrars to overcome any local resistance that persisted. The results were stunning. For the first time in a century, a majority of African Americans in the South qualified for suffrage, and by the end of the 1960s, the percentage of enrolled blacks approached two-thirds. Nowhere was progress swifter than in Mississippi, one of the covered states, which saw the percentage of black registrants soar from slightly under 7 percent in 1964 to just over 54 percent in 1968. Even in Texas, where the white primary had initially fallen but which did not come under the special, remedial provisions of the law, the Voting Rights Act helped stimulate black enrollment from 58 percent to 83 percent within four years.[20]

Despite this dramatic progress, civil rights advocates discovered that whites entrenched in power did not intend to relinquish it easily. In fact, even after passage of the Voting Rights Act and its successive renewals in 1970, 1975, and 1982, the struggle over political participation continued in the South in a different form. Literacy tests and poll taxes became relics of the past, but efforts to thwart voter registration did not end. Those who attempted to retard black enrollment did so in ways that made the process less convenient. However, the

---

20. The seven southern states were Alabama, Georgia, Louisiana, Mississippi, North Carolina, South Carolina, and Virginia; see ibid., 81, 223.

major point of contention no longer centered on voter registration but on vote dilution. From the late 1960s through the beginning of the next millennium, the remnants of the Civil Rights movement fought to defeat electoral rules that diminished the strength of black ballots. Some of these electoral obstacles had existed before the Voting Rights Act; others were fashioned after 1965 to deprive the newly enfranchised of fair representation on municipal, state, and federal governing bodies. Procedures such as at-large elections, instead of single-member districts, meant that in racially polarized contests, which existed extensively throughout the South, the odds of minority candidates winning office were slim if not impossible. In addition, white-controlled legislatures and assemblies had the power to reapportion these bodies in a manner that minimized the impact of the black electorate. They did so by fracturing contiguous black populations into separate districts that left them in the minority. Or, conversely, they clustered a large portion of black voters into one district where they held a majority, but reduced their potential power by not scattering them over two or more districts where they might have had sufficient strength to elect additional candidates of their choice.[21]

Starting in 1969, the Supreme Court ruled that the Voting Rights Act could be used to challenge electoral arrangements that were intended to or had the effect of diluting the African American vote. In effect, the majority of the Supreme Court decided that the 1965 law was not simply a voter registration statute but also applied to protecting the value of the ballots blacks cast. Thus, systems of representation that operated to handicap African Americans had to be reconfigured to allow blacks the opportunity to compete successfully for electoral office. As previous history had shown, it took a vigilant Civil Rights Division in the Justice Department and dedicated civil rights attorneys hired by private litigants to ensure the implementation of favorable Supreme Court decisions at the state and local levels. Over several decades, as reform efforts succeeded in replacing at-large elections with single-member districts and forced lawmakers to reapportion their legislatures to afford blacks increased representation and seats, the number of African American elected officials in the South zoomed from under seventy-five in 1965 to around five thousand by the turn of the century.[22]

21. Washington Research Project, *Shameful Blight: The Survival of Racial Discrimination in Voting in the South* (Washington, D.C., 1972); Frank R. Parker, *Black Votes Count: Political Empowerment in Mississippi after 1965* (Chapel Hill: University of North Carolina Press, 1990).
22. *Allen v. State Board of Elections* 393 U.S. 544 (1969); Steven F. Lawson, *In Pursuit of Power: Southern Black and Electoral Politics, 1965–1982* (New York: Columbia University

By the year 2002, while blacks did not risk losing their hard-earned right to vote or returning to the dark days following Reconstruction, they nonetheless faced the real prospect of seeing their gains in electoral representation come to a standstill and wither. In the mid-1990s, the Supreme Court, consisting of a majority of members who had been appointed by conservative Republican presidents, began pulling back from approving the kind of legal remedies that led to the election of a record number of black candidates. In following the dictates of the Voting Rights Act and prior Supreme Court decisions, state legislatures had created so-called minority-majority legislative districts for state and federal elections. This required that lawmakers, where feasible, deliberately redrew district lines to provide blacks with a voting majority that best expressed their electoral choice. On occasion, this led to the fashioning of strangely shaped districts, which a majority of the justices found offensive. Beginning with a series of cases in 1993, a narrowly divided court ruled that state legislatures could not cobble together a district with race as the predominant consideration in the design.

Five conservative justices, with Sandra Day O'Connor the swing vote, engaged in this version of judicial activism. They upheld the claim of white plaintiffs, who had neither lost their right to vote nor suffered racial discrimination, that they had been deprived of the equal protection of the law. In reaching this conclusion, the court's majority apparently believed that race was a category that applied to African Americans but not to whites. They failed to recognize that lawmakers also took the whiteness of the electorate into account when they concocted districts to ensure that white candidates win election, whether they belonged to a particular political party or ethnic group. In effect, the court declared that the Constitution required racial-blind policies for blacks though not for Caucasians; according to this thinking, predominantly black districts reflected a system of racial apartheid, but majority-white districts did not. However, all was not lost, as the court did not follow the suggestion of Justices Clarence Thomas and Antonin Scalia to limit the Voting Rights Act strictly to voter registration and not voter-dilution issues.[23]

With the expansive interpretation of the Voting Rights Act coming to a close and the real possibilities for creating majority black districts reaching their ge-

---

Press, 1985). For a different and negative account, see Abigail Thernstrom, *Whose Votes Count: Affirmative Action and Minority Voting Rights* (Cambridge: Harvard University Press, 1987).

23. J. Morgan Kousser, *Colorblind Injustice: Minority Voting Rights and the Undoing of the Second Reconstruction* (Chapel Hill: University of North Carolina Press, 1999), chapter 8.

ographical limits, it is appropriate to assess the results of what *Smith* v. *All-wright* set in motion. Statistics related to voter registration and black elected officials confirm enormous advancement since 1944. There is still a good deal of room for improvement, as African Americans rarely sit in governor's mansions or in the United States Senate and never in the White House. Yet sixty years ago it would have been unthinkable that just a year into the new century a white president from Texas would rely most heavily in dealing with world crises on two African Americans, one the secretary of state and the other the national security advisor. The fact that the latter, Condoleeza Rice, grew up in strife-torn Birmingham during the heyday of the Civil Rights movement adds even greater poignancy to the story. African Americans, in choosing enfranchisement as their first priority, held great expectations for the right to vote. Hine explains the consensus that motivated the Texas pioneers in the struggle: "The ballot meant protection. With the vote blacks could defend themselves, their property, and their futures by electing those politicians most responsive to their needs."[24] With the election of black mayors in such former civil rights battlegrounds as Birmingham, Selma, New Orleans, and Atlanta, African Americans have experienced a greater measure of physical security in their lives and obtained increased opportunities to determine their own political and economic destinies.

Still, it is undoubtedly true that blacks placed too much faith in the remedial qualities of the ballot. Given their history and the available alternatives, it is understandable that they did so. However, obtaining the franchise did not guarantee that black candidates who won election would possess either the skills or power to reverse the centuries of racial advantages that whites had institutionalized in the political, social, and economic institutions of the city, state, and nation. Black mayors, who held positions closest to their constituents and therefore would be most sensitive to their needs, soon found their options narrowed by the reality that economic power most often remained in the hands of whites. They also faced a bureaucracy of civil servants that restricted their room to maneuver. Within these limitations, black public officials succeeded most in creating opportunities for the middle class to expand, but they were much less successful in breaking the cycle of low-paying jobs and inadequate housing that affected the poor.

Of course, many of these problems lay beyond the command of any local official, black or white, and had to be addressed by national leaders in Washington. In this respect, the right to vote proved a disappointing victory. One

---

24. Hine, *Black Victory*, 235.

of the main assumptions of black voting-rights activists was that in obtaining the ballot and exercising it effectively, African Americans would join with sympathetic whites and reshape the landscape of the South and the nation in progressive ways. Protected by a deliberately shrunken electorate and bloated by the political seniority they received as a result, white southern Democratic politicians had pursued a conservative agenda in Washington that worked against blacks and the impoverished. The stranglehold that white oligarchs had in keeping down poor southerners of both races would be broken once their tight grip on ballot boxes was shattered.

What the most optimistic of voting-rights proponents failed to predict was that enfranchisement of black southerners would lead to a countermobilization of white voters. Although newly enfranchised African American voters did manage to liberalize the Democratic party in the South, the expansion of the black electorate set in motion the revitalization of the Republican party in Dixie, a virtual outcast in the region since the end of Reconstruction.[25] This metamorphosis produced a Democratic party more sympathetic to black interests, but it created a powerful GOP that embraced the economic positions and recast in modified form the racial concerns associated with pre–Civil Rights–era Democrats. With the rise of conservative Republicans in statehouses throughout the region and in considerable numbers in Congress, the dream of a liberal South invigorated by newly enfranchised black and white voters has yet to materialize. The same Texas that led the way in overturning the white primary and produced Lyndon Johnson, the greatest civil rights president, two decades later would vault into the White House the two George Bushes, father and son, whose brand of southern Republicanism spotlighted the need for a Third Reconstruction.

If the vision embedded in the reenfranchisement movement and spurred on by the black victory against the white primary is finally to succeed, then the story recounted by Darlene Clark Hine retains its significance. The vote alone is not enough. And as the presidential election of 2000 shows, the South, and Florida in particular, still employs the means to make black ballots count less or not at all. African Americans have been down this road before and have demonstrated that sheer persistence and creative strategies can yield triumphs. Hine shows that if they are once again to achieve success, African

25. When President Lyndon Johnson signed the 1964 Civil Rights Act into law, he already realized the potential danger for the Democrats from a white electoral backlash. He remarked to his assistant, Bill Moyers: "Bill, I think we just delivered the South to the Republican Party for a long time to come." See Tom Wicker, "Remembering the Johnson Treatment," *New York Times,* May 9, 2002, A39.

Americans will have to mobilize their communities, find common ground with others who share similar grievances, and establish coalitions that bring their voices more fully to bear in the arena of national government. After all, the long history of African Americans battling for suffrage demonstrates that the power of the right to vote comes not from the ritual of individuals routinely marking their ballots, but from the purposeful, collective action of an engaged electorate.

# In Retrospect

## Darlene Clark Hine's *Black Victory*

### Merline Pitre

*Black Victory* is the exhilarating story of the struggle to declare the white democratic primary statute of Texas unconstitutional. The white primary was as simple as it was effective. Since the Democratic party was the dominant party in Texas, and since the winner of that primary was inevitably the winner of the general election, the way to prevent blacks from having any real effect on the election of officeholders was to prevent them from joining the Democratic party. This was done by stipulating (via statute) that only "white males" could vote in the party's primary election. Thankfully, Darlene Clark Hine broadened our understanding of black Texans' roles in removing this subterfuge to voting. While *Black Victory* is an account of the successful effort by blacks and the NAACP to challenge the white primary statute, the real focus of this work is the maneuvering within the NAACP and between that organization and local blacks over strategies and tactics. Hine is at her best when she discusses those differences. In doing so, she goes beyond legalistic details and reveals the emergence of a popular black leadership. The talented lawyers, journalists, ministers, and business professionals who rose to challenge the white primary and sought to change judicial attitudes occupy the heart of this story. "What brought these and other black people together and ultimately united them was the belief that without the right to vote all their aspirations would be thwarted."[1]

---

1. See Barbara Thompson Day, review of *Black Victory: The Rise and Fall of the White Primary of Texas,* in *Journal of Southern History* 47 (May 1951): 309–10.

## Black Victory and Black Female Leadership

While Hine's study is certainly an inspiration and beginning point for ex-amining black leadership in the struggle to retrieve the ballot, it is far less il-luminating of black female leadership. Until the publication of my volume *In Struggle against Jim Crow: Lulu White and the NAACP, 1900–1957,* little, if any, recognition had been afforded black females, especially those who worked shoulder to shoulder with male leaders to destroy the constitutional basis for Jim Crow (in this particular case, the Texas white primary). Yet the claim of "shoulder to shoulder" would suggest that one views leadership through the lens of gender and as a social construction.[2]

Both in Hine's study and in popular memory and public recognition, lead-ership in the years associated with the movement to eliminate the white pri-mary was viewed as the domain of the black male. Because black men and women shared a history of suffering and resistance, it was assumed that women would be involved in the twenty-two-year struggle to retrieve the bal-lot, but that black men would and should be at the forefront of the movement. However, as we learn more about citizenship classes, club movement, and neighborhood organizing, for which women bore special responsibilities, an entirely different picture emerges. Women such as Lulu B. White, Christia Adair, Ora Lee Terry, Irma Leroy, Hazel Young, and Thelma Bryant could be considered pioneers, paving the way for action that brought male leaders to prominence. Yet we know very little about who these women were and what they wanted, did, and achieved.

One of the things that these women had in common is that they were all organizers. As Charles Payne has argued, in the Civil Rights movement, "men led, but women organized." This is a very useful assessment in part because in the past decade, feminist scholars of the movement have been concerned with revaluing the important contributions female organizers made to the movement. In recent scholarship, organizing is being recognized as a critical movement activity in its own right and has been redefined as an important form of leadership. Today a number of scholars, including Belinda Robnett, Vickie Crawford, Jacqueline Rouse, Guida West, and Rhoda Lois Blumberg, have been concerned with revaluing the important contributions of female leadership.[3]

---

2. Merline Pitre, *In Struggle against Jim Crow: Lulu B. White and the NAACP, 1900–1957* (College Station: Texas A&M University Press, 1999).

3. Charles Payne, "Men Led but Women Organized: Movement Participation of Women

In her study *How Long? How Long?* Belinda Robnett focuses primarily on the leadership of African Americans in the Civil Rights movement, distinguishing the formal leaders of the movement, who were almost always men, from the grassroots or bridge leaders, who were primarily, although not always, women. Robnett's explanation of how individuals rose to positions of formal leadership is most intriguing. She contends that most men had access to structural and institutional power, while most women's access was based on their community work or extraordinary activism within the movement. More often than not, these women were bridge leaders—individuals who fostered ties between the social movement and the black community. Within this context, Robnett identified four types of female bridge leaders: (1) the professional leader, one who had significant civil rights experience prior to the movement's activities and whose concern went beyond local issues; (2) the community leader, who was concerned with local civil rights activities; (3) the indigenous leader, who worked in concert with community leaders; and (4) the "main street" bridge leaders, who were white females. Robnett maintains that all of these leaders focused on developing the potential for reflection and action in others. Their goal was to empower participation and to bring those they led not only to action, but also into decision making.[4]

If one looks seriously at the difference women made in retrieving the ballot in Texas, a scholarly redefinition of leadership is therefore in order. It is important not only for the recovery of a lost political past of women but also because it raises other questions: Why is it necessary to reexamine female leadership? Why hasn't organizing been valued as much as traditional leadership, or recognized as a form of leadership; was it always this way? The case study that follows on Lulu B. White's activism and leadership role in the Civil Rights movement in Houston and Texas during the 1930s, 1940s, and 1950s suggests that the problem of not acknowledging women's leadership is one of historical memory—somebody forgot to tell somebody something. To be sure, we

---

in the Mississippi Delta," in *Women in the Civil Rights Movement: Trailblazers and Torchbearers, 1941–1965,* ed. Vicki L. Crawford, Jacqueline Anne Rouse, and Barbara Woods (Brooklyn: Carlson Publishing, 1990), 1–12; Belinda Robnett, *How Long? How Long? African American Women in the Struggle for Civil Rights* (New York: Oxford University Press 1997); Guida West and Rhoda Lois Blumberg, eds., *Women and Social Protest* (New York: Oxford University Press, 1990); Jo Freeman, "The Origin of Women's Liberation Movement," *American Journal of Sociology* 78, no. 4: 792–811; Myra Marx Feree and Beth Hess, *Controversy and Coalition: The New Feminist Movement* (Boston: Twayne, 1983). See also Thelma S. Bryant, *Pioneer Families of Houston: Early 1900s.* (Houston: privately printed, 1997).

4. Robnett, *How Long? How Long?* 19–23.

have inherited a composite portrait of the civil rights leadership that has a male face. Yet if we go back to contemporary accounts of that period, we see that women were indeed effective mobilizers and organizers, and they were often recognized as leaders by their contemporaries. Such was the case of Lulu Belle Madison White.

The tenth of twelve children, Lulu was born in Elmo, Texas, in 1900 to Henry Madison, a landowner, and Easter Madison, a domestic worker. Lulu received her early education in the Elmo and Terrell public schools. Following her high school graduation, she attended Butler College for one year, then transferred to Prairie View College, where she received a bachelor's degree in English in 1928. In that same year, she married a prominent Houston businessman, Julius White, who had a great deal of liquid capital, was a longtime member of the NAACP, and had funded and served as plaintiff in several white primary cases. This marriage had both advantages and disadvantages. Unable to find a teaching job in the Houston Independent School District because of what some called "her husband's involvement in civil rights," Lulu White secured a position in Lufkin, Texas. After teaching school for nine years, White resigned her post and became an activist with the NAACP in the struggle to eliminate the Texas white democratic primary.[5]

It is important to note that Lulu White did not join the NAACP thoughtlessly or simply as an extension of her husband's involvement. While still a student at Prairie View, she was involved in almost every movement for social change on campus—active in the YWCA and serving as dormitory spokesperson and vice president of her class. Also, as she pursued her degree, she became keenly aware of the broader issue of race. She talked with other blacks who had suffered some of the same indignities that confronted her. She witnessed acts of discrimination and violence meted out to African Americans, and she also read books, articles, and magazines about the black struggle for equality. Conversely, during her tenure as a student, she also saw signs of change. She observed aggressiveness, assertiveness, and boldness on the part of black Texans who were trying to overturn the white primary. The lawsuits filed by these individuals were inspiring displays of fearlessness by people who were determined to stand up for their civil rights. So when White did not become a member of the Biracial Committee of Houston as she had envisioned, no one was surprised when she joined the NAACP.[6]

When White left Prairie View, she was more convinced than ever that she

5. Pitre, *In Struggle against Jim Crow,* 1–19.
6. Ibid., 19–22.

must become an agent of change. On her way to accomplishing this goal, although she worked in Lufkin, she found it necessary to establish a home and a power base in Houston. It is well to note that domesticity was never White's sole reason for creating a home. Home was not simply a physical structure, a dwelling where she lived. It was also where she found a necessary psychological space, where she felt a sense of belonging, of being special. Her "marital" home was politically empowering and socially and emotionally satisfying. Very often the White home served as a meeting place for fraternal orders or social clubs of which Lulu was a member—the Grand Court of Calanthe, the Eastern Star, the 1906 Art, Literary, and Charity Club, the Married Ladies Social Club, the Ethel Ransom Art and Literary Club, and the Metropolitan Council of Negro Women. Like her experience in the dormitories at Prairie View, these clubs provided White with a sustained interaction with women with whom she shared hard work and the common goals of fighting against Jim Crow and "lifting as we climb."[7]

The most pressing problem that African Americans faced while Lulu White taught school in Lufkin, Texas, from 1928 to 1935, was the elimination of the white democratic primary. At that time, White wanted to have her "say" on the issue of retrieving the ballot, but her personal situation never fully allowed her the opportunity to achieve this desire. Her distance from and limited time spent in Houston, as well as her exclusion from the all-male Negro Democratic Club, served as barriers. Her occupation and gender also mitigated against her becoming a public reform activist, a role for which she was temperamentally suited. So White contented herself by serving as a bridge leader, fostering ties in the community with local leaders and working in the background with her husband and other NAACP members to map out strategies.[8]

White enlarged upon her role as a community bridge leader in 1935 when the local NAACP chapter ignored the advice of the national office and proceeded to take their own case to court *(Grovey* v. *Townsend)*. The struggle to

---

7. Ibid., 133–35; Houston *Informer,* November 4, 1944, and January 12, 1946. Known among blacks as the "fraternal capital" of the U.S., Texas had over five hundred African American lodges at the turn of the century. The most noted of these were the Masons, the Eastern Star, the Invincible Sons and Daughters of Commerce, and the Grand Court of Calanthe. Lulu B. White belonged to the True Heart Chapter 193 Order of Eastern Star and the Pride of Houston Chapter 244 of Grand Court of Calanthe. The Grand Court of Calanthe was the richest of the women's fraternal orders. Founded in 1897 in Texas, the Grand Court of Calanthe served as a benevolent burial insurance association. In 1933, when most insurance companies went bankrupt, the Grand Court had an assets of $611,540 and loaned thousands of dollars to members to pay their taxes.

8. Houston *Informer,* July 22, 1932.

eliminate the white primary gained momentum with the *Grovey* case. The fact that Richard Grovey, the plaintiff, was a "homeboy" with a long record in civil rights made it easier for black Houstonians to put their trust in him and the cause for which he was fighting. No doubt, the *Grovey* case unified Houston's black community along class, gender, education, and economic lines. Support came from everywhere—labor leaders, ministers, women, the church, and the press, to name a few. Carter Wesley used his black newspaper, the Houston *Informer,* to emphasize the need for close cooperation of the total black population. Similarly, Lulu White galvanized women's organizations around the *Grovey* case—the YWCA, the Metropolitan Council of Negro Women, the Eastern Star, and the Grand Court of Calanthe. These women knocked on doors, raised funds, attended mass meetings, and participated in demonstrations. Although Grovey's pleas were rejected by the Supreme Court on April 1, 1935, the case provided Lulu White with a window of opportunity to express her political views on suffrage and racial oppression, as well as enabling her to share strategies on eliminating the white primary with a plethora of groups all working toward a common goal.[9]

The chilling effect of the *Grovey* decision resulted in the reorganization of the local NAACP branch and Lulu White emerging a formal secondary leader. In 1935, the Houston branch of the NAACP was at a crossroads. It had fallen behind other self-help and civil rights organizations in popularity, financial support, and members. The group attempted to rectify this situation in 1937 by placing Lulu White as director of the Youth Council and Clifford Richardson as senior branch president.[10] White was pleased with this career change because she had long aspired to be a "race woman," to make a career of social activism, raising racial and political consciousness. Inspired by the interest of Houston's young people in the NAACP, White soon began to envision her role as a youth director. It was not to be at all an ordinary task, but one where she would travel across the city and state garnering support for the organization and working with the leadership of the senior branch, the state branch, and the national office.

Although the job as youth director elevated her status, it did not bring with it any monetary gains. The love of her work and her satisfaction with it com-

9. Pitre, *In Struggle against Jim Crow,* 21–26; see also Robert Haynes, "Black Houstonians and the White Democratic Party, 1920–1945," in Howard Beeth and Cary Wintz, eds., *Black Dixie: Afro Texas History and Culture* (College Station: Texas A&M University Press, 1992), 192–210; Walter Lindsey, "Black Houstonians Fight against the Texas White Primary" (master's thesis, University of Houston, 1971).
10. Pitre, *In Struggle against Jim Crow,* 23–24.

pensated for the loss of her teacher's salary. This job gave her access to the NAACP hierarchy and provided her an opportunity to create her own space in the organization. Equally, it served as a recruiting mechanism that enabled White to help revive and strengthen the senior branch. It also provided a platform for her to sponsor popular programs on civil rights, literary topics, and current events. Very often, Lulu White's ideas for such programs came from the literary and social clubs of which she was a member. Each year, to provide programs for the community, these clubs sought out new books and public figures or authorities on the race issue. Lulu White capitalized on the activities of these clubs by inviting their guests to her regularly sponsored Sunday afternoon teas. Consequently, she recruited new members and advanced the NAACP's agenda. These Sunday socials became so regular that people knew that they could drop by during certain hours and expect to meet interesting people who were discussing civil rights issues. Lulu White was at ease in this setting, and she communicated effectively across generational lines to market her product—the NAACP.[11]

Despite Lulu White's efforts to build a strong NAACP in Houston, the local chapter, like many other branches, excluded females from the decision-making positions in the organization. With the exception of Ora Lee Terry, who served as assistant secretary, women usually worked as committee members, field workers, or volunteers. Lulu White's position as director of the Youth Council was a token one. While this post was higher than those held by most women in the organization, it was below those of most male officers. To change this situation, White decided to use her position to become part of the "inner circle." As such, she was not threatening to usurp the achievements of her male superiors, nor was she estranged from the men. Rather, she became increasingly close to them as colleagues, role models, and mentors. No longer solely dependent upon her husband for social contacts, Lulu White was now in a position to interact directly with the upper echelon. From 1937 to 1940, she cemented her relationship with Clifford Richardson and Albert A. Lucas, future branch presidents; with A. Maceo Smith, the director of state branches; with Thurgood Marshall, an NAACP counsel; with Daisy Lampkin, a national field worker; with Walter White, the executive director; and with Roy Wilkins, the assistant executive director.[12]

Recognizing the impact that White played in bridging the community to the

11. Houston *Informer,* March 25, 1937, December 16, 1939; see also 1906 Art, Literary, and Charity Club [Houston] Minutes, 1906–1953, in the Houston Metropolitan Library.
12. Pitre, *In Struggle against Jim Crow,* 29.

movement, the all-male leadership asked White to serve as interim president upon the death of Clifford Richardson in August 1939. When she assumed this post the following month, the Houston chapter was beset with financial and management problems. Concerned with the image and credibility of the organization, White immediately called for an investigation by the national office. "Some existing conditions in the branch are quite out of line with the aims and purpose of the Association," Lulu White told the national executive director. "A visit from you would mean saving our branch." Rather than making the trip himself, Walter White sent the national field worker Daisy Lampkin, who confirmed Lulu White's suspicions. After Lampkin's investigation was completed, a slate of new officers was elected without Lulu White, who refused the nomination. Instead, she became a local field worker and director of the membership drive.[13]

Meanwhile, between 1940 and 1943, as black Texans, especially those in Houston, began to prepare for what they hoped would be the final assault on the white primary, the need for more money, members, and workers became apparent. Consequently, in the fall of 1942, the executive board of the Houston chapter voted to set a goal of five thousand members for its upcoming membership drive. Initially, many thought this goal was unrealistic, but they quickly changed their minds as they witnessed the enthusiasm generated by *Smith* v. *Allwright*. But if the organization were to fulfill its objectives and reach its goal, it needed an executive secretary to handle the day-to-day operations of the branch in order to free the president of some responsibilities. So, amidst increased activities of political awareness and an increase in membership, Lulu Belle White was selected as the first full-time salaried secretary of the Houston branch, making her the first female of the South to hold such a post.

With experience as an advantage, Lulu White was ready for the challenge. Exuberant upon hearing the news that she would become executive secretary, she exclaimed in a letter to Walter White: "Give me five years, and I'll be darned if I do not give you 5,000 members in Houston. I won't be a bit surprised if you . . . move your headquarters here." True to her words, in six years Lulu White moved the organization from the brink of ruin to the pinnacle of success in terms of racial advancement, from a fledgling organization into one that was second in size only to the group in Detroit, and from a civil rights or-

13. Lulu B. White to Walter White, September 15, 1939, in Pitre, *In Struggle against Jim Crow*, 32–33. Lampkin to White, October 1934; Report of Meeting of the Board of Directors, NAACP Archives, Manuscript Division, Library of Congress (hereafter cited as MDLC). All letters to and from Lulu White come from that file. See also Houston *Informer*, September 1939.

ganization that dealt with legal issues to one that also employed direct action.[14]

Lulu White was now a formal primary leader with a title and power. In many instances in the Civil Rights movement, women had power without title or title without power, but rarely did one have both. Armed with institutional and organizational backing, White was a high-profile leader whose position in a male-dominated organization rendered her an anomaly. Still she did not seek to alter her role as a female in a man's world. But in fact she challenged the usual gender roles as she fought for civil rights with her male peers, acting as an equal, addressing the issues of goals and tactics, voting rights, and discrimination. According to Belinda Robnett, leadership within the context of social movement is not limited to making decisions regarding goals, tactics, and strategies, but includes the ability to influence leaders and organizational constituencies, to harness emotion, and to inspire collective action. This definition of leadership reflects Lulu White's actions as she assumed the helm of the local chapter of the NAACP.[15]

In the spring of 1943, Lulu White began the most remarkable period of her public life. She was embarking upon her work as executive secretary of the Houston chapter of the NAACP at a time when the organization's fate was bound up with the white primary struggle and only sixteen months after the United States entered World War II. While the war affected the Civil Rights movement positively in many ways, it exacerbated racism and racial discrimination in Texas and throughout the South. Within this racial and wartime environment, Lulu White seemed determined to make a name for herself among civil rights activists. Confident and enthusiastic, she felt that she was equal to the task. In size and appearance, Lulu White was a likely candidate to challenge the State of Texas. Standing five feet, six inches tall and weighing over 250 pounds, she was bold, brave, and loud, but also amiable, dignified, and respected by friends and foes alike. An acid-tongued individual who was not afraid to speak her mind to powerful whites and to differing black factions, White combined political radicalism with the administrative skills needed to effect change. When milder techniques did not work, she became openly defiant. To many, she seemed exactly what the doctor ordered for the Civil Rights movement in Houston and Texas in the 1940s and 1950s.

A professional bridge leader with deep ties in the community, Lulu White

14. Lulu B. White to Walter White, April 13, 1943; see also Memorandum—Financing Regional Office, December 17, 1944, in NAACP files, MDLC.
15. Robnett, *How Long? How Long?* 113–14.

understood her centrality in the movement that was gripping the state. Her social location within the movement as a member of two marginalized groups, black and female, enabled her to be an effective purveyor of public consciousness, racial identity, and group solidarity. Imbued with a determination to destroy the constitutional basis of Jim Crow, and empowered by the movement's activities, more often than not White operated in "free spaces" without any clear standard of conduct. For instance, during her first year as secretary, White made good on her promise that she would not fit the conventional mold of executive secretary. Many of her followers, who had been members of the NAACP for decades and who looked upon the organization as an elite club, soon found White overturning traditions. White concentrated a great deal of her effort on recruiting new members and on starting new chapters in cities as well as in the "hinterland." She defied tradition by going to both churches and nightclubs to get new members. While she continued the legalistic strategy used by the NAACP in the past to secure civil rights for blacks, she also employed a more direct form of protest by boycotting, picketing, demonstrating, and simply "raising hell" in order to achieve her objectives. For example, in 1943, White led an NAACP boycott against Winegarten Store that resulted in the dismissal of one of the store's security guards, who had struck a black customer. Another protest led to the establishment of Reserve Officer Training Corps units in some of the city's black high schools. Similarly, an NAACP-led demonstration made it possible for blacks to attend a production of *Porgy and Bess* at the Houston Music Hall and to be seated on the same floor levels as whites. White also staged solo demonstrations to try on women's apparel in department stores. When told by the manager she could not, White would usually respond "I have" and walk out.[16]

Lulu White's boldness created the movement culture for the elimination of the white primary. If the movement were to succeed, it needed risk taking, passion, and spontaneity. While grievance and frustration may spark collective action, they do not sustain it. The movement, therefore, needed mobilization of people and resources—grassroots, community, and professional activists, as well as money and institutional backing. Yet central to any mobilization effort is its leadership. One of the things that the movement sorely needed was a professional bridge leader who had the time, resources, and energy to bridge, expand, and transform the techniques needed to encourage people to join the NAACP. The movement found that leader in Lulu White.

16. See History of the Houston Branch in NAACP in Branch Annual Reports of 1943 and 1944, both in NAACP Files, MDLC; Houston *Informer* February 5, 1944. Lulu's husband was a nightclub owner, and many celebrities and noncelebrities visited his club.

When Lulu White assumed the post of executive secretary of the Houston chapter in 1943, her job description included managing the office, conducting branch activities, helping to organize other branches, and especially directing membership and fund-raising drives. On a salary of eighty-nine dollars per month and gasoline money for her automobile (which was provided by her husband), White immediately set out to make Houston's branch one of the largest in the nation. Under her tutelage, the Houston branch grew from 5,679 members in 1943, to 10,705 in 1944, to 12,700 in 1945. Elated over White's performance, Daisy Lampkin wrote to her: "Each day, I marvel at the amount of work you are able to accomplish." A. Maceo Smith, executive secretary of the state branches, was equally pleased with White for winning first place in the national membership drive in 1943. Walter White said of Lulu, "She has brought fine quality of leadership to Houston and has given many techniques and ideas to other branches." Acknowledging her role in recruitment for the organization, Thurgood Marshall said: "Her courage, wisdom and tremendous energy are considered by us in the national office as one of the greatest assets in our ever increasing membership." Partly because of White's efforts, 23,000 new members enrolled in the national association between 1943 and 1945, thereby expanding the number of state branches from 36 to 104. This increase in membership enabled the Houston chapter to pay a subsidy to the national office for three consecutive years: five hundred dollars in 1945, seven hundred dollars in 1946, and five hundred dollars in 1947.[17]

White's role in helping to build the NAACP might be better understood by looking at it through what can be called "layers of leadership," the transcending of leadership wherein leaders engage and create new "leader-followers." By engaging ministers and presidents of civic, political, professional, educational, labor, and women's groups early in her career, the executive secretary was able to establish a "leader-followership." It was mainly through White's association and work with individuals such as these that she was able to keep the association healthy via membership and fund-raising. Enjoying herself immensely as she went about creating new branches and reviving old, White told Ella Baker, a national field worker, "I get a big kick out of these people wanting branches. So, I say get as many as fifty and you may have your own and

17. See Duties of Executive Secretary in Houston Constitution and Bylaws 5–6 in NAACP files, MDLC; Houston *Informer,* February 5, 1944; Walter White to L. P. Lubin Byras, January 11, 1946; Thurgood Marshall to L. P. Lubin Byras, January 24, 1946; and A. Maceo Smith to Lulu White, October 26, 1943; see also August Meier and John Bracey, Jr., "The NAACP as a Reform Movement 1909–1965: To Reach the Conscience of America," *Journal of Southern History* 59 (February 1993): 3–30.

they start hustling for members." It was this kind of infectious charisma and knowing how to "sell" the NAACP that enabled White to develop the loyal following so necessary to the movement in the 1940s.[18]

It should not come as a surprise that Lulu White capitalized on the foundation laid by the Rev. A. A. Lucas, the president of the Houston chapter, in soliciting membership from the churches. As an organizational tool in the struggle for civil rights, the church was second to none. It provided informational networks and furnished the meeting places and fund-raising machinery. The church was the oldest and most respected institution in the black community. Central to black culture, the symbol of black historical experience, and the expression of African Americans' hopes and aspirations, the church gave blacks a sense of solidarity, self-identity, and self-respect. And when it came to arousing and manipulating an audience, the combination of black preachers and Lulu White had few rivals.

White's effectiveness in soliciting memberships and monies was connected to the transcendent leadership styles of black ministers. These ministers developed a "behind the scenes" local leadership cadre whose style was the antithesis of the "out front" style of Lulu White. The Texas Civil Rights movement of the forties is replete with the image of Lulu White at the podium and black ministers and labor leaders down in the trenches organizing. These ministers were effective organizers because they knew their congregations and how to motivate them; they also could identify potential local leaders and inspire them to action. They knew how to delegate responsibilities by placing members of their congregation in an auxiliary, thus giving those individuals a sense of importance while simultaneously extracting loyalty and work from them. Likewise, Lulu knew how to stir the ministers and members to action. In her membership campaigns, she offered incentives for leadership roles to ministers and merit certificates to the members. White usually placed workers into groups of five to twenty, with a minister as captain of each group. One could argue that White, by employing such techniques, trapped these ministers into leadership positions: If they dropped out of the campaign, they would be branded as cowards and traitors, but if the membership increased, they would enjoy an increased status in the community. To reinforce the bond between ministers and followers, White often pointed out that "A voteless people is a voiceless people and a voiceless people is a hopeless people."[19]

---

18. Pitre, *In Struggle against Jim Crow,* 170; Lulu White to Ella Baker, March 18, 1946.

19. Pitre, *In Struggle against Jim Crow,* 110–11; see also Merline Pitre, "Building and Selling the NAACP: Lulu B. White as Organizer and Mobilizer," *East Texas Historical Journal* 39 (spring 2001): 22–32.

The above model does not mean that the clergy were the only leaders and organizers and that everyone else was a follower. While the church played a tremendous role in providing organizational leaders and in motivating the masses at rallies, church rosters do not adequately reflect all who provided leadership on a daily basis, selling dinners, holding meetings at their houses to select plaintiffs, knocking on doors and passing out flyers, housing and providing meals for out-of-town NAACP officials, and influencing other blacks who were not members of Protestant churches to join the movement. It was not always the church network that provided mobilization. Some of it came via the women's network.

Women's groups provided a powerful resource for recruitment and mobilization. Like Mary McLeod Bethune, Lulu White had developed a leader-followership among women's groups before she became executive secretary, and she capitalized on this network. Many of the women who became bridge leaders in the fight against the white primary were individuals who belonged to the same social clubs, women's organizations, or church as Lulu White. They had risen to positions of formal leaders, community organizers, or indigenous mobilizers mainly through their ability to network. When asked by White to join the membership campaign, they applied the same networking techniques. For example, when members of the Married Ladies Social Club met once a month to discuss community development and juvenile delinquency, they recruited for the NAACP. Likewise, the right to vote was discussed at meetings of the Metropolitan Council of Negro Women and the Art, Literary, and Charity Club. These women cast a wide recruitment net, inducing others to join the movement, especially those who found it difficult to join the NAACP or had other options or priorities. In Texas, for example, *NAACP* was a "dirty word" for black teachers. One could be fired for joining or for being publicly affiliated with it. Many female teachers got around this barrier by joining women's organizations, thus indirectly providing the NAACP with money and contacts needed for mobilization. The movement's message was spread via female networking at YWCA meetings, at beauty parlors, during Women's Day activities, and even on the bus, as domestic and laundry workers rode to and from work.

This one-on-one organizing manifested White's ability to create new leader-followers and enhanced her influence among women individually and collectively throughout the state. For example, a few years after Juanita Craft of Dallas joined the NAACP in 1940, she came to Houston to meet and consult with Lulu White about how to increase membership of the Dallas branch. The two quickly became mentor and "mentee" as they set out on a mission to help destroy the white democratic primary and to strengthen and expand the state NAACP. Their work at recruitment greatly impressed state officials. Consequently, White was named Director of State Branches while Craft was given the post of State Organizer in 1946.[20]

In recruitment, White applied the same model to her relationship with labor unions as she had with ministers. The labor movement among blacks in Houston included public spokespersons and network activators. White was essentially a network activator and a gadfly, whose sharp tongue and philosophy of economic parity made her very popular among workers. Her effectiveness was closely connected to the work of labor movement advance men—Richard Grovey, Sid Hillard, Sidney Hasgett, Heman Marion Sweatt, and Moses Leroy—individuals who were responsible for citizenship classes. The purpose of these classes was to teach individuals about voting rights, civil rights, economic rights, and black history. These classes empowered black people to take control of their destiny, challenged them to become active and effective in addressing injustices in their lives, and helped them to learn about the power of the vote. These men worked publicly to organize black workers while their wives worked privately alongside them, teaching in the citizenship classes, recruiting for the NAACP, and informing Lulu White of the progress.[21]

With a cadre of labor unions, fraternal, political, social, and church leaders going door-to-door spreading the word about the NAACP and seeking new recruits, the task of soliciting membership became easier for White. From the beginning, such organizing efforts were the keys to the success of the movement and to Lulu White's leadership. As a result, whenever the NAACP called

20. Pitre, *In Struggle against Jim Crow,* 133–35. In 1947, Lulu B. White and Juanita Craft had a conference with the mayor of Bay City, in Matagorda County, Texas, regarding the existence of a white man's union primary. After the meeting, the mayor assured these women that he was fully behind the NAACP and requested that an attorney and photographer be on the scene on election day, April 10, 1948. White also worked closely with Craft on Dallas's November 1948 NAACP membership drive. See also Lulu B. White to Wilkins, March 9, 1948. Lois Wood, interview by author, Houston, Texas, 1976.

Craft was the first black woman deputized to sell poll taxes in Texas and was a pioneer in helping to break down racial barriers in Dallas's public facilities. At age seventy-three, she won a seat on the Dallas City Council and served for two consecutive terms, 1975 to 1979. She died in 1985 at age eighty-three, after receiving the Eleanor Roosevelt Pioneer Award from the University of Texas. See Juanita J. S. Craft Collection, Dallas Public Library; Dorothy Robinson, "Interview with Juanita Craft," January 20, 1977, in the Black Woman Oral History Project (Schlesinger Library at Radcliffe College, Cambridge, Mass., and K. C. Saur Verlag); Thelma Bryant, interview by author, Houston, Texas, March 10, 1990; Lois Wood, interview by author, Houston, Texas, 1996, transcripts in author's collection.

21. Pitre, *In Struggle against Jim Crow,* 44–45; Houston *Informer,* January 24, 1946.

a rally to discuss an issue, much of the work was already done. The ministers, union leaders, and fraternal and social organization presidents provided an audience, generated enthusiasm, and brought legitimacy to the movement that White so ably articulated.

Lulu B. White was admired by a large number of blacks as she traveled throughout Texas organizing and reviving branches. Noted for her dynamic speaking and her capacity to impart courage and to chase timidity, White literally moved people to action. She motivated crowds to fight for civil rights and developed strategies with branch presidents and executive boards to achieve the desired results. Lulu White anticipated a favorable decision in the NAACP's final assault on the white primary, *Smith* v. *Allwright* (1944); two months prior to that decision, in which the Supreme Court rendered the white primary unconstitutional, Lulu White mounted a "pay your poll tax" campaign. When "black victory" came, White joined in jubilant celebration with other NAACP officials, hailed the decision as a second emancipation, and looked forward to the day when African Americans would recognize its full impact. If Lulu White had known how her fighting spirit and effort would influence the future, she would have found even her symbolic victories gratifying. Her last campaign for blacks to run for public office, before her death in 1957, resulted in the election of Hattie M. White to the Houston school board, making her the first black Texan to be elected to public office since Reconstruction. And it is upon Lulu White's and Hattie White's shoulders that Barbara Jordan stood in 1966, when she became the first black female elected to the Texas Senate, and in 1972, when she became the first black from the twentieth-century South to sit in the U.S. Congress.

It is clear that Lulu White's leadership was not hampered by her gender. Rather, she was strengthened by the movement's activities. Her attributes and wide range of skills prepared her to meet the internal and external demands of the Civil Rights movement. White's understanding of the black world came from her day-to-day involvement in the community, her access to its institutions, and her local, regional, and national network within the NAACP. It may be that White's greatest strength as a leader was her ability to mobilize the black community—its people, financial resources, and leaders—and to promote the NAACP by bringing in new members to the organization. In doing so, she gained the respect of many self-reliant grassroots leaders, many of whom were unconcerned with who got the credit for success. Their triple devotion to civil rights, the NAACP, and Lulu White contributed mightily toward black victory. White's leadership, alongside that of the men, illustrates the many strategies and tactics that led to the elimination of the white primary.

## The Legacy of Black Victory in Texas

It would be difficult to exaggerate the political significance of the overthrow of the white Democratic primary. *Smith* v. *Allwright* helped open up the political system and changed the political map for African Americans. For example, Texas had only 30,000 blacks who were registered voters in 1940. By 1948, this number had increased to 100,000. Black voter registration in the state reached 345,000, 57 percent of the voting-age population in 1964, and this number increased even more when the Twenty-fourth Amendment and the Voting Rights Act of 1965 struck down the poll tax as a requirement in national elections and when the Supreme Court in 1966 declared the Texas poll tax in state elections unconstitutional. As a result, the number of black elected officials increased from 45 in 1971 to 472 in 2002. Today, 35 blacks sit in the Texas legislature, and 2 have held mayoral posts in the largest cities in the state, Houston and Dallas.[22]

The mass movement for first-class citizenship that gave rise to *Smith* v. *Allwright* did not happen in a vacuum. It was and is a continuum that includes males and females, traditional and nontraditional leaders, and grassroots and professional activists. It is therefore quite appropriate that Darlene Clark Hine's *Black Victory* be reissued. Her study makes for compelling reading and deepens our understanding of the connection between the past and present struggles for the right to vote and shows us how such struggles are complicated by race and gender constructions. *Black Victory* will continue to be a starting point and one of the best sources for scholars and students seeking to understand how black Texans secured a political weapon—the vote—that they so effectively use today.

22. Robert Calvert, *The Civil Rights Movement in Texas,* in *The Texas Heritage,* ed. Ben Procter and Archie P. McDonald (Wheeling, Ill.: Harlan Davidson, 1998), 183; see also Alwyn Barr, *Black Texans: A History of the Negro in Texas, 1528–1995* (Norman: University of Oklahoma Press, 1995).

# Black Victory

# *P̶reface
## to the First Edition

This story has a simple beginning. One day in 1923 a middle-aged, middle-class black man, Dr. Lawrence A. Nixon of El Paso, Texas, decided that he would vote! He collected his poll tax receipt, went to the local precinct and requested a ballot that he might vote in the Democratic primary election. The election official refused his request, informing him that he, Nixon, could not vote in the primary as maintained by state law because he was a Negro. For more than two decades thereafter, Nixon and a small cadre of black lawyers and leaders in Houston, Texas, with the strong financial and moral backing of a large number of local blacks and the NAACP, would continue to challenge the constitutionality of the exclusion of blacks from Democratic primary elections. These challenges resulted in four major U.S. Supreme Court cases: *Nixon* v. *Herndon*, 1927, *Nixon* v. *Condon*, 1932, *Grovey* v. *Townsend*, 1935, and *Smith* v. *Allwright*, 1944.

In the 1944 *Smith* v. *Allwright* case, the Supreme Court declared unconstitutional the Texas Democratic white primary. The white primary was the most effective scheme used in southern states to strip blacks of the vote and render them politically impotent. The *Smith* decision represented a significant political victory for black Texans and the NAACP. But the *Smith* decision symbolized more than either blacks or whites could know then. Had blacks known what the decision portended for the future, their victory would have been, undoubtedly, even sweeter. For in their long, relentless, costly, and often frustrating pursuit of free access to the polls in the primary elections that counted most, they propelled the United States Supreme Court to embark upon a bold new course of judicial interpretation of the Fourteenth and Fifteenth Amendments that would ultimately revolutionize the American political process. *Smith* v. *Allwright* infused subsequent Supreme Court decisions dealing with residential segregation, educational discrimination, and reapportionment, issues that continue to affect our political lives.

Chapter 1 discusses major nineteenth-century Supreme Court decisions pertaining to the meaning and intent of the Fourteenth and Fifteenth Amendments. In these decisions the Court severely restricted the usefulness of these amendments—originally designed as instruments to protect the civil and political rights of blacks—by inventing the theory of state action. The Supreme Court, by the close of the nineteenth century, had come to view these amendments as prohibiting states from abridging the rights of its citizens because of race or previous condition of servitude. The amendments did not, in the Court's view, govern private groups or individual interference with black civil and voting rights. The cumulative effect of the Court's restrictive pronouncements was to establish the constitutional foundation for black second-class citizenship and disfranchisement.

The second chapter traces the rise of the Democratic white primary in Texas. Mandatory statewide direct primaries replaced the corrupt convention system of selecting party candidates during the early decades of the twentieth century. They were widely heralded as a "progressive" reform. In Texas, however, local county primaries existed as early as the 1880s and had always been open to whites only. Because the major white primaries cases originated in Texas, it is necessary to place Texas in the broader southern and national context and to answer the basic question: Why Texas?

Chapter 3 identifies the black participants in the white primary battle: black Texans and the NAACP. Black Texans were unusually assertive in their efforts to enter the Democratic primaries. Their level of political activism far exceeded that of their counterparts in other southern states. What factors made black Texans behave differently? The NAACP provided the chief legal expertise in the white primary cases. However, in handling the Texas cases, the NAACP discovered that as an organization it had to make significant changes in its approach to dealing with blacks, particularly black Texans, on the local level. The changes in approach that occurred within the NAACP are treated throughout the book. They provide at least a partial explanation for the continued survival of the NAACP as an organization while other groups equally committed to black advancement were short-lived.

The remaining seven chapters deal largely with each of the major and minor white primaries cases. When the NAACP first asked the Supreme Court in 1927 to declare Democratic white primary elections a violation of the Fifteenth Amendment, the justices were apparently befuddled. There were serious questions that had to be answered. Primaries had not existed when the Reconstruction amendments were adopted. Were primaries "elections" in the constitutional sense and thus open to congressional regulations? Could a political party be a private organization as the Democrats claimed? Did the Fourteenth and Fifteenth Amendments, which stated that "no state" shall abridge the rights of citizens because of race and so on, apply to the actions of private individuals? What constituted state action? What was the original intent and understanding of the framers of the Fourteenth Amendment? Did the Fifteenth Amendment confer the right to vote upon anyone?

The white primaries cases reflect the Court's slow and laborious progress toward answers to these and other questions. The first three white primary cases caught the justices ill prepared to break ties with nineteenth-century precedents. Nineteenth-century Supreme Court decisions were in harmony with the larger society's disinclination to intervene in and halt assaults on black civil and political rights. To what extent did the Supreme Court from 1927 to 1944 reflect fundamental accord with prevailing national sentiments on black disfranchisement in the South?

By 1944 the Court breathed new life into the Fifteenth Amendment and was ready to give to the Fourteenth Amendment the breadth and scope its framers intended. The Supreme Court's path to this position and the political and social significance of the 1944 *Smith* v. *Allwright* case are the central foci of this study.

# *Acknowledgments*
## to the First Edition

I welcome this opportunity to convey my deepest appreciation to groups of individuals in overlapping categories: professors and friends with whom I share my life, and my family, who make everything and every day worthwhile. All have given me the encouragement and assistance that made working on this project a meaningful and exciting adventure.

August Meier suggested the topic and gave unstintingly of his time and expertise in directing the dissertation upon which this book is based. Professors John T. Hubbell, Elliott Rudwick, and James Louis served on the dissertation committee and made many substantive and organizational suggestions.

Several of my Purdue colleagues read various portions of the manuscript during successive stages of the revising process: Don Berthrong, Harold Woodman, and the members of "Gibbon," Les Cohen, Linda Levy Peck, Phil VanderMeer, Charles Ingrao, Jon Teaford, Regina Wolkoff, and Lois Magner. Martha Gentry proofread the entire manuscript and offered the right amount of support when I most needed it. Lamont Yeakey spent hours listening to me conceptualize, which helped to sharpen many of my arguments. Graduate assistants Mim Jackson and Kate Wittenstein lent a helping hand when deadlines loomed frustratingly near. Joyce Good and secretaries in the history department typed numerous drafts of this study with skill and patience.

Librarians at the Library of Congress, Kent State University, the University of Houston, Lyndon B. Johnson Library, the Eugene Barker Library at the University of Texas, and Texas Southern University were especially cooperative. Their collective professionalism greatly eased the trials and tribulation of a traveling researcher.

The late Judge William H. Hastie, Roy Wilkins, and James M. Nabrit graciously consented to interviews and spent hours recalling personal experiences during the white primary fight. A special tribute is due to the other courageous blacks and whites who dedicated their lives to the cause of freedom and human dignity.

Harold M. Hyman, in addition to being a fine scholar, is an adroit editor. Working with him on the final preparation of this book has been a valuable educational experience.

Friends are golden, and they become more valuable when they believe in and support your efforts. My special thanks go to a special friend and colleague, James D. Anderson, who read the manuscript with a keen and critical eye. Friends Jimmie Franklin and Otey Scruggs likewise took the time to read portions of the manuscript. Deciding on an appropriate title for the book, in surroundings not exactly conducive to clear thinking, required the assistance of friends John Blassingame, Charles Vincent, Juliet Walker, Armsted Robinson, and Nathan Huggins. While space does not permit me to name all significant others, I must acknowledge the friends who were seemingly always there—Murry De Pillars, Walter Steindl, Bobby Jackson, Luther S. Williams, Thelma Queens, and Mary Berry.

The most delightful part of any acknowledgment comes when it's time to recognize family contributions. There are never enough opportunities adequately to express my appreciation to my parents, Levester and Lottie; siblings, Barbara, Alma, Orlando; and Bridgie, Sylvester, and Dorothy for their warmth, support, love, confidence, and prayers. The existence of this book is, I hope, one of many symbols of our mutual admiration and appreciation. And to William C. Hine, thanks, sincerely, for always being in my corner.

I also acknowledge the *Southwestern Historical Quarterly* and the *Journal of Negro History* for permission to include portions of articles that first appeared in their journals.

I share the credit for all that is good in this book with my former professors, friends, colleagues, and family. Of course, errors of commission or omission are my sole responsibility.

# Black Victory

# 1

# The Supreme Court and the Black Ballot

## From Reconstruction Reality to New South Myth

The vote has been the most effective, prized means by which Americans made their wills felt in politics. For the black man the vote has meant much more. Through the exercise of the franchise he could make his political will felt, and protect his physical being and his basic human and civil rights. To be without the ballot was catastrophic.

In the closing years of the nineteenth and the opening decades of the twentieth centuries, blacks and their white allies organized pressure groups and civil rights organizations such as the National Association for the Advancement of Colored People (NAACP), and fought to retrieve ballot rights lost since Reconstruction. They persevered against the seemingly insuperable odds of entrenched racism, northern indifference, southern violence, congressional inaction, and judicial blindness.

This study examines the black struggle to regain the ballot, a struggle which affected both jurisprudence and the shape and form of national and southern politics in the twentieth century. Blacks under the aegis of the NAACP initiated litigation to persuade the United States Supreme Court to declare unconstitutional Democratic "white primary" laws. White primary laws were among the most effective and blatantly discriminatory disfranchisement schemes adopted in one-party southern states. The successful conclusion of this thirty years of legal struggle rendered a decisive blow to the edifice of southern "white supremacy" politics.

To appreciate this struggle fully, in its numerous ramifications and complexities, a brief look at political and constitutional developments in the Civil War and Reconstruction era is in order.

The Civil War and Reconstruction altered the status of more than three million slaves. Under the Military Reconstruction Act of 1867 and the watchful supervision of federal troops in southern states, approximately 700,000 blacks qualified as voters and participated in the political affairs of local, state, and national governments; between 1865 and 1900, twenty-two blacks were elected to the United States Congress. A decade later (1875), however, this limited participation had dribbled to an end. The disputed Hayes-Tilden presidential election of 1876 led Republicans and Democrats to a "compromise" which portended ominously for the future of black Americans. In exchange for permitting Rutherford B. Hayes to occupy the White House, Republicans acquiesced in the demands of Democrats and promised to withdraw the few remaining federal troops from the South. This arrangement, at least in symbolic terms, effectively signalled the collapse of one phase of the Reconstruction experiment.[1]

As the last troops left, the hopes and aspirations of blacks for first-class citizenship plummeted. Republican party leaders conceded that the chances of building a strong southern Republican party were slim if not hopeless, and ultimately unnecessary. Increasingly, the party reflected more interest in tariff and monetary policies than in colorblind citizenship equality. The cause of the black man dropped in Republican political priorities. Supreme Court decisions, negating national laws passed from 1866 to 1875 to protect the civil and political rights of black people, further exacerbated their deteriorating plight. Blacks experienced an increasing number of physical assaults and a mounting sense of political abandonment and judicial betrayal. By 1883 one outraged and totally exasperated black was moved to declare the Constitution "a dirty rag, a cheat, a libel" which "ought to be spit upon by every Negro in the land."[2] The absence of the physical and symbolic presence of federal troops coupled with unsympathetic and unnecessarily restrictive judicial pronouncements kept blacks effectively subordinated, in economic and power terms, to whites. The outcome was predictable. Former masters and unreconstructed white

1. C. Vann Woodward, *Reunion and Reaction: The Compromise of 1877 and the End of Reconstruction,* 1st ed. (Boston: Little, Brown, 1951), 14–15, 211–15; John Hope Franklin, *Reconstruction: After the Civil War* (Chicago: University of Chicago Press, 1961), 218–24; Stanley P. Hirshson, *Farewell to the Bloody Shirt: Northern Republicans and the Southern Negro, 1877–1893* (Bloomington: Indiana University Press, 1962), 28–29; quote from Earl Warren, "Fourteenth Amendment: Retrospect and Prospect," in Bernard Schwartz, ed., *The Fourteenth Amendment: A Centennial Volume* (New York: New York University Press, 1970), 212–13.

2. H. M. Turner, *The Barbarous Decision of the Supreme Court Declaring the Civil Rights Act Unconstitutional* (pamphlet; Atlanta, 1883), quoted in Edwin S. Redkey, *Black Exodus: Black Nationalist and Back-to-Africa Movements, 1890–1910* (New Haven: Yale University Press, 1969), 41–42.

southerners, with the implicit sanction of uninterested northerners, systematically stripped black men of the rights and privileges so recently bestowed by national policies and laid the foundation for the so-called New South. For the remainder of the nineteenth century and first half of the twentieth, the promises of Reconstruction became empty words and painful reminders of what could have been. Many blacks came to view Reconstruction as a sham, and attributed to the Supreme Court of the United States a large share of the blame for the fraud perpetrated upon them. Frederick Douglass, the nineteenth-century black activist, expressed the sentiments of many when he exclaimed, "O For a Supreme Court of the United States which shall be as true to the claims of humanity, as the Supreme Court formerly was to the demands of slavery."[3]

From the perspective of the ex-slave, the extremity of the loss of civil and political rights and of social status after the collapse of Reconstruction was even greater considering the breadth and scope of the Thirteenth, Fourteenth, and Fifteenth Amendments to the federal Constitution and the laws enacted to enforce their provisions. The Bill of Rights had prohibited federal infringements upon the rights of the states and their citizens. The Reconstruction amendments altered accepted notions of the relationship between states, citizens (who now became national citizens as well), and the federal government. For the first time, the federal government had an interest in the protection of state citizens against the state itself. The safeguarding of state-defined political and civil rights was to remain primarily a state function.[4]

The Thirteenth Amendment, ratified on December 18, 1865, settled the slavery issue. "Neither slavery nor involuntary servitude," it proclaimed, "except as punishment for crime whereof the party shall have been duly convicted shall exist in the United States, or any place under their jurisdiction." It also invalidated the original basis for congressional representation, which had counted a slave as three-fifths of a man. Three years later, after tremendous debate, the Thirty-ninth Congress hammered out, and the states ratified, the controversial Fourteenth Amendment. The Fourteenth Amendment conferred national and state citizenship upon ex-slaves. Thereby the amendment

---

3. *Proceedings of the Civil Rights Mass Meeting Held at Lincoln Hall, October 22, 1883* (pamphlet; Washington, D.C., 1883), 4–14. Frederick Douglass's speech included in LaWanda and John H. Cox, *Reconstruction, the Negro, and the New South* (New York: Harper and Row, 1973), 144–51.

4. Bernard Schwartz, "The Fourteenth Amendment in Operation: A Historical Overview," in Schwartz, *The Fourteenth Amendment*, 31; and Erwin N. Griswold, "Due Process Problems Today in the United States," ibid., 162.

negated the infamous 1857 Dred Scott Supreme Court decision which had declared, in effect, that the black man was not a citizen of the United States or of any state and, consequently, had no rights.

The first section of the Fourteenth Amendment provided that "No State shall make or enforce any law which shall abridge the privileges or immunities of citizens of the United States; nor shall any State deprive any person of life, liberty, or property, without due process of law; nor deny to any person within its jurisdiction the equal protection of the laws [Note: meaning equal protection of states' laws]." In an oblique attempt to coerce states toward enfranchisement of black state citizens, Section 2 prescribed penalties for states interfering with or denying voting rights to state citizens, including blacks. It read, in part, "But when the right to vote at any election for the choice of electors for President and Vice-President of the United States, Representatives in Congress, the Executive and Judicial officers of a State, or the members of the Legislature thereof, is denied to any of the male inhabitants of such State, being twenty-one years of age, and citizens of the United States or in any way abridged, except for participation in rebellion, or other crime, the basis of representation therein shall be reduced in the proportion which the number of such male citizens shall bear to the whole number of male citizens twenty-one years of age in such State." And on March 30, 1870, the Fifteenth Amendment was added to the Constitution. It had as its primary objective the enfranchisement of northern as well as southern blacks.[5] This last of the Reconstruction amendments prohibited all state racial restrictions on voting: "The right of citizens to vote shall not be denied or abridged by the United States or by any State on account of race, color, or previous condition of servitude." Each of the three amendments contained virtually identical concluding sections: "The Congress shall have the power to enforce this article by appropriate legislation."

In spite of the vigor and determination with which Congress proceeded to seek state-defined civil and political rights for the black man, popular sentiment in the North and especially in the South remained divided on the question of black suffrage and equality.

Still, the Reconstruction amendments enlarged federal interest in rights. Congress enacted legislation to enforce the provisions of the Thirteenth, Four-

5. Alfred H. Kelly and Winfred A. Harbison, *The American Constitution: Its Origins and Development* 3d ed. (New York: Norton, 1963), 493–94; William Gillette, *The Right to Vote: Politics and Passage of the Fifteenth Amendment* (Baltimore: Johns Hopkins University Press, 1965), 77–78.

teenth, and Fifteenth Amendments. On May 31, 1870, Congress passed the First Enforcement Act which detailed civil rights and attempted to protect the right to vote against state infringement. Blacks were to enjoy equally state-defined rights to enter into contractual relationships, to acquire, and convey, real and personal property,[6] and to enforce legal rights in courts of law. The February 1871 Second Enforcement Act, dealing primarily with northern cities, placed congressional elections under direct federal supervision. Federal criminal penalties were prescribed for those who, under "any [state or local] law, statute, ordinance, regulation or custom" interfered with the black man's right to vote on account of race, color, or previous condition of servitude.[7] The Third Enforcement Act, the so-called Ku Klux Klan Act, became law in April 1871. It granted blacks federal protection against private conspiracies "to injure, oppress, threaten or intimidate any citizen with intent to hinder his free exercise of any right or privilege granted by the Constitution."[8] Congress completed the protective legislative process with the Civil Rights Act of 1875. It guaranteed blacks protection against private interference and the same access to public accommodations that whites enjoyed: "All persons within the jurisdiction of the United States shall be entitled to the full and equal enjoyment of the accommodations, advantages, facilities, and privilege of inns, public conveyances on land or water, theaters, and other places of public amusements; subject only to the conditions and limitations established by law, and applicable alike to citizens of every race and color, regardless of any previous condition of servitude."[9]

While white congressmen debated the constitutionality of the Enforcement Acts, their black counterparts correctly perceived them as necessary insurance to preserve rights so recently and painfully gained. The speeches of black congressmen in the House of Representatives reflected their concern over the potential for state and private subversion of the Fourteenth and Fifteenth Amendments. One black South Carolina representative, Robert Brown Elliott, urged that the Enforcement Bill be speedily enacted and "be quickly enforced." He observed, "In one section of the Union crime is stronger than law. Murder, unabashed, stalks abroad in many of the southern states." Elliott concluded, "If you cannot now protect the loyal men of the South then have the loyal peo-

6. 16 Stat. 140 (1870); Stanley I. Kutler, *Judicial Power and Reconstruction Politics* (Chicago: University of Chicago Press, 1968), 143.
7. 16 Stat. 444 (1871); see also Albie Burke, "Federal Regulation of Congressional Elections in Northern Cities, 1871–1894" (Ph.D. diss., University of Chicago, 1968).
8. 17 Stat. 13 (1871).
9. 18 Stat. 335 (1875).

ple of this great Republic done and suffered much in vain, and your free Constitution is a mockery and a snare." Another black congressman from South Carolina, Richard H. Cain, in a February 3, 1875, speech in the House of Representatives, was even more insistent in advocating passage of the Civil Rights Bill of 1875. "These five millions of people for whom I speak are waiting for its passage. Their hopes, their prospects, their lives to a certain extent depend upon it. And I think this country owes it to them." He concluded, "Having lifted them out of slavery, having emancipated them, having given them manhood in a sense, I regard it as essential to the interests of this country that they shall make them citizens of this country, with all that that word imports, and that they shall guarantee to them the protection necessary for their lives and for their property." Cain warned that failure to enact the Civil Rights Bill would result in "strife all over this land as long as five millions of black men, women and children are deprived of their rights. There will be no real and enduring peace so long as the rights of any class of men are trampled under foot. . . ."[10] That their concerns were justified is shown in the number of outrages committed against blacks by the Ku Klux Klan and like terrorists. Between 1865 and 1871, anti-rights activists killed hundreds of blacks and their supporters. Grand promises of equality and justice looked good on paper, but freedmen's lives continued to be governed by violence, intimidation, and fear.

Scholars still disagree on the understanding and intent of the framers and sponsors of the Fourteenth Amendment. Two fundamental questions central to this study are: Was Section 1 of the Fourteenth Amendment intended to protect voting rights? Do the Fourteenth and Fifteenth Amendments govern private or individual interference with voting rights? The current controversy surrounding these questions echoes, to a large extent, the same uncertainties of a hundred years ago. Then Supreme Court justice John Marshall Harlan III, dissenting in the 1964 reapportionment case, *Reynolds* v. *Sims*,[11] concluded after a lengthy review of the legislative history of Section 2 of the Fourteenth Amendment that Section 1 did not address or protect voting rights. For that matter, Section 1, he said, had nothing to do with voting rights.

Duke University law professor William W. Van Alstyne took exception to Justice Harlan's reading of the original understanding and intent of the Fourteenth Amendment and suggested that the right to vote had, on the contrary,

10. Robert Brown Elliott's speech in favor of the Enforcement Bill in 42d Cong., 1st sess., *Congressional Globe,* 102; Richard H. Cain, *Congressional Record,* 43d Cong., 2d sess., pp. 956–57, in Leslie H. Fishel, Jr., and Benjamin Quarles, eds., *The Black American: A Documentary History* (Glenview, Ill.: Scott, Foresman, 1970), 283–89.

11. *Reynolds* v. *Sims,* 377 U.S. 533 (1964).

been the single most deliberately considered subject at that time. Van Alstyne also asserted that the Republican sponsors of the amendment had been intensely aware that it would offer great possibilities for differing future interpretations at least insofar as voting rights were concerned. He noted that "in spite of complaints that it might lead to future protection of voting rights, the proponents refused to adopt an amendment to preclude that effect even while denying that such an effect was intended." Van Alstyne concluded his analysis by arguing that the Fourteenth Amendment should be broadly interpreted to include protection of citizenship rights including the right to vote.[12] Historian Harold Hyman concurs with Van Alstyne's assertions. He contends, speaking of civil rights, that "instead of formulating positively national civil rights minima the Fourteenth Amendment forbade unequal deprivation of the broad, uncodified, vague mass of civil rights practices which a state professed to afford equally to the generality of its citizens."[13]

An opposite view, expressed by Ward E. Y. Elliott in his recent study of the Supreme Court's role in voting rights disputes, cautions against efforts to argue or attempts to convert terms like "equal protection" and "due process" into "blank checks for posterity." Elliott asserted that the Fourteenth Amendment's legislative history was a series of attempts to secure general federal protection for voting rights—all of which Congress rejected decisively. Sponsors of the amendment, likewise, denied accusations by opponents, complaining that its broad language might permit Congress to intervene with state control of the franchise.[14]

To contemporary blacks, the questions could be answered simply. The important issue was not the original understanding or intent, but the Supreme Court's interpretations of the amendments in post-Reconstruction litigation, and the impact of those decisions on the lives and political fortunes of blacks. In 1875, black congressman-lawyer Robert Brown Elliott declared, "These amendments, one and all . . . have as their all-pervading design and end the security of the recently enslaved race, not only for their nominal freedom, but their complete protection from those who had formerly exercised unlimited

12. William W. Van Alstyne, "The Fourteenth Amendment, the 'Right' to Vote, and the Understanding of the Thirty-Ninth Congress," *Supreme Court Review* (1965): 36–76.

13. Harold M. Hyman, *A More Perfect Union: The Impact of the Civil War and Reconstruction on the Constitution* (New York: Alfred A. Knopf, 1973), 467.

14. Ward E. Y. Elliott, *The Rise of Guardian Democracy: The Supreme Court and Voting Rights Disputes* (Cambridge: Harvard University Press, 1974), 61; for similar arguments, see Raoul Berger, *Government by Judiciary: The Transformation of the Fourteenth Amendment* (Cambridge: Harvard University Press, 1977).

dominion over them. It is in this broad light that these amendments must be read, the purpose to secure the perfect equality before the law of all citizens of the United States."[15]

The debate over the original understanding and intent of the Fourteenth Amendment is warranted. The language of both amendments regarding citizenship and suffrage had been necessarily cast negatively and ambiguously. Several crucial questions were either indirectly addressed, left unresolved, or left open to speculation. Among other things, the ambiguity and evasiveness of the wording of the amendments that facilitated their ratification also, paradoxically, permitted southerners later to devise effective disfranchisement mechanisms. Quasi-constitutional state policies such as literary-understanding clauses, complex registration laws, poll taxes, white primaries, and "grandfather clauses" reduced the black vote and, in some areas, left the black man politically impotent. These laws were frequently buttressed by resort to extralegal local customs and practices: intimidation, fraud, violence, and assassination. White southerners received assistance from decisions and interpretations made by the Supreme Court during the quarter century following the withdrawal of federal troops. These decisions, concerning the nature, intent, and scope of the Reconstruction amendments and the constitutionality of the Enforcement and Civil Rights laws, contributed to the process of black disfranchisement.[16]

The initial test of the meaning of the first section of the Fourteenth Amendment came in 1873 in the "Slaughterhouse Cases."[17] The Court's decision in these cases, which, ironically, had nothing to do with blacks, severely crippled the "privileges and immunities" clause and represented a significant development in the history of judicial construction of the Fourteenth Amendment. The cases involved a thousand New Orleans butchers who sought redress from

15. Robert Brown Elliott, "Speech on the Civil Rights Bill," reprinted from *The Congressional Record*, part 2, 43d Cong., 1st sess., pp. 407–10, in Daniel J. O'Neill, ed., *Speeches by Black Americans* (Encino, Calif.: Dickenson Publishing, 1971), 70; John P. Frank and Robert F. Munro, "The Original Understanding of 'Equal Protection of the Laws,'" *Columbia Law Review* 50 (1950): 31–169; Laurent B. Frantz, "Congressional Power to Enforce the Fourteenth Amendment against Private Acts," *Yale Law Journal* 73 (1964): 1353–84.

16. Kutler asserts, "The minority party, frustrated in its attempts to stem the tide of Republican Reconstruction, chose to rely on the rubrics of 'constitutionality' and judicial determination as a last-ditch defense. Confidently, the Democrats predicted judicial nullification of the Republican legislation and the vindication of their own opposition," in *Judicial Power and Reconstruction Politics*, 30; Loren Miller, *The Petitioners: The Story of the Supreme Court of the United States and the Negro* (New York: Pantheon Books, 1966), 85ff.

17. Slaughterhouse Cases, 16 Wall 36 (1873).

a 1869 Louisiana public health statute that had favored the monopolization of the city's slaughterhouses by a favored corporation, created by the state legislature. The butchers claimed that protection of their privilege to engage in business fell into the category of rights protected against the states. Speaking for the Court, Justice Samuel F. Miller drew a sharp distinction between privileges and immunities that were derived from state citizenship and those derived from United States citizenship. Of the rights safeguarded by the federal government, he observed incidentally that the right to vote in federal elections had been secured by the original Constitution and was indirectly protected by the Fifteenth Amendment. In sum, while the ruling stressed Negro rights and the protective purpose of the Fourteenth Amendment, it also declared that the privileges and immunities clause protected only those rights arising out of national, not state, citizenship. This interpretation of the privileges and immunities clause weakened subsequent attacks upon the constitutionality of various contemporary discriminatory state statutes.[18]

In 1876, the year of the disputed Hayes-Tilden election, the Court ruled in a significant case, *United States* v. *Cruikshank*,[19] on the constitutionality of the Enforcement Act of 1870, enacted under the Fourteenth Amendment. The case concerned 96 indictments arising from a massacre of 60 blacks who had been participating in a political meeting in Colfax, Louisiana, in 1873. Cruikshank and the other whites were charged with the violation of the sections of the Enforcement Act which made it a crime if two or more persons conspired "to injure, oppress, threaten or intimidate any citizen with intent to hinder his free exercise and enjoyment of any right or privilege granted or secured to him by the Constitution of the United States. . . ." The Supreme Court had to determine, therefore, what rights and privileges the Constitution granted.

The Court echoed its "Slaughterhouse" ruling. Chief Justice Morrison R. Waite observed that "The Fourteenth Amendment prohibits a State from depriving any person within its jurisdiction of the equal protection of the laws; but this provision does not add anything to the fundamental rights of one citizen under the Constitution as against another." The Fourteenth Amendment, as the Court interpreted it, limited the power of the national government to the enforcement of the guarantee that all citizens enjoy equality of state-defined rights against encroachment by the states. In response to the government's contention that the blacks had been denied equal protection of the laws

---

18. Claude, *The Supreme Court*, 47–48; G. Edward White, *The American Judicial Tradition: Profiles of Leading American Judges* (New York: Oxford University Press, 1976), 103.
19. *United States* v. *Cruikshank*, 92 U.S. 542–69 (1876).

because the state had failed in its duty to protect them against mob violence, the Court held that the Fourteenth Amendment prohibited states, not individuals, from denying the equal protection of the state's laws. The *Cruikshank* decision also touched upon voting rights, holding, "The right to suffrage is not a necessary attribute of national citizenship, but exemption from discrimination in the exercise of that right on account of race, etc. is." In other words, the Court viewed the Fifteenth Amendment as conferring suffrage on no one: "The right to vote in the States comes from the States, but the right of exemption from the prohibited discrimination comes from the United States."[20]

In the same 1876 term, the Supreme Court rendered a heavy blow to the Fifteenth Amendment in *United States* v. *Reese.*[21] The defendant, a Kentucky state election official, had refused to receive and count the vote of William Garner, a black, and had been indicted under the third and fourth sections of the Enforcement Act of 1870. Sections 1 and 2 of the Act required that administrative preliminaries to state elections be conducted without regard to race, color, or prior condition of servitude. Sections 3 and 4 forbade wrongful refusal to register, receive, and count votes where a prerequisite act "required to be as aforesaid" had been omitted.

Chief Justice Waite delivered the Court's opinion reversing Reese's conviction. The Court held that sections 3 and 4 were defective and inoperative because they did not repeat the amendment's language about race, color, and servitude and the words "as aforesaid" would not suffice. According to the Court, Congress had not yet provided "appropriate legislation" for the punishment of said offenses.

The fundamental issue at stake concerned the scope of the Fifteenth Amendment and the extent to which Congress was empowered to legislate under the amendment. Justice Waite declared that "The Fifteenth Amendment does not confer the right of suffrage upon anyone." He continued: "It prevents the States, or the United States, however, from giving preference . . . to one citizen of the United States over another, on account of race, color or previous condition of servitude." Congress did not possess the power or authority to regulate or control all interference with a citizen's right to vote. Thus, the Enforcement statute could be considered operative only if the federal attorney proved that the defendant had operated under the color of state law and used race as a basis for discrimination. This decision practically emasculated the Fifteenth Amendment and virtually assured the disfranchisement of the

20. Claude, *The Supreme Court,* 55.
21. *United States* v. *Reese,* 92 U.S. 214–56 (1876).

black man. With it, as one scholar contends, "the victory of the counter-revolutionists was made complete."[22] The work of the Supreme Court, however, was not complete.

In an effort to retrieve the ground lost in the *Cruikshank* decision, the government carefully prepared another case under the provisions of Section 2 of the 1871 Enforcement Act. On August 14, 1876, after taking four blacks from the custody of a Tennessee sheriff, an armed mob had critically injured one of the blacks and had severely beaten the others. The government had indicted twenty whites, charging them with violation of Section 2 of the so-called Klan Act. The issues raised in *United States* v. *Harris*[23] were almost identical to the *Cruikshank* case. Harris and the others were charged with conspiring to deprive the four black men of their rights to the due and equal protection of state laws and to protection while under state arrest. The key question raised was whether Congress had possessed the power to enact the legislation under which the indictments had been framed.

Justice William B. Wood announced the Court's decision. "The legislation under consideration finds no warrant for its enactment in the Fourteenth Amendment." He continued: "When the State has been guilty of no violation of its provisions; when it has not made or enforced any law abridging the privileges and immunities of citizens of the United States; when no one of its departments has deprived any person of life, liberty, or property, without due process of law, nor denied to any person within its jurisdiction equal protection of the law; when on the contrary, the laws of the States, as enacted by its legislative and construed by its judicial and administered by its executive departments, recognize and protect the rights of all persons, the Amendment imposes no duty and confers no power upon Congress." The key pronouncement of the Court in this case was that the equal protection of the laws clause of the Fourteenth Amendment was limited to a "guaranty of protection against the acts of State Government itself." He continued: "It was never supposed that the section under consideration conferred on Congress the power to enact a law which would punish a private citizen for an invasion of the rights of his fellow citizen."[24]

The climactic blow against the rights of blacks was struck in the five 1883 Civil Rights cases.[25] The Supreme Court declared that the public accommo-

---

22. Franklin, *Reconstruction*, 208–9.
23. *United States* v. *Harris*, 106 U.S. 629–44 (1883).
24. Ibid., at 639, 644.
25. Civil Rights Cases, 109 U.S. 3, S. Ct. 18 (1883).

dations provisions of the Civil Rights Act of 1875 were unconstitutional. Justice Joseph Bradley viewed the Thirteenth Amendment as inapplicable to the case and held, further, that the Fourteenth Amendment prohibited discriminatory action only by the states and not by private persons. He elaborated: "An individual cannot deprive a man of his right to vote, to hold property, to buy and to sell, to sue in the courts or to be a witness or a juror; he may commit an assault against the person or commit murder, or use ruffian violence at the polls . . . but, unless protected in these wrongful acts by some shield of state or state authority, he cannot destroy or injure the right. . . ." Therefore, under the Fourteenth Amendment, Congress only has "power to counteract and render nugatory all state laws and proceedings which have the effect to abridge any of the privileges or immunities of citizens of the United States, or to deprive them of life, liberty or property without due process of law, or to deny them the equal protection of the laws." In the concluding section Bradley, in harmony with the times, commented on the whole body of protective legislation for blacks: "When a man has emerged from slavery, and by the aid of beneficent legislation has shaken off the inseparable concomitants of that state, there must be some stage in the progress of his elevation when he takes the rank of a mere citizen, and ceases to be the special favorite of the laws, and when his rights as a citizen or a man, are to be protected in the ordinary modes by which other men's rights are protected."[26]

From this decision emerged the doctrine of state action that "doomed the heart of the Fourteenth Amendment to death [by] judicial limitation."[27] Hyman maintains that "almost no one anticipated, when formulating the Fourteenth Amendment in 1866 or when ratifying the Fifteenth in 1870, that the rights specified by both post war amendments would be interpreted to affect only the public acts of the small number of state officials rather than private actions."[28] This decision reflected the extent to which judicial power had been enlarged. The Supreme Court decided that Congress could not enforce citizenship guarantees conferred on blacks by the Reconstruction amendments. What this meant in reality was that the system of "white supremacy" would now exist without fear of federal interference, since the southern social order rested mainly upon private, person-to-person relationships. The southern po-

26. Ibid.; White, *The Judicial Tradition,* 106; Kelly and Harbison, *The American Constitution,* 491–92; for an analysis of the Civil Rights cases, see Milton R. Konvitz, *The Constitution and Civil Rights* (New York: Columbia University Press, 1947), 8–28.

27. Silard, "A Constitutional Forecast: Demise of the 'State Action' Limit on the Equal Protection Guarantee," 66 *Columbia Law Review* 855, 857 (1966).

28. Hyman, *A More Perfect Union,* 439.

litical order likewise received support from these decisions, which in effect set the stage for the disfranchisement legislation that emerged in the South after 1880.[29]

The Supreme Court's Civil Rights cases decision struck black America like a thunderclap and left most blacks momentarily stunned. Ten years of adverse and restrictive Supreme Court decisions had left them unprepared for this latest jolt. With this decision, the Supreme Court had written with broad strokes that the black man was now on his own. Although the reactions of blacks ranged from fury to complacency—with one significant exception, Booker T. Washington—black leaders unanimously condemned the Supreme Court and the American judicial system.

His voice filled with regret and sorrow, Frederick Douglass spoke before a mass meeting of blacks in Washington, D.C., shortly after the Civil Rights decision was announced. "This decision has inflicted a heavy calamity upon seven millions of the people of this country," he said, "and left them naked and defenseless against the action of a malignant, vulgar, and pitiless prejudice." He likened the decision to "a moral cyclone" sweeping over the land, "leaving moral desolation in its tracks." Douglass focused on the sheer absurdity of the opinion. He asked, rhetorically, "What does it matter to a colored citizen that a State may not insult and outrage him, if a citizen of a State may?" And again, "What is a State in the absence of the people who compose it? Land, air and water. That's all." He complained that the Supreme Court had "utterly ignored and rejected the force and application of object and intention as a rule of interpretation." Speaking of the judicial emasculation of the Fourteenth Amendment, Douglass accused the Supreme Court of construing "the Constitution in defiant disregard of what was the object and intention of the adoption of the Fourteenth Amendment." He declared that the Court had been guided by "the narrowest and most restricted rules of legal interpretation."[30]

T. Thomas Fortune, militant black editor of the New York *Globe* (and later of the New York *Age*), responded with much less restraint. Infuriated, Fortune angrily editorialized, "The colored people today feel as if they have been baptized in ice water. . . ." He asked his readers: "What is the position in which the Supreme Court has left us?" His reply: "Simply this—we have the ballot without any law to protect us in the enjoyment of it; we are declared to be created equal, and entitled to certain rights . . . but there is no law to protect us in the enjoyment of them." He bitterly proclaimed, "We are aliens in our own land."

29. White, *The American Judicial Tradition*, 105–7.
30. Quoted in Cox, *Reconstruction, the Negro, and the New South*, 144–51.

Fortune often lamented the apparent servility and docility of black men and advised his readers to stand up and fight for their rights. In response to criticisms of his intemperate remarks and accusations as incendiary, Fortune declared, "We do not counsel violence; we counsel manly retaliation. We do not counsel a breach of the law, but in the absence of the law, in the absence of proper police regulation, we maintain that the individual has every right in law and equity to use every means in his power to protect himself." In Fortune's opinion, there was "no law in the United States for the Negro." He said, "The whole thing is a beggaredly [sic] farce." He saw the federal government as being "simply a puppet which each state treats with contempt or reverence as the spirit moves it."[31]

While Fortune described the United States Constitution as "disjointed," black nationalist leader Bishop Henry McNeal Turner called it a "dirty rag." The Civil Rights decisions reaffirmed Turner's conviction that the United States was an undesirable place for the black man. He threatened that if the government could not protect the black man's freedom then black men would no longer "enlist in the armies of the government" and were effectively absolved of all allegiance to the United States. He advised black people: "If the Court's decision is right and is accepted by the country, then prepare to return to Africa or get ready for extermination."[32]

Teacher, newspaperwoman, and anti-lynching crusader Ida B. Wells purchased a railroad ticket in Memphis, Tennessee, and took a seat in the section now by state policy legally and constitutionally reserved for whites. When she refused to move, she was bodily thrown off the train, whereupon she hired a lawyer and sued the Chesapeake and Ohio Railroad for damages. The *Memphis Daily Appeal* headlined the federal circuit court's verdict: "Darky Damsel Obtains a Verdict for Damages Against the Chesapeake and Ohio Railroad— What it Cost to Put a Colored School Teacher in a Smoking Car—Verdict for $500." Upon appeal, the Supreme Court of Tennessee reversed the lower court's ruling, concluding: "We think it is evident that the purpose of the defendant in error was to harass with a view to this suit, and that her persistence was not in good faith to obtain a comfortable seat for the short ride."[33] Wells

31. New York *Globe*, October 20, 1883, quoted in Emma Lou Thornbrough, *T. Thomas Fortune: Militant Journalist* (Chicago: University of Chicago Press, 1972), 47–48.

32. Redkey, *Black Exodus*, 41–42.

33. *Chesapeake and Ohio and Southwestern Railroad Company v. Wells,* Tennessee Reports: 85 Cases Argued and Determined in the Supreme Court of Tennessee for the Western Division, Jackson, April Term 1887, p. 615, quoted in Ida B. Wells, *Crusade for Justice: The Autobiography of Ida B. Wells,* ed. Alfreda M. Duster (Chicago: University of Chicago Press, 1970), 19–20.

noted in her autobiography, "The Supreme Court of the nation had told us to go to the state court for redress of grievances; when I did so I was given the brand of justice Charles Sumner knew Negroes would get when he fathered the Civil Rights Bill during the Reconstruction period."[34]

At least one black leader handled the Civil Rights decision complacently. The "great accommodator," Booker T. Washington, observed simply, "Brains, property, and character for the Negro will settle the question of civil rights." Washington felt that good schoolteachers and adequate funds with which to pay them would be "more potent in settling the race questions than many civil rights bills." He professed the unshaken belief that the southern people had "a good deal of human nature."[35] Washington's mild pronouncements elicited some negative comments from some blacks. One well-known Afro-American wrote, "It is not a pleasing spectacle to see the robbed applaud the robber. Silence were better."[36] The 1883 decision signalled another curtain call for the Reconstruction experiment.

In subsequent years, the Supreme Court responded to the applause of southern white audiences with judicial encores. The 1896 *Plessy* v. *Ferguson* decision was, however, more than a repeat performance. It went beyond previous cases to enunciate a new judicial doctrine. The case involved the constitutionality of a Louisiana statute requiring separate railway coaches for whites and blacks. Speaking for the Court, Justice Brown held that the state law did not deprive blacks of the equal protection of the laws, provided that blacks were furnished accommodations equal to those for whites. The ruling was both a culmination of processes begun earlier and also a qualitative step in its own significance. The decision held that state segregation policy was compatible with legal rights equality. Justice Harlan's lone dissent reflected how far the clock had been turned backward: "In my opinion, the judgement this day rendered will, in time, prove to be quite as pernicious as the decision made by this tribunal in the *Dred Scott* case."[37]

The results of the Supreme Court's decisions were: The Fourteenth Amend-

34. Wells, *Crusade,* 20.

35. Quoted in Louis Harlan, *Booker T. Washington: The Making of a Black Leader, 1856–1901* (New York: Oxford University Press, 1972), 160–61.

36. Charles W. Chesnutt, "The Disfranchisement of the Negro," in *The Negro Problem: A Series of Articles by Representative American Negroes of Today* (1903; reprint, Miami: Mnemosyne Publishing, 1969), 111.

37. *Plessy* v. *Ferguson,* 163 U.S. 537, 165 S. Ct. 559 (1896); the Court ruled, "A state statute providing for separate railway carriages for the white and colored races by railway companies carrying passengers in their coaches in the state, and the assignment of passengers to the coaches according to their race by conductors does not deprive a colored person of any rights under the 14th Amendment of the Federal Constitution."

ment prohibited states from interfering with or abridging the rights and privileges of their citizens in a discriminatory manner on account of race, color, or previous condition of servitude. The Fifteenth Amendment, not conferring the right to vote on anyone, only prohibited each state from discriminating racially against or interfering with the exercise of suffrage once granted by a state. Congress did not have the authority to regulate actions of, or to punish, private individuals who interfered with the voting rights of, or discriminated against, other private citizens. In short, state laws which did not overtly discriminate or disfranchise on the basis of color, race, or previous condition of servitude would not be considered unconstitutional by a Supreme Court whose members measured substance by form. The activities of individuals, in the absence of the "color of [state] law," were outside the purview of federal regulation. Former black representative and political leader John R. Lynch of Mississippi cogently assessed the consequences of the Court's restrictive and "unwise" interpretation of the Reconstruction amendments and laws: "By the unfortunate and fatal decisions the vicious and mischievous doctrine of States' rights, called by some State sovereignty, by others self-government, which was believed to have perished upon the battlefield of the country, was given new life, strength and audacity. . . ."[38]

Southern legislatures, now fortified, settled upon five basic schemes by which disfranchisement of blacks could be achieved without apparent violation of the Constitution: the literacy test, complex registration laws, the poll tax, the "grandfather clause," and the "white primary." The Supreme Court promptly validated the first three devices. In *Williams* v. *Mississippi* (1898), the Court upheld the constitutionality of the Mississippi literacy provision. The state law permitted the mass disfranchisement of blacks, since local officers could determine whether any "undesirable" voter had passed the test.

The Court, likewise, found it no violation of the Constitution to require payment of a poll tax as a prerequisite for the franchise. The poll tax had a negative impact on both black and poor white voters.[39] Five years later the Court

38. John R. Lynch, "Some Historical Errors of James Ford Rhodes," *Journal of Negro History* (October 1917): 366.

39. *Williams* v. *Mississippi*, 170 U.S. 213 (1898); Kelly and Harbison, *The American Constitution*, 493; Richard Bardolph, ed., *The Civil Rights Record: Black Americans and the Law, 1849–1970* (New York: Crowell, 1970), 147; letter of registrar to Rep. Harry D. Flood (D., Va.), quoted in Andrew Buni, *The Negro in Virginia Politics, 1902–1925* (Charlottesville: University Press of Virginia, 1967), 21. One such voting official wrote, "All right will sirtunly do my best to get the Dem voters to register & vita versa I am one of the registrars they seems to be verry little interest taken in the registrations but I think they are awakening to the necesity pretty fast There wont be no negro registered that aint entitled to You bet."

spread its protective cloak around Alabama's complex and discriminatory registration procedures.[40] By 1908, the majority of southern states had written
constitutional provisions for black disfranchisement; by 1915, practically all
of the southern states had provided for white primaries. One historian of suffrage restrictions notes, "the cross-fertilization and coordination between the
movements to restrict the suffrage in the Southern States amounted to a public conspiracy."[41]

By 1900, the black man hung suspended between slavery and citizenship.
The specter of white men voting when black men could not reminded them
of their inferior status. Hope, however, did not die completely, and in many,
the will to be free, really free, grew stronger. Black leaders frequently debated
with each other and struggled to reach a solution and decide upon a course of
action which would enable blacks to retrieve the ground lost in the post-
Reconstruction era. The United States Justice Department had been of no
assistance since 1893. One young scholar forcefully argues that "the ultimate
failure to prevent the disfranchisement of the freedman was as much an administrative failure as it was a political, social and moral one. The Justice Department as a law-enforcement agency was not equipped to hold back in the
long run the concerted efforts of white Southern Democrats to deny the freedman his civil and political rights."[42]

Black author Charles W. Chesnutt, in a forceful essay on the disfranchisement of the Afro-American, outlined the strategy he felt blacks should pursue
to retrieve the ballot. He wrote, "To try to read any good thing into these fraudulent Southern Constitutions, or to accept them as an accomplished fact, is to
condone a crime against one's race. . . ." He declared that the struggle should
continue before the national Supreme Court: "This Court should be bom-
barded with suits . . . on the broad question of the Constitutionality of the disfranchising Constitutions of the Southern States." He maintained further that
"the direct remedy for the disfranchisement of the Negro lies through political action." Chesnutt also expressed hope in the potential for the acquisition
of and the effective use of power by northern blacks. "There are many colored

40. *Giles* v. *Harris*, 189 U.S. 475 (1903); Miller, *The Petitioners*, 158–59; see Louis R. Harlan, "The Secret Life of Booker T. Washington," *Journal of Southern History* 37 (August
1971): 397–98, for an interesting discussion on Washington's surreptitious role in financing and supervising the Giles case.

41. J. Morgan Kousser, *The Shaping of Southern Politics: Suffrage Restriction and the Establishment of the One-Party South, 1880–1910* (New Haven: Yale University Press, 1974),
39, 45–62.

42. Robert Michael Goldman, "'A Free Ballot and a Fair Count': The Enforcement of
Voting Rights in the South, 1877–1893" (Ph.D. diss., Michigan State University, 1976),
303–4.

men at the North, where their civil and political rights in the main are respected," he said, and "when this race develops a sufficient power of combination, under adequate leadership—and there are signs already that this time is near at hand—the Northern vote can be wielded irresistibly for the defense of the rights of their Southern brethren."[43]

By 1903, the fiery T. Thomas Fortune was expressing similar views concerning the strategy blacks should pursue. He wrote, "Under the circumstances, there is no alternative for the Negro Citizen but to work out his salvation under the Constitution." He predicted pessimistically, however, that it would "take the Afro-American people fully a century to recover what they had lost of civil and political equality. . . ."[44] Fortune was tragically accurate.

The gloom of political powerlessness lifted briefly for black Americans in 1915. In *Guinn* v. *United States* the Supreme Court, after a twelve-year silence on the issue of black voting rights and disfranchisement, outlawed the Oklahoma grandfather clause.[45] The victorious moment was short-lived. Blacks became increasingly aware that the fight for the ballot had only just begun. Disfranchisers were ingenious, if nothing else.

The most effective of the disfranchisement subterfuges, the white primary, still stood as a bulwark between blacks and the ballot. Overthrowing the white primary would prove to be very complicated, time-consuming, and costly, necessitating carefully coordinated, unified, and sustained efforts by blacks and their white allies.

Blacks had to persuade the United States Supreme Court that the white primary was an integral part of the southern election process. This task was made more difficult because of the fact that primaries, not to mention "white primaries," had not been in existence at the time of the framing or adoption of the Fourteenth and Fifteenth Amendments. Moreover, to have the white primary declared unconstitutional entailed convincing the Supreme Court of the error of its past interpretations of the original understanding, intent, and provisions of the Reconstruction amendments. This struggle would take thirty years. Part of its significance lies in the fact that only with the demise of the white primary would the entire system of black disfranchisement in the South begin to crumble. The white primary, therefore, stood, constitutionally and politically, as the most important of all the disfranchisement devices. Its history deserves telling, and this account now turns to the rise of the white primary.

43. Chesnutt, "The Disfranchisement of the Negro," in *The Negro Problem,* 115–20.
44. T. Thomas Fortune, "The Negro's Place in American Life at the Present," *The Negro Problem,* 219–20.
45. *Guinn* v. *United States,* 238 U.S. 347 (1915).

# 2

# The Rise of the Texas
# Democratic White Primary

When the Texas legislature resolved in 1923 to eliminate blacks completely from state politics, it enacted a white primary statute. The law proclaimed that all qualified voters belonging to the Democratic party, the only effective political organization in Texas, were eligible to participate in its primary elections. Under no circumstances, however, was a Negro eligible to vote in a Democratic primary. Election judges were ordered to discard the ballot of any Negro who attempted to vote.[1]

Texas was the only ex-Confederate state to take this action. With little regard for congressional or judicial consequences, it passed a law that explicitly discriminated against black state citizens on the basis of color. The state assumed the responsibility for black disfranchisement because the Democratic primary was in fact, if not in law, the real election machinery in Texas. The open general election simply rubber-stamped the choice made in the primary election. For black Texans the 1923 statute ended their already limited involvement and influence in state and local politics. The white primary was like an iron curtain, for even if blacks became literate, acquired property, and paid poll taxes, they could not conceal or change the color of their skins. Thus they could never, as long as the "white primary" stood, take part in what became the most critical step in the Texas electoral process.

Other states had adopted techniques such as the poll tax, literary tests, understanding and good character clauses, and complex registration laws. These subterfuges appeared to be in harmony with the United States Constitution

---

1. General Laws of Texas, *38th Legislature Journal,* 2d Called Session (Austin, 1923), p. 74; *Texas Revised Civil Statutes,* Article 3107 (1935); J. Alston Atkins, *The Texas Negro and His Political Rights: A History of the Fight of Negroes to Enter the Democratic Primaries of Texas* (Houston: Webster Publishing, 1932), 6–24.

and the Fourteenth and Fifteenth Amendments as interpreted by the Supreme Court during the last quarter of the nineteenth century. Texas bypassed these constitutionally sanctioned and politically restrictive techniques and relied exclusively upon the poll tax and the "white primary." The white primary was, ironically, a mutant form of the direct primary that had been widely heralded as a reform instrument to purge southern elections of the corruption that had typically disgraced them.[2]

Many southern states, starting in the late 1890s, adopted limited forms of the direct primary. South Carolina adopted primary legislation in 1896, Arkansas followed in 1897, Georgia in 1898, Florida and Tennessee in 1901, Alabama and Mississippi in 1902, Kentucky and Texas in 1903, Louisiana in 1906, Oklahoma in 1907, Virginia in 1913, and North Carolina in 1915.[3] Essentially, direct primary laws established the time for holding the primary election, the party test for qualification, the method of placing names on the ballot, the order of the names on the ballot, the vote necessary to elect, offices covered, and the drafting of the party platforms.[4] Following the adoption of direct primary legislation, each southern state passed laws granting the party the right to establish membership qualifications. The tacit understanding being, of course, that blacks would by this means be denied party membership and thus access to the Democratic primaries.

Florida, for example, passed legislation in 1902 amending its primary law to make provisions for state-wide nominations and for a second runoff primary. Blacks were excluded from the Democratic primary with little difficulty. The law provided that primary voters should meet the same qualifications as for the general election and, most importantly, be members of the party. Later that year, the Florida Democratic Executive Committee sent out announcements for the party's first state-wide primary and limited its membership to whites.[5]

Disfranchisement of blacks through the adoption of "white primary" resolutions followed much the same pattern in Georgia. The Democratic party, not the state, established and financed the primaries. Consequently the general assembly hesitated to pass laws regulating them. In 1891, it passed a law to pro-

---

2. C. Vann Woodward, *The Strange Career of Jim Crow* 2d ed. (New York: Oxford University Press, 1957), 66–67.

3. Ibid., 68.

4. Charles Edward Merriam and Louise Overacker, *Primary Elections* (Chicago: University of Chicago Press, 1928), 66ff.

5. H. D. Price, *The Negro and Southern Politics: A Chapter in Florida History* (New York: New York University Press, 1957), 18.

tect the primaries from certain corrupt practices. It expressly left the formulation of qualifying rules, however, to the political party holding the primary. This made the party, rather than the state, responsible for the exclusion of blacks.[6] By removing the state from the actual establishment of qualifying rules for participation in primaries, Florida and Georgia skillfully averted a possible judicial challenge to their legislation. Texas, however, ignored these precautions and thus left the door open for a legal attack.

Black Texans never acquiesced in disfranchisement nor completely relinquished their tenuous grasp on the ballot. Unlike blacks in other southern states, black Texans remained a numerically small but viable force in state and local politics until the turn of the century. Each subterfuge to wrest the ballot from their hands met with individual or group opposition. Two central questions remain to be answered: Why Texas? Where did Texas fit in the spectrum of southern and national politics at the time of its adoption of the 1923 white primary law? The answers may be found in a brief examination of political developments in Texas from Reconstruction through World War I.

During and after Reconstruction black Texans were deeply involved in county and state politics. Most, though not all, black elected officials were Republicans and represented a group of black belt counties in East Texas. From 160,000 in 1860 the black population rose to 690,000 by 1910, roughly 18 percent of the state's population.[7] Most of this black population was concentrated in 74 to 80 counties in the southeast, a pattern largely due to slavery. The degree of concentration varied: in 14 counties blacks were a majority. The four counties with the largest concentration of blacks (over 60 percent) were Fort Bend, Harrison, Marion, and Matagorda. From this area came the chief opposition to black voting.[8]

Beginning in the late 1870s, whites in the black belt counties organized associations, unions, and clubs with the express purpose of ousting blacks from local, county, and state politics. The constitutions and by-laws of all groups admitted only whites to membership and required that all participants adhere to the principles of white supremacy. These associations organized under the

---

6. Olive Hall Shadgett, *The Republican Party in Georgia: From Reconstruction through 1900* (Athens: University of Georgia Press, 1964), 153–54.

7. Charles William Ramsdell, *Reconstruction in Texas* (1910; reprint, Austin: University of Texas Press, 1969), 11; Lawrence D. Rice, *The Negro in Texas 1874–1900* (Baton Rouge: Louisiana State University Press, 1971), 4–5.

8. Alwyn Barr, *Reconstruction to Reform: Texas Politics 1876–1906* (Austin: University of Texas Press, 1971), 17; Melvin James Banks, "The Pursuit of Equality: The Movement for First Class Citizenship among Negroes in Texas, 1920–1959" (Ph.D. diss., Syracuse University, 1962), 7.

banner of the Democratic party and legitimized their existence by holding county-wide nominating elections months before the general elections. The club members selected the Democratic nominee who, in the general elections held in November, was pitted against the Republican or third party candidate.

Although all white members pledged complete support to the Democratic nominee, as long as blacks were in the majority, the chances of a Democrat winning the general election where blacks could participate without hindrance were minimal.

To break black political power, local whites, as in other parts of the South, resorted to extra-legal devices such as fraud, intimidation, intrigue, and murder. Harrison County in northeast Texas was the first to suppress the black vote. Blacks represented 68 percent of Harrison County's population. In 1876, local whites organized a White Citizen's Club and attempted to wrest control of county offices from the Republicans, many of whom were black. The White Citizen's Club drew up ballots similar to the Republicans' and distributed them on election day in an unsuccessful attempt to confuse illiterate voters. Nevertheless, Republicans retained control of the county. White club leaders thereupon challenged the returns from a key precinct on the grounds that the voting box had been improperly situated. A Democratic district judge granted them an injunction that the Republican county judge refused to recognize. What they failed to win by "legal" means the white club members took by force. They seized control of the sheriff's and county clerk's office, organized their own court, counted "duplicate" returns for the unchallenged precincts, and issued themselves certificates of election. The Republicans appealed to the governor's office, but to no avail. The White Citizen's Club members armed themselves and dared the rightfully elected Republican officials to attempt to take their offices.[9]

The leaders of these essentially black-disfranchising associations, clubs, and unions were reputable members of the local communities. They felt that they had lost status by the wholesale enfranchisement of blacks and were willing to take the law into their own hands to reverse the changes imposed upon them by outside forces, e.g., the Republican party and congressional legislation. In Robertson County, for example, Judge O. D. Cannon assisted local whites in barring black elected officials from taking office. Judge Cannon stood at the election booth on election day with a drawn six-shooter and prevented blacks and many other "undesirables" from voting. During his tenure as county judge (1890–1900), he killed three whites and one black and wounded another

9. Barr, *Reconstruction to Reform,* 194–95; Rice, *Negro in Texas,* 114–19.

black. Hariel Geiger, a black lawyer and member of the 1881 state legislature, was defending an accused man in Judge Cannon's court when he purportedly made an "insolent remark." The judge drew his gun and shot Geiger five times. Understandably, by 1900 black political participation in Robertson County virtually disappeared.[10]

The rise of white men's associations and county white primaries reflected the increasing fear and uncertainty that plagued white Texans during the postwar years. Whites in black belt counties tended to exaggerate the numbers and power of black politicians and degree of black political influence. Much of the power blacks allegedly possessed can be attributed to the attitudes and actions of whites themselves. There was never any real threat of black ascendancy, certainly not to the extent imagined by local white Texas Democrats. Many whites, as Forrest Wood has observed, all too often wallowed in self pity and were too consumed with indignation and apathy to participate fully in neighborhood political affairs. Some refused to vote and stayed away from the polls in order to avoid an implied recognition of racial equality.[11] The myth of black domination and white powerlessness once introduced into political discussions, however, enjoyed widespread currency and was frequently used by white leaders to manipulate the white masses.

The fear of black domination was further buttressed by the extreme fluidity of Texas politics during the post Civil War and Reconstruction periods. Difficult economic conditions, with depressions at ten-year intervals, nurtured the development of third parties such as the Greenback Independent Movement in the 1880s and the Populist revolt in the 1890s. In each of the postwar decades, Texas Democrats had to confront serious threats to their political hegemony as each new party attempted to woo the black vote.[12] The rise of each new party led to louder complaints of black participation. As Wood explains, white southerners in general defined black majority in a peculiar way: "The freedman did not need a numerical majority in order to enjoy a political majority. Rather, if the total number of eligible Negro voters was greater than the difference in the number cast for each party, the Negroes had a 'majority.'"[13] Presumably, by either selling votes to one candidate or bloc voting

10. Richard Denny Parker, *Historical Recollections of Robertson County, Texas,* ed. Nona Clement Parker (Salada, Tex.: Anson Jones Press, 1955), 48–49.

11. Forrest G. Wood, "On Revising Reconstruction History: Negro Suffrage, White Disfranchisement, and Common Sense," *Journal of Negro History* 51 (April 1966): 108–11.

12. J. Morgan Kousser, *The Shaping of Southern Politics: Suffrage Restrictions and the Establishment of the One-Party South 1880–1910* (New Haven: Yale University Press, 1974), 209.

13. Wood, "On Revising Reconstruction History," 111.

for another, blacks could, in that case, hold the balance of power. The rise of third parties in Texas, then, increased anxiety and exacerbated the fear that when white men divided politically black power flourished.

The demonetization of silver and other financial policies of the Grant administration resulted in a money scarcity and gave impetus to the organization of the Greenback party. Formed in Waco, Texas, on August 7–8, 1878, the party was comprised of an equal number of dissident Democrats and Republicans. The Greenbackers openly appealed to black voters by espousing the "free vote and a fair count" slogan, but they did not in any way imply support for social equality. The Greenback party enjoyed tremendous success in the 1878 election, polling 55,000 votes for governor, more than one-third of the Democratic vote and double the Republican. Blacks were repaid for their support. The Greenback party was primarily responsible for the election of several blacks to the Texas State Legislature, either by fusing with Republicans or by splitting the white vote to allow other blacks to be elected on the Republican ticket.[14]

In 1884 the Democrats overcame the Greenback challenge. Within three years, however, another third party made its presence felt. In 1886 the Prohibition party made its first respectable showing on a state ticket. The Prohibitionists polled in excess of 19,000 votes for their candidate for governor. Although much less impressive than previous Greenback showings, the election was fraught with intense vituperation and violence. The party was ultimately unsuccessful, and it would be another twenty years before Prohibition again became an important issue in almost every state election.[15]

The Democratic party's most serious confrontation with a third party occurred in the 1890s with the Populist agrarian revolt. The resolution of this threat to the Democrats held serious consequences for the future of black participation in Texas politics. The People's party was comprised of many Democrats, independents, ex-Greenbackers, Republicans, some Prohibitionists, and radical agricultural interest groups. Its stronghold was clearly among white farmers. Initially, the People's party's economic and political ideology was elaborate. Populists desired a strong, active federal government, a subtreasury plan which would have provided farmers with short-term credit for

14. Dabney White, ed., *East Texas: Its History and Its Makers* (New York: Lewis Historical Publishing, 1940), 335; Rice, *Negro in Texas,* 106; C. Vann Woodward, *Origins of the New South 1877–1913* (Baton Rouge: Louisiana State University Press, 1951), 84–85; Kousser, *Shaping Southern Politics,* 25.

15. Lewis Gould, *Progressives and Prohibitionists: Texas Democrats in the Age of Wilson* (Austin: University of Texas Press, 1975), 28; White, *East Texans,* 140.

agricultural products stored in government warehouses. They wanted an increased and more elastic currency supply. Populists also favored stringently enforced antitrust laws. But as recent scholarship suggests, farmers were fundamentally concerned about the exclusion of agrarian representation in local and national politics. They wanted to be more actively involved in the direction of society. This desire, in addition to cultural and economic factors, gave rise to the political alienation which produced the fervors of Populism.[16]

While the Populist party did not attract a majority of Texas black voters, Populist leaders nevertheless made an open bid for the black vote. In August 1891, at the first state convention of the People's party the convention president declared: "He [the Negro] is a citizen just as much as we are, and the party that acts on that fact will gain the colored vote of the South."[17] One party member summed up the position of many white Populists on the black vote/membership issue: "They are in the ditch just like we are."[18]

Although many blacks participated in third party movements in Texas, quite a few expressed some reservations about jumping onto the People's party bandwagon. The black leader of Texas Republicanism, Norris Wright Cuney of Galveston, opposed Populism. Cuney was much more concerned with the consolidation and maintenance of the black man's power and with his own power and position within the Republican party—a party which had increasingly become disinterested in and unresponsive to black demands. Indeed, during the 1890s the "lily white" faction of the Republican party increased in strength and vigorously attempted to sever all association with blacks. One "lily white" Republican leader declared, "The Negro is an incubus, a millstone on the neck of the Republican Party. We must drop him. Give him his legal rights but let him remain in the background where he belongs."[19] Cuney preferred to regard the agrarian movement as an adjunct of "lily white" Republicanism. Joining the Populists represented a serious political gamble. If blacks relinquished their power base within the Republican party—and it was the

16. Peter H. Argersinger, *Populism and Politics: William Alfred Peffer and the People's Party* (Lexington: University of Kentucky Press, 1974), 59, 67–93; Stanley B. Parsons, *The Populist Context: Rural versus Urban Power on a Great Plains Frontier* (Westport, Conn.: Greenwood Press, 1973), 31; Lawrence Corbett Goodwyn, "The Origins and Development of American Populism" (Ph.D. diss., University of Texas, 1971), 20, 114, 187.

17. Dallas *Morning News,* August 18, 1891, quoted in Rice, *Negro in Texas,* 70.

18. Dallas *Morning News,* August 18, 1892, quoted in Woodward, *Origins of the New South,* 25.

19. Dallas *Daily Times Herald,* July 15, 1892, Houston *Daily Post,* April 20, 1890, quoted in Virginia Neal Hinze, "Norris Wright Cuney" (master's thesis, Rice University, 1965), 96–102.

only real political base black men had in Texas—only to discover that the movement was "unsuccessful" both from the standpoint of becoming a majority party and its continued existence, blacks would consequently have no personal foothold at all in the political process. Cuney was convinced that the stakes were too high.[20]

Cuney's position aside, many blacks by 1892 could no longer rationalize continued allegiance to the party of Lincoln. They had witnessed a steady deterioration of the northern Republican commitment to civil rights after 1875, the splintering of the southern Republican party into "lily whites" and "black and tans" factions, as well as the increasing business orientation of the party.[21] One black leader, John B. Rayner, a schoolteacher from Calvert, in East Texas, severed ties with the Republicans and became the leading black spokesman for the Populists. Rayner, a superb organizer and speaker, brought 25,000 black voters into the Populist camp by 1896.[22]

The Democrats were so consumed by internal divisions during this period that the appearance of the Populist party did not at first cause them much concern. In 1892, two factions, the dominant "reform" wing, largely based on Alliance voters and headed by Governor James S. Hogg, and the conservative "goldbug" faction, led by railroad lawyer George Clark, vied for control of Texas politics. A railroad-baiting, anti-corporation "man of the people," Hogg appealed to discontented agrarians and moderate Democrats. He called for active governmental participation in Texas economic life but stressed the state-oriented nature of this intervention.[23]

During the hotly contested 1892 gubernatorial campaign, Hogg, the incumbent, confronted two challengers: Clark and T. L. Nugent, the Populist candidate. Hogg won the election with less than a majority and was more than a little shaken by the Populist showing: Hogg, 44 percent; Clark, 31 percent; Nugent, 25 percent. All three candidates competed fiercely for, and received, portions of the black vote. Black organizers established several Hogg clubs, and the Governor's supporters took pains to establish his record on race rela-

20. Goodwyn, "Origins of American Populism," 281; Jack Abramowitz, "The Negro in the Populist Movement," *Journal of Negro History* 38 (July 1953): 269; Hinze, "Norris Wright Cuney," 70–79.

21. Goodwyn, "Origins of American Populism," 232–33; Maud Cuney Hare, *Norris Wright Cuney: A Tribute of the Black People* (1913; reprint, Austin: Steck-Vaughn, 1968), 143–66.

22. Douglass Geraldyne Perry, "Black Populism: The Negro in the People's Party in Texas" (master's thesis, Prairie View University, 1945), 35–36; Abramowitz, "The Negro in the Populist Movement," 270.

23. Gould, *Progressives and Prohibitionists,* 8–9.

tions. They cited the rewards he had offered for the apprehension of lynchers and his numerous pardons of black offenders. Clark likewise solicited the black and relied heavily on the Republican vote. Ironically, both during and after the election, Clark and Hogg attacked each other for appealing to the black vote and the old refrain of blacks-will-hold-the-balance-of-power-if-white-men-divide was heard repeatedly. By 1894 the two Democratic factions were sufficiently impressed with the seriousness of the Populist challenge to reconcile their differences and attempt to forge a united front of white supremacy.[24]

After the 1896 gubernatorial election it was obvious that the Populist movement in Texas and in the nation was on the decline. A number of factors contributed to its collapse. One recent scholar argues that "Populism died because it failed to transcend the American political system. It was killed by those very factors of politics, that its founders had intended to kill: prejudice, elite manipulation, corruption." Farmers were unable to overcome their poverty, isolation, and political inexperience. As the Populist party became increasingly oligarchic, its leaders became primarily concerned with winning office; votes became more important than principles as in the Republican and Democratic parties. At heart, the farmer, or agrarian radical, was a frustrated, pragmatic capitalist. As one scholar maintained, "One good crop year sent them scurrying back to the major parties."[25] In the southern states, violence, fraud, bribery, and the "humbug" about "Negro domination" were important in undermining the Populist party and brought an end to the interracial cooperation that it symbolized.

Once white Democrats overcame the Populist challenge, agitation for the enactment of measures to prevent further threats to the hegemony of the "white man's party" escalated. Hogg and State Representative Alexander Watkins Terrell came to view mandatory primary elections as the ultimate solution. The joker was that the Democratic party's primaries would be for whites only. A poll tax would further restrict the electorate. In sum, three motivational factors operated simultaneously. First, white Democrats desired to restrict the franchise in order to ensure that the "right" class of white men ruled. The state enjoyed an extremely fluid social structure, and because of the money made from railroads, banking, cattle, oil, sulfur, and gas, the upper economic orders increased considerably. These newly rich individuals were quite

24. Ibid., 10; Rice, *Negro in Texas*, 69–82; White, *East Texas*, 344–47.
25. First quote from Argersinger, *Populism and Politics*, 303; second quote from Parsons, *The Populist Context*, 147–48.

concerned about protecting their economic advantages from the political influence of the "have-nots." Second, certain white Democrats were determined
to expand and secure their political dominance in state affairs. They emphasized the need for a white united front or "white solidarity." Third, there was
a sincere desire among some to purify elections and to prevent the sins that
white men committed when they vied for the black vote. The accomplishment
of these objectives depended upon the total elimination of the black man from
the body politic. The effects may be judged racist but the motivations leading
up to and resulting in black disfranchisement are much more complex. Events
in Fort Bend and Grimes Counties illustrate the complexities.

Blacks outnumbered whites about four to one in Fort Bend and had held
many political offices from 1868 to 1888. During Reconstruction, Fort Bend
elected more blacks to political office than any other Texas county. For approximately twenty-five years, black Republicans controlled many important
county offices. Some local whites, in 1888, initiated plans to end black political participation in the county. They formed an ostensible literary and social
club which quickly evolved into the Young Men's Democratic Club of Fort
Bend County. While they agreed upon the desirability of wresting control of
the political machinery of the county from blacks, the whites could not agree
among themselves which whites would rule once black disfranchisement occurred. The club split into two factions, the Jaybirds and the Woodpeckers.

The Jaybirds represented wealthier property owners and the Woodpeckers
were the less affluent who frequently cooperated with blacks, solicited their
votes, and depended upon their support in order to retain offices. Blacks were
caught in the middle. Woodpeckers and Jaybirds, on more than one occasion,
fought out their differences in a style reminiscent of the old wild west. Woodpeckers generally lost most of the shootouts and many others fled the county.
By their first annual meeting in March 1890, the Jaybird Democratic Association was left in complete control. Realizing the profound shift in the political
winds, many blacks left the county. Although other factors, such as the desire
for economic advancement, the search for better educational opportunities,
and the lure of urban areas may have contributed to the subsequent black exodus from Fort Bend, the contemporary precipitous drop in the black population is noteworthy. From a high of 78 percent, by 1910 blacks comprised only
62 percent of the total population. By the end of the second decade of the
twentieth century, blacks were in the minority in Fort Bend, with approximately 12,000 whites to 10,000 blacks.[26]

26. Millie L. Kochan, "The Jaybird-Woodpecker Feud" (master's thesis, University of

A similar picture prevailed in Grimes County. After the collapse of the Populist movement, local whites in Grimes County moved to disfranchise its black residents. From the close of the Civil War to the mid-nineties, Grimes County blacks maintained an indigenous political structure which sent a few black legislators to Austin. The county in 1890 was comprised of 21,213 whites and 11,664 blacks. Out of legitimate self-interest during the high point of the Populist period, Grimes County blacks supported the People's party and were able to win many elected positions. In the spring of 1899, defeated Democratic candidate for county judge J. G. McDonald organized a clandestine meeting with other prominent local citizens and disappointed Democratic office seekers and founded a covert political institution, the White Man's Union. The organization's charter declared that no person could be nominated for office who was not a member of the Union and no person could be a member who refused to subscribe to its racially exclusionary by-laws. To participate in the organization's activities, so adequately expressed in its formal title, as a policy matter one had to support black disfranchisement. These by-laws were reinforced by intimidation and bloodshed. Members of the Union murdered a number of black Populist leaders, organizers, and white sympathizers. For whatever reasons, as had been the case in Fort Bend County, blacks "left by train, by horse and cart, by day and by night." Over 4,500 votes had been cast in Grimes in 1898. On November 6, 1900, only 1,800 persons ventured to the polls. These figures may, to a large degree, reflect the effect of various suffrage restriction legislation in addition to disfranchisement through fear, violence, and intimidation. The 1910 Census revealed the extent of the emigration. Grimes County's black population declined by almost 30 percent from the 1900 total.[27] During the 1890s the adoption of Democratic white primaries became a common phenomenon in most black belt counties.[28]

The 1890s also witnessed increased pressure for a statewide mandatory poll tax as a suffrage restriction measure. Proposals had been offered in the Constitutional Convention of 1875 to make a poll tax a requirement for voting. Poll tax advocates argued that it would eliminate presumably irresponsible nontaxpayers whose votes were often purchasable. This effort was led by

---

Texas, 1929), 35; Pauline Yelderman, "The Jaybird Democratic Association of Fort Bend County" (master's thesis, University of Texas, 1938), 30–38, 49, 66; Clarence R. Wharton, *History of Fort Bend County* (San Antonio: Naylor, 1939), 184, 196–97, 222; Rice, *Negro in Texas,* 121–26.

27. Lawrence C. Goodwyn, "Populist Dreams and Negro Rights: East Texas as a Case Study," *American Historical Review* 76 (December 1971): 1435–56.

28. Annie Lee Williams, *A History of Wharton County 1846–1961* (Austin: Von Voeckman-Jones, 1964), 111–12, 127–33; Rice, *Negro in Texas,* 133.

former Confederate postmaster general and future United States congressman John H. Reagan of Anderson County (44.7 percent black in 1880) and by W. L. Crawford of Marion County (65.6 percent black). Many white Democratic legislators, almost all of whom were members of the farmers' organization, the Grange, opposed the imposition of the poll tax and joined with Republicans to block its enactment. They argued that suffrage was a natural right and correctly predicted that a capitation tax would disfranchise many poor whites.[29] The poll tax measure was defeated.

In 1879 Alexander Watkins Terrell introduced another poll tax amendment and successfully pushed it through the state senate. Terrell argued that linking the tax to suffrage would end the high rate of delinquency in its payment. That was not all he desired to accomplish, however, for in November 1878 he had written, "Unless some flank movement can be made on the mass of ignorant negro voters, we will soon be at sea in Texas." Terrell was unable to amass enough support in the House to pass his bill. Undaunted, he reintroduced poll tax bills in the 1881 and 1883 legislatures—both were defeated. After the last failure, poll tax bills disappeared for a short period. During the 1890s, however, poll tax bills reappeared with predictable regularity.[30]

A more concerted effort in 1889 to pass a poll tax bill also failed. During the 1888 presidential campaign the Republican candidate, Benjamin Harrison, secured more southern votes than any Republican nominee for the presidency since the end of Reconstruction. Republicans also won firm control in both branches of the Congress. Shortly after taking control, Republican senator Henry Cabot Lodge introduced the proposal for a bill (the Force Bill) to provide federal supervision of congressional elections. The federal supervisor would have been authorized to control voter registration, pass on qualifications of challenged voters, and to decide between federal and state canvassers. It is likely that had the bill been enacted the number of southern Republicans and Populists in Congress would have increased. Most importantly the Force Bill would have ended questionable southern election practices. This, coupled with the increased strength in Congress of southerners hostile to the Democratic party, might well have further eroded Democratic power.[31] The Force Bill created a flurry of excitement, and the alarm spread quickly throughout the South. Conservative Democrats employed the threat of the Force Bill to

29. Kousser, *Shaping Southern Politics*, 200.
30. Terrell, quoted in Barr, *Reconstruction to Reform*, 204; Dale Brown Wood, "The Poll Tax as a Voting Requirement" (master's thesis, University of Texas, 1942), 47–48.
31. Kousser, *Shaping Southern Politics*, 29–30; Key, *Southern Politics*, 537; Woodward, *Origins of the New South*, 254.

support their efforts to divide members and potential members of third parties along the color line.[32] Although the Force Bill was defeated in the Senate
in January 1891, it clearly encouraged southerners to search for more constitutional means of disfranchising blacks.

Texans found the closing years of the nineteenth century to be relatively quiet ones. Some Democrats, however, refused to give up on the idea of enacting
a poll tax. In 1899 Representative, and future governor, Pat Neff of McLennon
County (24 percent black) and Senator A. B. Davidson of De Witt County (23
percent black) introduced a new poll tax measure into the state legislature. The
measure was defeated, but in 1902 its Democratic supporters were more successful. The general electorate adopted a poll tax amendment to the state constitution which required all voters to pay the tax at least eight months prior to
the general election. Blacks, Populists, some Republicans, and the State Feder-
ation of Labor blasted the amendment. The few remaining Populists charged
that the poll tax was a plot to rob the laboring people of their liberties at the
ballot box. Labor union men denounced the tax as a ploy used by wealthier
whites to disfranchise poorer classes. Blacks, many of whom were less disposed
to vote by this time, turned out in large numbers in East Texas to register their
opposition to the poll tax.[33] The combined opposition to poll tax legislation
was of little consequence. The enactment of the tax, coupled with the death of
Norris Wright Cuney and continued Republican intra-party squabbling and
the growing pre-eminence of the "lily whites," caused black political power almost to disappear. J. Morgan Kousser concludes that "the adoption of the poll
tax in Texas then, was neither part of a general 'reform' program nor the result
of a frantic racist upsurge. It was the quiet climax of a long drive by a few men,
a drive which succeeded when the opposition became dormant." It could be
added that it succeeded when the opposition was worn out by the use of unfair methods of political competition: bribery, coercion, intimidation, fraud,
and murder.[34]

While black participation in Texas politics was declining, ardent disfranchisers remained unsatisfied. Alexander Watkins Terrell led the fight for the
further "purification" of the Texas electorate through the adoption of a statewide mandatory primary law. Terrell, staunch advocate of the poll tax
throughout the 1870s and 1880s, became, in 1895, one of the most forceful
proponents for the adoption of direct primary legislation. Born in Virginia in

32. Woodward, *Origins of the New South,* 255.
33. Kousser, *Shaping Southern Politics,* 69–71, 206; Wood, "The Poll Tax," 49–50; Barr,
*Reconstruction to Reform,* 205.
34. Kousser, *Shaping Southern Politics,* 205.

1829 to a slaveholding family, Terrell earned a law degree from the University of Missouri. After being admitted to the bar he worked as a city attorney in St. Joseph, Missouri, prior to moving to Austin, Texas, in 1852. Within a short time Terrell entered politics. He served as a district judge and became a Confederate general during the Civil War. After the war Terrell served as a state senator from 1876 to 1884. He served in the lower house from 1890 to 1892 and again from 1902 to 1906. Unlike most disfranchisers, Terrell resided in a predominantly white county (Travis). He possessed a strong and unchanging antipathy towards blacks, decried all vestiges of racial equality, and from 1867 to 1871 gave up practicing law because blacks were permitted to serve on some juries. Terrell blamed blacks for the mob violence that often erupted in Texas. He felt that blacks were intellectually incapable of advanced education and vehemently declared that the greatest mistake in the nineteenth century was the North's "forcing the ballot into the hands of the negro." Terrell was only slightly less biased towards poorer whites. He attempted to destroy the whole system of public elementary education in Texas while serving in the legislature. Terrell was, throughout his career, a consistent proponent of suffrage restriction for whites and disfranchisement for blacks. The Fifteenth Amendment, he said, amounted to "the political blunder of the century," and he later asserted that only the poll tax could eliminate "the thriftless, idle and semivagrant element of both races." In 1906 he summed up the views he articulated throughout his life. "Whether universal manhood suffrage is good for the country depends entirely on the sort of men who vote."[35] For Terrell, who was a racist with strong feelings of having been somehow wronged and degraded by Reconstruction policies, the poll tax and the white primary would ensure that the right sort of men not only voted but controlled all the political, educational, and economic affairs of the state. His "right sort" of man was, undoubtedly, white, native-born, of the upper socioeconomic class, and a Democratic party loyalist.

While "reform" Governor James Hogg was in office, Terrell met with him daily to write laws and map out strategies designed to foster white solidarity and preserve white supremacy. Hogg shared many of Terrell's views. During his two terms as governor he blatantly endorsed segregation and used his power shrewdly and ruthlessly to destroy political opposition.[36] One of the mea-

35. Biographical sketch drawn from Charles Kincheloe Chamberlain, "Alexander Watkins Terrell, Citizen, Statesman" (Ph.D. diss., University of Texas, 1956), 3–108, 493–94; Kousser, *Shaping Southern Politics*, 201–2.
36. Gould, *Progressives and Prohibitionists*, 10–11; Kousser, *Shaping Southern Politics*, 202.

sures which the governor and Terrell labored over was later approved by Hogg's successor Charles Culberson. The Texas legislature, in 1895, in its first effort to regulate primaries enacted a law declaring it a misdemeanor to vote more than once; buy votes; vote outside one's home precinct; attempt to bribe voters or election officials; or to make a false return.[37] Passage of the law cannot be attributed solely to racist motives. In part, it reflected a general concern and desire to "purify" the electoral process. This becomes clearer, perhaps, by examining the law's defects. The law did not specify who could or could not vote in primaries. This lack of specification permitted any reasonably qualified male to vote if he desired to do so.

Culberson's law was direct primary legislation more so than a "white" primary law. During the time of its enactment a nationwide agitation developed for the "democratization" and "purification" of American politics. A growing belief existed among progressive Americans that their political system was infected with a corruption that threatened to contaminate not only business and social relations but the whole fabric of American society. American imperialism involved concomitant control over masses of nonwhite people. This, coupled with the specter of hordes of poor, illiterate, unpropertied whites joining political hands with blacks, and unstable economic conditions, explains the demand for a series of changes in the mechanics of political life—direct primaries, popular election of senators, initiative, referendum, recall, and the secret ballot. Richard Hofstadter argued that the push for the adoption of the direct primary can be viewed as an effort to restore popular government as it was "imagined . . . to exist in an earlier and purer age."[38]

Every Texas state legislature that convened from 1895 to 1923 amended the primary election law. In 1897 the legislature amended the 1895 law to establish definite times for holding elections and the manner of handling election returns. Subsequent laws specified qualifications of voters. The 1899 law declared that the voter had to be twenty-one years old, male, U.S. citizen, and resident of county or precinct six months prior to the election. The 1901 amendment required males over twenty-one years of age to pay their poll taxes before the first of February of each year in order to vote in the primary.[39]

37. Chamberlain, "Alexander Terrell," 452–55, 461–94; Barr, *Reconstruction to Reform*, 203.

38. Richard Hofstadter, *The Age of Reform: From Bryan to F.D.R.* (New York: Vantage Books, 1960), 255.

39. Howard Mell Greene, "Legal Regulation of Political Parties in Texas" (master's thesis, University of Texas, 1923), 79; W. T. Garner, "The Primaries in Texas" (master's thesis, University of Texas, 1920), 48–51.

Terrell remained dissatisfied. In early 1902, he ran for the state legislature from Travis County. He promised during his campaign that he "would try to see whether laws and penalties could be adopted which would restore the pure ballot." True to his word, as soon as he took his seat in the house, Terrell introduced a primary election reform bill. The law provided for a first and second primary, for official ballots, and a voter declaration of party membership. Second or "runoff" primaries were often necessary because as the Democratic party gradually became the only functioning party it was not uncommon to have as many as six or more aspirants for each of the more important state offices. A candidate received the party's nomination if he received a majority of the total votes cast in his contest. If no candidate received a majority, the two highest in the polls became contenders in the runoff primary. Terrell's law further stipulated that tax collectors could not deliver poll tax receipts or exemptions to any person other than the one whose name appeared on the certificate. Expenses for holding the primary election were to be paid jointly by the counties and the state. In a two-hour speech before the legislature on February 27, 1903, Terrell argued that once the election bill was passed it would make it impossible for men to barter their ballots. "The objective of the bill," he said, "was to make elections as pure as the snow that fell on the earth." His plea won support from Representative Thomas B. Love of Dallas, who proposed "that the county executive committee of each party may prescribe further qualifications." Like Terrell, Love was an ardent disfranchiser who believed that blacks and ballots, particularly Democratic primary ballots, did not mix. The Terrell Election Bill passed the senate 22 to 8 and the house 66 to 46.[40] Although the statute did not mention blacks specifically, it was understood that blacks would be barred from voting in the Democratic party's primaries. But even this did not produce the desired results and Terrell was soon before the legislature again.

Because white Democrats never unanimously agreed upon the effectiveness or indeed the desirability of this method of black disfranchisement, many county executive committee chairmen were opposed to the proscription, and white candidates continued to solicit the black vote. Beaumont, Texas, provides one example of how the Terrell Election Law was circumvented and ignored. According to the Beaumont *Enterprise,* both blacks and whites regularly participated in ballot bartering. During the 1904 elections, the paper reported that at least 500 people committed penitentiary offenses in violation of the Terrell Election Law. Two white election judges were removed because they

40. Chamberlain, "Alexander Terrell," 462–65.

allegedly assisted an illiterate black in marking his ballot. These events high-lighted the defects of the 1903 law.[41]

On January 12, 1905, Terrell introduced a bill amending his 1903 statute. The new law made the practice of paying poll taxes of blacks a misdemeanor. But most importantly, the new law gave the party's executive committees the right to determine eligibility for party membership and thus voting privileges in primary elections.[42] Again, Beaumont is instructive. The Jefferson County Democratic Committee of the city of Beaumont immediately arranged a city primary in accordance with the 1905 law. The city's Democratic leaders draft-ed an oath which became the test for party membership: "I am a white quali-fied voter in the city of Beaumont under the laws of Texas and said city, and hereby pledge myself to support the nominees of the democratic primary and abide by the results of said primary." The immediate effect of this test of par-ty membership was the almost total removal of blacks from city politics. In 1902 more than 1,000 blacks had registered to vote; in 1904 approximately 800 paid poll taxes. By 1906 only 200 paid poll taxes and in 1908 only one black voter was reported to have attempted to vote. He went away when asked to sign an affidavit that he was a Democrat.[43] Thus, in at least one Texas city, Terrell's objective was finally realized when his laws bore the fruit of black disfran-chisement.

Subsequent amendments to the primary election laws followed in 1907 and at two-year intervals thereafter. Some of the amendments attempted to restrict corrupt or illegal corporate involvement in primary elections. One gave women the right to vote in primary elections. Others prescribed uniform tests for voters in the form of party loyalty oaths. A series of amendments regulat-ed the runoff primaries and alternately gave and retracted the right of coun-ty executive committees to decide whether candidates for precinct and coun-ty offices should be nominated by plurality or majority vote.[44] The Texas Supreme Court later declared unconstitutional a 1913 primary law requiring each county to pay its share of primary election expenditures. The Court held that public revenue could only be expended for public purposes and that the primary was not a public affair.[45] This court decision justified the continued privacy of the Democratic primary.

41. Paul E. Isaac, "Municipal Reform in Beaumont, Texas, 1902–1909," *Southwestern Historical Quarterly* 78 (April 1975), 421–22.

42. Rice, *Negro in Texas,* 136.

43. Isaac, "Municipal Reform," 421–22.

44. Garner, "The Primaries in Texas," 56–57.

45. *Waples* v. *Marrast,* 184 S.W. 180 (1916); Garner, "The Primaries in Texas," 59.

Why Texas did not employ all of the disfranchisement and suffrage restriction techniques used in other southern states is open to speculation. V. O. Key points to many characteristics that differentiated Texas from the remainder of the South. Unlike other southern states, Texas had two groups of distinctive national origins—Mexican-Americans and German-Americans. The Mexican vote was effectively controlled by machine ward leaders. Mexicans also suffered from economic dependency, many did not speak English, and most possessed only a rudimentary conception of Anglo-American governmental institutions. There was apparently little reason to fear the Mexican vote because it was so tightly controlled. The Germans, on the other hand, took American democracy literally. As a rule they had never been slaveholders (indeed, slavery in Texas was of relatively short duration—20 years—as compared to the length of time it existed—200 years—in older southern states), were liberal, and inclined toward Republicanism but did not support coalition with the Populists during the nineties.[46] The Germans did not condone efforts to restrict suffrage or disfranchisement. Their presence, perhaps, in at least a few of the counties, had a mediating influence on Texas politics.

Another factor is the size of the state. The great distances handicapped the consultation and negotiation necessary to forge and maintain unanimity on issues. East Texas, while being the site of the greatest concentration of the black population, was still interspersed with counties in which blacks were outnumbered by whites more than three to one. By 1910 only 8 of 217 Texas counties had black majorities. There were likewise no factional cleavages based on geographical or regional conflict. Class and economic considerations were ultimately the most important determinants of political behavior. Furthermore, as Key observes, the settlement of West Texas after 1900 created a huge territory with few blacks and thereby reduced even further the significance in the state as a whole of those counties immediately and intensely concerned with questions of race.[47] All of these factors combined thus mitigated against the adoption of the complete baggage of antidemocratic assaults on the black ballot. Given that it was all they had, this perhaps explains why a few Texas leaders worked so hard to strengthen, and preserve, the poll tax and white primary legislation once adopted. These two measures constituted the only legal tools Texas disfranchisers possessed to achieve their twin goals of restricting certain whites and eliminating all blacks from active participation in the state

46. V. O. Key, Jr., *Southern Politics in State and Nation* (New York: Alfred A. Knopf, 1949), 271–73.

47. Ibid., 259–61, 275–76; Kousser, *Shaping Southern Politics*, 196.

political process, as well as impeding the development of third party opposition.

Although the issue of disfranchisement was resolved, in the main, during the first two decades of the twentieth century, some white Texans nevertheless remained haunted by the black presence. As the one-party system became a reality, factions and intra-party feuds erupted frequently over other issues and personalities. At an almost subliminal level the white man's fear of the omnipresent, but now politically impotent, black man continued directly and indirectly to influence his political decisions.

From 1911 to 1921 the Prohibition issue split the Democratic leadership into two contending camps—the "Wets" versus the "Drys." The Dallas *Morning News* in 1916 observed, "Prohibition is as perennial as it is paramount as an issue in our politics. The methods devised to keep it outside party councils have failed utterly. It determines most other decisions and influences all of them, until it would hardly exaggerate to say that no question is considered on its own merits." Interestingly both "Wets" and "Drys" on occasion defended their positions with references to the black presence. Ardent anti-Prohibitionist Senator James Weldon Bailey spoke against the passage of a national Prohibition amendment out of a fear that it would invite federal intervention into the social and political affairs of the state. He was obsessed with the specter of miscegenation and at one point asserted, "Pass a national prohibition amendment and there will not be a square foot of territory in the United States where it will be unlawful for negroes and white people to intermarry." The "Drys," from a different and often contradictory perspective, also based their arguments in support of a federal Prohibition amendment upon the black presence. "Drys" charged that blacks voted against Prohibition and were decisive in the closely fought liquor battles because they received financial assistance and supervision from the brewing interests. Senator Thomas B. Love concluded that "the Negro ought not be permitted to vote on the question of whether or not liquor shall be sold in Texas any more than the Indian should be permitted to vote on the question of whether or not liquor shall be sold in Indian country."[48]

Although informal arrangements and local laws in most counties kept blacks out of the Democratic primaries, they could vote in presidential and national elections and in contests over federal constitutional amendments.

48. Dallas *Morning News,* August 10, 1916; speeches by Senator Joseph Weldon Bailey and comments by Thomas B. Love, quoted in Gould, *Progressives and Prohibitionists,* 23–24, 48–49; Rupert Norval Richardson, *Texas: The Lone Star State* (New York: Prentice Hall, 1943), 286–87.

Even this limited political participation irked both "Drys" and "Wets." Prohibitionists were particularly incensed when they lost the battle to enact a liquor amendment in July 1911. The "Drys" blamed the black vote for the defeat and accused the liquor camp of employing a slush fund to produce the outcome.[49]

A second hotly debated and divisive issue in Texas politics centered around the women's suffrage question. White Texans reflected much of the ambivalence, self-serving perspectives, and status anxiety expressed in the national women's suffrage movement. On the state level, the faction opposed to the proposed women's suffrage amendment argued that passage would open the door to increased federal supervision over suffrage and would grant the franchise to black women. One influential white Texan sent a warning from Washington, D.C., declaring that the suffrage amendment pending in Congress meant "more than the mere extension of the franchise to women." He explained, "It means that the Federal Government shall supervise our elections and of course in all the states of the South where negroes are in the majority, the negroes will again be placed in control just as they were after the war when the white people were practically disfranchised."[50]

On the national scene, northern and southern white women worked hard to disassociate the "Negro question" from women's suffrage. Southern white women based their appeal for the vote on the argument that the enfranchisement of women would greatly increase the white majority, ensure white supremacy, and was in fact, they claimed, a solution to the race problem. White women also effectively capitalized on the growing nativism in the country. They emphasized the objectionable fact and alleged injustice of making refined white women the political inferiors of former slaves and "unfit" immigrants.[51] Women's suffrage and the white primary were two sides of the same coin. Both had the desired effect of expanding the power of certain elements or groups in the white electorate, the one by increasing the number of likeminded white voters and the other by eliminating black voting.

The debates over black disfranchisement, Prohibition, and women's suffrage exacerbated the already tense social relations between the two races in Texas. While historians have labeled the period between 1898 and 1910 as a period of relative quiet in Texas history, this description is certainly not ap-

49. Richardson, *Texas: The Lone Star State,* 49, 55–56.

50. John H. Kirby to J. A. Mooney, August 15, 1914, Kirby Papers, quoted in Gould, *Progressives and Prohibitionists,* 24–25.

51. Alan P. Grimes, *The Puritan Ethic and Woman Suffrage* (New York: Oxford University Press, 1967), 111, 125; Aileen S. Kraditor, *The Ideas of the Woman Suffrage Movement, 1890–1920* (New York: Columbia University Press, 1965), 164–68, 196.

plicable to the second decade when the numbers of riots, lynchings, and violent interracial clashes reached their highest level ever. The years immediately following World War I were particularly bloody ones not only in Texas but in the entire country.

Waco, Texas, was the location of a horrible lynching in 1916. The lynching reflected so much brutality that the National Association for the Advancement of Colored People published a supplement to the regular edition of *The Crisis* entitled, "The Waco Horror." A crowd of over 10,000 people was present for the lynching of Jesse Washington, a Negro charged with assault and murder. His body was beaten, stabbed, and mutilated beyond recognition before he was hanged and finally burned by the citizens of Waco. Women and children were present in large numbers with children held high so they could better view the spectacle.[52]

A year later a riot occurred in Houston, Texas, which left twenty persons wounded or dead. The Twenty-fourth Infantry arrived as military guards in rigidly segregated Houston on July, 18, 1917. Whites were openly hostile and resented the presence of the black soldiers. After a series of insulting exchanges and other indignities inflicted by the local whites and the police, a riot broke out on August 23, 1917. The black soldiers were accused of inciting the riot, and there was a clamor of public opinion demanding vengeance. At least one white man was killed. Following the largest court-martial in American history, thirteen black soldiers were executed at Camp Travis on December 11, 1917. Forty-one others were sentenced to life in prison. Apparently not satisfied with this, the army tried fifty-five more soldiers in two additional court-martials. Sixteen were sentenced to hang and twelve to life terms. President Wilson saved ten of the sixteen sentenced to be executed and commuted their terms to life imprisonment on August 22, 1918. Blacks across the country were shocked at what was, in essence, a mockery of justice.[53]

Black blood continued to flow in the postwar years. What James Weldon Johnson called "The Red Summer of 1919" began early in July when whites invaded the black section of Longview, Texas, seeking Lemuel Walters, who had allegedly accused a white woman of a liaison with a black man. Later the *Chicago Defender* (a black newspaper), with a dateline from Longview, reported that the white girl had in fact lived with Walters. Longview whites de-

52. Galveston *Daily News,* May 16, 1916; Dallas *Morning News,* May 16, 1916; "The Waco Horror," *The Crisis* 12, no. 3 (July 1916, supplement): 18.

53. Robert V. Haynes, "The Houston Mutiny and Riot of 1917," *Southwestern Historical Quarterly* 76 (April 1973): 418–39; and *A Night of Violence, Houston Riot of 1917* (Baton Rouge: Louisiana State University Press, 1976), 1–15.

cided that a black schoolteacher had written the article. They organized a mob and went searching for the black teacher to drive him out of town after he had been taught the appropriate lesson. The mob approached the home of a black physician who supposedly was harboring the individual who authored the story. When the whites met with a show of black resistance, they waited for reinforcements to arrive. As the mob grew larger and more confident, it moved into the black community, beating and shooting blacks and burning homes and other buildings. The riot ended only after the state militia arrived and restored order.[54]

The state attorney general's office contended that certain black publications had incited the riot. The National Association for the Advancement of Colored People responded to the thinly veiled accusation that its journal *The Crisis* was in any way connected to the occurrences. The national headquarters immediately issued a call demanding an end to segregation. White officials in Austin, in the meantime, ordered the local NAACP branch to disband and the state attorney general subpoenaed the records of the organization. NAACP executive secretary John R. Shillady, a white, went to investigate the situation and to learn "what had occasioned the inquiry which had been conducted in Austin into the Association's and the local branch's affairs, to ascertain what legal objections, if any, had been raised against the Association." Shillady did not get very far in his mission. On a street in Austin, Shillady was assaulted and severely beaten by a mob that included County Judge Dave Pickle and constable Charles Hamby. The national office was outraged by the attack and immediately demanded an investigation and proper punishment of Shillady's assailants. The unsympathetic governor W. P. Hobby responded, "I believe in sending any narrow-brained, double-chinned reformer who comes here with the end of stirring up racial discontent back to the North where he came from with a broken jaw if necessary." Hobby advised the NAACP that it could "contribute more to the advancement of both races by keeping your representatives and their propaganda out of this state than in any other way."[55] Shillady's assailants were never punished and race relations in Texas steadily deteriorated.

A general air of hostility and fear prevailed in the state, which provided fertile ground for the rise of the new Ku Klux Klan. Nowhere, with the possible

54. Arthur I. Waskow, *From Race Riot to Sit-In, 1919 and the 1960's: A Study in the Connections between Conflict and Violence* (Garden City, N.Y.: Doubleday, 1967), 16–20; "The Race Riot at Longview, Texas," *The Crisis* 18 (October 1919): 297–98.

55. *The Mobbing of John R. Shillady, Secretary of the National Association for the Advancement of Colored People, Austin, Texas, August 22, 1919* (New York: NAACP, 1919), 2–5, 11; Gould, *Progressives and Prohibitionists,* 253.

exception of Indiana or Oklahoma, would the Klan command more respect and wield more power than in Texas. World War I had intensified racial antipathies. Armed black soldiers who had enjoyed new levels of freedom of contact with whites in France, for example, returned in the postwar years with a decided unwillingness to endure white oppression. The Klan quickly capitalized on the feelings of those whites who believed they saw signs of Negro "uppitiness" everywhere. From 1922 to 1924 the Klan was one of the paramount issues in Texas politics. The Klan successfully elected Earl B. Mayfield to the United States Congress and won many local offices. The Klan also gained extensive control of city governments in Fort Worth, Dallas, and Wichita Falls during the municipal elections of 1924. A majority of the 38th Texas State Legislature were Klan members and sympathizers.[56] Thus when new pressure mounted for a more stringently exclusive white primary law, the legislature was receptive.

In 1905 the state legislature had amended the 1903 white primary statute to permit the county Democratic executive committees to establish voting qualifications. It was implicitly understood that blacks would be barred from voting in the party's primaries. Because white Democrats never unanimously agreed upon the efficacy of black disfranchisement, many county executive committee chairmen were opposed to the proscription, and white candidates continued to solicit the black vote. This was particularly true in counties where blacks were numerically significant. The uncertainty surrounding the issue created a climate by 1918 which motivated various factions and personalities within the Democratic party to intensify agitation for universal black disfranchisement and the enactment of a law which would remove the question from the political arena altogether.[57]

The immediate demand for a stronger white primary statute grew out of a factional feud within the Democratic organization of Bexar County. Bexar County was one of the few counties that continued to permit blacks to vote in the Democratic primaries in spite of the Terrell Election Law of 1905. During the election campaign of 1922, D. A. McAskill, the incumbent district attor-

56. Arnold S. Rice, *The Ku Klux Klan in American Politics* (Washington, D.C.: Public Affairs Press, 1962), 15; Charles C. Alexander, *The Crusade for Conformity: The Ku Klux Klan in the Southwest* (Houston: Texas Gulf Coast Historical Association, 1962), v; Charles D. Alexander, *The Ku Klux Klan in the Southwest* (Lexington: University of Kentucky Press, 1966), 121; Kenneth T. Jackson, *The Ku Klux Klan in the City, 1915–1930* (New York: Oxford University Press, 1967), 71–73.

57. Conrey Bryson, *Dr. Lawrence A. Nixon and the White Primary* (El Paso: Texas Western Press and University of Texas at El Paso, 1974), 2; Atkins, *The Texas Negro and His Political Rights,* 6; Rice, *Negro in Texas,* 136.

ney, ran against Frank Williams for re-election. While both candidates had on previous occasions solicited support from blacks, McAskill chose to make an issue of black voting in this particular campaign. McAskill accused his opponent of inflaming blacks against him because of his prosecution of a black man accused of raping a white woman. He charged that his opponent's behavior was undemocratic and that "any white man who would ask black folk for their votes was not a Democrat." He warned of the "direful domination of local government affairs by the colored people" of San Antonio who, in reality, were less than one-twelfth of the population.[58]

McAskill's statements and agitation for a statutory white primary bar aroused the consternation of the black citizens of Bexar County. One black, H. M. Tarver, in an open letter to the district attorney, attempted to refresh McAskill's memory of his past solicitation of the black vote when he first ran for public office. McAskill had made a special appeal to blacks for their support in a primary election. Tarver quoted McAskill's speeches during which he swore that he was "a life-long Democrat of the sort that believed all men regardless of race had a just right to the equal protection of the law and likewise the selection of public officials." In a revealing passage Tarver noted that blacks had come "in recent years to think it right and praiseworthy not to oppose or antagonize their neighbors in matters of politics without reason, if at all, but from motives entirely correct and lofty they have voted regularly for candidates and measures put forward by the Democratic party."[59]

Black protests notwithstanding, McAskill, after winning the election, kept his campaign promise and immediately pressured the state legislature to enact a statutory bar against black participation in the Democratic primary. It was widely publicized that Governor Pat Neff approved of and supported enactment of a white primary law. The state chairman of the Democratic executive committee, Frank C. Davis, announced his wholehearted support.[60] A recent United States Supreme Court decision in the *Newberry* v. *United States* case may have been interpreted as giving constitutional sanction to the proposed statute. The Newberry case involved the federal Corrupt Practices Act

58. San Antonio *Express*, May 11, 1923, July 23, 1922; Paul Lewinson, *Race, Class and Party: A History of Negro Suffrage and White Politics in the South* (New York: Oxford University Press, 1932), 113.

59. Harold M. Tarver, "The Whiteman's Primary (An open letter to D. A. McAskill, 1922)." See copy of this letter in the Eugene V. Barker Library, Texas State Historical Library at the University of Texas in Austin, Texas. Letter listed in the card catalogue under author's name.

60. San Antonio *Express*, May 11, July 23, 1923.

of 1910 which limited by criminal penalties the amount of money that might be spent in congressional election campaigns. The act required that all interstate political committees keep finances aboveboard and report on the source of campaign contributions in excess of $100 and expenditures exceeding $10. Truman Newberry of Michigan successfully defeated Henry Ford in a race for a seat in the United States Senate in 1918. Charges were lodged against Newberry on the grounds that during the campaign he violated the Corrupt Practices Act. The Supreme Court ruled in favor of Newberry and in so doing maintained that congressional power did not extend to regulation of primary elections. Primaries therefore were not considered to be elections for an office but merely methods by which party adherents agreed upon a candidate whom they intended to support in the general elections.[61] The convergence of these events encouraged the Texas legislature to take an unprecedented step.

There were a couple of obstacles but almost no opposition to the enactment of the white primary bill of 1923 introduced in the Senate by Senator R. S. Bowers of Caldwell, Texas, and in the House of Representatives by D. S. Davenport of Dallas and Clifton E. Beagley of Sulfur Springs. The supporters of the bill encountered their first obstacle when the lieutenant governor ruled that the bill was out of order because it was not listed on Governor Neff's call for a special session of the legislature. After a short delay, Governor Neff obligingly submitted an amended call for the special session so that the proposed bill could be enacted. Only one member of the House, R. A. Baldwin of Slaton, Texas, expressed reservations about the bill. He confessed, "I seriously doubt the constitutionality of Senate Bill, Number 44, expressly disfranchising negroes in primary elections, and see in it possibilities for serious legal complications and many contests of primary elections. For these reasons I cannot vote for it." Baldwin did not vote against the bill either; he simply voted "present."

The bill was presented to Governor Neff for his approval on May 10. The Governor had the option of vetoing the measure or letting it become law without his signature. Governor Neff decided to take no action and after ten days the following white primary measure became law:[62]

61. *Newberry v. United States*, 256 U.S. 232, 65 L. ed. 913 (1921); Richard Claude, *The Supreme Court and the Electoral Process* (Baltimore: Johns Hopkins University Press, 1970), 32–33.

62. House Journal, *38 Legislature*, 2d Called Session (Austin, 1923), April 25, 1923, p. 1295; Senate Journal, *38th Legislature*, 2d Called Session (Austin, 1923), May 1, 1923, pp. 112, 378, 458; Bryson, *Dr. Lawrence A. Nixon*, 13–16.

Any qualified voter under the laws of the Constitution of the State of Texas who is a bonafide member of the Democratic Party shall be eligible to participate in any Democratic primary election provided such voter complies with all laws and rules governing party primary elections; however, in no event shall a negro be eligible to participate in a Democratic Party primary election held in the State of Texas and should a negro vote in a Democratic primary election such ballot shall be void and election officials are herein directed to throw out such ballot and not count the same.[63]

Representative Baldwin's cautionary remarks were prophetic, for challenges to the bill were, indeed, immediately forthcoming.

63. General Laws of Texas, *38th Legislature Journal,* 2d Called Session (Austin, 1923), p. 74.

# 3

# Black Texans and the
# Rise of the NAACP

Throughout the first two decades of the twentieth century, as white Texans struggled to enact white primary disfranchisement legislation, blacks were equally determined that such proscriptions be declared unconstitutional by the courts. By 1921 the political climate in Texas had changed considerably. The post–World War I outbreaks of racial violence had led to new heights of fear and increased demands for mechanisms to control blacks and "keep them in their place." The Klan amassed noteworthy support across the state that culminated in the election of a number of sympathizers to local and state offices.[1] Blacks were developing a more militant and assertive mode of behavior and thought. Across the country talk was heard of the emerging "New Negro," who would rather "fight" and "nobly die" for his rights than submit to second-class citizenship.

In spite of the Terrell Election Law of 1905, blacks continued to participate in nonpartisan municipal elections in cities such as El Paso, San Antonio, Galveston, Houston, Dallas, and Fort Worth.[2] In 1921, white Democrats in Houston, however, decided to end even this limited participation. The City Democratic Executive Committee of Houston, on January 27, 1921, adopted a resolution excluding blacks from the primary election scheduled for February 9, 1921. This assault on the black ballot precipitated a mobilization of black leaders who immediately initiated legal proceedings for an injunction.

Black Houstonians were psychologically predisposed to counteract the

---

1. Charles C. Alexander, *The Ku Klux Klan in the Southwest* (Lexington: University of Kentucky Press, 1966), 121.
2. Ralph J. Bunche, *The Political Status of The Negro in the Age of FDR*, ed. Dewey W. Grantham (Chicago: University of Chicago Press, 1973), 78–79, 152–54; Melvin James Banks, "The Pursuit of Equality: The Movement for First Class Citizenship among Negroes in Texas, 1920–1950" (Ph.D. diss., Syracuse University, 1962), 295–97.

white primary challenge and enjoyed enough economic freedom to respond quickly. In many important respects, black Texans in general differed from blacks in other southern states. Donald R. Matthews and James W. Prothro, in a remarkable statistical study of blacks in southern politics, identified and analyzed variables which inhibited black political activity in the South. They asked, "Why are southern Negroes, in most but not all respects, less politically active than are southern whites?" Ironically, the factors they isolated to explain the absence of political activity among some southern blacks are useful in accounting for the pronounced political activity of black Houstonians.

Although locked out of participation in Democratic primaries, black Houstonians in particular and black Texans in general were, nevertheless, politically active. Black newspapers carefully reported political developments. Social, religious, economic, and political clubs and organizations all paid some attention to the political instruction of the masses of black Texans. Black leaders urged the payment of poll taxes and participation in the open general elections. The most important factor responsible for maintaining high levels of political interest and activity among rank-and-file blacks, as will be shown, became the fight against the Democratic white primary. Yet these factors combined only partly explain why black Houstonians and Texans were so politically assertive.

Personal characteristics such as sex, age, education, occupation, and income relate directly to political activity. Most political activists are male, aged twenty and above, who become especially active during their forties. They are reasonably well educated, and are in the comfortable-to-high income brackets. Matthews and Prothro argue that southern blacks who acquire either a college education or employment in professional or white-collar jobs are much more likely than other blacks to take some part in politics. A higher income is particularly conducive to increased political participation: "First, it can pay a poll tax," buys greater leisure time, helps to build greater self-confidence in coping with one's environment, provides more daily experience in making choices, and leads to greater recognition by whites. Simultaneously, a pool of educated, skilled, and economically independent blacks in one community can have "a multiplier effect." "Not only are those Negroes in white-collar employment more likely to be political participants," Matthews and Prothro assert, "but their presence in an area also seems to lead other Negroes to participate." They observed that "the kind of county in which Negroes win nominal jobs is the sort of place where a Negro middle class has an opportunity to exert some political leadership."[3]

3. Donald R. Matthews and James W. Prothro, *Negroes and the New Southern Politics* (New York: Harcourt, Brace and World, 1966), 68–95, 133.

Houston had such a pool of well-educated black professionals and entrepreneurs economically independent of whites. As early as 1902, there were 9
lawyers, 4 dentists, 16 doctors, 10 real estate agents, 5 black newspapers, 30
restaurants, and 40 stores. It would be difficult to duplicate such a conglomer-
ation of blacks in almost any southern city outside of Texas (and the other five
states of the peripheral South—Arkansas, Florida, Virginia, North Carolina,
and Tennessee).[4] The illiteracy rate among the masses of black Texans was also
on the decline. In 1890, 53.2 percent of black Texans ten years old and over
were illiterate. In 1920, the level of illiteracy had dropped to 17.8 percent, and
by 1930, only 13.4 percent were illiterate. It is also significant to note that Texas
had a relatively larger urban black population than any other southern state,
although the total population was quite small. The black population grew
from 741,694 in 1920 to 854,964 in 1930, with blacks comprising 14.7 percent
of the total population in the latter year. Approximately 40 percent of the
blacks, by 1930, resided in urban areas.[5]

Matthews and Prothro suggest that the larger the proportion of blacks in a
southern community, the smaller the proportion who are politically active.
Conversely, the fewer the number of blacks, as compared to white residents,
the greater the degree of political activity. As the proportion of blacks climbs
to 40 percent and above, "the proportion of whites favoring the abstract notion of Negro voting drops very rapidly." The black commitment to voting cor-
respondingly declines, as white disapproval of such activity increases.[6] Black
Houstonians were safely within the population ratio/white approval margin.
In 1920, blacks comprised 24.6 percent of Houston's total population (138,276
white, 33,960 blacks).[7] Third Circuit Court Justice William Henry Hastie, and
the former president of Howard University, attorney James M. Nabrit (who
was also a leading figure in the white primary fight in Texas during the 1930s),
expanded on these observations. Hastie maintained that "the black community in Houston had more financial resources than most black communities.
Texas was already beginning to be a prosperous place as far as the oil industry
[was concerned]. There were some black businesses developing and even those
who were on salary jobs were probably better paid than people doing compa-
rable things in many other places in the South." Nabrit felt that the economic

---

4. *The Crisis* 5 (November 1912): 8; U.S. Bureau of the Census, *Negroes in the United
States, 1920–1932* (Washington, D.C.: U.S. Government Printing Office, 1935), 48; Matthews and Prothro, *Negroes and the New Southern Politics,* 169.

5. U.S. Bureau of the Census, *Negroes in the United States,* 813.

6. Matthews and Prothro, *Negroes and the New Southern Politics,* 115–18.

7. Chandler Davidson, *Biracial Politics: Conflict and Coalition in the Metropolitan South*
(Baton Rouge: Louisiana State University Press, 1972), 18.

situation of many blacks provided immunity from white retaliation. He added, "It was these individuals [the black middle class] who put up the money for the litigations and who volunteered to become plaintiffs in the cases."[8] Factors other than personal ones, however, play an equally important role in promoting black political activity.

According to Matthews and Prothro, certain characteristics of a given community are also important factors determining the extent of black political activity. The most favorable characteristics are social heterogeneity, economic diversity, a community ethos which does not glorify the (largely mythical) good old antebellum days, and a political multifactionalism of the "every man for himself" variety that gives blacks someone to bargain with. In Texas, blacks were usually able to distinguish one or more candidates as favorably disposed to their interests—despite the candidates' best efforts to avoid being labeled by whites as "Negro candidates."[9] Nabrit described Texas as "still a frontierlike society as late as 1930." He said, "most people carried pistols, and you were expected to defend yourself." Consequently, "whites would have more respect for you if you were able to or attempted to take care of yourself." Nabrit felt that this attitude and the fact that the majority of the whites were more concerned with making money and getting rich than suppressing the small number of blacks in their midst helped to create an atmosphere which encouraged blacks to fight for their rights.[10]

A major factor that, when absent, inhibited black political activity but, when present, acted as a stimulant was the existence of black organizations which could be either political or nonpolitical in form. For any "underdog" group, the value of organization is incalculable, and constitutes a major political resource (especially when wealth, prestige, and knowledge are absent).[11] It is evident that unorganized masses of people have little impact on the political forces that govern their lives. If black Houstonians and Texans were anything, they were organized.

The plethora of black organizations in Texas can be divided into roughly four categories. The first type was comprised of affiliates of national civil rights organizations such as the NAACP. The Houston chapter was founded in 1912 and by 1918 had 414 members. The total state membership was 2,652.

8. Interview with Judge William Henry Hastie, Associate Justice of the Third Circuit Court of Appeals, Philadelphia, Pa., November 27, 1973; interview with Dr. James M. Nabrit, former president of Howard University, Washington, D.C., April 6, 1974.

9. Matthews and Prothro, *Negroes in the New Southern Politics,* 159, 234.

10. Interview with Nabrit, April 6, 1974.

11. Matthews and Prothro, *Negroes in the New Southern Politics,* 203.

Local political clubs and leagues made up the second category. In Houston, the two major black political organizations were the Progressive Voters League and the Independent Voters League. Both were formed during the early and mid-twenties in reaction to the increased hostility of "lily-white" Republicanism. Thirdly, there were the social, civic, business, and religious groups. Almost every black Houstonian belonged to a church, fraternal organization, or social club. Black ministers, in 1938, organized the Interdenominational Ministerial Alliance which had three strong committees on education, civic improvement, and political action. Most black entrepreneurs were affiliated with the Texas Negro Chamber of Commerce, founded in Dallas in 1926. It established branches in many of the larger cities and fought for the economic advancement of blacks. The fourth category consisted of interracial organizations. For those blacks who desired to work for change in conjunction with sympathetic whites there was, for example, the Texas Inter-racial Commission. In the early 1940s representatives of nineteen black organizations would meet in Dallas to found the Texas Council of Negro Organizations to serve as a coordinating agency and spearhead for the all-out, long- and short-range attack on discrimination and segregation.[12]

All of the above factors combined dictated the type of leaders, strategies, objectives and direction, and, to some extent, the effectiveness of the political activity in a given city, county, or state. Black men were rarely, during the period under consideration, leaders in the sense of being governmental office-holders (the positional definition) or in the sense of having power to influence general public policy (the policy-influence definition of leader). The simplest way to define black leaders is to assert that they are generally those individuals most frequently thought of as leaders by blacks. These individuals are most frequently the ministers, businessmen, lawyers, and doctors of the black community.

Again, Matthews' and Prothro's conceptual framework is useful. There are three basic types of black leaders: traditional, moderate, and militant. The traditional black leader is generally economically dependent upon whites with either high or low educational and occupational attainments. The goal of the traditional black leader is the amelioration of conditions within the parameters of the segregated system. His strategies are basically ad hoc, covert, and individualistic. He depends on ingratiation and supplication and is influential with whites to the extent of his indispensability. Blacks look up to him because

---

12. Davidson, *Biracial Politics*, 18; Banks, "The Pursuit of Equality," 163, 181, 197, 244; NAACP, *9th Annual Report* (1918), 86–87.

of his access or his prestige. The moderate leader enjoys a high educational level and is economically independent of whites. He works for the improvement in the welfare of all blacks and for the gradual end of segregation. His strategies can be characterized as continuous, overt, organized efforts, with emphasis on legal attacks on segregation, disfranchisement, and discrimination. His influence with whites derives from his legal challenges and control over black votes. Blacks judge him on the basis of his political ability and performance. The militant leader possesses either a high or low educational and occupational level within the community but is economically independent of whites. His goals are essentially status goals; that is, symbolic victories for all blacks and the immediate destruction of segregation. His strategies involve the use of mass protest demonstrations and movements. His influence with whites derives from their fear of adverse publicity, boycotts, violence, and federal intervention. His influence with blacks is based upon his agitation and forensic abilities, or, in other words, his power to sway the masses and the extent to which he symbolizes their discontent.[13] As will be illustrated throughout the remainder of this study, the black Texans who fought and led the struggle against the Democratic white primary were moderate-to-militant leaders. While strategies may have differed from time to time, there was, at base, a homogeneous political ideology founded upon the premise that "a voteless people is a hopeless people."[14]

After the City Democratic Executive Committee of Houston adopted the white primary resolution in 1921, the black leadership of Houston filed for an injunction. At the forefront was Charles N. Love, the tall, slender, albino editor of the *Texas Freeman,* which he had founded January 1, 1902. Among his co-plaintiffs was W. L. Davis, editor of the *Western Star* of Houston and former secretary of the executive board of the Negro Division of the Federal Foods Administration during 1918. Love persuaded Davis to join him in testing the "validity" of the white primary resolution. Since 1919 both editors had waged a campaign to encourage black Texans to pay their poll taxes and vote. This action of white Houstonians provided Love and Davis the opportunity to practice what they preached. Love wrote Davis: "We must develop the leadership and awaken the inward powers of the masses and we must once more place the problem of the Negro squarely upon the conscience of the nation. I believe our ultimate hope lies in the Federal Courts. It was the Supreme Court that opened the way for the South to develop the dual system and the Supreme

13. Matthews and Prothro, *Negroes in the New Southern Politics,* 196–200.
14. Banks, "Pursuit of Equality," 161.

Court alone can reverse the trend."[15] Love and Davis retained a young black graduate of Yale University Law School, R. D. Evans of Waco, Texas, to handle the case.

On behalf of his clients C. N. Love, W. L. Davis, William Nickerson, Jr., Newman Dudley, Jr., and Perry Mack, Evans filed for an injunction against G. W. Griffith, chairman of the Harris County Democratic Executive Committee, to restrain the committee from executing the disfranchisement resolution. An adverse ruling in the District Court of Harris County was followed by an unsuccessful appeal to the Court of Civil Appeals for the first Judicial District of Texas. The Appeals Court held that at the date of its decision, which was months after the election, the cause of action had ceased to exist and the question was, thus, moot.[16]

Undaunted, Evans, Love, and Davis resolved to continue with the case and were granted a hearing before the United States Supreme Court. Evans, a young and relatively inexperienced lawyer, sought assistance in the preparation of the case he was to present before the Supreme Court from seasoned attorney James A. Cobb of Washington, D.C. Cobb, a graduate of Fisk University, earned his LL.B. from Howard University Law School. A Special Assistant United States Attorney from 1907 to 1915, Cobb was a member of the Howard University Law School faculty and had been instrumental in developing the NAACP's cases against residential segregation and restrictive covenants during the early 1920s. Cobb was anxious to assist Evans because he had long desired to test the constitutionality of the disfranchisement schemes developed in the South.[17] He shared with Evans background material he had collected on disfranchisement laws.

15. C. N. Love to W. L. Davis, March 18, 1922, Davis Papers, quoted in Banks, "The Pursuit of Equality," 144; Charles William Grose, "Black Newspapers in Texas, 1868–1970" (Ph.D. diss., University of Texas, 1972), 111.

16. *Love* v. *Griffith*, 236 S.W. 239 (Texas Civ. App. 1922); Arthur B. Spingarn to W. E. B. Du Bois, October 31, 1934, A. B. Spingarn Papers, Box 3, Library of Congress.

17. Fitzhugh Lee Styles, *Negroes and the Law in the Race's Battle for Liberty, Equality, and Justice under the Constitution of the United States* (Boston: Christopher Publishing House, 1937), 148; Richard Kluger, *Simple Justice: The History of* Brown *v.* Board of Education *and Black America's Struggle for Equality* (New York: Alfred A. Knopf, 1976), 118; Clement Vose, *Caucasians Only: The Supreme Court, the NAACP, and the Restrictive Covenant Cases* (Berkeley: University of California Press, 1967), 52. Cobb represented the NAACP in the *Corrigan* v. *Buckley* (1922) restrictive covenant case. August Meier and Elliott Rudwick, "Attorneys Black and White: A Case Study of Race Relations within the NAACP," *Journal of American History* 62, no. 4 (March 1976): 913–46; Walter White, secretary of the NAACP, described Cobb as "one of the best informed men of the country on Southern election laws, having made a special study of them." Walter White to Fred C. Knollenberg, March 13, 1925, NAACP Papers, Box D-63, Library of Congress.

Cobb's enthusiasm and optimism concerning the outcome of the case decreased after he observed the young lawyer before the Court. Evans, in Cobb's opinion, made a serious blunder when "he stated to the Court that there was a statute in Texas regulating the primaries. The Court adjourned for him to find the statute. He was not able to do so. The Court suggested for him to send it back to them from Texas." Cobb remained convinced that Evans could have proven the state's role in the primaries had he pointed out that officers and official representatives of the state of Texas had actually supervised and worked in the primaries.[18]

Blunders notwithstanding, the Supreme Court, too, decided that the case was moot because the cause of action had ceased to exist. The rule promulgated by the Democratic committee had been for a single election only and the Court ruled that it would be impossible to enjoin the Houston committee from doing something that it had done in February 1921. Though the decision was adverse, the opinion, however, ended on an encouraging note. Black Texans and the national officers of the NAACP paid particular attention to the Court's speculation that, if the case had been presented to the Supreme Court as it had been presented to the District Court of Harris County, "it would present a grave question of Constitutional law."[19]

Although the Supreme Court ruled against Evans, Love, Davis, et al., *Love* v. *Griffith* was not a complete loss. The case attracted the attention of individuals who were appalled at the blatant discrimination inherent in the white primary. The only organized body financially equipped and possessing the legal expertise to launch a sustained attack on the white primary, and as Love put it, to "place the problem of the Negro squarely upon the conscience of the Nation," was the National Association for the Advancement of Colored People.

The NAACP originated from a conference called in response to William English Walling's vivid newspaper coverage of the bloody 1908 race riot in Springfield, Illinois, and his denunciation of the type of blatant, nationwide, anti-black attitude and behavior that the riot represented. Mary White Ovington, Walling, and a few others met in 1909 to organize a "large and powerful body of citizens" to fight for the rights of blacks. The organization was formally established in 1910 and in the following year the founders incorporated it under the laws of New York State. The white members of the interracial organization were primarily middle-class professionals: businessmen, clergy-

18. James A. Cobb to James Weldon Johnson, October 7, 1924, October 10, 1924, NAACP Papers, Box G-35.
19. *Love* v. *Griffith*, 266 U.S. 32, 45 Sup. Ct. 12 (1924); A. B. Spingarn to Du Bois, October 31, 1924, A. B. Spingarn Papers, Box 3.

men, educators, social workers, journalists, and lawyers of various political persuasions ranging from conservative Republicans to democratic Socialists to Progressives. They joined in the founding of the Association out of a desire to alleviate the social, political, and educational injustices that blacks suffered.[20]

The black members of the Association likewise reflected a wide range of careers but were more uniform in their political expressions. Many had belonged to the short-lived Niagara Movement formed in 1905 under the leadership of Monroe Trotter, editor of the *Boston Guardian,* and W. E. B. Du Bois, a Harvard-trained sociology professor at Atlanta University. Blacks in the Niagara Movement were characterized by their unwillingness to accept second-class citizenship and their opposition to the accommodationist philosophy of Booker T. Washington. Washington, the most powerful black leader in America at that time, had advised blacks to cease in the agitation of questions of social and political equality. Washington had declared in 1895, at the Cotton States and International Exposition in Atlanta, that blacks must cease in the agitation of questions of social equality and must realize that progress and the enjoyment of all the privileges of citizenship would come to blacks as a "result of severe struggle rather than of artificial forcing."[21]

But Washington's approach had not stemmed the tide of racial proscription. In the year following his famous "Atlanta Compromise" speech, the United States Supreme Court had handed down the *Plessy* v. *Ferguson* decision. In this decision the Supreme Court had given constitutional sanction to the doctrine of "separate-but-equal" facilities for the races.[22] By 1910, blacks in northern and southern communities shared the common experiences of second-class citizenship, segregation in housing and places of public accommodation, and interracial violence.

The black leaders of the Niagara Movement were determined to fight and protest the continuing assault upon their human and civil rights. The Move-

20. Jack Abramowitz, "Origins of the NAACP," *Social Education* 15 (January 1951): 21–23; Charles Flint Kellogg, *NAACP: A History of the Association for the Advancement of Colored People* (Baltimore: Johns Hopkins University Press, 1967), 9–25; Mary White Ovington, *The Walls Came Tumbling Down* (New York: Harcourt, Brace and World, 1947), 100–108.

21. W. E. B. Du Bois, *The Autobiography of W. E. B. Du Bois* (New York: International Publishers, 1968), 254–58; Stephen R. Fox, *The Guardian of Boston, William Monroe Trotter* (New York: Atheneum, 1971), 126–39; Elliott M. Rudwick, "The Niagara Movement," *Journal of Negro History* 42 (July 1957): 177–200; E. Davidson Washington, ed., *Selected Speeches of Booker T. Washington* (Garden City, N.J.: Doubleday, 1932), 31–36.

22. *Plessy* v. *Ferguson,* 163 U.S. 537 (1896).

ment was torn asunder by 1907, however, because of internal dissension, chronic financial difficulties, and outside pressure from Booker T. Washington. As short-lived as it was, however, the Niagara Movement did leave a major legacy not readily apparent at the time of its demise. It had had a "catalytic role in the shift of the consensus of black thought from the Washington brand of accommodation to a return to the protest tradition." This shift affected both black and white men and women as was to be reflected in the work later undertaken by the National Association for the Advancement of Colored People. In the new and infinitely more resourceful organization, W. E. B. Du Bois became its top black salaried official and the editor of its organ, *The Crisis;* Moorfield Storey, national president; William Walling, chairman of the executive committee; John E. Milholland, treasurer; and Oswald Garrison Villard, disbursing treasurer. Conspicuously absent from the new organization's roster of leaders and members were Washington and Trotter.[23]

The Association sought to launch a formal attack against the social, educational, and political discrimination that oppressed blacks, and to persuade the judicial and legislative branches of government properly to enforce the Fourteenth and Fifteenth Amendments. Problems of racism, segregation, and interracial violence transcended differences of regions and sections and were "national in character." To attack these problems and to utilize fully the increasing powers of the courts and the executive and legislative branches of the federal government, the NAACP had to develop a systematic and tightly coordinated organizational structure. Its leaders were convinced that only a strong organization would be able to defend in the press, on the platform, at the ballot box, and in the courts the constitutional rights of colored people.[24]

The formal hierarchical structure of the new association consisted of a board of directors, the general officers, the secretary, and the principal personnel in the national office. Authority, responsibility, and decision-making power emanated from the board of directors. Its principal agency was the national office. The secretary became the key figure in the national office and controlled the day-to-day operations of the Association. The national office, acting for the board, scrutinized and supervised the major activities of the branches and collegiate chapters.[25]

23. Fox, *The Guardian of Boston,* 126–39; Rudwick, "The Niagara Movement," 177–200.

24. "The Power of Organization," *9th Annual Report of the NAACP, 1918* (New York: NAACP, 1919), 22.

25. Nathaniel Patrick Tillman, "Walter Francis White: A Study in Interest Group Leadership" (Ph.D. diss., University of Wisconsin, 1961), 39–40; B. Joyce Ross, *J. E. Spingarn and the Rise of the NAACP* (New York: Atheneum, 1972), 339–401.

By 1916, requests for assistance so burdened the Association that the officers felt it mandatory to enunciate a clear general policy of operational strategy. The Association decided to take no cases except those which showed actual discrimination because of color; it would limit itself in legal matters to those cases which involved broad principles.[26] The Association's legal advisers examined each case to determine "whether it is a case in which injustice has been done or is threatened because of race and color and . . . whether entrance of the Association will establish a precedent which will affect the basic citizenship rights of Negroes and other Americans."[27]

While legal action became the central thrust of the NAACP, its officers recognized that sustained publicity, peaceful agitation, organized protest, unrelenting propaganda, and the careful compilation of data on all questions of discrimination were essential adjuncts to the successful execution of the Association's work. For example, when a lynching occurred, an investigator would be dispatched; where congressional legislation was concerned, lobbying and letters of protest to congressmen were to become the patterns of response.[28] Due to the magnitude of the work that needed the Association's attention and because of its limited financial resources, publicity and agitation were greatly emphasized. The first black secretary of the Association, James Weldon Johnson, noted the significance of publicity and agitation as valuable tools in the growth of the NAACP. "During the first seven years . . . the organization was lacking in funds and the strength that comes from numbers, but it made use of the only effective weapon available—agitation." *Crisis* editor Du Bois elaborated: "We advertise the cases in which the public is interested in order to keep and increase interest. We arrange our programs for our meetings and conferences with a wary eye to the headliner whose appearance will get us on the front page of newspapers." He added, "We use propaganda and ballyhoo, and to some extent, we are compelled to do this as the sheer price of survival. . . ."[29]

To develop, organize, and conduct the legal program, the board of directors established the National Legal Committee. From 1914 to 1939, Arthur Spingarn, a 1901 graduate of Columbia Law School and an expert in the field of

26. Report of the Chairman of the National Legal Committee (Arthur B. Spingarn) at the NAACP Annual Meeting in 1916, NAACP Papers, Box A-23.

27. Walter White, *A Man Called White* (New York: Viking Press, 1948), 142.

28. Ross, *J. E. Spingarn*, 399.

29. "What Is Wrong with the NAACP?," an address delivered by W. E. B. Du Bois at the 1932 Annual Conference of the NAACP in Washington, D.C., NAACP Papers, Box B-7; minutes of NAACP Meeting of the Board of Directors, May 5, 1910, NAACP Papers, Box A-1.

copyright law, headed the legal committee. The committee was composed of several eminent volunteer attorneys. Indeed, during the formative years, one of the Association's more important assets was its access to the talents and services of some of the most outstanding attorneys in the country. Until 1929, the Association received invaluable assistance from Moorfield Storey. A Harvard graduate and former secretary to Senator Charles Sumner, Storey was president of the American Bar Association in 1895 and was the NAACP'S president for the first twenty years of its existence.[30] In the 1920s another successful and competent New York constitutional lawyer, Louis Marshall, played a significant role in helping to institutionalize the Association's approach to cases involving discrimination and violations of the constitutional rights of blacks. Marshall, like Storey, had an unshakable faith in the Court as interpreter of the Constitution. To Marshall, the Court as final arbiter would justly decide any case presented to it clearly and logically based upon a precise understanding and interpretation of the meaning of the Constitution. Marshall viewed the Constitution of the United States as a "holy of holies, an instrument of sacred import." His legal career was dominated by an attitude of respect and reverence for what he regarded as a body of law based on the Constitution.[31]

Not only did white attorneys such as Storey, Spingarn, and Marshall represent the Association free of charge, but their relationship with the young organization also gave to it social respectability, integrity, and stability. Their usefulness transcended the value of their legal services. Because of their prestige and personal and professional contacts, they were able to bring the agitation for black rights to a wider audience and ultimately broaden the base for financial support. The relative unavailability of black legal talent during the Association's formative years made the contribution of these lawyers even more valuable.[32]

Due to the fact that both Storey and Marshall had thriving practices in Boston and New York respectively, and were already old men, they were ini-

30. William B. Hixson, Jr., *Moorfield Storey and the Abolitionist Tradition* (New York: Oxford University Press, 1972), 134.

31. Morton Rosenstock, *Louis Marshall, Defender of Jewish Rights* (Detroit: Wayne State University Press, 1965), 7, 28–29; Hixson, *Moorfield Storey,* 145.

32. Interview with James M. Nabrit, April 6, 1974. Interview with Roy Wilkins, executive director of the NAACP, New York, April 19, 1972. Meier and Rudwick, in "Attorneys Black and White," 915, point out that in 1910, "of about 114,000 lawyers in the country, only 795, or .7 percent, were black. Twenty years later, Negroes formed only about .8 percent of the country's attorneys."

tially removed from the daily administration of the Association.[33] Consequently, Storey and Marshall relied quite heavily on James Weldon Johnson, NAACP secretary from 1920 to 1929. Johnson, a poet, a musician, and prominent literary figure during the Harlem Renaissance, was born in 1871 in Jacksonville, Florida. He served as United States Consul at Puerto Cabello, Venezuela, from 1906 to 1909, and from 1909 to 1912 he was Consul at Corinto, Nicaragua. In 1916, Johnson joined the Association as field secretary and helped to organize 131 NAACP branches throughout the South. It was while he worked in this capacity that he met Walter White, a blond, blue-eyed Negro from Atlanta, Georgia, who subsequently, at Johnson's insistence, joined the national office staff in 1918 as assistant secretary. Johnson assumed the secretary's post after John Shillady was incapacitated as a result of the severe beating he received in Austin, Texas, in 1919.[34]

Spingarn and Johnson worked together to select the cases that the Association supported. The secretary frequently made important decisions concerning the Association's financial commitment to each litigation. Spingarn was often involved with a case from the beginning and assisted local lawyers in preparing briefs and records in the district and federal courts. While the branches and the local lawyers were primarily responsible for preliminary investigations, once a case reached the Supreme Court of the United States, either Spingarn, Storey, or Marshall would argue the case or act in supervisory capacities.

After the deaths of Storey and Marshall in 1929, the NAACP secured the services of Nathan Margold and of Marshall's son, James. A young, talented lawyer, Margold was an instructor of law at Harvard University and an assistant United States attorney general in New York. In the mid-thirties, the Association, with money provided by the Charles Garland Fund, formally known as the American Fund for Public Service, hired as special counsel a young, dynamic black lawyer with impressive credentials, Charles Houston. Houston, a Phi Beta Kappa graduate of Amherst College, received a law degree from Harvard Law School and a doctorate of civil law from the University of Madrid. As vice dean of Howard University Law School from 1929 to 1935, Houston turned it into "a living laboratory where civil-rights law was invented by teamwork."[35] One of his most distinguished proteges, Thurgood Marshall, gradu-

33. Hixson, *Moorfield Storey,* 134.

34. James Weldon Johnson, *Along This Way: The Autobiography of James Weldon Johnson* (New York: Viking Press, 1933), 8, 223, 257–73, 314–43.

35. Biographical sketch of Charles Houston, Special Correspondence of Charles Houston, NAACP Papers, Box C-65; Kluger, *Simple Justice,* 173–84.

ated from Howard Law School at the top of his class in 1933 and, after three years of struggle as a private lawyer in Baltimore, Maryland, joined Houston as assistant special counsel for the NAACP.[36] Houston's retention as special counsel heralded the rise of the black lawyer. He was successful in engaging a number of the few black attorneys in the country in the Association's work.

From the outset, the Association declared that one of its primary goals was the destruction of the various schemes designed to disfranchise blacks. Its leaders planned to show the courts, particularly the United States Supreme Court, clearly and precisely the unconstitutionality of all of the subterfuges used to destroy the rights and privileges of blacks delineated in the Fourteenth and Fifteenth Amendments. Its organizers believed that the black man had to obtain his right to vote in the South; this was an essential step in achieving tolerable living conditions in sections where the black man was deprived of any, if not all, rights as a citizen and as a human being.[37] Moorfield Storey spoke strongly of the need for the black man to have the vote. "In the long run only voters have rights in this country. The politicians whether they hold executive offices or sit in legislatures . . . have no thought to spare for any class that has no vote. . . ."[38] Hastie explained why the NAACP placed top priority upon combating disfranchisement: "We all felt then that the things we were doing in education or housing or residential segregation and so on, would not amount to much unless the blacks in the South were effectively franchised . . . even though the courts may decide in our favor on any number of those basic and important rights. Unless blacks had the power as voters to influence their local governments, the enforcement of these other rights would be so unsatisfactory that we wouldn't have gained very much by winning those other battles."[39]

The Association's first move against disfranchisement was a limited involvement in the 1915 *Guinn* v. *United States* case which challenged the constitutionality of the Oklahoma grandfather clause. This case originated when a United States government attorney instigated proceedings against Oklahoma voting registrars Guinn and Beale for their refusal to permit blacks to register and to vote in federal elections. The registrars had acted in compliance with the 1910 amendment to the Oklahoma Constitution, which had exempted from literacy tests all those who were "on January 1, 1866, or at any

36. Biographical sketch of Thurgood Marshall, Special Correspondence of Thurgood Marshall, NAACP Papers, Box C-84; Kluger, *Simple Justice,* 173–84.

37. *The Crisis* 31, no. 2 (December 1925): 72.

38. Address delivered by Moorfield Storey at NAACP Annual Conference, 1920, in Atlanta, Georgia, NAACP Papers, Box B-3.

39. Interview with Judge William H. Hastie, November 27, 1973.

time prior thereto, entitled to vote under any form of government" or anyone who was a "lineal descendant of such person." While blacks were not specifically mentioned, few, if any, voted or were able to vote prior to 1866. The U.S. attorney accused Guinn and Beale of violation of the 1871 federal act passed to enforce the Fifteenth Amendment. The solicitor general, John W. Davis, presented the government's position before the Supreme Court. A former United States senator and ardent racist, James W. Bailey of Texas argued Oklahoma's case. Davis demonstrated to the Court that the Fifteenth Amendment provided that under no conditions could a member of any race be excluded from voting for racial reasons, and that such an exclusion was the purpose of Oklahoma's grandfather clause. Bailey, who styled himself the "last Democrat," was a staunch defender of state rights. He used his considerable oratorical abilities to protest the extension of federal authority that would unravel the customary social arrangements in the South that kept the black man "in his place." The United States Supreme Court upheld the decision of the lower court and ruled that the grandfather clause adopted by the state of Oklahoma was unconstitutional under the Fifteenth Amendment.[40]

The *Guinn* decision reflected the Court's new willingness to look beyond the "nondiscriminatory form" of disfranchisement legislation and to recognize its "discriminatory substance." In this sense, the *Guinn* case was the first really modern voting rights decision. For 45 years, the Court had declined to intervene against racist voting laws such as the literacy requirement and other subterfuges, and had demonstrated general adherence to the national preference of letting the South solve, through segregation, disfranchisement, and intimidation, its racial problems.[41] Moorfield Storey, representing the NAACP, filed an *amicus curiae* (friend of the court) brief that endorsed the government's position. After the Supreme Court rendered its decision, the NAACP proclaimed the case to be the Association's first and most significant victory. Spingarn maintained that "the Association is to be congratulated on the fact that it has had placed at its services, on this and many other occasions, the legal learning of one of the most distinguished members of the American Bar, without whose effort this happy result could hardly have been attained."[42]

40. *Guinn* v. *The United States,* 238 U.S. 347, 363, 365 (1915); Hixson, *Moorfield Storey,* 138; Kluger, *Simple Justice,* 104; for a detailed biographical sketch of Joseph Bailey, see Lewis L. Gould, *Progressives and Prohibitionists: Texas Democrats in the Wilson Era* (Austin: University of Texas Press, 1973), 16–25.

41. Ward E. Y. Elliott, *The Rise of Guardian Democracy: The Supreme Court's Role in Voting Rights Disputes, 1845–1969* (Cambridge: Harvard University Press, 1974), 70–71.

42. Report of the Chairman of the National Legal Committee to the Board of Directors, 1916, NAACP Papers, Box A-23.

The favorable decision and the apparent change in the Court's attitude encouraged NAACP officials to increase their efforts against disfranchisement. The Texas white primary law, because of its discriminatory form and substance and even more dubious constitutionality, opened the door to deeper NAACP involvement in voting rights litigation. Association officials anxiously awaited the right case. After the *Love* decision, Du Bois had observed, "there is a chance to bring this matter of the white primaries directly before the Supreme Court when a proper case can be framed."[43] The *Crisis* editor and his colleagues at the national office did not have long to wait. The "proper case" was already in the making.

43. *The Crisis* 29 (February 1925): 156.

# 4

# *Nixon v. Herndon, 1927*

By the time the United States Supreme Court delivered its opinion on *Love v. Griffith*, the Texas legislature in 1923 had enacted the white primary statute. The *Love* challenge had concentrated only on the actions of the Democratic Executive Committee of the city of Houston. The new legislation was more far-reaching. It made the state a leading participant in the disfranchisement of blacks. The emergence of a literate and economically viable black professional and business class meant that an increasing number of blacks could pay the poll tax. White Texas politicians feared the black vote not because blacks really threatened the political domination of whites, but because blacks perhaps could be used by the "outs" to defeat the "in" group and bring about a shift in political power and control.[1] This fear was particularly evident among those politicians who resided in counties that were predominantly black.

The 1923 statute was challenged immediately by Hurley C. Chandler, a black resident of San Antonio. Chandler sought to enjoin the enforcement of the statute on the grounds that it abridged his privileges and immunities and denied him equal protection of the laws in violation of the Fourteenth Amendment. He charged that the statute also violated the Fifteenth Amendment because it abridged his right to vote on the basis of color. The federal district court's decision in *Chandler* v. *Neff* relied heavily on the 1921 United States Supreme Court's decision in *Newberry* v. *United States.* The *Newberry* case had not been a white primary case, but a prosecution under the Corrupt Practices Act of 1910, which limited the expenditures of congressional candidates. Nevertheless, the ruling had touched upon the question of primary elec-

1. Robert H. Brisbane, *The Black Vanguard: Origins of the Negro Social Revolution, 1900– 1960* (Valley Forge, Pa.: Judson Press, 1970), 128–31; Ralph J. Bunche, *The Political Status of the Negro in the Age of F.D.R.,* ed. Dewey W. Grantham (Chicago: University of Chicago Press, 1973), 55.

tions. Justice McReynolds had held that when the Constitution had been adopted primaries had been unknown:

> Moreover, they are in no sense elections for an office, but merely methods by which party adherents agree upon candidates whom they intend to offer and support for ultimate choice by all qualified electors. General provisions touching elections in Constitutions or statutes are not necessarily applicable to primaries—the two things are radically different.[2]

The federal district court based its decision on *Newberry*. Because a primary election was not in the same category as a general election, denial of voting privileges to blacks could not be viewed as abridgment of a right guaranteed by provisions of the Fourteenth and Fifteenth Amendments. The primary was merely the procedure of selecting party candidates. The court's position accepted the reasoning that the Fourteenth and Fifteenth Amendments prohibited only state action and could not be applied to the actions of voluntary associations such as political parties. The district court added that it was within the state's reserved powers to regulate internal political affairs. The state was free to prescribe any reasonable test of political affiliation and Chandler's claims were unfounded.[3] Chandler did not appeal the decision.

The *Chandler* v. *Neff* and *Love* v. *Griffith* decisions illustrated the futility of asking for an injunction or a mandamus affirmative action. In both instances the question became moot the day after the election. Subsequent challengers of the white primary deduced from this fact that the best procedure would be to sue for damages. Shortly after the Chandler decision had been delivered, blacks in El Paso decided to launch their own attack against the offending statute.

In 1923, L. W. Washington, president of the El Paso NAACP branch, at-

2. Le Marquis De Jarmon, "Voting: One Hundred Years to the Beginning," in *Legal Aspects of the Civil Rights Movement*, ed. Donald B. King and Charles W. Quick (Detroit: Wayne State University Press, 1965), 59–77; *Newberry* v. *United States*, 256 U.S. 232, 65 L.Ed. 913 (1921).

3. *Chandler* v. *Neff*, 298 Fed. 515 (W.D. Texas, 1924); O. Douglas Weeks, "The White Primary," *Mississippi Law Journal* 8 (December 1935): 145–46. Luther Harris Evans, "Primary Elections and the Constitution," *Michigan Law Review* 32 (February 1934): 451–56. The Texas courts since 1916 have established through a series of cases the position that primary elections were private affairs of political parties; see *Waples* v. *Marrast*, 184 S.W. 180 (1916), a party is a voluntary association; *Kay* v. *Schneider*, 218 S.W. 479 (1920), a party is an instrument of a private group; *Walker* v. *Hopping*, 266 S.W. 146 (1920), party officers are not government officials; Melvin James Banks, "The Pursuit of Equality" (Ph.D. diss., Syracuse University, 1962), 301.

tended the Association's annual conference and spoke to William Pickens, NAACP field representative, about the white primary in Texas. Pickens instructed Washington to "go back to El Paso and find a black Democrat and have him present himself at the polls at the time of the election."[4] With little difficulty, Washington found a man who was willing to go to the polls on July 26, 1924, and request a ballot to vote in the Democratic primary. That man was Lawrence A. Nixon, an El Paso physician.

Dr. Nixon, a forty-one-year-old resident of Texas, had lived and voted in the city and county of El Paso for fourteen years. Born on February 9, 1883, in Marshall, Texas, the county seat of Harrison County, the first county to exclude its majority (68 percent) black population from the Democratic primary in 1876–1881, Nixon was educated in private schools in New Orleans, attended Wiley College, and earned his medical degree at Meharry Medical College in Nashville, Tennessee, in 1906. When he moved to El Paso in 1910, the black population amounted to approximately 3.0 percent of the total population of the county.[5]

Most of the black residents of the city were employed in service occupations—maids, porters, waiters, etc. There was nevertheless a small group of entrepreneurs—owners of eating establishments, drugstores, and barber shops. The latter group comprised El Paso's black middle class and provided leadership through fraternal and religious organizations. Nixon helped organize a branch of the NAACP in 1910, which remained one of the most active chapters in the state. Segregated, and largely left to develop their own resources, blacks in El Paso possessed a keen political consciousness. In addition to building a thriving medical practice, Nixon owned a drugstore that became a gathering place where discussions often dealt with political issues. Because of their meager numbers, blacks had posed no threat to the whites and consequently were permitted to vote in both general and primary elections,[6] prior to the enactment of the white primary statute in 1923.

Nixon's decision to serve as plaintiff in the case created great excitement among blacks in El Paso and generated more political discourse. L. W. Washington described the prevailing sentiments of the black residents: "During our fourteen years residence in El Paso, we have not been denied the right to vote in any election until July 26, 1924. . . . Since no other party has been strong

4. Speech delivered by L. W. Washington before the 25th Annual Conference of the NAACP in Oklahoma City, Oklahoma, June 28, 1934, NAACP Papers, Box B-10.

5. Conrad Bryson, *Dr. Lawrence A. Nixon and the White Primary* (El Paso: University of Texas at El Paso, 1971), 1–17, 27; Banks, "The Pursuit of Equality," 303.

6. Bryson, *Dr. Lawrence A. Nixon,* 1–17.

enough here to make a showing at the polls, the elections for city, county and state officers for the most part, have been held with one faction of Democrats against another." Reflecting an understanding of the political realities, Washington added, "The Negro vote had been sought and his vote the last fourteen years has been cast for those whom he knew to be better disposed to the entire citizenship."[7]

Nixon, a lone black figure, stood before the election booth on July 26, 1924, fully cognizant of the significance of his simple request for a ballot. Election judges C. C. Herndon and Charles Porras refused his request. Nixon recalled the event many years later: "The judges were friends of mine, they inquired after my health, and when I presented my poll-tax receipt, one of them said, 'Dr. Nixon, you know we can't let you vote.'"[8] Herndon and Porras signed a statement Nixon had with him attesting that they had denied Nixon a ballot solely because of his color. "Nixon's position made him invulnerable to the reactions of the whites. They could not fire him or penalize him in other ways for standing up like a man," explained Roy Wilkins, former executive director of the NAACP. Wilkins observed that Dr. Nixon was a man with a "social conscience" and "wanted to do things, not necessarily for himself. He could have gone through life and not voted again, but he attempted to vote because he was in a position to challenge this ruling."[9]

To aid in the handling of the case, the El Paso NAACP branch employed Fred C. Knollenberg, a forty-eight-year-old white attorney and member of the Republican party. Knollenberg was Nixon's personal attorney and the one lawyer in El Paso who frequently represented blacks when they needed legal assistance. Knollenberg, born January 10, 1877, in Quincy, Illinois, received his LL.B. from the University of Michigan Law School in 1901 and specialized in tax law. He was a member of the local NAACP branch and was held in high esteem by L. W. Washington both for his "legal ability" and his "moral character." The branch paid him $100 to represent Nixon in the federal district court and agreed to raise most of the $2,500 fee Knollenberg requested should he have to present the case before the United States Supreme Court.[10]

Washington collected the pertinent data concerning the primary case, summarized their negotiations with Knollenberg and forwarded the information

7. L. W. Washington to Robert Bagnall, August 2, 1924; Washington to Walter White, January 6, 1925.

8. Quoted in Bryson, *Dr. Lawrence A. Nixon,* 23.

9. Interview with Roy Wilkins, April 19, 1972.

10. Ibid.; memorandum on Fred C. Knollenberg, no date; Washington to White, January 26, 1925; Washington to Bagnall, December 18, 1928, NAACP Papers, Box D-63.

to the national office. After some deliberation the NAACP board of directors voted unanimously to take up the case.[11] Spingarn, chairman of the National Legal Committee, felt the case to be well prepared. He offered the opinion that if the Association believed that this was "the time to push this particular case, perhaps a test could be made of it. . . ." He cautioned: "This is a very important issue and cannot be taken up lightly. If we decide to get behind it, it will mean the expenditure of a great deal of money, because no matter how competent these El Paso lawyers are, we would have to hire additional counsel when we get to the United States Supreme Court."[12] NAACP president Storey believed that there were many merits in the case. He maintained that "such a statute as that which the legislature of Texas has passed is absurd, but if it is upheld there is no limit to the laws that can be passed against the colored people. I think the Supreme Court will sustain this case."[13] Attorney James Cobb also felt that the Association should take up the case. "I believe that the primary law in question is right in the teeth of the Fifteenth Amendment and such a case would do the Association a great amount of good."[14]

The national office subsequently contracted with Knollenberg to handle the case on the local level. It agreed to pay him $2,000 and allow $500 for court costs. The El Paso branch promised to forward to the national office half of this amount and all monies raised locally for the case. The national office impressed on Knollenberg its desire to have "one or more eminent lawyers associated with . . . the case." Cobb was asked to serve as legal consultant for the national office because of his familiarity with the proceedings in the *Love* case, and his knowledge of southern election laws. In addition, he lived in Washington, D.C., and could easily handle details relating to the case should it go as far as the Supreme Court.[15]

When the national officials and their legal advisers had clearly delineated their responsibilities and commitments, they instructed Knollenberg to file a $5,000 damage suit against election judges Herndon and Porras in the federal district court. Knollenberg charged in his brief that the law violated the Fifteenth Amendment and Sections 1979 and 2004 of the federal law that pro-

11. Extract from Minutes of the February 9, 1925, Meeting of the Board of Directors, NAACP Papers, Box D-63.

12. Spingarn to White, January 6, 1925, NAACP Papers, Box D-63.

13. Moorfield Storey to White, January 10, 1925, NAACP Papers, Box D-63.

14. James A. Cobb to White, January 29, 1925, NAACP Papers, Box D-63.

15. White to Storey, March 13, 1925, NAACP Papers, Box D-63; White to Knollenberg, March 13, 1925; James Weldon Johnson to F. C. Knollenberg, November 25, 1925, L. A. Nixon Papers, Lyndon Baines Johnson Library at the University of Texas, Austin, Texas, Box No. 1.

vided that all qualified voters be permitted to vote. The defendants, represented by attorneys W. H. Fryer and R. E. Cunningham, moved to dismiss the
complaint, alleging that the refusal of a ballot to Nixon had not violated any
of the abovementioned statutes. They argued that the primary election merely took the place of a Democratic convention and was thus a party affair. Judge
Du Val West, then sitting on the San Antonio Court of the Western District,
agreed with the defendants and dismissed the case at the plaintiff's expense on
December 4, 1924.[16] The NAACP's National Legal Committee representatives
entered the case once the Supreme Court of the United States agreed to hear
it on a writ of error.[17]

Cobb, Spingarn, and Storey made recommendations and suggestions to
Knollenberg as he prepared the brief he planned to present before the United
States Supreme Court. Cobb recommended that he call the Court's attention
to *Love* v. *Griffith* and establish the fact that the primary election in Texas was
a public election; thus any restriction of voting privileges was a violation of
the Fifteenth Amendment.[18] Storey was particularly concerned that the *Nixon*
case be handled differently from the *Love* case, since, in both instances, "the
primary election had already occurred."[19] White, after conferring with Knollenberg and Spingarn, assured Storey that the two cases differed significantly.
Nixon, after all, was challenging "a state statute prohibiting participation by
any Negro, whether qualified or not, in a white primary."[20] Storey reviewed
Knollenberg's brief and pronounced it adequate to present before the Supreme
Court. Storey, due to failing health, did not travel to Washington. Spingarn,
however, did go and participate. James Weldon Johnson, out of a desire to provide moral support for the El Paso attorney and to show the Court that blacks
were acutely concerned about the white primary issue, arranged with the
Washington, D.C., branch to have "a representative delegation of colored people" present in the Court.[21]

The presence of the black delegation, however, did little to avert the disas-

16. *Nixon* v. *Herndon and Porras,* 994 Law, U.S. District Court, Western District of Texas;
Bryson, *Dr. Lawrence A. Nixon,* 38–39.
17. Copy of brief filed before the Supreme Court of the United States, October Term,
1925; *L. A. Nixon, Plaintiff in Error* v. *C. C. Herndon and Charles Porras,* No. 480, NAACP
Papers, Box D-64; Walter White to Fred Knollenberg, April 8, 1926, Nixon Papers.
18. Cobb to Knollenberg, April 7, 1926, NAACP Papers, Box D-63.
19. Storey to White, February 16, 1926, NAACP Papers, Box C-76.
20. White to Storey, March 5, 1926, NAACP Papers, Box C-77.
21. Storey to Johnson, April 20, 1926, December 13, 1926; special correspondence of
Moorfield Storey, NAACP Papers, Box C-76; NAACP Press Release, December 17, 1926,
Secretary, District of Columbia Branch, December 18, 1926, NAACP Papers, Box G-35.

ter which followed. Knollenberg was ill at ease. In his first appearance before the Supreme Court, he "legally stubbed his toe once or twice" because "he was aiming more after the psychological effect upon the Court than upon the legal effect."[22] Neither Cobb nor Spingarn was impressed with Knollenberg's performance. Cobb accused him of not presenting the case well and of possessing minimal acquaintance with the brief. For example, the El Paso attorney was not, in Cobb's opinion, as familiar with the *Love* v. *Griffith* and the *Newberry* v. *United States* cases as he should have been.[23]

Knollenberg, in a letter to Storey, assessed his own appearance before the Supreme Court:

> The question being new and novel, the Court took me to task quite a little, and really the entire time allotted was used in answering questions propounded by different members.
>
> The Chief Justice and Justice Holmes and Brandeis seemed to be in sympathy with our position, and I feel justice Stone is as well. However, Justice Butler and Justice McReynolds took issue with me and judging from the position they took in the argument, I feel that they will file a report adverse to our position. My only hope is that they do not write the majority opinion.
>
> Mr. Spingarn discussed the *Newberry* case, as justice McReynolds seemed to feel that it was binding upon us, and that the United States Government had no authority under the Constitution over primary elections.[24]

From the observations of the national officers and, implicitly, in his own statements, it is obvious that Knollenberg was well-meaning but incompetent.

An unexpected development helped the NAACP salvage the case. The attorney general of Texas, Dan Moody, appeared unexpectedly before the Supreme Court and requested permission to file a brief. The thirty-three-year-old, red-haired Moody was the youngest governor-elect in the history of Texas. His substantial victory in the 1926 Democratic primary over Miriam (Ma) Ferguson reflected voter approval of his strict law enforcement image, which he had established earlier as a county attorney, district attorney, and attorney general. The Supreme Court granted his request and allowed him thirty days to prepare a brief. The NAACP was granted two weeks thereafter in which to reply.[25]

22. Johnson to Cobb, January 10, 1927, NAACP Papers, Box D-63.
23. Louis Marshall to James Weldon Johnson, January 13, 1927, NAACP Papers, Box D-64; Cobb to Johnson, January 11, 1927, NAACP Papers, Box D-64.
24. Knollenberg to Storey, January 20, 1927, Nixon Papers.
25. "The White Primary, the NAACP Attack on Disfranchisement," *The Crisis* (March

The legal committee removed Knollenberg from the case and appealed to attorney Louis Marshall to write the reply brief and to reargue the case before the Supreme Court. Marshall possessed a brilliant mind and a deep sense of social responsibility. He had become a member of the NAACP's National Legal Committee in 1923.[26] Marshall replied to the plea for assistance stating, "I shall be very glad indeed to examine the brief to be submitted by the Attorney General of Texas and to prepare the reply brief thereto. I recognize the importance and difficulty of the case and therefore deem it to be my duty to give due consideration to the presentation of the case to the Court."[27]

Marshall's strategy in the reply brief was to show the Court that the primary was the most important and, in effect, the only Texas election worth participating in. Marshall argued that the Fifteenth Amendment protected the right to vote in all its forms. He contended that nomination in the primary was equivalent to election. As Marshall illustrated, the vote cast in the runoff primary election on August 28, 1926, for governor had been 703,766, whereas the vote cast for the Democratic candidate in the general election had been only 89,263, or a little less than 13 percent of the vote cast in the primary runoff. Marshall argued that the Texas statute created an arbitrary classification by race and color, and that it therefore constituted a complete deprivation of the equal protection of the laws, abridging the privileges and immunities clause of the Fourteenth Amendment.[28]

The Texas attorney general's brief posited the same arguments raised in the lower court. He maintained that, as a consequence of the *Newberry* Supreme Court decision, the primary election of party candidates did not constitute an election and that the right to vote therein was not, therefore, within the protection of the Fourteenth and Fifteenth Amendments. The decision of the Texas Federal Court in *Chandler* v. *Neff* was used to support the assertion that the present case involved a political question not within the province of the judiciary.[29]

---

1927): 9–10; Walter B. Moore, *Governors of Texas* (Dallas: *Dallas Morning News,* 1973), 29; Knollenberg to Dan Moody, January 15, 1927, Dan Moody Papers, Archives Division, Texas State Library, Austin, Texas, Box 152. There is very little information in the Moody Papers concerning the white primary.

26. Morton Rosenstock, *Louis Marshall, Defender of Jewish Rights* (Detroit: Wayne State University Press, 1965), 7.

27. Marshall to Johnson, January 13, 1927, NAACP Papers, Box D-64.

28. Reply Brief in *Nixon* v. *Herndon* by Louis Marshall, February 1927; NAACP Press Release, "Negro Body Answers Texas in 'White Primary' Case," February 21, 1927, NAACP Papers, Box D-64.

29. Texas attorney general's brief summarized in *Nixon* v. *Herndon,* 273 U.S. at 538, 539, 47 Sup. Ct. 446 (1927).

Justice Oliver Wendell Holmes delivered the unanimous opinion of the Supreme Court on March 7, 1927. Although the ruling granted Nixon and the NAACP what they desired, the victory was incomplete. The Court remained uncertain about the precise status of primaries. The Court's doubt led Justice Holmes to base the decision on the Fourteenth Amendment, which provided much weaker ground for judicial intervention in voting rights disputes of this kind. Yet the Fourteenth Amendment as construed in the Court's interpretation furnished the Court the avenue to sidestep the issue. Regardless of whether primaries were elections and the right to vote was involved, there had been state action denying the equal protection of the laws to blacks. This was expressly prohibited by the Fourteenth Amendment.

It was unnecessary to consider the Fifteenth Amendment, Holmes declared, because the Texas white primary law so clearly violated the provisions of the Fourteenth Amendment. According to the Court, the state of Texas was guilty of using its power to withhold from blacks "the equal protection of the laws." The Court held:

> We find it unnecessary to consider the Fifteenth Amendment, because it seems to us hard to imagine a more direct infringement of the Fourteenth. . . . That Amendment not only gave citizenship to persons of color, but it denied to any State the power to withhold from them the equal protection of the laws.[30]

The Court concluded, "States may do a good deal of classifying that it is difficult to believe rational but there are limits, and it is too clear for extended argument that color cannot be made the basis of a statutory classification affecting the right set up in this case."[31]

Justice Holmes recognized that Texans were denying the substance of a voting right while granting it in form by allowing blacks to vote in the less important general elections. By sidestepping the questions raised about the Fifteenth Amendment, however, Holmes weakened the constitutional foundation of his decision. The construction of the decision provided Texas Democrats with an escape hatch. The decision failed to answer the question whether the primary election was an election or an essential part of an election, in the constitutional sense, that involved a right to vote. Justice Holmes was, perhaps, aware that his narrowly based decision offered little real relief to blacks. "He was reported to have said, in a wry aside after delivering his opinion, 'I know that our good brethren, the Negroes of Texas, will now rejoice that

30. Ibid., at 541.
31. Ibid.

they possess at the primary the rights which they heretofore have enjoyed in the general election.'"[32]

Editors of law journals, NAACP attorneys, and white Texas politicians were aware of the defects of the ruling. The law journals noted that Texas whites could easily nullify the Court's ruling. The *Michigan Law Review* observed that the Court appeared to have argued against the discriminatory effect of the statute rather than for the right of blacks to vote in primaries.[33] The *Yale Law Journal* pointed out that the Court had failed to take into consideration the realities of Texas politics and had left the way clear for whites to continue to exclude blacks—by repealing all state laws pertaining to primary elections and leaving the task of exclusion to the party.[34] Storey predicted that further action would be necessary because white Texans would probably try to "accomplish the same thing [disfranchisement] in a less brutally frank way."[35] White Texans, as expected, emphatically declared that "Negroes will never vote in Texas Democratic Primaries." R. E. Cunningham, chairman of the El Paso City Democratic Executive Committee, announced, and County Judge E. B. McClintock agreed, "Supreme Court or no Supreme Court, here is one executive chairman who will see that they do not vote. The Supreme Court has held the Texas Democratic primary law prohibiting negroes from voting unconstitutional, but they can't keep the various local executive committees from passing rules prohibiting the negro vote."[36]

Whether further action would be undertaken would be considered at a later date. The staff in the NAACP national office ignored the shortcomings of the decision and hastily announced that the "white primary" had been dealt a death blow. Walter White later admitted, "In our jubilation over the victory, we naively believed that disfranchisement by means of 'white Democratic primaries' was settled."[37] The case possessed a dual significance for the NAACP. It was important because it represented the Association's first complete handling of a case attacking black disfranchisement. It had provided all of the money and the legal expertise required to execute the litigation. Of equal importance was the way in which the Association leaders could use the case to further the development of the NAACP as an organization. The publicity ac-

---

32. Ward E. Y. Elliott, *The Rise of Guardian Democracy: The Supreme Court's Role in Voting Rights Disputes 1845–1969* (Cambridge: Harvard University Press, 1974), 74.

33. *Michigan Law Review* 28 (1930): 613.

34. *Yale Law Journal* 41 (1932): 1218–19.

35. Storey to Johnson, March 9, 1927, NAACP Papers, Box C-76.

36. El Paso *Herald,* March 10, 1927.

37. White, *A Man Called White,* 86.

corded the case generated a great deal of enthusiasm and support among blacks and whites in the work of the Association. In short, the creation of a strong organization was as important as the eradication of barriers to first-class citizenship and equality.

In October 1925, the NAACP announced the launching of a $50,000 Legal Defense Fund Drive. The American Fund for Public Service donated $5,000 and promised an additional $15,000 on the condition that $30,000 was raised to match the offer.[38] Secretary James Weldon Johnson organized the nation-wide campaign to solicit money from the "great Negro business enterprises, the powerful fraternal orders, and the various professional and other organizations." In a direct appeal to the Grand Exalted Ruler of the Elks, Johnson noted, "The colored Doctors of the country have already responded and are getting their machinery in motion. The National Association of Colored Women has also signified its intention of raising money toward this Fund." He suggested, "We feel that our powerful fraternal organizations can do nothing better than to give the NAACP the means to carry out the purposes which these organizations wish to see executed, but which they themselves are not specifically organized to carry out."[39]

During the 1920s the Association leaders buttressed the appeal for funds by stressing a trio of citizenship rights cases. The first case concerned Dr. Ossian Sweet, a prominent black doctor in Detroit who had taken up residence in a white neighborhood. The white neighbors, incensed by his presence, assembled an angry mob, and on a late Saturday afternoon in September 1925, surrounded his house and threatened to burn him out. Shots were fired—no one ever determined how many—and one white man was killed. Dr. and Mrs. Sweet and several relatives and friends who were in the house at the time were arrested and charged with murder. The NAACP entered the case and employed one of the best lawyers in the country, Clarence Darrow, to defend Sweet. The principle they sought to establish in this case was that every man, regardless of the color of his skin, had a legal right to defend his home from a mob. A mistrial was called in the first trial. Dr. Sweet's brother Henry was tried and acquitted. His acquittal led to the dismissal of the other cases but not before the Association had spent $37,849.[40]

38. NAACP Press Release: "Negroes Start $50,000 Defense Fund for Detroit Riot Victim: Will Also Finance Segregation and White Primary Contests Coming Before the United States Supreme Court," October 29, 1925, NAACP Papers, Box C-156.

39. Johnson to J. Finley Wilson, November 6, 1925, NAACP Papers, Box C-156.

40. Mary White Ovington, *The Walls Came Tumbling Down* (1947; reprint, New York: Schocken Books, 1970), 200–203; White, *A Man Called White,* 79.

The second citizenship rights case, *Corrigan* v. *Buckley*, focused on the question whether a group of landlords could contract never to sell, rent, or lease property to a Negro and then be able to punish in the courts any of their number who changed his mind, or a subsequent buyer who desired to sell to a black. In 1921, thirty white residents in Washington, D.C., including a certain Corrigan and a certain Buckley, signed an agreement which restricted the sale or occupancy of their property to Negroes for twenty-one years. Later, Corrigan violated the agreement and sold his restricted property to a black named Curtis. Buckley applied to a federal court of the District of Columbia for an injunction to void the sale. Corrigan and Curtis in turn filed a motion to dismiss. The lower court upheld the restrictive covenant and the NAACP entered the case and appealed it to the United States Supreme Court. The Supreme Court dismissed the appeal with an opinion, stating, in part, that the questions raised were "so insubstantial as to be plainly without color of merit and frivolous."[41] The decision was the Association's first major setback. The third of the trio of citizenship rights cases was the white primary case, *Nixon* v. *Herndon*.

By November 27, 1927, the NAACP had collected $14,364.71 towards the $30,000 goal,[42] and had worked out a successful strategy for soliciting funds, publicizing its activities and accomplishments, and building the organization. In the days following the *Nixon* victory, Association leaders developed itineraries for cross-country lecture tours and speaking engagements. Following Johnson's lead, they stressed that the victory in the *Nixon* case would have been impossible for any individual to have attained and was only possible through the generous and high-minded public service of the eminent counsel whose aid the Association had been able to enlist.[43] Branch officers were instructed to concentrate their efforts upon arousing black people and persuading them of the importance of supporting the Association. The black and white press

41. Clement E. Vose, *Caucasians Only: The Supreme Court, the NAACP, and the Restrictive Covenant Cases* (Berkeley: University of California Press, 1967), 17–18; *Corrigan* v. *Buckley* 271 U.S. 323 (1926).

42. NAACP Press Release: "NAACP Fund Nears Half-Way Mark to Require $30,000," November 27, 1927, NAACP Papers, Box C-156. Eventually the Association raised a defense fund of $79,000 which was used to finance "the defense activities of the Association for . . . eleven years." Of the $79,000 about $30,000 was contributed by the Garland Fund. Approximately $40,000 was spent on the Sweet case and the remainder was used on other cases, notably the white primary cases. Walter White to Mrs. Grace Hamilton, July 23, 1936, NAACP Papers, Box C-156.

43. NAACP Press Release: "Texas White Primary Victory Cost NAACP Only $2,909.31," March 25, 1927, NAACP Papers, Box D-64.

was fed a steady stream of press releases detailing the NAACP's involvement in the case.

A great deal of its effort was directed toward Texas blacks, particularly those who lived in communities where they dared not openly express favor toward or organize NAACP branches.[44] Dr. Nixon supported this focus and wrote the national office that "other parts of Texas could show their appreciation . . . in no better way than by sending cash."[45] Johnson encouraged both Nixon and Knollenberg to conduct a statewide campaign in Texas to win 10,000 to 20,000 new members for the Association. He encouraged Knollenberg to go on speaking engagements in the black community and to emphasize the necessity of taking an active part in the work of the NAACP:

> It is splendid that you are going to speak for the local branch. I judge that the thing they will be most interested in will be the *Nixon* case and, of course, you can tell them more about that than anyone else. I hope, however, that you will stress this fact: that the colored people of Texas ought to bestir themselves and take an active part in the work of the NAACP. There ought to be a state-wide campaign on the strength of the *Nixon* case which would result in ten to twenty thousand members in the great state of Texas. I wish you would emphasize this.[46]

The black press also provided a mechanism through which the NAACP could reach a large number of blacks. Black editors and columnists thoughtfully emphasized the Association's involvement in the cases and encouraged blacks to join and support the organization. In the 1928 *Annual Report,* the national office noted, "With the 250 colored editors to whom the Association sends weekly news reports, relations have continued most cordial. Both editorially and in their news columns these editors have been most helpful in forwarding the Association's program." The following year, the Association again praised the black press and added, "The strong and loyal support accorded to the Association's work and program by the colored editors of the country remains one of the foundation's support of its activity."[47] As the circulation of the black newspapers increased between the two World Wars, so did their coverage of the NAACP. Protest was a constant theme of the editorials. Sociolo-

---

44. Johnson to Nixon, March 17, 1927, NAACP Papers, Box D-64.
45. Nixon to Johnson, March 12, 1927, NAACP Papers, Box D-64.
46. Johnson to Knollenberg, January 24, 1927, NAACP Papers, Box D-64.
47. *19th Annual Report* (New York: NAACP, 1928), 19; *20th Annual Report* (New York: NAACP, 1929), 42.

gist E. Franklin Frazier observed, "The Negro Newspaper came into existence as an organ of 'Negro protest' and it grew in importance because the white press ignored what was considered 'news' in the Negro Community."[48] The relationship between the NAACP and the black press was mutually beneficial. The NAACP provided it with copy and the press provided the organization with much-needed publicity.

The black press provided widespread coverage of the *Nixon* decision and the NAACP's role in the case. The Richmond *Planet* proclaimed the victory "a virtual proclamation of a new era in the political history of this section." It declared the ruling to be "the most far reaching decision upon the questions of constitutional rights that had been delivered by that august tribunal in fifty years."[49] The New York *Age* likewise provided front page coverage of the NAACP's white primary fight. It, too, heralded the *Nixon* case as "significant and far reaching, and perhaps of greater importance even than appears on the surface. . . ."[50] The Dallas *Express* asserted that "this new attempt [*Nixon* v. *Herndon*] should cause the immediate rallying of Negroes all over the State to the assistance of this organization which has so effectually fought other racial battles to the gates of success, and which more than any of its kind, has the reputation of never quitting until the last opportunity of winning success has been taken advantage of. . . ."[51]

The major white dailies were less effusive in their reports of the *Nixon* decision. Indeed, a major source of aggravation suffered by James Weldon Johnson was due to the fact that most of the white newspapers neglected to mention the NAACP's role in the case. Johnson wrote the editor of the New York *World*: "In view of the fact that *The World* gave front-page space to the Supreme Court's decision in the Texas 'white primary' case; that it published an editorial two-thirds of a column long . . . I feel sure it would be interested in knowing that it was the National Association for the Advancement of Colored People which carried this case through from beginning to end."[52] Similarly, Johnson took the editor of the New York *Herald-Tribune* to task: "In your excellent editorial on the Texas White Primary case, there is one slight omis-

48. E. Franklin Frazier, *Black Bourgeoisie* (New York: Collier Books, 1962), 148–49. For a more extensive treatment of the black press, see Roland E. Wolseley, *The Black Press in the United States* (Ames: Iowa State University Press, 1971); Charles William Grose, "Black Newspapers in Texas, 1868–1970" (Ph.D. diss., University of Texas, 1972), 196.

49. Richmond *Planet*, March 12, 1927.

50. New York *Age*, March 12, 1927.

51. Dallas *Express*, April 18, 1927.

52. Johnson to editor of *The World*, March 9, 1927, NAACP Papers, Box D-64.

sion which I should like the privilege of rectifying. You say that the suit was brought against the Texas election officers by Dr. Nixon. Technically this is true. Actually this case was financed from beginning to end and fought by attorneys for the NAACP."[53] It is interesting to note that the white press in El Paso, both the *Herald* and the *Times,* referred to Dr. Nixon as simply L. A. or A. L. Nixon and refused to give his address or acknowledge that he was a doctor and had practiced in the city for seventeen years.[54]

Johnson's concern about the white press's failure to acknowledge the NAACP's role in *Nixon* v. *Herndon* underscores the dual significance of the case to the Association. The white press was obviously one of the best forums through which the plight of blacks and the value of the NAACP could be brought to the attention of the whole country. *Nixon* v. *Herndon* was the first in a series of NAACP cases that challenged the constitutionality of the white primary and forced the courts and nation to reexamine the quasi-legal subterfuges devised to negate meaningful black participation in the American political process. Realists such as James Weldon Johnson and Walter White, however, had also to make the cases serve the Association. They were charged with the responsibility of developing sophisticated and successful strategies to solicit funds for the NAACP's work and to ensure its survival as an organization.

53. Johnson to editor of New York *Herald Tribune,* March 9, 1927, NAACP Papers, Box D-64.

54. Bryson, *Dr. Lawrence A. Nixon,* 51.

# 5

# An Overview of White Primary Cases in Virginia, Arkansas, and Florida, 1928–1930

Although the NAACP proclaimed the *Nixon* v. *Herndon* decision to be the death knell of the white primary in Texas and in other southern states, the obsequies were a bit premature. The campaign against the white primary parallels the Association's approach to handling issues and relating to its black constituency. While this study focuses principally upon the NAACP's fight against the white primary in Texas, a brief look at its efforts in Virginia, Arkansas, and Florida from 1928 to 1930 provides insight into the difficulty it confronted in attempting to make favorable court decisions mean more than paper victories. By examining NAACP actions against the white primary in these three states, one can better understand the NAACP's internal organization and its relationship with some of the branches.

During the 1890s Florida enacted registration, poll tax, eight box law (provided for separate boxes for the various national, state, and local offices as a form of literacy test; the voter had to choose the correctly labeled box), and secret ballot laws in efforts to eliminate the black vote and to curtail the political participation of a sizable number of illiterate whites. By the turn of the century the Democratic party reigned supreme. The Virginia disfranchisement package required each voter to satisfy lengthy residence requirements and advance payment of poll taxes. Individuals who belonged to one of three categories could register to vote before 1904: soldiers and their sons, those who held $333 worth of assessed property, and men who could interpret selected portions of the Constitution. After 1904 new registrants were required to prove their literacy by completing a complex blank registration form. J. Morgan Kousser points out that in Virginia "the active electorate was so small that from 1905 to 1948 state employees and officeholders cast approximately one-third of the votes in state elections." Disfranchisement of blacks in Arkansas was achieved with the adoption of the "secret ballot" in 1891. The law prohibited all party designations from appearing on the ballot and effectively purged blacks and illiterate whites from the electorate.[1]

In these three states, the adoption of white primary legislation was anticlimactic. In contrast to the actions of the Texas legislature, Democratic leaders in Virginia, Arkansas, and Florida enacted white primary laws granting the Democratic executive committees power to call conventions and establish party membership and voting qualifications. It was tacitly understood that blacks would be excluded: this precaution made the party rather than the state responsible for Negro exclusion. By removing the state from the actual establishment of qualification rules for participation in the primaries, and by delegating that responsibility to the executive committees of the party, Democratic leaders effectively, or so they reasoned, precluded the possibility of any judicial challenge to their primary legislation.[2]

The Florida legislature, in 1902, provided for statewide nominations by a primary election and if necessary a runoff. The law further stipulated that all voters in the primary be members of the party. A short time thereafter the Democratic executive committee of the state announced a statewide primary election and specifically restricted party membership and voting privileges to whites.[3] The Virginia Primary Law of 1912 bore strong similarities to that of Florida. The Virginia General Assembly empowered the Democratic party to formulate rules, establish membership qualifications, and call conventions. Unlike Florida, however, Virginia continued to finance the party's primaries. The Virginia Democratic party subsequently adopted a resolution restricting voting privileges in its primary to Democrats who had voted in the last general election for the Democratic nominees. Historically, most black Virginians

---

1. J. Morgan Kousser, *The Shaping of Southern Politics: Suffrage Restrictions and the Establishment of the One-Party South, 1880–1910* (New Haven: Yale University, 1974), 55, 91–103, 180–81. John Williams Grave, "Negro Disfranchisement in Arkansas," *Arkansas Historical Quarterly* 26 (1967): 212–13.

2. Paul Lewinson, *Race, Class, and Party: A History of Negro Suffrage and White Politics in the South* (New York: Oxford University Press, 1932), 112–13; Ralph J. Bunche, *The Political Status of the Negro in the Age of FDR*, ed. Dewey W. Grantham (Chicago: University of Chicago Press, 1973), 31; V. O. Key, Jr., *Southern Politics in State and Nation* (New York: Alfred A. Knopf, 1949), 620–21.

3. Hugh Douglas Price, *The Negro and Southern Politics: A Chapter in Florida History* (New York: New York University Press, 1957), 19.

claimed allegiance to the Republican party and were, therefore, unqualified to vote in Democratic primaries.[4]

The *Nixon* decision had held that Texas could not pass a law prohibiting blacks from voting in Democratic primaries. Did it also prohibit legislative sanction of the party's restrictive regulations? Louis Marshall was determined to force the courts to clarify this issue. He believed that the laws of Virginia, Florida, and Arkansas amounted to "state action" in violation of the Fourteenth and Fifteenth Amendments. Marshall maintained, "What has been done in Virginia is only to pursue in a round about manner the same vicious method of holding a primary as was sought to be effected in a more brutal but more honest fashion by the Legislature of Texas."[5]

Blacks in Richmond, Virginia, motivated in part by the *Nixon* decision, attempted on April 3, 1928, to vote in the city's Democratic mayoral primary. White election officials A. C. Bliley, William Boltz, and William Ricker refused to give ballots to James 0. West and other blacks. West, with the Richmond NAACP branch's approval, retained black attorney Joseph R. Pollard and, upon his recommendation, white attorney Alfred E. Cohen. Both Pollard and Cohen had assisted the local NAACP branch in fights against residential segregation ordinances.[6] The attorneys filed West's complaint against election judge Bliley before the local Richmond court and asked for $5,000 in damages.

Pollard and Cohen argued that the state itself had never passed a law using a racial or color criterion to restrict the right of its citizens to vote in elections. They maintained that the state was without constitutional authority to deny the right to vote and certainly could not delegate an authority it did not possess.[7] The defendants asserted that they received their authority to deny West a ballot under the general laws regulating primaries: Section 227 of the 1919 Annotated Codes of Virginia gave each political party the power to make its own regulations and to provide for, in any way it deemed appropriate, the nomination of its candidate. On June 11, 1924, the Democratic Party leaders adopted "The Primary Plan of the Democratic Party." The Primary Plan did not mention blacks specifically; it merely stated that all qualified white persons could vote in the primary election. The lower court decided in West's fa-

4. Andrew Buni, *The Negro in Virginia Politics, 1902–1965* (Charlottesville: University Press of Virginia, 1967), 60–61.

5. Louis Marshall to William T. Andrews, September 5, 1928, Louis Marshall Papers, The Jewish Union Theological Seminary, Cincinnati, Ohio, Letter 150.

6. Memorandum on the visit of acting secretary (Walter White) to Richmond, Virginia, February 25, 1929, NAACP Papers, Box D-67.

7. Joseph Pollard to William T. Andrews, May 12, 1928, NAACP Papers, Box D-67.

vor, and the election judges immediately appealed to the Eastern District Court in Virginia.[8]

As counsel for West, Pollard and Cohen informed the national office of these developments. The Association's newly appointed Special Legal Assistant William T. Andrews was the liaison between the National Legal Committee members and the lawyers handling the various local cases. Andrews forwarded correspondence concerning the white primary to Louis Marshall. The limitations of the *Nixon* decision had dissatisfied Marshall to the extent that he maintained a keen interest in the white primary for the rest of his life. Marshall was unable to review the brief before Pollard and Cohen submitted it on April 11, 1929, to the United States District Court. When he did examine it, he became extremely annoyed and demanded that Pollard and Cohen immediately file an amended complaint before Judge Lawrence D. Groner delivered his decision.

Marshall found the Pollard and Cohen brief "quite inadequate." To correct its defects, he prepared a detailed outline of major points that should be stressed in the revised complaint. Marshall emphasized the importance of Section 21 of the 1912 Primary Law, which made the state financially responsible for the cost of the primary. He maintained that because state funds financed party primaries, all taxpayers in reality paid for the holding of elections. Therefore those elections were considered valid state functions and were subject to the rules governing general elections. Marshall urged Cohen and Pollard to underscore the state's legislative sanctioning of the Democratic Party's restriction of the franchise to whites only. This "state action" violated the Fourteenth and Fifteenth Amendments. The amended complaint, Marshall concluded, should rest upon the premise that the Democratic Party Plan of 1924 was simply a more sophisticated method of achieving the same goal the Supreme Court's *Nixon* decision prohibited Texas from accomplishing.[9]

On June 5, 1929, Judge Groner, favorably impressed with the amended complaint, ruled on behalf of the NAACP and West. The judge declared that a state was required to protect the equal rights of suffrage of all its citizens in both primary and general elections. The decision transcended Justice Holmes's *Nixon* opinion. Judge Groner held that the "Democratic Party Plan" was contrary to both the Fourteenth and the Fifteenth Amendments. A state which delegated authority to a political party to prescribe restrictive voting regula-

8. *West* v. *Bliley,* 33f (2d) 177 (E. D. Va. 1929); Marshall to Andrews, May 28, 1928, NAACP Papers, Box D-67.
9. Marshall to Andrews, May 28, 1928, NAACP Papers, Box D-67.

tions violated the provisions of the Amendments.[10] To the delight of the National Legal Committee, which desired to go again before the United States Supreme Court, the Virginia Democrats appealed the decision to the Circuit Court of Appeals.

On May 2, 1930, Cohen and Pollard argued West's case before the Fourth Circuit Court of Appeals. Marshall had died in late September 1929; his son James, along with Spingarn, assisted in the preparation of the appeals brief.[11] The circuit court, on June 13, affirmed Judge Groner's decision. Judge Elliott Northcutt authored the opinion, which observed that "if all the political parties in the State of Virginia incorporated the same qualifications in their rules and regulations as did the Democratic Party, nobody could participate in the primary except white persons and other persons would be deprived of a material right guaranteed to them under the Constitution as amended."[12] Virginia Democratic party leaders decided not to appeal the decision. They also preferred not to assume the costs of financing their own primaries. Therefore, blacks who so desired could vote. For the second time in three years, the NAACP was victorious in its campaign against the white primary.

While the NAACP national office contributed only token monetary assistance in the case, it compensated by providing local attorneys with the expertise of Marshall and Spingarn. The returns to the Association in terms of increased membership and more local support were minimal. Unlike the El Paso black community and its very active branch, Richmond blacks were neither very enthusiastic about nor supportive of the white primary case. The Richmond branch had pledged to raise the money for *West* v. *Bliley*, yet, as of October 1929, it had succeeded in raising only $250. One member of the Richmond branch, Dr. Leon A. Reid, complained to Walter White that it was difficult to impress upon black Virginians the significance of the efforts to overthrow the white primary. He wrote, "They really think it is a joke that Negroes should want to vote as a Democrat. Maybe they will realize what it is all about some day and wake up, though I am beginning to doubt it."[13] Attorney Cohen also commented on the lack of financial support of or interest in the case: "It is important for me to know just what stand to take in the matter, for

10. *West* v. *Bliley*, 33f (2d) 177 (E. D. Va. 1929); NAACP Press Release, June 5, 1929; Secretary Report to the Board of Directors, June 1929, NAACP Papers, Box A-16.

11. Secretary Report to the Board of Directors, February 1920, NAACP Papers, Box A-17.

12. *West* v. *Bliley*, 42f (2d) 101 (1930); Secretary Report to Board of Directors, July 1930, NAACP Papers, Box A-17.

13. Dr. Leon Reid to Walter White, October 2, 1929, NAACP Papers, Box A-16.

if any further fighting is to be done in the case I have been assured by Dr. Reid that the people in this vicinity will not back it up financially."[14]

Walter White, the new secretary of the NAACP after James Weldon Johnson's resignation, was caught between the reality of an apathetic branch in Richmond and the need to continue the fight against the white primary. By 1929 the Association was suffering a severe shortage of money which would become more acute in the coming years. The $500 pledged to the *West* case meant an additional drain on meager resources. White seriously questioned the value of spending a great deal of money in Virginia given the branch's moribund condition.[15]

Little rejoicing followed the announcement of the *West* victory. White attributed the branch's inactivity to its president, C. V. Kelly, the conservative editor of the black weekly, *St. Luke's Herald*. Although Secretary White described Kelly as a "very charming and affable man," Kelly apparently was unable to organize or convince many people to support the Association's program. White specifically recalled one very serious instance of Kelly's obvious lack of leadership: "Mr. Kelly failed absolutely to take any action when the segregation ordinance [in Richmond, Virginia] was proposed. When . . . a delegation of about a dozen citizens went to the Council Chambers to protest, neither Mr. Kelly nor any other representative of the Richmond branch went. Mr. Kelly stated that on that evening he was busy."[16]

In addition to the lack of forceful leadership, a divided black community questioned the utility of protest and the efficacy of the NAACP. Some leading blacks, as White pointed out, relied quite heavily upon the "good white people" and simply did not want anything to disturb the tenuous harmony they had painfully established. This sentiment or class bias was evidenced in an editorial in the black-owned Richmond *Planet* immediately following the *Nixon* decision. At that time, editor John Mitchell cautiously wrote that progress could come "certainly if colored folks show their appreciation of white folks by helping to nominate them, while at the same time pledging themselves to aid in electing this same class of people against all comers." Mitchell stated in the same editorial that *Nixon* v. *Herndon* was "the beginning of the fulfillment of our prophesy made over a decade ago that the time would come when the Southern white man would be ready and willing to protect the black man in

14. Cohen to Andrews, October 10, 1929, NAACP Papers, Box D-67.

15. White to Pollard, October 29, 1929, NAACP Papers, Box D-67; Secretary Report to Board of Directors, February 1930, NAACP Papers, Box A-17.

16. Memorandum: Visit of Assistant Secretary to Richmond, Virginia, Re: Richmond Segregation Ordinance, February 25, 1929, NAACP Papers, Box D-67.

his vote while the Northern one might be indifferent in according him the same privileges."[17]

After their initial exclusion from the primary, little action was undertaken by Virginia blacks from 1912 through 1925 to contest the law. The *West* decision did little, in any case, to alter the general political situation. One study calculated that although there were approximately 385,000 Virginia Negroes of voting age, only about 10,000 voted in 1930, so that the percentage who registered for Democratic primaries must have been exceedingly low. According to the Richmond *Times-Dispatch,* a year after blacks had won the right to participate in the Democratic primary only a few bothered to do so.[18]

The circumstances surrounding the development of the Arkansas white primary case resembled the Richmond effort. In November 1928, Dr. J. M. Robinson and a few other blacks in Little Rock, emboldened by the *Nixon* decision, attempted to vote in Democratic primaries. The election officials, as expected, refused them ballots. Dr. Robinson, with the support of the local NAACP branch, retained black attorneys John A. Hibbler and W. A. Booker and filed for an injunction in the Pulaski County Chancery Court. Judge Mann, a temporary replacement for Chancellor Dodge, ordered the election officials to refrain from denying ballots to qualified black Democrats. Election officials gave the appearance of compliance. They allowed eight blacks to vote, counted their ballots separately, and quickly arranged with Chancellor Dodge to dissolve the restraining order.[19] Chancellor Dodge complied with the wishes of the Democratic party leaders, whereupon Robinson and his attorneys decided to appeal the case, *Robinson* v. *Holman,* to a higher court.[20]

Andrews learned of the case from newspaper reports. He wrote to Robinson's attorneys requesting copies of the pleadings and stressed that the NAACP was "extremely interested in the political rights" of black people. Nibbler complied with the request and informed the Special Assistant that his strategy in the suit was to make the state chairman and secretary of the Democratic Central Committee, and their successors in office, defendants. He used this approach in order to prevent the court from considering the question moot.[21]

The NAACP, in spite of repeated requests for financial assistance, remained rather aloof from the Robinson case. Secretary White felt the costs (approxi-

---

17. Richmond *Planet,* March 12, 1927.
18. Buni, *The Negro in Virginia Politics,* 117–20.
19. *Arkansas Gazette,* December 2, 1928.
20. Andrews to W. A. Booker, December 7, 1928; Andrews to John A. Hibbler, December 18, 1928, NAACP Papers, Box D-44.
21. Hibbler to Andrews, December 22, 1928, NAACP Papers, Box D-44.

mately $600) of the case to be excessive and that if the Association contributed anything to it, it should be no more than one dollar for every three dollars raised by the local community.[22] Legal committee chairman Spingarn agreed with White but for different reasons. Spingarn felt that large expenditures in the litigation could not be justified because of the strong similarities between it, *Love* v. *Griffith,* and the cases being adjudicated in Virginia, Florida, and Texas. He favored sending some symbolic sum to indicate interest in, but not commitment to, the case.[23]

There were other reasons why White and Spingarn expressed reluctance to take over the major part of the financial responsibilities of this case. White explained to Hibbler that "the National Office has spent, with one exception, more money in Arkansas than in any other state. Yet the Negroes of Arkansas have given very little towards the work of the National Association for the Advancement of Colored People." Essentially White felt that the Association had to be very selective in the cases it designated for support. It made sense to him that the Association take up cases from areas where its work produced reasonable local support: "Our assistance in worthwhile cases is, of course, not conditioned upon contributions but . . . it is not fair to other states who have by their contributions enabled the Association to continue in existence that we should give disproportionate amounts in cases in states where little has been done to help the Association carry on its work." White added, "We know that there are enough colored men of means in Little Rock alone to finance this case with ease and we certainly do not feel that we ought to be called upon to bear all of the major portion of the cost from this office."[24]

Luther W. Moore, head of the Citizens Defense Fund Committee that had assisted the Little Rock NAACP branch's fund-raising efforts, responded to White's criticisms. He informed White that "the Little Rock branch of the NAACP associated with a special Committee" had assumed the responsibility of helping to finance the Democratic primary case through the state Supreme Court and the United States Supreme Court. Moore resented White's insinuations that Arkansas had not supported the Association. To set the record straight, Moore assured White that if he consulted his files again he would discover "that Arkansas has also helped herself greatly in raising money to carry

22. Hibbler to Andrews, August 30, 1929; White to Hibbler, September 5, 1929; memorandum from White to Andrews, Re: Arkansas White Primary Case, September 20, 1929, NAACP Papers, Box D-44.

23. Andrews to Luther W. Moore, September 24, 1929; Arthur Spingarn to Andrews, October 1, 1929, NAACP Papers, Box D-44.

24. White to Hibbler, September 5, 1929, NAACP Papers, Box D-44.

on law suits, both in the state courts and in the United States Supreme Court in which our people have been involved."[25] White eventually relented and suggested to Spingarn that he recommend to the legal committee and the NAACP a contribution of $50 to $100. Spingarn agreed to do this and left the matter up to White, who sent a $50 check to Moore. The pragmatic secretary made the contribution to ensure that the NAACP would at least receive some of the credit in the event a definitive decision was rendered in the case.[26]

This amount was insufficient to aid significantly Hibbler and Booker, who were hampered by lack of funds throughout the case. By the time the case reached the Supreme Court of Arkansas, it had become evident that blacks in Little Rock would not raise the necessary funds. Most blacks had apparently lost interest in the deliberations, which they viewed as a "political rather than a racial fight."[27] Blacks in other parts of Arkansas, notably Hot Springs, had promised to contribute some money to the primary case, but they too failed to live up to their commitment. The president of the Hot Springs NAACP branch wrote Hibbler about their monetary problems. The branch found it difficult to send its yearly dues to the national office: "The promise to send you $25 on the primary case was contingent upon my being able to convert the Executive Committee of our local NAACP branch to that view. I have not been able to do so. . . ."[28] Hibbler confided to Andrews, "Insofar as raising money in Arkansas from the Negroes to carry on the fight it seems that we are hopeless."[29]

Hibbler and Booker argued the case before the Arkansas Supreme Court on March 17, 1930. One week later, the Court upheld Chancellor Dodge's decision. The state Supreme Court saw the Democratic Party not as an agency of the state but as a voluntary political organization with the right to prescribe the rules and regulations defining membership qualifications. It was inconsequential that Dr. Robinson and his associates claimed to be Democrats. Indeed, the justices maintained that there was no more reason to say that the Democratic party in Arkansas could not make its primaries restrictive than there was to say that the Masonic bodies in Arkansas could not exclude Negroes on the basis of color.[30] Hibbler and Booker immediately filed an appeal

25. Moore to White, September 17, 1929, NAACP Papers, Box D-44.

26. White to Spingarn, November 7, 1929; Spingarn to White, November 8, 1929; White to Moore, November 13, 1929, NAACP Papers, Box D-14.

27. Hibbler to White, May 5, 1930, NAACP Papers, Box D-44.

28. Dr. Harand H. Phills to Hibbler, August 25, 1930, NAACP Papers, Box D-44.

29. Hibbler to Andrews, August 27, 1930, NAACP Papers, Box D-44.

30. *Law Reporter* 41, no. 9 (March 24, 1930): 713–14. Copy is in NAACP Legal Files, Box D-44.

motion to the Supreme Court of the United States, which, on November 24, 1930, declined to review the case. Without elaboration, Walter White reported to the board of directors that the decision of the Supreme Court was based largely on technicalities.[31]

In both Arkansas and Virginia some blacks failed to comprehend why other blacks should want to vote as Democrats under any circumstances. Blacks had never voted in appreciable numbers in the Democratic primary elections in either of the states. Moreover, few lower-class blacks could see any value in supporting these apparently "middle-class aspirations."

The National Association, aware of the situation in Arkansas, was naturally not very receptive to subsequent pleas for money.[32] The Arkansas attorneys were forced to spend some of their own funds to docket the case before the Supreme Court and print the records and briefs.[33] At the last moment, Spingarn approved a contribution of $200.[34]

When the United States Supreme Court refused to review, White observed that the case was unfortunate and disappointing but that it was not a permanent setback. He let it be known that the Association had given some support to the Arkansas case but that it had more directly supervised the one in Virginia. He remarked that the *West* v. *Bliley* case had been the one which set forth most clearly the basic point under dispute—the validity of so-called enabling acts granting to political parties the right to determine their own qualifications for membership.[35]

The NAACP attempted to persuade the courts of Florida to deal with the same issue. The Pensacola branch issued a circular following the *Nixon* decision, which stated: "Taking the recent decision of the United States Supreme Court . . . at face value, we are determined to have the law applied to Florida. We believe that political freedom is as essential as economic freedom and the right to vote for any party of our choice should not be denied us." Branch president Nathan A. Jones and the president of the Escambia County Voters League, A. M. Johnson, organized a registration campaign that resulted in the registration of 1,500 blacks for the Democratic primary scheduled for April 10, 1928. White Democrats, led by J. H. Baylis, mayor of Pensacola, an-

31. *Robinson* v. *Holman*, 282 U.S. 804, 75 L. ed. (1930); Secretary Report to Board of Directors, December 1930, NAACP Papers, Box A-17.

32. Andrews to White, May 20, 1930; White to Andrews, May 26, 1930, NAACP Papers, Box D-44.

33. Hibbler to Andrews, August 12, 1930, NAACP Papers, Box D-44.

34. Memorandum from Andrews to White, October 1, 1930, NAACP Papers, Box D-14.

35. White to Mr. Billikopf, November 28, 1930, NAACP Papers, Box D-44.

ticipated black attempts to vote and organized to resist any effort of the city's black residents to topple the white primary. When the white election judges denied ballots to black Democrats on primary election day, H. G. Goode, a member of the local NAACP branch, and others retained white attorney Fred Marsh and asked for a writ of mandamus in the Circuit Court of Escambia County.[36]

Prior to the election, the attorney general of Florida had suggested to whites certain measures by which they could counter the blacks' attempt to vote. He stated that blacks could not vote in the statewide primary because Florida law gave the executive committee authority to establish primary voting qualifications. Whites, he maintained, could legally charge the Negroes with perjury on the grounds that they could not be Democrats since they had not voted as Democrats in the previous election. The attorney general, as the black newspaper the Savannah *Tribune* observed, conveniently overlooked the fact that blacks could not vote in the previous election because of the same restrictive ruling. Nevertheless, he advised the whites that perjury could be charged if any Negro swore to an election official that he had voted a Democratic ticket in the last election.[37]

When the returns from the April 10, 1928, primary election were counted, Mayor J. H. Baylis was renominated as a member of the city commission. Baylis, a strong advocate of black disfranchisement, called a number of meetings of the white citizens to discuss their strategy in the pending suit. At the first meeting, the whites voted to ask that any surplus funds remaining after the second primary election in June be used to pay attorneys to oppose the Negroes.[38]

Nathan Jones informed the national office of the developments in the case and in June 1928 the NAACP donated $100 to help finance the litigation. Marshall was asked to supervise the litigation and the preparation of the complaint. Because the Virginia and Florida white primary cases were being handled simultaneously, Marshall's recommendations were applicable to both. He asserted that the Virginia and Florida state statutes were unconstitutional because political parties could not be empowered to adopt resolutions determining the terms and conditions under which legal voters became members of the party and could vote. "It necessarily follows," he suggested to Andrews, "that the res-

36. Savannah *Tribune,* April 12, 1928 (a black newspaper); NAACP Press Release: "Florida Negroes Push Fight on Primary Disfranchisement," May 11, 1928; NAACP Press Release, December 2, 1928, NAACP Papers, Box C-285.

37. Savannah *Tribune,* April 12, 1928.

38. NAACP Press Release: "Florida Whites Excited over Negro Primary Vote Fight," June 1, 1928, NAACP Papers, Box C-285.

olutions so adopted are dependent for their validity upon the act of the Legislature, and that the act of the Legislature is therefore to be read as though it in so many words sanctioned the provisions contained in the resolutions."[39]

Marshall found attorney Marsh's complaint inadequate. According to Marshall, there was no suggestion of the constitutional questions involved. Marsh had not anticipated or formulated answers to the defendants' possible contention that, under the regulations adopted by the Democratic Party in Florida, the plaintiff had no right to vote and thus his ballot was rejected. Marsh's complaint simply posited "that the plaintiff is a citizen of the United States and of the State of Florida, qualified to vote at primary elections, that he registered as a member of the Democratic party and had offered to vote at a primary election held by that Party, and that the defendants denied him the right to vote . . . without warrant of law or legal excuse."[40]

Before Marshall could convince Marsh of the necessity to recast and otherwise improve the brief, Judge Thomas West of the Circuit Court of Escambia County ruled that blacks could not vote in Democratic primary elections in Pensacola as long as the Democratic party limited voting to white persons.[41] Incensed, Marshall vented his anger upon Andrews. Marshall informed the Special Assistant of his regret that "the case had come up for hearing on a complaint so unsatisfactory" and added, "I am greatly displeased with the manner in which this case has been handled." Marshall complained that, in spite of his continued correspondence, "not a suggestion [he] made has been given the slightest consideration." He blamed Andrews for the "nearly two months" delay in forwarding to him related records and materials. He ruefully concluded, "The best cases in the world are sometimes lost because of a failure to start right and because the question which is to be decided has not been properly presented."[42]

On October 11, 1929, Marsh presented an unchanged version of the brief before the Florida Supreme Court. The Court was more than eighteen months behind in its docket[43] and consequently did not deliver a decision on the case until three years later. In October 1932, the Florida Supreme Court ruled in favor of the plaintiffs in *H. G. Goode* v. *Thomas A. Johnson et al.* According to reports sent to the national office, the Court based its decision largely on *Nixon*

39. Marshall to Andrews, August 2, 1928, NAACP Papers, Box C-69.

40. Marshall to Andrews, September 5, 1928, NAACP Papers, Box C-69.

41. Secretary Report to the Board of Directors, September 1928, NAACP Papers, Box A-16.

42. Marshall to Andrews, October 29, 1928, Louis Marshall Papers, Letter 536.

43. *20th NAACP Annual Report* (New York: NAACP, 1930); Marsh to Andrews, January 28, 1929, NAACP Papers, Box D-65.

v. *Herndon* in holding the Democratic Party's resolution and the state's enforcement of it to be in violation of the Fourteenth Amendment.[44]

Initially, leaders in the Florida case of *Goode* v. *Johnson* aroused the enthusiastic support of the black community in Pensacola and received encouragement from the national office. The Pensacola NAACP branch had forged a
coalition with the Escambia County Voter's League leadership and had established a measure of functional unity. However, by the time the Florida
Supreme Court delivered its opinion, little of the original enthusiasm remained. Blacks, as in the Virginia case, had won only a hollow victory.

Of the three cases considered in this brief overview, two ended in victory
for the NAACP. *West* v. *Bliley* was by far the most significant. It established a
very important precedent that NAACP attorneys would cite frequently in later
cases. A state could not use its powers or machinery of government to enforce
the restrictive resolutions barring blacks from the Democratic primaries. The
*West* victory was limited, however, because it was not binding on actions in
other states, as illustrated in the Arkansas litigation. In order to obtain a ruling enforceable throughout the South it was, thus, mandatory that the Association plead a new case before the United States Supreme Court.

The heated interactions between the national office and the local branches
during the Florida, Virginia, and Arkansas litigations proved to be typical of
the organizational problems that confronted the Association during the 1930s.
Approximately 55 percent of the Association's branches frequently defaulted
on fund-raising commitments and were often delinquent in attracting new
members.[45] Both Spingarn and White were cognizant (as indicated above) of
the moribund state of the Richmond and Little Rock branches. Recent critics
of the Association attribute its failure to reach and mobilize, in an enduring
way, the broad mass of lower socioeconomic black Americans to several factors. One student of the Association argues that the NAACP's leadership with
its "somewhat elitist orientation" was a product of "middle- and upper-class,
professional, educated, traditionally oriented America." Accordingly, its leadership possessed a strong belief in the efficacy of reform and was more re-
formist than revolutionary. One scholar observes that the NAACP's ideological orientation, which differed little from that of the dominant white society,
propelled it to develop strategies and an organizational structure designed to
operate well within the very political, economic, and social arena it sought to

44. *24th NAACP Annual Report* (New York: NAACP, 1933), 37.
45. B. Joyce Ross, *J. E. Spingarn and the Rise of the NAACP* (New York: Atheneum, 1972),
59.

change. This factor, added to the reluctance of white America to grant the black man his rights, contributed decisively to the Association's failure to attract massive local black support for its programs.[46]

Another analyst of the NAACP emphasizes the organization's structure, which "closely paralleled the corporate arrangement" common to both the business community and many nonprofit voluntary associations. From its inception, the NAACP's administrative system was more oligarchic than democratic. It was administered from the top down with little input from the average rank-and-file member. During its formative years all decision-making power resided in the hands of a few wealthy white liberals and their black counterparts. There was no effective mechanism through which members of the lower socioeconomic class could influence critical decision-making processes. For example, as one scholar argues, "The constitutional provision that the national office was to receive up to 50 percent of the proceeds accruing to the branches from membership fees and donations not only regulated the number and kinds of programs in which the branches could engage but also reinforced the concept of their subordination to the parent body."[47] Perhaps, to some extent, this arrangement worked to stifle initiative and confidence in the members' ability to carry on those activities the branches did attempt. The institutionalization of the NAACP's organizational structure during the 1920s led to the growth of indifference to, if not outright alienation from, its programs among the rank-and-file membership.[48]

The white primary campaigns in Florida, Arkansas, Virginia, and Texas substantiate the leading scholarly analyses of strained relationship between the NAACP leadership and its rank-and-file membership. The white primary, adopted in the closing years of the nineteenth century, assumed increased significance after World War I. Other disfranchisement devices such as the poll tax, complex registration forms, literacy requirements, etc., already had successfully eliminated the overwhelming majority of potential black voters.

By the 1920s, however, there were a growing number of blacks who could afford to pay the poll taxes, successfully fill out complex registration forms, and adequately interpret portions of the Constitution. These few blacks, essentially middle class in orientation, outlook, and skills, desired to re-enter the political arena and cast their vote for those candidates most responsive to the needs and interests of black people. The national officers of the NAACP were completely sympathetic to their aspirations.

46. Robert L. Zangrando, "The 'Organized Negro,'" in *The Black Experience in America*, ed. James C. Curtis and Lewis L. Gould (Austin: University of Texas, 1970), 145–71.
47. Ross, *J. E. Spingarn*, 58.
48. Ibid., 59, 145.

The Texas white primary campaign provided the Association leaders the medium through which many of the problems revealed within the Virginia, Arkansas, and Florida branches could be worked out. Later, during the 1930s and 1940s, the NAACP would evolve the more successful but nonrevolutionary practice of national control with local-level consultation. National officers would identify those local blacks whom the blacks in a given community recognized as their leaders. They would forge a close working relationship with those leaders who in effect were to become the liaison between the national office and the rank-and-file.

Recognizing the emergence of a "New Negro," white Democrats developed intense fears. They were not really afraid of "black domination," despite the usual rhetoric—only one-seventh of the population of Texas was black.[49] Ultimately what mattered was the achievement of white solidarity and the preservation of white supremacy. To allow a few blacks the vote would challenge that basic ideological posture that held that all blacks were inferior and only Anglo-Saxons were fit to rule. The Dallas *Morning News,* a major white newspaper in Texas, analyzed the desire of blacks to enter the white primary and suggested that it was quite understandable because "the Democratic primary in ninety-nine cases out of a hundred, determines in this state what men shall rule over the Negro citizen." More revealing, however, was the discussion of the whites' belief in their right to political dominance and the inference that the idea of party would break down if a party could not restrict its membership.[50] Just as slave masters had viewed the existence of a class of free blacks as a threat to the preservation and justification of the institution of slavery, so the proponents of disfranchisement found the existence of a few blacks who qualified to vote in general elections, despite virtually insurmountable obstacles, to threaten the concept of white supremacy. If one black were allowed to vote, then it would be possible for most of them to do so. Black disfranchisement could only be justified if all blacks were excluded. In this context there is little wonder that white politicians fought hard to preserve the white primary to the extent of nullifying United States Supreme Court decisions.

The NAACP pursued its legalistic attack on disfranchisement with varying degrees of success. For example, the Association's attack on the white primary was initially more successful than its effort to have Congress enact an anti-poll-tax law. Yet gains from the campaign against the white primary, in terms of massive black support or increased membership during the 1920s, were

49. Houston *Informer,* March 12, 17, 1927.
50. Dallas *Morning News,* February 4, 1930.

minimal. Blacks in the lower socioeconomic groups, as shown in Richmond and Little Rock, did not identify with the struggle against the white primary. They viewed the campaign as being essentially a middle-class, politically oriented struggle, as opposed to a racially oriented one. This is one of the major differences between blacks in Texas and in Virginia, Florida, and Arkansas. To continue the struggle against the white primary, the NAACP once again focused on Texas.

# 6

# *Nixon v. Condon, 1932*

The *Nixon* v. *Herndon* victory did not alter the political status of black Texans. White Democratic stalwarts and Governor Dan Moody realized that the decision posed no fundamental threat to the white primary and could easily be circumvented by legislative adjustments. Moody announced hours after the decision that "some legislation will be necessary to protect the ballot and give that guaranty of good government" the displaced statute was "designed to offer." He assured white Texans that "certainly the legislature can give to the committees of the party the power to fix qualifications for participation in a Democratic primary and the same end will be reached as by the statute" recently declared unconstitutional. He confidently concluded, "I take it that such a provision will not contravene the amendment [Fourteenth] to the Constitution."[1]

Moody's strategy won the endorsement of many high-ranking white Democrats. Walter A. Kneeling, a former state attorney general, supported the contention that political parties could and should choose their own members.[2] A leading white El Paso Democrat, W. H. Burgess, sent a strongly worded telegram to the governor urging that "no action be taken by legislature affecting rights of Negroes to vote in Democratic Primaries except unconditional repeal of clause forbidding same." Burgess insisted that this "be done before legislature adjourns otherwise Federal Courts and Congress will probably hold primaries under absolute control of Congress thereby excluding all state control or regulation under decision in Nixon case. . . ." From Houston, Richard T. Fleming, secretary of the state Democratic executive committee, surmised that if the offending Article 3107 were removed, "it appears the party, independent of statutes, could make its own rules and regulations."[3]

1. Austin *Statesman,* March 7, 1927; Ward E. Y. Elliott, *The Rise of Guardian Democracy: The Supreme Court's Role in Voting Rights Disputes, 1845–1969* (Cambridge: Harvard University Press, 1974), 74.
2. Dallas *Morning News,* March 9, 1927.
3. W. H. Burgess to Dan Moody, March 11, 1927, Post-Telegraph Commercial Cables, in

In late May 1927, Governor Moody impressed upon the state legislature the need to repeal Article 3107. He asserted that a political party was a voluntary group, an association of citizens acting of their own initiative, free from state control. Moody urged the legislature to enact "a statute which will invest power in the Executive Committee of the several political parties to determine the qualifications requisite to membership in such parties."[4]

The Governor's wishes were quickly drafted into a bill. It passed the house on a vote of 83 to 17. One opponent, Hubert T. Faulk of Quitman, Wood County, declared that while he would "support any reasonable bill to curb the negro vote he could not endorse the new legislation." He objected to the fact that "the act empowers the state executive committee to prescribe without limit the qualifications of a voter." Faulk felt that the act bestowed too much power upon the thirty-one members of the executive committee. He protested that "they have ample power under this act to say that a man must be a Methodist, a Mason, and a millionaire." Representative A. R. Stout of Ennis, Ellis County, was even more critical of the proposed bill. He pointedly exclaimed, "I had rather take my chances on handling the 'nigger' than I would on thirty-one men who would have final authority to determine who should vote and who should not vote, and who should be a Democrat and not be a Democrat."[5]

The House bill was introduced in the Senate by R. S. Bowers of Caldwell, who had previously introduced the 1923 white primary statute. After some debate the Senate passed a slightly altered version of the House bill which allayed many of the fears expressed by the House opposition. Section 1 of the new law read:

> Every political party in this State through its State Executive Committee shall have the power to prescribe qualifications of its own members and shall in its own way determine who shall be qualified to vote or otherwise participate in such political party provided that *no person shall ever be denied the right to participate because of former political views or membership in organizations other than the political party.*

While the first section did not mention blacks, Section 2 left little doubt of the statute's intent:

---

Dan Moody Correspondence, Texas State Library, Austin, Texas (cable sent from El Paso); Austin *Statesman,* March 8, 1927.

4. House Journal, *40th Legislature,* 1st Called Session (Austin, 1927), p. 207.

5. Ibid., 246, 302; Conrey Bryson, *Dr. Lawrence A. Nixon and the White Primary* (El Paso: Texas Western Press and University of Texas at El Paso, 1974), 53–55.

The fact that the Supreme Court of the United States has recently held Article 3107 invalid, creates an emergency and an imperative public necessity that the constitutional rule requiring bills to be read on three several days in each house be suspended and be in force from and after its passage, and it is so enacted.[6]

It was tacitly understood that the "emergency" dealt with black voting and that the state executive committee would undertake the necessary action to ensure denial of party membership to blacks. Thus would blacks continue to be barred from participation in the only election that mattered in Texas.

The new law, however, was fraught with difficulties. A few whites remained uneasy over the potential dangers of concentrating so much power in the hands of a few. Even the restrictive clause in the law prohibiting the state executive committee from denying to any person the right to participate in primary elections because of prior political affiliations did not completely stifle criticism. Four months after the *Nixon* v. *Herndon* decision, however, the executive committee of the Democratic party adopted a resolution drafted by member W. A. Kneeling, a former attorney general of Texas. The resolution declared that "all white Democrats . . . and none other" be allowed to participate in the forthcoming primary election. The chairman and secretary of the state Democratic executive committee were directed to forward a copy of the resolution to each Democratic county chairman in Texas and the white press.[7] At this point, the new Texas law was virtually identical to the ones blacks in Virginia, Florida, and Arkansas were currently attacking.[8]

The white and black press produced mixed reactions to the entire series of events beginning with the Supreme Court's decision and culminating in the Democratic executive committee's resolution. One white paper found Moody's legislative maneuverings and the law enacted feeble and ludicrous. The Houston *Post-Dispatch* chided, "It would be hard to find a sillier belief than the one that white supremacy in Texas is endangered to the slightest ex-

6. House Journal, *40th Legislature*, 1st Called Session (Austin, 1927), p. 228, 268–71, 328–31; General and Special Laws of the State of Texas, *40th Legislature*, 1st Called Session (Austin, 1927), p. 193; Bryson, *Dr. Lawrence A. Nixon*, 55.

7. *Yale Law Journal*, p. 1212. See *Nixon* v. *Condon*, 286 U.S. 73, 90, 52, Supreme Court 484 (1932); Knollenberg to James Marshall, March 5, 1929, Nixon Papers.

8. Louis Marshall to William T. Andrews, October 29, 1928, Louis Marshall Papers, Jewish Union Theological Seminary, Cincinnati, Ohio, Letter 536; NAACP Press Release: "NAACP to Fight Newest Texas Attempt at Negro Disfranchisement: Subterfuge Similar to That in Virginia, Florida and Other Southern States," July 27, 1928, NAACP Papers, Box D-64.

tent by a straggling corporal's guard made up of negro democrats."[9] The black editor of the Houston *Informer*, C. F. Richardson, mockingly asked, "Is 'white supremacy' endangered by a few thousand black men and women casting their votes for democratic candidates in a state that is overwhelmingly white and democratic . . . ?"[10] The editor of the Austin *Statesman* clarified the issue: "This is a white man's government way down here in Texas. This is a white man's country . . . the Texas negro . . . is popular in his place—that of hewer of wood and drawer of water."[11]

To the dismay and consternation of many white Democrats, the first legal challenge to the new law and party resolution came not from black Texans but from within their own ranks. The coming Democratic primaries, which would, incidentally, involve Governor Moody in a re-election campaign, were but a minor part of the political activity scheduled for the presidential election year of 1928. The Democratic national convention held in Houston elected Al Smith as the Democratic nominee for president of the United States. Smith's nomination precipitated a major split within the Texas Democratic party, led to a revival of the Klan and an outbreak of intense anti-Catholic hysteria. Klansmen in Texas and many Democratic politicians who were neither anti- nor pro-Klan hated everything Smith purportedly represented—the city, liquor, Catholicism, and foreignism. Smith was depicted as a tool of the Pope, of the Tammany Hall machine, and as a friend of the Negro.[12] The ensuing presidential campaign marked a revival of concern over the appropriate status of the black man in southern politics. As a result of a series of misunderstandings, the black man became a heated topic in Texas politics from 1928 to 1930.

In an unprecedented move, a number of eminent white Democrats bolted the party and energetically worked to foster the election of the Republican presidential candidate, Herbert Hoover. The leaders of the Hoovercrats, as they became known, were former state representative Thomas B. Love and former governor Oscar B. Colquitt. Love, a native of Webster County, Missouri, born June 23, 1870, moved to Texas in the late 1880s and became involved in Dallas political affairs. Admitted to the bar in 1892, Love specialized in cor-

9. Houston *Post-Dispatch*, June 3, 1927; see also San Antonio *Light*, June 1, 1928, and El Paso *Post*, June 18, 1928.

10. Houston *Informer*, March 12, 1927.

11. Austin *Statesman*, January 7, 1927.

12. Charles Alexander, "The Crusade for Conformity: The Ku Klux Klan in Texas," *Texas Gulf Coast Historical Association* 6, no. 1 (August 1962): 78; Doris Asbury, "Negro Participation in the Primary and General Elections in Texas" (master's thesis, Boston University, 1951), 68–69; Dallas *Morning News*, February 3, 1930.

porate and insurance law until he was elected in 1902 to the House of Representatives. Elected on a campaign calling for primary election reform, Love worked closely with Alexander Terrell to revise the state's primary election laws. A leading figure in state and national politics during the Woodrow Wilson administration, Love in 1928 turned his considerable talents to the organization of Hoover clubs throughout Texas.[13] Love never expressed interest in building a strong Republican party and consistently proclaimed his allegiance to the Democratic party. He simply desired to defeat the "sachem of Tammany Hall" and the liquor interests and thus purify the Democratic party. Love and the Hoovercrats carried the state for Hoover, the first time Texas supported a Republican presidential nominee since Reconstruction.[14]

Love's defection was not without consequences. While supporting Hoover's candidacy, Love attempted to run for the lieutenant governorship of Texas. On the eve of the Democratic primary, the primary subcommittee of Cameron County decided that Love was no longer a member of the party because he had broken his pledge to support the party's nominee. After a district judge denied Love's request to compel the county committee to add his name to the ticket, Love, unable to obtain a rehearing before the Court of Civil Appeals, dropped the whole issue and concentrated on aiding his friend, Dan Moody, in his bid for renomination to the governor's office.[15]

Two years later, Love attempted to run in the gubernatorial primary and was again denied permission to have his name included on the ticket. The state Democratic executive committee met in late January 1930 and adopted a new resolution. All qualified voters, regardless of previous political affiliations, were invited to participate in the 1930 primaries as voters and candidates. The resolution, however, barred those who had previously been affiliated with other political parties from running as Democratic candidates for state office. Love took this to be a slap in the face and retaliated with a civil suit against Democratic party chairman, N. M. Wilcox. The press gave widespread coverage to the ensuing legal and political battle.

Love charged that the committee barred "nobody except the white men and women who voted against Al Smith . . . and having done this, the committee

---

13. Sue E. Winston Moore, "Thomas B. Love, Texas Democrat, 1901–1949" (master's thesis, University of Texas, 1971), 1–25; Donley E. Watt, Jr., "The Presidential Election of 1928 in Texas" (master's thesis, University of Texas, 1970), 1–30; Lewis Gould, *Progressives and Prohibitionists: Texas Democrats in the Wilson Era* (Austin: University of Texas Press, 1973), 279–82; Knollenberg to the NAACP, June 12, 1930, Nixon Papers.
14. Moore, "Thomas B. Love," 25; Gould, *Progressives and Prohibitionists*, 279–82.
15. Moore, "Thomas B. Love," 23–24.

deliberately invited every negro in Texas who is a qualified voter to participate in the Democratic primary." An angry Love lashed out that "for the first time, our Texas Democratic primaries are thrown open, wide open, to negroes under the operation of a Statute passed solely for the purpose of enabling the State committee to bar negroes." Love warned his opponent: "I have just begun to fight. From an intensive study of the election laws of Texas, covering the last thirty years, I am prepared to say that the action of the State committee, barring the Anti-Tammany Democrats, is undoubtedly void, and will be so held by the courts."[16]

Wilcox took "sharp issue" with Senator Love's accusations and incorrect reading of the committee's resolution. He admitted that the resolution inviting those who voted the Republican national ticket in 1928 to vote in the Democratic primaries this year was "on its face" subject to the construction that the committee had invited Negroes to vote but, said Wilcox, "that was not the intent of the resolution." He went on to point out that the question of whether blacks would be allowed to vote would be before the committee at its regular meeting in June "and there is no doubt about the fact that, as in the past, negroes will be allowed to vote in our primaries." Ex-bolters anxiously awaited the Court's decision. There was a good chance of another bolt should the Court uphold the state Democratic executive committee's right to keep bolters off the state party ticket.[17]

The crisis was averted when Associate Justice Thomas B. Greenwood of the state Supreme Court issued a writ of mandamus, ordering the state executive committee to certify Love as a candidate on the Democratic ticket. The Court decreed that the committee did not have the power to prohibit party participation because of past political affiliations.

> Moreover, the language of Article 3107 is fairly susceptible of no other interpretation than that the legislature intended the same qualifications to be prescribed by the State Committee for all participating in a party primary, whether as voters or candidates, and further that the same qualifications must be prescribed for all candidates. By the resolutions of February, 1930, all qualified voters, regardless of previous political views or affiliations, are

---

16. Ibid., 27–28; *Love* v. *Wilcox*, 28 Southwestern Reporter (2d) 515 (1930); "Love's Views on Barring of Bolters Given" [in an Austin statement, February 2, 1930], Dallas *Morning News*, February 3, 1930.

17. "Wilcox Makes Reply to Love," Dallas *Morning News*, February 5, 1930; Escal Franklin Duke, "The Political Career of Morris Sheppard, 1875–1941" (Ph.D. diss., University of Texas, 1958), 395–98.

expressly invited to participate in the 1930 primaries as are all candidates save those State offices. Because of the attempted discrimination between candidates and between certain candidates and voters, in violation of the statute, the resolution can not be upheld.[18]

Some blacks interpreted the *Love* decision to be an indication that the Texas Supreme Court would disallow the portions of the executive committee's resolution which pertained to them should a proper case be presented. Black attorney Carter Wesley of Houston excitedly wrote El Paso attorney Fred Knollenberg's office: "Now, this Love case, the Court definitely answers the one big question in our favor, for the court says the executive committee does not have the power to make any regulations which encroach upon the constitutional rights of an individual."[19] The fact that the Court had not actually said this was beside the point. The resolution had been invalidated not because it exceeded any constitutional limitation, not because the legislature could not do indirectly what it was prohibited from doing directly, nor because it could not delegate authority which it did not possess. The resolution was invalidated because the legislature had in fact authorized the executive committee to adopt the same qualifications for all alike. Wesley and other blacks would soon discover that black participation in white primaries did not naturally follow in the wake of the *Love* decision.

Blacks had not passively accepted the fact that the state Democratic executive committee's resolution prohibited their participation in the primary elections of 1928. In most major Texas cities, blacks challenged the restriction. J. B. Grigsby, president of the American Mutual Insurance Company, and O. P. De Walt, president of the Houston NAACP branch and proprietor and manager of the Lincoln Theater in Houston, quickly retained R. D. Evans, president of the Independent Colored Voters League and attorney in the *Love* v. *Griffith* case. They filed suit in the district court asking for an injunction against the Harris County Democratic Executive Committee. Judge Joseph Hutcheson, Jr., a former mayor of Houston who generally regarded blacks as if they were "a lower type of individual and an inferior race," decided that black exclusion from the Democratic primary violated no constitutional provisions. Hutcheson pointed out that the Texas legislature had taken precautions to re-

18. *Love* v. *Wilcox*, 28 Southwestern Reporter (2d) 515 (1930); Knollenberg to the NAACP, June 12, 1930; William T. Andrews to Knollenberg, June 20, 1930, Nixon Papers, Box 2.

19. Carter Wesley to E. F. Cameron, July 9, 1930; E. F. Cameron to Wesley, July 2, 1930, Nixon Papers, Box 2.

move itself from the establishment of primary voting qualifications and had placed that power in the executive committees of the various parties.[20]

San Antonio blacks also indicated a desire to challenge the new white primary subterfuge. Local NAACP branch president J. R. Morris and attorney R. A. Campbell contacted the national office and El Paso attorney Fred C. Knollenberg with requests for assistance. Special Legal Assistant William T. Andrews avoided responding directly to their requests. Knollenberg, however, advised the branch to drop the idea of starting a suit in San Antonio and urged it to support the national office in the case it had decided to take up with Nixon as plaintiff. Knollenberg reminded Campbell that if he persisted in developing the suit he would eventually have to present it before Judge Du Val West, who had previously delivered the *Chandler* v. *Neff* decision. The El Paso attorney confidently added, "I do not think that you will be able to accomplish as much there as we can from here."[21]

The Houston and San Antonio branches' request for assistance arrived at NAACP headquarters much too late for consideration. The national office had already made plans to handle the case that Knollenberg, Nixon, and branch president L. W. Washington were initiating in El Paso. In mid-June 1928, Washington informed the national office: "We will attempt to set the stage as before and keep your department informed of each step."[22] Their plans worked smoothly. At approximately 10:00 A.M., on July 28, Nixon went to the Ninth Precinct polling place in El Paso. He presented his poll tax receipt to precinct judge James Condon. Condon accepted the receipt, referred to his voters' list and returned it to Nixon, explaining, "This is a Democratic Primary, you will have to get an order from Mr. Cregor," the chairman of the Democratic Executive Committee of El Paso County. Nixon attempted to reach

20. Interview with Dr. James M. Nabrit, Washington, D.C., April 6, 1974; description of Hutcheson found in memorandum on telephone conversation with Mac Lowenthal, formerly of the Wickersham Commission, and Walter White, Re: Individuals mentioned for the United States Supreme Court bench as successor to Mr. Justice Holmes, January 15, 1932, NAACP Papers, Box C-399; *Grigsby* v. *Harris* 27 Fed. (2d) 942 (S. D. Texas, 1928); for biographical sketch of O. P. De Walt, see A. W. Jackson, *A Sure Foundation and a Sketch of Negro Life in Texas* (Houston: Yates Publishing, 1940), 385. O. P. De Walt was born in East Texas near Livingston, Polk County. He worked his way through Prairie View College and after graduating in 1910 he secured a job as a real estate salesman in Houston. After a brief two months as a high school principal, De Walt opened the first exclusively black theater in Houston. He served as president of the Houston branch of the NAACP until his death, April 24, 1933.

21. Andrews to J. R. Morris, June 8, 1928; Knollenberg to R. A. Campbell, June 28, 1928, NAACP Papers, Box D-64.

22. L. W. Washington to Andrews, June 20, 1928, NAACP Papers, Box D-64.

Cregor first by phone and later at his headquarters at the El Paso Drug Company. Unable to locate the county chairman, Nixon returned to the voting place and once again requested a ballot. Condon refused but agreed to sign a statement admitting that he and the associate judge C. H. Kolle "refused to permit him [Nixon] to vote in said primary . . . for the reason that he is a negro, and because we were instructed by the Democratic Executive Committee of the State of Texas to permit no one to vote except white Democrats."[23] Armed with this document, Nixon and Knollenberg filed a damage suit for $5,000 against election judges Condon and Kolle in the Western United States District Court. The national office, after much correspondence and debate, agreed to pay Knollenberg $2,500 to handle the case in the local courts. The attorney originally demanded $4,000 in fees.[24]

Interbranch rivalry quickly erupted as De Walt and Grigsby and other black Houstonians expressed disappointment that their case, *Grigsby* v. *Harris,* had not been taken up by the national association.[25] The discontented grumbling worried the national office. Louis Marshall of the legal committee feared that the Houstonians would persist with their case and that it would reach the Supreme Court of the United States before the second *Nixon* case. Marshall urged Walter White to convince Grigsby and De Walt to drop their case, adding, "I know of nothing which is more important to our organization than to see to it at once that this inexcusable snarl is disentangled."[26]

The national office asked Robert W. Bagnall, director of branches, to resolve this potentially disruptive situation. After weeks of correspondence Bagnall finally convinced Evans, Grigsby, and De Walt to drop the case. He shared with them Marshall's opinion that the Houston case as presently structured would not be reviewed by the Supreme Court because the election had passed and there was no longer a need for an injunction, thus rendering the question moot. Bagnall suggested that De Walt and the others work to involve "other groups in Texas . . . fraternal orders, clubs and churches, in contributing towards the expense of the Nixon case."[27]

23. L. A. Nixon to Knollenberg, August 24, 1928; statement signed by James Condon, Presiding Judge in Ninth Precinct and C. H. Kolle, Associate Judge in Ninth Precinct, July 28, 1928, Nixon Papers, Box 3; White, *A Man Called White,* 87.

24. Knollenberg to NAACP, July 10, 1928; James Weldon Johnson to Knollenberg, July 19, 1928, NAACP Papers, Box D-64.

25. O. P. De Walt to Robert Bagnall, September 8, 1928, NAACP Papers, Box D-64.

26. Marshall to Andrews, October 29, 1928, NAACP Papers, Box C-69.

27. Robert W. Bagnall to De Walt, September 13, 1928, October 31, 1928; Bagnall to R. D. Evans, August 29, 1928; De Walt to Bagnall, November 3, 1928, NAACP Papers, Box D-64.

Assured that the Houstonians would not press ahead with their case, Marshall turned his attention to Knollenberg's brief for the second *Nixon* case. The two attorneys clashed almost from the start, primarily over procedural matters. Knollenberg desired to include the county chairmen and each of the thirty-one members of the Democratic state executive committee in the suit, in addition to the election judges. According to Knollenberg, the county chairmen had instructed the election judges to deny Nixon the ballot in compliance with the executive committee's rule. The El Paso attorney reasoned that the most effective way to proceed was to compel the entire executive committee to travel to El Paso. He explained, "Now just imagine yourself being placed in this position, and if they are at the next election members of this Committee, they will consider it inadvisable to pass such damn fool instructions."[28]

Marshall was not amused by Knollenberg's idea and generally found the brief he submitted "unsatisfactory." Marshall patiently explained that there was no reason to take action against the members of the committee and that to make all of them parties in the suit would tend to obscure the true nature and significance of the litigation. Moreover, he added, "The chances would be that the complaint would be dismissed as to each member of the Committee, with costs, which amounts to a large sum if each of the members of the Committee were to appear by different lawyers."[29] Marshall threatened that if Knollenberg insisted upon proceeding along the lines put forth in his complaint, the NAACP board of directors would have "to take the responsibility of exercising its functions."[30] Andrews strongly advised Knollenberg to withhold processing the papers until he incorporated Marshall's recommendations. In the end, Knollenberg reluctantly filed the brief making the two election judges the sole defendants in the damage suit.[31]

Meanwhile, Condon and Kolle and their attorney, Ben Howell, moved to dismiss the suit in the United States District Court. They argued that the primary election held on July 26 in El Paso was not an election within the meaning of the United States Constitution. In the motion to dismiss, the defendants claimed that the subject of Nixon's suit was political in nature, and that the Court was without jurisdiction to determine the issues involved. They insisted that Nixon was not the proper party to have initiated this suit and that he failed to name the necessary defendants, i.e., the members of the Executive

28. Knollenberg to Arthur B. Spingarn, September 22, 1928, NAACP Papers, Box D-64.
29. Louis Marshall to Andrews, November 9, 1928, NAACP Papers, Box D-64.
30. Marshall to Andrews, February 27, 1929, Louis Marshall Papers, Letter 291.
31. Andrews to Knollenberg, November 9, 1928, NAACP Papers, Box D-64; Knollenberg to the national office, March 16, 1929, NAACP Papers, Box D-65.

Committee of the Democratic Party of the State of Texas. Furthermore, they asserted that the matters and allegations in question were not sufficient to constitute a cause of action against the defendants, who had violated neither the Fourteenth and Fifteenth Amendments nor the laws or constitution of Texas.[32]

Marshall was "pleased" that the defendants had argued in this fashion. He told Knollenberg that it was likely that the district court would follow Judge Hutcheson's decision in *Grigsby* v. *Harris.* This would enable the NAACP to appeal to the United States Circuit Court of Appeals and from there to the United States Supreme Court.[33]

Hearings on *Nixon* v. *Condon* were conducted in the district court on May 20, 1929. Approximately nine weeks later, Judge Charles A. Boynton delivered his opinion. During this waiting period Knollenberg became exceedingly agitated and anxious. One week he pessimistically believed that the judge would rule against them. The next week he was equally disturbed over the possibility that the judge would rule in their favor and upset the Association's plan to take the case to the Supreme Court. Knollenberg shared his ambivalence with Andrews: "I am hoping . . . that the lower Court decides against us; then we will have the appeal in the same condition that we had it in the case of *Nixon* v. *Herndon.*" Yet he felt simultaneously that "Judge Boynton was with us from the legal standpoint." And if the judge ruled in the NAACP's favor on the motion to dismiss, the case would simply "die."[34]

Knollenberg's distress subsided when Judge Boynton ruled in favor of the defendants and dismissed the case. Boynton decided that, first, the primary was not an election and that the Democratic party had a right to deprive Negroes, Jews, Catholics, Methodists, or anyone it desired of the right to vote in Democratic party primaries. Second, the Fourteenth and Fifteenth Amendments prohibited only states from depriving a man of his right to vote and did not apply to private citizens. The judge concluded that the Executive Committee of the Democratic Party of the State of Texas and the primary election judges were not public officials because they did not get their pay from the state.[35]

32. Copy of motion to dismiss in NAACP Legal Files; Knollenberg to Marshall, April 3, 1929, NAACP Papers, Box D-65.

33. Marshall to Knollenberg, April 8, 1929, NAACP Papers, Box D-65.

34. Washington to James Weldon Johnson, May 22, 1929; Knollenberg to Andrews, July 13, 1929, Knollenberg to Andrews, July 19, 1929, NAACP Papers, Box D-65.

35. *Nixon* v. *Condon*, 34F (2d) 464 (W.D. Texas, 1929); Knollenberg to Marshall, August 2, 1929, NAACP Papers, Box D-65.

Following the ruling Knollenberg attempted to persuade the legal commit-tee to appeal directly to the United States Supreme Court instead of the cir-cuit court of appeals. He pleaded, "This southern country is not going to al-low a negro to vote if they can help it and it would be natural for members of the Court of Appeals of the Fifth Circuit to look at this case the same way as Judge Boynton did." Marshall, Spingarn, and Andrews disagreed with Knol-lenberg and instructed him to file the appeal in the circuit court. This issue was scarcely resolved when Knollenberg raised another objection. He thought it an unwise expenditure of money to pay to go all the way to the circuit court and argue the case orally, "for all of these fellows are from the South and they will all be against us. . . ." With waning patience White explained that "the chief advantage of oral argument would be publicity by means of which our side of the case and arguments in substantiation . . . may be widely spread through-out the South."[36]

In addition to resolving Knollenberg's problems, the Association had to ad-just, in late 1929, to the deaths of two of its most ardent legal fighters: Moor-field Storey and Louis Marshall. Marshall's son, James, continued work on the white primary. James Marshall eagerly pitched in to help write the brief in the case that was to be argued before the circuit court of appeals in November 1930.[37] Knollenberg wrote the first draft and sent it to the national office for revision. James Marshall, like his father, suggested additions and deletions in the brief. Like his father, he also experienced the frustration of having the lo-cal attorney ignore his pertinent suggestions.[38]

Knollenberg did not take Marshall's suggestions seriously. The brief he prepared and forwarded to the national office contained none of Marshall's recommendations. Marshall complained to Spingarn: "It is difficult to know when one is fairly criticizing someone else's brief and when one is merely pushing one's own stylistic idiosyncrasy. Still I feel that the brief has too much skeleton and too little cartilage." He reiterated that a study of the state legisla-ture and contemporary statements of politicians would demonstrate that di-rect primaries were adopted to make nominations democratic and to give vot-ers a chance to name their own candidates. He stressed that this was important to tie up the main arguments in *Nixon* v. *Condon* and to "defeat the suggestion

36. Knollenberg to Marshall, August 2, 1929; Andrews to Marshall, August 14, 1929; Knollenberg to the national office, November 14, 1949, NAACP Papers, Box D-65. Spin-garn to White, January 28, 1930; White to Knollenberg, January 30, 1930, NAACP Papers, Box D-62.
37. Spingarn to White, February 1, 1930, NAACP Papers, Box D-62.
38. James Marshall to White, February 15, 1930, NAACP Papers, Box D-62.

that political parties are to be regarded as private lunch clubs which can govern the activities of their members."[39]

By August, with the hearings only three months away, Marshall resigned himself to the realization that it was too late to recast the entire brief. He strongly urged, however, that his suggestions be incorporated in the brief if it went up to the United States Supreme Court. White conveyed the essence of Marshall's criticisms to Knollenberg and warned him that "by the time this case reaches the Supreme Court there ought to be in the brief a table showing the vote for the Governor in Texas at each election during the last thirty years and the vote for primary contestants to show that the primary is really the most important thing."[40] Knollenberg replied in self-defense that he and his associate had prepared the brief to present to judges on the bench who were prejudiced against them and who would not give them fair consideration. Knollenberg admitted that "the brief . . . probably is not such a one as should be filed in the Supreme Court. However, we realize the conditions that we have to meet, and we presented it for the purpose of meeting the judges who are now on the bench." Knollenberg believed that inclusion of "all these facts" would not help their case with the circuit court judges or any southern judge for that matter.[41]

At this juncture, shortly before the circuit court hearings, the NAACP retained Nathan Margold "to direct its proposed legal campaign under the Garland Fund appropriations,"[42] and a copy of the *Nixon* brief was submitted to him for suggestions. Margold, a Harvard Law School graduate and a student of Felix Frankfurter, had already had a distinguished career as an assistant United States attorney in New York though still a young man. In 1930, he acted as special counsel to the Pueblo Indians in pressing their land-title claims. Because Margold was new on the job, Spingarn painstakingly brought him up to date on the *Nixon* v. *Condon* case. Explaining the shortcomings of Knollenberg's brief, Spingarn said: "Mr. Knollenberg sent a copy of his proposed brief to the National Office this summer when Mr. James Marshall was at his camp in the country and in view of the fact that the brief had to be filed in a very short time, neither he nor I was able to do more than make a few perfunctory suggestions." Spingarn defensively added, "Although my name ap-

39. J. Marshall to Spingarn, August 18, 1930, NAACP Papers, Box D-62.

40. White to Knollenberg, August 20, 1930, NAACP Papers, Box D-62.

41. Knollenberg to White, August 23, 1930; Knollenberg to Spingarn, September 2, 1930, NAACP Papers, Box D-62.

42. Nathan Margold to Knollenberg, October 21, 1930, A. B. Spingarn Papers, Library of Congress, Washington D.C., Box 5.

pears in the brief it is not in any sense my brief and my name is only on it so that the colored people of the country may know that the National Association is sponsoring the case." The legal committee chairman confided, "It is an unfortunate fact that in choosing a lawyer in a Southern state to undertake causes as unpopular as ours, we have not the same freedom of selection that we should like. Some day I should like to talk to you about this problem."[43]

After the circuit court hearings, Knollenberg reported to the national office that the court consisted of "Judge Bryan, a Florida Democrat and ex-Senator appointed to the bench by President Woodrow Wilson and Judge Foster, a southern Republican, both Circuit Court judges; and Judge Dauthet, a District judge from Louisiana and formerly a member of the Supreme Court of Louisiana." When Judge Foster asked, "Has not that case been decided by the Supreme Court?" Knollenberg wrote, "We explained to him that we were contending that it had been, and after explaining the difference between the 1923 Statute and the 1927 Statute, we referred to the West-Bailey [*sic*] case from the Fourth Circuit. . . ." Knollenberg lamented that "in rather an active practice in the Court-room for many years, I never in my life before felt such prejudice."[44] A few weeks later Knollenberg, still obviously upset and hurt by his recent experience in the circuit court, wrote White that he should not have been caught so off guard. He confided, "at my last appearance, while I was doing my best to present the case, two of the judges turned around in their chairs and presented their sides, or backs to me."[45]

On May 16, 1931, the circuit court of appeals affirmed Judge Boynton's decision handed down in the district court. Boynton had declared that the Democratic state executive committee, in passing the resolution excluding blacks from membership and voting in the primary, had not acted as an agent of the state.[46] The Association was "pleased" with the decision. White and Herbert Seligman (director of publicity) collaborated on a press release proclaiming: "In some respects it is advantageous to be able to carry the case for a definitive decision from the Supreme Court, inasmuch as the other similar case, won in Virginia last year . . . *West* v. *Bliley* . . . never had to go to the United States Supreme Court."[47]

43. Spingarn to Margold, October 16, 1930, A. B. Spingarn Papers, Box 5.

44. Knollenberg to Margold, November 13, 1930; William Andrews' report for the month of November 1930, December 3, 1930, NAACP Papers, Box D-62.

45. Knollenberg to White, November 17, 1930, Nixon Papers, Box 3.

46. *Nixon* v. *Condon*, 49F (2d) 1012 (C. C. A. 5th, 1931).

47. Memorandum from White to Herbert Seligman, May 20, 1921; NAACP Press Release, May 1931, NAACP Papers, Box D-62.

Seizing this opportunity, the Association attorneys appealed for a writ of certiorari from the Supreme Court. Margold and Marshall in conjunction with Knollenberg and his assistant, E. F. Cameron, prepared the brief.[48] As the date for oral argument before the Court drew near, some rivalry developed between Marshall and Margold as to who would represent the NAACP before the Supreme Court. Walter White was placed in the unenviable position of trying to placate both men. White had sent out a memorandum announcing that the oral argument would be made either by Margold or some other member of the Association's legal committee. Margold took exception to this and announced: "I am going to make the argument and it is always bad for more than one person to argue." White asked Spingarn, "How are we going to get over to him that Jimmie is going to join in the argument?" He left the matter up to the "great tact and wisdom of the Chairman of the Legal Committee." After a week of silence, White informed Spingarn that Marshall was "getting nervous because of the nearness of the argument and the fact that he can get no word out of Margold." Once again White suggested, "I think it would be an excellent idea if you wrote a tactful letter to Mr. Margold pointing out that *Nixon* v. *Condon* is not one of the cases coming under the Garland Fund appropriation and that since Mr. Marshall is contributing his services we wish him considered as chief counsel." White desired to have this potentially troublesome issue resolved in such a way "that we should have a little leeway of our own in case we should want some other member of the Legal Committee or some other attorney to argue in a given case."[49]

Apparently Spingarn was able to ease the situation because on January 7, 1932, Marshall argued the case with Spingarn and Margold present in the Court. The attorney general of Texas had informed the clerk of the Supreme Court that he would submit a brief, but by the start of the hearings he had not done so. Knollenberg informed Marshall that the Texas attorney general had not entered the case so as to avoid the appearance of defending the state's actions. The Court wanted to hear both sides of the case, however, so it scheduled a reargument of the case on March 14, 1932. Ben Howell decided to appear to represent the Texas Democratic party's interests.[50]

48. NAACP Press Release: "Primary Bar on Negroes Put Up to United States High Court," July 30, 1931, NAACP Papers, Box D-62.

49. White to Spingarn, November 2, 1931, November 11, 1931, NAACP Papers, Box D-62.

50. NAACP Press Release, January 8, 1932; Knollenberg to White, January 26, 1932, NAACP Papers, Box D-63; Knollenberg to Marshall, January 26, 1932, Nixon Papers.

On the date of the reargument, both Margold and Marshall participated although "Marshall made the first and principal argument." Margold later commented to his former professor, Felix Frankfurter, concerning Marshall's performance, "I thought he did quite well, until a series of questions put to him by the Chief Justice and Justices McReynolds and Sutherland at the end of his argument indicated that they, at least, had not grasped some of the vital points he should have driven home." Elaborating, Margold stated, "His answers to the questions were weak and I had to abandon my own plan of argument in order to cover the points he left doubtful." Evaluating his own performance, Margold offered, "I was not at all satisfied with the turn the argument took, but I hope to do much better in future appearances before the Supreme Court."[51] White, who was also present in the Court, made a complimentary report on both attorneys to Johnson: "Jimmie made a superb argument as did Margold, while the lawyers representing the State of Texas made a very poor showing."[52]

During the rearguments, Marshall and Margold attempted to show that the state Democratic executive committee received whatever power it had from Article 3107 of the Revised Civil Statutes of Texas. The state Democratic executive committee, in this case, had not in fact undertaken to fix qualifications of members of the Democratic party. The NAACP attorneys maintained, "The resolution makes no attempt to say who shall be Democrats, but rather what Democrats may exercise their legal rights and what Democrats shall be deprived of their legal rights." They concluded, "It is interesting to note that while denying Texas has anything to do with excluding Negroes from the statutory primary, the State gives the full force of all of its sovereign powers in recognizing and protecting defendants in such exclusion."[53]

Ben Howell, attorney for Condon and Kolle and, implicitly, the state of Texas and its Democratic party, contended that the Fourteenth and Fifteenth Amendments applied only to the power of a state. These amendments did not affect private individuals or private associations. More specifically, Howell claimed that by enacting chapter 67 of the laws of 1927, the Texas Legislature had merely withdrawn the state from an attempted unlawful interference with the right of the Democratic party to determine the qualifications of its mem-

51. Margold to Felix Frankfurter, April 4, 1932, Felix Frankfurter Papers, Manuscript Division, Library of Congress, Washington D.C., Box 82.

52. White to Johnson, March 19, 1932, NAACP Papers, Box D-63.

53. Motion for leave to file briefs and argue the case *Nixon* v. *Condon,* Supreme Court of the United States October Term, 1931, No. 265, copy in NAACP Legal Files Box D-62. A copy of the brief is also in this box of the legal files.

bers. The Fifteenth Amendment, he asserted, was a limitation only upon states, thus the state had not deprived the petitioner of his vote.[54]

White speculated, after the arguments, that "McReynolds seemed hostile... and we aren't sure about Sanford. Hughes, Stone, Brandeis, Roberts and Cardozo seem to be with us. We don't know about Van Devanter and Sutherland."[55] White's judgment proved to be substantially accurate. On May 2, 1932, the Supreme Court, in a five to four decision reflecting the social attitude divisions between the justices, once again ruled in favor of Nixon and the NAACP. Recently appointed Supreme Court justice Benjamin Cardozo delivered the ruling of the Court, in which Justices Stone, Brandeis, Hughes, and Sanford concurred.[56] McReynolds, with Van Devanter, Sutherland, and Butler concurring, wrote the dissenting opinion. The majority opinion left undecided two of the most significant issues relating to the white primary. Cardozo stressed that the Court was not ready to rule upon the questions of "whether a political party in Texas has the inherent power today without restraint by any law to determine its membership..." and "whether the effect of the Texas legislature has been to work so complete a transformation of the concept of a political party as a voluntary association...."[57]

Following these opening disclaimers, Cardozo went on to say that the State Executive Committee of the Texas Democratic Party did not have the right to bar Negroes from admission to party ranks. "The State Executive Committee if it is the sovereign organ of the party, it is not by virtue of any power inherent in its being. It is, as its name imports a Committee and nothing more, a Committee to be chosen by the Convention and to consist of a Chairman and thirty-one members, one from each senatorial district of the State." The very

54. *Nixon* v. *Condon*, 286 U.S. 73–106 (1932).

55. White to Johnson, March 19, 1932, NAACP Papers, Box D-63.

56. In 1930 White vigorously and successfully led and organized a campaign to block the confirmation of Judge John J. Parker of North Carolina, a Hoover nominee, to the Supreme Court on the grounds that Parker was a racist and would not be fair to blacks coming before the High Court for justice. After Parker's defeat, Justice Owen Roberts was appointed to the bench. In 1932, on the very day of the *Nixon* v. *Condon* hearings, a NAACP press release announced, "the newly confirmed liberal Supreme Court Justice Benjamin N. Cardozo is being inducted in office," February 16, 1932. Immediately after the decision was announced White wired the seven major black newspapers, "TEXAS WHITE PRIMARY VICTORY IN USSC BY FIVE TO FOUR VOTE DEMONSTRATES WISDOM NAACP IN EXCLUDING PARKER FROM BENCH..." Ironically the future performance of both judges would prove Parker to be much more sensitive and favorable to the black cause than Justice Roberts! See May 3, 1932, NAACP Papers, Box D-63.

57. *Nixon* v. *Condon*, 286 U.S. 73–106 (1932); Henry J. Abraham, *Freedom and the Court: Civil Rights and Liberties in the United States*, 2d ed. (New York: Oxford University Press, 1972), 330.

fact that Texas legislation was thought necessary was a token that the committee was without inherent powers. Cardozo added, "The pitch of the matter is simply this, that when those agencies are invested with an authority independent of the will of the association in whose name they undertake to speak, they become to that extent the organs of the State itself, the repositories of official powers." Accordingly, Cardozo maintained, "Delegates of the State's power have discharged their official functions in such a way as to discriminate invidiously between white citizens and blacks" and in so doing abridged the Fourteenth Amendment. "The Fourteenth Amendment, adopted as it was with special solicitude for the equal protection of members of the Negro race, lays a duty upon the Court to level by its judgment these barriers of color."[58] Once again the Supreme Court declined to base its decision on the much firmer ground afforded by the Fifteenth Amendment.

But insofar as the political fortunes of blacks were concerned, a critical flaw marred Cardozo's opinion. He had held that the state executive committee was only a part of the state Democratic convention and had no right to pass the resolution barring blacks from participation in Democratic primaries. The only body having the right, by implication, was the state Democratic party convention which elected the state Democratic executive committee. The state convention had not given the committee that power; the state legislature had done so. According to Cardozo, this made the state Democratic executive committee an agency of the state. The resolution subsequently passed had to be considered "state action," and not action of individuals.

> The suggestion is offered that in default of inherent power or of statutory grant the committee may have been armed with the requisite authority by vote of the Convention. Neither at our bar nor in the trial was the case presented on that theory. At every stage of the case the assumption has been made that authority, if there was any, was either the product of the statute or was inherent in the Committee under the law of its creation.[59]

In the dissenting opinion, McReynolds, Van Devanter, Sutherland, and Butler maintained that political parties were "fruits of voluntary action" and citizens could create them at will and limit their membership. Condon and Kolle had inflicted no wrong upon Nixon when they obeyed the orders of the executive committee to bar Negroes. In their opinion, the Texas legislature by adopting the new law in 1927 had not given the executive committee new pow-

58. *Nixon v. Condon,* 286 U.S. 73–106 (1932).
59. Ibid.

er but had simply recognized the right to establish membership and voting qualifications as existing inherently in the party. The dissenters contended that the new act had merely attempted to reestablish the situation that existed before the enactment of the first 1923 white primary law.[60]

*Nixon* v. *Condon* was a narrow and incomplete victory. The majority decision rested upon a technical point. The Court was sharply divided. Its ambiguous attitude toward the "inherent power" of a state political party to determine membership opened the door for future legislation whereby white Texans could again sidestep its decision. Margold, for example, was acutely aware of the limitations of the decision. He confided to Frankfurter that the majority opinion had left a path open "for new litigation to determine whether the Democratic Party, acting without statutory sanction or authorization can exclude Negro voters from its primaries by means of a resolution, adopted in State Conventions, limiting party membership to white voters." Margold predicted that if the convention did take such a step and another case was started in the state court, "it is a foregone conclusion that the Texas statutes will be held not to interfere with the existence of inherent power in the Party itself to prescribe the qualifications of its members."[61]

The NAACP hailed the decision as another victory. An elated James Weldon Johnson said that it re-emphasized "the power and vital worth of the Association." He stated, "The decision will, of course, have far-reaching effects on the civil status of the race, and I think it ought to have immediate good effects on the fortune of the Association."[62] In this instance Johnson perhaps spoke too quickly. Not only was the victory clouded by the limitations of the decision, but a growing dissatisfaction with NAACP national leadership among portions of the Texas black population soon began to make its presence felt in the NAACP's national office.

Three young black attorneys in Houston (Carter Wesley, J. Alston Atkins, and James Nabrit) and a gambler with a reputation of being "completely without fear" (Julius White),[63] had become disturbed by the seemingly lofty manner of the NAACP in conducting the case. White was described as an "underworld character" who would fight at the drop of a hat. "He had attributes that all of us," said Nabrit, "should have—a willingness to go to bat for the people, was without fear." Elaborating on White's character and reputation, Nabrit added, "He was a hustler with no high school education, he ran women and

60. Ibid.
61. Margold to Frankfurter, May 5, 1932, NAACP Papers, Box D-63.
62. Johnson to White, March 16, 1932, NAACP Papers, Box D-63.
63. Interview with James M. Nabrit, April 6, 1974.

had shot two policemen and was generally considered to be crazy." Houston's white population avoided Julius White. The national office discovered after *Nixon* v. *Condon* that more than court battles and victories were needed to win the allegiance and support of this Texas black community.

The national office in 1928 had successfully persuaded the members of the San Antonio branch and president O. P. De Walt of the Houston branch to drop their suits and support *Nixon* v. *Condon*. Other individuals in Houston's black community chose to ignore the national office and continued in their separate efforts to overthrow the white primary. The leaders of this Houston-based struggle were Carter Wesley, J. Alston Atkins, James Nabrit, Julius White, and Richard Randolph Grovey.

A native Houstonian, Wesley was born on April 29, 1892, and graduated from Fisk University and, in 1922, from Northwestern University Law School. Wesley moved to Oklahoma, where he became "the first Negro on record up to that time to pass the Oklahoma bar on his first try." He opened a law office in Muskogee at the same time that an old friend of his, J. Alston Atkins, also a graduate of Fisk University who received his law degree from Yale, was beginning practice in Tulsa. Wesley built up a fairly lucrative practice and in time persuaded Atkins to form in Muskogee the law firm of Wesley and Atkins. A successful lawyer, Wesley was purported to have won eleven of thirteen cases he argued before the Oklahoma Supreme Court.[64]

The lawyers prospered until they became involved in a case that brought them unwanted notoriety. A half-black, half-Creek ex-slave, Leonard Ingram, hired Wesley and Atkins to control and administer his finances and secure his land claims when he discovered oil on his 160 acres in Oklahoma. Wesley and Atkins defended Ingram's claim and took charge of other administrative and legal affairs, billing Ingram approximately $40,000 for their services. Many blacks and whites believed that Wesley and Atkins had taken advantage of Ingram in charging such exorbitant fees. Another black lawyer, appalled by the deal, sued Wesley and Atkins in an attempt to help Ingram recover some of his money.[65]

Shortly after the Ingram affair, Wesley and Atkins moved to Houston. Wesley had prepared for the move by taking correspondence courses in business and finance. In March 1927, he and Atkins joined C. F. Richardson, black editor of *The Informer*, and two black businessmen, George H. Webster and S. B.

---

64. Ibid.; Charles William Grose, "Black Newspapers in Texas, 1868–1970" (Ph.D. diss., University of Texas, 1972), 141.

65. Grose, "Black Newspapers in Texas," 141.

Williams, raised $25,000 in cash, and established the Safety Loan and Broker-age Company, Inc. The corporation specialized in buying, selling, and managing real estate. The business paid off handsomely—making loans, offering investment advice, selling insurance, and drawing up wills. The bottom fell out when the stock market crashed in 1929. Wesley and Atkins recovered eventually from their losses by concentrating their attention on the Webster-Richardson Publishing Company, which they had also established in 1927 along with Webster, Williams, and Richardson. The company absorbed the Houston *Informer,* retaining Richardson as editor and Webster as general manager and treasurer. Wesley served as auditor and Atkins became the secretary.[66]

This small group of men proceeded virtually to revolutionize the black newspaper business in Texas. They installed a modern printing plant, increased the paper's circulation until it surpassed all black newspapers in Texas, retained academically trained journalists and expanded the staff from a one-man enterprise to ten. The new venture was not without problems. Competition was intense. There were at least four other black newspapers in Houston. Personality conflicts and dissension afflicted the *Informer* leadership. The Ku Klux Klan expressed open hostility to the militant tone of the newspaper, and was believed to have been responsible for damaging the *Informer* press and burning its files. Wesley and Richardson vied for power within the organization from the beginning. Wesley eventually won when on January 14, 1931, a majority of the stockholders in the Webster-Richardson Publishing Company voted to change its name to Webster Publishing Company, deleting Richardson's name entirely. Competition from other papers was reduced when Richardson was replaced by C. N. Love on the board of directors and Love's paper, *The Texas Freeman,* merged with the Houston *Informer.* The paper became known by 1931 as *The Houston Informer and Texas Freeman.*[67] Richardson founded another paper called *The Houston Defender.* The power struggle within the Webster Publishing Company continued, however, as Webster and Wesley clashed over the paper's financial policies. In 1933 Webster withdrew from the company and established the Webster Printing Company. Wesley, now with the controlling voice, encouraged the stockholders of the Webster Publishing Company to change its name to the Informer Publishing Company.[68] By 1937 local editions of *The Informer* were being printed for Austin, Corpus Christi, Galveston, Longview, Lovelady, Marshall, Palestine, Texar-

66. Ibid., 138–42.
67. Ibid., 143–44, 170.
68. Ibid., 171; Dallas *Express,* May 2, 1942.

kana, Tyler, and Beaumont. Approximately 50 adults and 400 youngsters worked statewide for the newspaper at that time. By the mid-forties Wesley had organized the *Informer* group of newspapers into a Texas-wide chain, including the Dallas *Express* and the San Antonio *Informer,* and had founded the National Newspaper Publishers' Association.[69]

The editor of the Dallas *Express* described Wesley as "a hardheaded, almost cold-blooded business man, [who] kept alive the Informer chain many times by making personal sacrifices." The editor further assessed Wesley's personality, stating: "One of the factors which has contributed heavily to Carter Wesley's success is his strong will power. Once he sets himself out on a course there is nothing that can turn him away from it."[70] A former colleague described Atkins in much the same fashion. "Atkins was quiet but ruthless, in any purpose he set himself on he would brook no opposition."[71]

After Wesley and Atkins moved to Houston, they invited another young black lawyer, James M. Nabrit, to join them in setting up a law firm. In 1930, Atlanta-born Nabrit, a graduate of Morehouse College and Northwestern University Law School, became a partner in the law firm of Nabrit, Atkins, and Wesley. Nabrit handled most of the legal work while Wesley and Atkins devoted a large share of their energies to running the *Informer* newspaper, building a power base and making money. Nabrit and the others saw Houston as the ideal place for black lawyers to fight for civil rights. Nabrit described the city as "a place where blacks were comparatively free from the intense racial animosity that affected them in other southern states." Blacks in Houston, he continued, "had a better financial situation," which meant "that you weren't out there with no financial backing . . . you could get money from people who would put up whatever was necessary."[72]

Wesley remained a force in black Houston's political activities throughout his life, while Atkins moved to North Carolina in 1936 to become acting president of Winston-Salem Teachers College. Nabrit left Houston in 1935 and eventually became president of Howard University in Washington, D.C. But in 1930 these young, bright, ambitious men became deeply involved in the white primary fight. They joined forces with Richard Randolph Grovey, the leader of the most militant black grass-roots political organization in the city, the Third Ward Civic Club.

69. Roland E. Wolseley, *The Black Press in the United States of America* (Ames: Iowa State University, 1971), 50; Grose, "Black Newspapers in Texas," 170–75.
70. Dallas *Express,* May 2, 1942.
71. Interview with James M. Nabrit, April 6, 1974.
72. Ibid.

Grovey, born on Chances Prairie, near Sweeney, in Brazoria County, Texas, graduated from Moore High School in Waco in 1910 and, in 1914, Tillotson College in Austin, Texas. After a brief stint as principal of a rural school, he moved to Houston in 1917 and opened a barber shop. Financially independent of whites and relatively immune to economic reprisals, Grovey quickly became one of the most politically outspoken members of the black community. He frequently asserted, "I've lived as long as I want without a right to be a citizen; and I intend to fight to my dying day—in order that the Negro's right to be a man shall not be curtailed." Grovey organized the Third Ward Civic Club, composed primarily of working class blacks who wanted economic and political freedom. Grovey's organizational strategy helped to bridge cleavages between the black educated, professional class and the uneducated domestic or unskilled laboring classes. In describing the formation of the club he stated:

> We didn't go out and organize the school teachers and the doctors and write down a program for the "little" Negroes. We called the washerwoman, the maid, the ditch-digger, the business man, the cook, the preacher, the hod-carrier, the dentist, the bricklayer, the teacher, the longshoreman, and the gentlemen of the press.[73]

The Third Ward Civic Club was linked to a statewide black political organization. In order to coordinate the struggle for participation in political affairs within the state, a group of black leaders met in Austin in November 1927 and founded the Independent Colored Voters Leagues. Houstonians occupied prominent positions within the organization. Attorney R. D. Evans of Waco was elected president, and editor Richardson served as secretary. One of their immediate programs called for a massive campaign to persuade blacks to pay their poll taxes in spite of the fact that the white primary disfranchised them. The leaders emphasized that when armed with the ballot, "more justice in the courts, better peace officers, better wages to laborers, better public school buildings, better paid teachers, longer school terms . . . will come to the Negro of Texas . . . by paying this poll tax and paying it right now."[74] Richardson was convinced that one of the principal strategies to win political rights should be

---

73. Banks, "Struggle for Equality," 214; Jackson, *A Sure Foundation and A Sketch of Negro Life in Texas,* 681–83; Alwyn Barr, *Black Texans: A History of Negroes in Texas, 1528– 1971* (Austin: Jenkins Publishing, 1973), 136.

74. Banks, "Struggle for Equality" 204–5; Houston *Informer,* December 3, 10, 1927.

directed towards the courts. He believed "whenever any people establish a reputation for fighting in the courts of the country for their legal rights, those who
would disfranchise and oppress them think several times before acting, if they
ever act, along such discriminating lines."[75] Attorney Evans worked to broad-
en the scope of their tactics to combat disfranchisement, specifically the white
primary, by appealing to the United States Department of Justice. In 1930
Evans pressured the attorney general and his assistants to conduct a federal investigation of election practices in Texas.[76] His efforts were unsuccessful because the district attorney at San Antonio advised the United States attorney
general, William Mitchell, that "insofar as this District is concerned an investigation with reference to criminal responsibility of the heads of the Democratic Party in Texas is unwarranted."[77]

Wesley and Atkins used the *Informer* to raise the political consciousness of
black Houstonians. In so doing, they were continuing the tradition established
earlier by newspapermen C. N. Love, W. L. Davis, and C. F. Richardson. Love
contended "that after . . . the unlawful suppression of Negroes generally . . .
the Negro press was the only effective voice raised in their defense." Richardson likewise believed that "the three most important factors in the development of a race are preachers, teachers, and publishers or pulpit, pedagogy and
the press."[78]

Cognizant of the power and responsibility of the black press, Wesley and
Atkins called upon all "the self-respecting, liberty-loving Negroes in every
county in this state to organize leagues." They pledged that the *Informer* would
take the lead to launch "a concerted effort . . . to regain some of the political
ground lost by the race in this state during the past decade." In November 1930
the Houston *Informer* announced that "at its own expense" it had "employed
the law firm of Nabrit, Atkins and Wesley to fight the battle of the Negroes of
Houston in their effort to obtain the ballot in the coming city Democratic primary to be held January 23, 1931." According to the editorial, this action was
motivated by a statement made by G. W. Griffith, chairman of the city Dem-

75. Houston *Informer,* August 14, 1926; Banks, "Struggle for Equality," 144–46; Jackson,
*A Sure Foundation,* 238.
76. R. D. Evans to William D. Mitchell, attorney general of the United States, July 8, 1930;
O. R. Luhring, assistant U. S. attorney general to R. D. Evans, July 16, 1930; O. R. Luhring
to John D. Hartman, U.S. attorney at San Antonio, Texas, July 25, 1930; Hartman to the
U.S. attorney general, August 18, 1930, National Archives of the United States, Washington, D.C., File No. 72-76-0.
77. Hartman to U.S. attorney general, July 31, 1930, National Archives, File No. 72-
76-0.
78. Grose, "Black Newspapers in Texas," 127–30.

ocratic executive committee and the former defendant in *Love* v. *Griffith*. Griffith had remarked, "The Negroes asked me if it would not be all right for them to vote. They told me they were Democrats and are interested in city affairs. I told them that the Committee would not consider granting them the right to vote in the primary, that we conduct the primary the same as we would conduct a lodge and have a right to exclude membership to whomever we please."[79]

Attorney Nabrit was confident that they could force the courts to enjoin the Democratic party from pursuing the course of action outlined by Griffith. He argued, "In many respects the right of Negroes to vote in the city primary presents a much stronger case than in the county and state primary." On behalf of Love, a resident of Houston for 65 years, Nabrit filed suit for an injunction against the Democratic Executive Committee, City of Houston.

The case was argued on January 13th in the United States District Court before Judge J. C. Hutcheson.[80] During the hearings, Nabrit drove home two major points. First, he argued that the statute (Article 3164) under which the primary was held provided that "in all such city primary elections, the provisions of the law relating to primary election and general elections shall be observed." In other words, in the city of Houston both the primary and the general elections were regulated by the same law on the same basis. Secondly, Section 1 of Article V of the City Charter provided that all the legally qualified voters in the city should be permitted to vote in primary elections and if they were not then the primary should be absolutely illegal.[81]

Judge Hutcheson denied the injunction. Wesley editorialized in the *Informer* that blacks should not be discouraged because the case had "proven the ability, intelligence and integrity of the Negro." Wesley explained to his readers that Hutcheson held that the act of the Harris County Executive Committee excluding Negroes was an act of a private party and was not state action. Its resolution, in sum, had not violated any of Love's constitutional rights.[82]

Undaunted, the attorneys laid plans to establish a permanent organization specifically designed to coordinate the attack against the white primary. In early January 1932, the Texas secretary of state at Austin granted a charter to the Harris County Negro Democratic Club. Officers of the club were Julius White,

79. Houston *Informer*, May 5, 10, 1930, November 22, 1930.
80. Houston *Informer*, December 13, 1930, January 17, 1931.
81. Ibid.; copy of the Nabrit, Atkins, and Wesley brief in *C. N. Love* v. *The Democratic Executive Committee of the City of Houston, Texas,* in Nixon Papers, Box 2; Carter Wesley to Knollenberg, January 14, 1931, Nixon Papers.
82. Houston *Informer*, January 31, 1931.

president;[83] James Nabrit, chairman of the board of directors; C. A. Gilmore, secretary, and Leland D. Ewing, assistant secretary; Dr. M. Shadowens, Hobart Taylor, and Richard Randolph Grovey were elected first, second, and third vice president respectively. Carter Wesley was named treasurer and J. Alston Atkins was appointed general counsel.[84] Julius White was a plaintiff in a number of cases conducted by the Democratic club and became the figurehead of this organization.[85]

The club pledged to use every legitimate means to combat the subtle and undemocratic means of a "prejudiced group of party managers in taking away from the Negro every right as a citizen our State and Nation gives us." Grovey outlined the strategy of the club: "We plan to use reason, the public press and the Courts to let the world see Texas Democracy as it really is. We will broadcast these tactics of the Democratic Party managers to perpetuate civic injustice, unfairness in the Courts, police brutality—all behind the shibboleth: social equality."[86]

By the time this organization was firmly established, *Nixon* v. *Condon* was before the United States Supreme Court. The leaders of the Harris County Negro Democratic Club filed an *amicus curiae* brief in the case in much the same fashion that Storey had done in *Guinn* v. *United States* in 1915.[87] When the Supreme Court decided that reargument of the case was necessary in order to give Texas a chance to present its side, Wesley theorized that it had done so for another reason. He wrote: "After the justices had read the brief filed as *Amicus Curiae* by the *Houston Informer and Texas Freeman*, C. N. Love, and Julius White, the Court desired additional argument upon the propositions covered in that brief which were not contained in the brief, or in the argument submitted by Dr. Nixon's attorneys."[88] There is no evidence either to support or to disprove his contention.

83. White had also been the plaintiff in the white primary case *White* v. *Lubbock*, 30 S.W. (2d) 724 (Texas, 1930); White had sought a writ of mandamus from the Court of Civil Appeals of Texas at Galveston to prevent the enforcement of the party's resolution denying membership to blacks. The writ was denied. Barr, *Black Texans*, 136.

84. Houston *Informer*, January 9, 1932.

85. Interview with James M. Nabrit, April 6, 1974.

86. Houston *Post*, July 1, 1934 (a white newspaper).

87. Houston *Informer*, January 16, 1932; J. Alston Atkins to Knollenberg, August 14, 1931; Knollenberg to Atkins, September 16, 1931; Knollenberg to Marshall, August 17, 1931; Atkins to Knollenberg, September 14, 21, 1931, October 21, 1931; E. O. Smith to Knollenberg, November 2, 1931; Knollenberg to Smith, November 4, 1931; Atkins to Knollenberg, November 19, 1931, Nixon Papers, Box 1.

88. Houston *Informer*, January 23, 1932.

During the interim between Marshall's argument and the rearguments, a number of blacks across Texas began to pressure the National Association to permit J. Alston Atkins to take part in the' reargument. Telegrams and letters poured into the national office. The letters reflected what appears to have been a rather calculated outpouring of support for Atkins. One letter stated:

> This Committee [Harris County Negro Democratic Club Committee] believes that the next argument of this case should be done either in part or wholly by Mr. Atkins. . . . Mr. Atkins lives in Texas and has argued a similar case in the United States District Court here. Further than that he has had an intimate relation to the case and of disfranchisement himself. It is reasonable then to believe that he could and would lend more force and power to the prosecution of the case than one who had only had a chance to review the case from briefs, and that a far off.[89]

Another:

> If you were managing a ball club whose reputation was equal to that of St. Louis Cardinals, or New York "Yanks," and were playing another team of equal standing a three game series and the two games played stood tie-tie. And supposed in the deciding game the scores were tied in the last half of the ninth inning, with your men batting. With winning score on 3rd base, two men out, the next batter up having all through the game shown signs of weakness, What would you do? You would call for player A., the best pinch hitter on the club, of course. In this Primary Ball game right now a pinch hitter is needed. 800,000 Negroes in the Grandstand are crying let A., pinch hit. His name is Atkins. Let him strike at some of the curve balls that the Supreme Court inclines to throw. Judge Hutcheson admitted from the bench that he [Atkins] was a good batter. Call him and lets win the series.[90]

Association leaders were baffled by this unexpected show of discontent from black Houstonians. The eminent attorneys on the National Legal Committee were concerned, yet skeptical, as to J. Alston Atkins's legal ability. Marshall confided to Spingarn: "I am enclosing herewith a copy of a letter from Mr. Atkins,

89. Harris County Negro Democratic Club to O. E. Smith, January 27, 1932, copy forwarded to the NAACP National Office, NAACP Papers, Box D-63.

90. Dr. T. M. Shadowens, first vice president of the Harris County Negro Democratic Club, to Walter White, February 10, 1932, NAACP Papers, Box D-63.

also a copy of his motion for leave to participate in the reargument. I cannot understand what this muddy-minded person is thinking of. He is either abandoning the Constitution or the jurisdiction of the Supreme Court for some point that seems utterly meaningless to me." Although he realized the Association had been "caused considerable embarrassment by Atkins and his publicity" and that a defeat would undoubtedly elicit a great deal of criticism from the Atkins advocates, Marshall nevertheless felt "that he ought not to be permitted to join in our argument."[91]

Walter White's immediate reaction was to ignore the requests. As the volume of mail increased, he was forced to give the issue some consideration, however. He forwarded "copies of telegrams received asking that Mr. J. Alston Atkins be permitted to take part in the reargument of the Texas Primary Case" to Arthur Spingarn.[92] White felt it was unfortunate that the tactic of "bringing pressure" had been used in Atkins's behalf and expressed considerable anger and agitation. He wrote El Paso branch president Washington: "Frankly, reputable lawyers do not indulge or permit to be indulged in their behalf such tactics. Fortunately, for Mr. Atkins, the National Legal Committee is composed of men of such calibre that they have not let themselves be prejudiced against Mr. Atkins by those who thought they were doing him a favor." However, White went on to inform Washington that members of the legal committee (Marshall, Margold, and Spingarn) had "considered carefully and at very great length the demand that has been made upon us that the argument in the Supreme Court be turned over to Mr. Atkins. After deliberating the Legal Committee agreed that if the Supreme Court would grant additional time for Mr. Atkins, the Legal Committee would be willing to have him join in the argument."[93] The national office, however, decided not to ask the Supreme Court to permit Atkins time to participate in the reargument. Such a request, they felt, would possibly "prejudice the application for additional time" which Margold and Marshall thought it necessary to make for the NAACP.[94] Atkins, nevertheless, requested permission from the Court but was denied leave to participate orally. He later maintained that his denial resulted because he "was unable to get the consent of counsel for the petitioner."[95] The disagreement

91. Marshall to Spingarn, February 12, 1932, NAACP Papers, Box D-65.
92. White to Spingarn, January 22, 1932, NAACP Papers, Box D-63.
93. White to Washington, March 1, 1932, NAACP Papers, Box D-63.
94. Margold to Charles Houston, March 1, 1932, NAACP Papers, Box D-63.
95. J. Alston Atkins, *The Texas Negro and His Political Rights* (Houston: Webster Publishing, 1932), 50.

on this point created friction between the national office and the Atkins advocates for several months following the completion of the case.

Atkins, Wesley, and Nabrit now resigned themselves to filing an *amicus curiae* brief. NAACP secretary White asked that they forward a memorandum of points not contained in the NAACP brief which they felt should be included in the oral argument. "It is impossible, of course, for me to commit the lawyers who make the oral argument to acceptance of all these points," White stated, "but you may rest assured that they will be carefully and gratefully considered."[96] There is no indication that the NAACP attorneys ever used the Atkins brief.

Atkins, Wesley, and Nabrit concentrated in their brief on the alleged unconstitutionality of the Texas statute, which, they asserted, created an arbitrary, unreasonable, and unfair classification. It denied to the plaintiff the equal protection of the state's laws by authorizing discrimination on the grounds of color. The statute created a state-sanctioned political instrument whereby the plaintiff and all other qualified Negroes were barred from participation in "statutory" Democratic party primary elections.[97]

The major difference between Atkins's *amicus curiae* brief and that filed by the NAACP attorneys was one of approach and emphasis. Both were correct. Atkins asserted that the new statute, enabling the state executive committee to establish qualifications for voting and membership, constituted state action. Their brief discussed in some detail the history of the white primary cases which Atkins, Wesley, Nabrit, Love, and White had fought in Houston. Atkins stressed that the primary was the only meaningful election in the state of Texas and that the rights of 800,000 Texas Negroes were involved.[98]

The NAACP brief, on the other hand, did not focus primarily on the question of constitutionality or unconstitutionality of the new state statute. NAACP attorneys maintained that Nixon's right to vote had been abridged even if not specifically denied and that the state had not provided equal protection under the laws, thus violating the Fourteenth Amendment by its enforcement of the restrictive resolution. Margold was of the opinion that "if the question of state action is intimately bound up with the constitutionality of the statute, if we ourselves make it appear that we cannot succeed unless the statute is held unconstitutional, we make it easy for the other side to concentrate their argument on the statute and assume they have fully disposed of our

96. White to E. O. Smith, November 2, 1931, NAACP Papers, Box D-62.
97. *Nixon v. Condon*, 286 U.S. 73–106 (1932).
98. Copy of *amicus curiae* brief in *Nixon v. Condon*, A. B. Spingarn Papers, Box 65; Atkins, *The Texas Negro and His Political Rights*, 9.

case merely by establishing the validity of Article 3107."[99] The Supreme Court's eventual ruling in *Nixon* v. *Condon* appears to have been based more upon the arguments of the NAACP attorneys than upon Atkins when it declared that the state had violated the equal protection clause of the Fourteenth Amendment.[100]

With the conclusion of the *Nixon* v. *Condon* case, the NAACP officers found themselves immediately immersed in two new problems. The first problem developed from the limitations of the victory. The Supreme Court had declined to explore the public consequences of primary elections and had failed to consider the fact that nomination in the Democratic primary was tantamount to election. This reluctance to deal definitively with these questions, to look beyond form to substance, and to view the Fifteenth Amendment as best protecting the right to vote in Democratic primaries, made possible the eventual administrative nullification of its decision by resourceful Texas disfranchisers. Had not the majority opinion pointed out that the state Democratic convention could legally adopt a restrictive discriminatory resolution if it so desired? So, though the decision on its face seemed favorable to blacks, disfranchisers would soon show that they held aces. They were properly confident that the next round in the white primary fight would have a different outcome.

The second problem arose out of the rising dissatisfaction of black Houstonians. Men like Wesley and Atkins objected to the Association's organizational structure, but more profoundly, to the NAACP's manner of handling the white primary litigation and its apparent disinclination to involve them in the cases. Shortly after *Nixon* v. *Condon*, the NAACP officers were confronted with a potentially full-scale revolt of the very class of black leaders whose interests it ostensibly represented and served. The organization's somewhat inflexible structure and the elitism of some of its officers mitigated against an effective and quick resolution of the conflict. To be sure, many of the community leaders and attorneys employed to handle the white primary cases on the local level had exhibited degrees of incompetence and legal unsophistication. Many were bumbling and intellectually obtuse. But this was certainly not true of men like Atkins, Wesley, and Nabrit. The Association could not afford to ignore or dismiss their criticisms.

During the mid-thirties the Association leadership would be forced to modify some of its practices and solicit more input from black Texans and their local leaders, or would risk losing their allegiance. Black Houstonians who dared

---

99. Margold to Knollenberg, October 21, 1930, Nixon Papers.
100. *Nixon* v. *Condon*, 286 U.S. 73–106 (1932).

to take on white Texans certainly could not be intimidated by high-powered NAACP legal brass. Wesley and Atkins in particular were confident that they could fight white primary battles without NAACP assistance. The mix of somewhat overly confident black Texans and their determined white supremacist counterparts would not, as we shall see, bode well for the NAACP.

# 7

# The NAACP, Black Texans, and
# White Democrats, 1932–1934

NAACP officers soon discovered that they could not rest on their laurels. Black Houstonians Carter Wesley and J. Alston Atkins remained critical of the NAACP in spite of the successful *Nixon* v. *Condon*. They continued to question the Association's procedures. The renewed efforts of white Democrats to circumvent the Supreme Court's decision also challenged the legal gains of the Association made during the decade-long fight against the white primary. As tension between the national office and black Houstonians increased, one issue became prominent. Wesley and Atkins focused their attacks on the NAACP's failure to use black lawyers to argue its cases before the United States Supreme Court.

Wesley's annoyance with the Association had originated during the *Nixon* v. *Condon* case. Following the NAACP National Legal Committee's refusal to grant him permission to participate in the oral arguments before the Supreme Court, the Houston attorney had voiced objections to the NAACP's almost total reliance on white lawyers to argue its major cases before the high tribunal. Wesley was personally convinced that no one could "prepare or present Negro cases as well as a trained Negro." He insisted that the political future of blacks resided in the hands of the black lawyer and looked forward to the day when there would be a black federal judge. For the time being, he viewed the NAACP as the only organization capable of providing black lawyers the opportunity to present cases before the Supreme Court.[1]

---

1. Houston *Informer*, July 16, 1932. Interestingly, attorney Fred C. Knollenberg vigorously supported Wesley's and Atkins's efforts to participate in the arguments before the Supreme Court. Fred C. Knollenberg to J. Alston Atkins, September 16, 1931; Knollenberg to James Marshall, August 17, 1931, Nixon Papers, Box 3.

The Houston *Informer* became Wesley's chief vehicle to express the extent of his resentment, or, perhaps more accurately, injured pride. After the second *Nixon* decision, Seligman, NAACP director of publicity, reprimanded Wesley for failing to mention the NAACP in an *Informer* editorial on the white primary fight. Seligman, "with considerable astonishment," had read the editorial, entitled "A Second Emancipation." He informed Wesley that without the financial support and legal expertise of the Association, "no such victory would have been possible." Seligman indignantly asked, "Don't you think it was incumbent upon you to at least mention the NAACP in passing?"[2] Wesley's response was revealing. He replied that he was aware of the NAACP's role, but that he was equally cognizant of the part others had played. He reminded Seligman that the people associated with the *Informer* had filed briefs in support of the Association's application for a writ of certiorari and an *amicus curiae*. Wesley accused the NAACP of resisting their entrance as *amicus curiae* while its legal department had accepted material and information from J. Alston Atkins. Although he confessed that when he wrote the editorial he had not intended to slight the NAACP, he nevertheless strongly asserted that he felt it "unnecessary to imply that nobody else could do anything in order to have the work of the NAACP appreciated." Pointedly, he asked the director of publicity, "Don't you think it was incumbent upon you to at least mention . . . The Houston *Informer* and J. Alston Atkins . . . in passing?"[3]

Seligman, warming to the dialogue, answered, "I do not believe it was incumbent upon the Association to mention the Houston *Informer* and Mr. J. Alston Atkins, since their entrance in the case, while praiseworthy was not essential to the outcome." Furthermore, Seligman added, the history of the *Nixon* primary cases could not be written without reference to the NAACP, but it certainly could be written without reference to any other parties. Ironically, given the nature of the NAACP's involvement in the grandfather clause case, Seligman asserted that the Houstonian's filing as an *amicus curiae* had not been essential for the final result. From Seligman's vantage point, the credit for the *Nixon* victories belonged to the eminent white attorneys Spingarn, Margold, and Marshall.[4]

The dissatisfaction manifested in these exchanges disturbed and surprised secretary Walter White. Although sensitive enough to the plight of black lawyers, White was even more sensitive to criticisms of the NAACP. He could

2. Herbert Seligman to Carter Wesley, May 10, 1932, NAACP Papers, Box D-63.
3. Wesley to Seligman, May 20, 1932, NAACP Papers, Box D-63.
4. Seligman to Wesley, May 26, 1932, NAACP Papers, Box D-63.

not deny that historically the NAACP relied quite heavily upon the volunteer services of nationally prominent white attorneys. Nor could he dispute the fact the national officers made a conscious and deliberate attempt to obtain eminent white attorneys who possessed the talent, prestige, and integrity to handle their major cases. To be sure, the NAACP did solicit the services of black lawyers when they were available. For example, James A. Cobb of Washington, D.C., was consulted frequently.[5] The pragmatic secretary, while realizing the psychological value of having black attorneys associated with the organization's litigations, was, however, cognizant of the fact that a pool of black lawyers with the characteristics of a Storey, Spingarn, or Marshall did not exist.

In 1927 the Association hired its first salaried black legal assistant, W. T. Andrews, to link the national office and black lawyers in general. The high expectations with which he was hired never materialized and Andrews remained little more than a functionary at the national headquarters. While thus employed, Andrews did perform one noteworthy service. He worked on the compilation of a directory of black lawyers for the NAACP. The directory would enable the national office to contact quickly local black attorneys in emergency cases where it was impossible to rely on lawyers from the National Legal Committee.[6]

While Andrews was working on the directory, another young black attorney, Charles Houston, was making a comprehensive survey of black lawyers. Houston attempted to determine to what extent black lawyers participated in controversies involving race discrimination. In the process of completing his survey, Houston made wide contacts with a number of black lawyers throughout the South. His findings were not encouraging. Houston checked the census figures and discovered that at least 50 percent of the blacks listed as lawyers in 17 states were not actively engaged in the practice of law. They were working as mail carriers, real estate or insurance agents, ministers, and teachers. He found, further, that the lawyers who were actively pursuing the profession in the southern states concentrated in urban areas such as Richmond, Baltimore, Durham, and New Orleans.[7]

5. For a detailed examination of the views of Association leaders on the issue of white and black lawyers, see August Meier and Elliott Rudwick, "Attorneys Black and White: A Case Study of Race Relations within the NAACP," *Journal of American History* 62, no. 4 (March 1976): 913–46.

6. William T. Andrews to Charles A. Roberson in Shreveport, La., March 6, 1928, NAACP Papers, Box C-330.

7. Charles H. Houston to Andrews, April 19, 1929; Sidney S. Redmond to Andrews, March 13, 1929, NAACP Papers, Box C-330; Charles Houston, "Cooperation between the National Bar Association and the National Association for the Advancement of Colored

It was obvious that black lawyers had a long way to climb before they could enjoy the prominence and prestige of Storey, Marshall, and Spingarn. The vital link between fledgling black lawyers and the NAACP proved to be the National Legal Committee. Prior to the Atkins affair and the eruption of the black lawyer issue in 1932, White had become increasingly aware of the potential value of gaining black lawyers' cooperation with the work of the National Association. He lobbied to have a larger number of them placed on the National Legal Committee.

White could not personally appoint black or white lawyers to the legal committee. But Spingarn, chairman of the National Legal Committee, was usually receptive to White's suggestions about matters concerning the legal work. Spingarn responded favorably to White's diplomatically phrased recommendation that certain black men be appointed to the National Legal Committee. In October 1929, White informed Spingarn that he had reviewed the list of names on the legal committee and discovered only one "colored lawyer—James Cobb" on the list. Actually Cobb had not been a member of the National Legal Committee since 1926, when he was appointed a federal judge in the District of Columbia. White inquired, "What do you think, as Chairman, of the idea of asking T. G. Nutter of Charleston, West Virginia and Francis E. Rivers of New York to serve on the Committee?"[8] Spingarn agreed that it would be a good idea to add Nutter to the committee, but he objected to Rivers because he was "too young and unproven." Nutter accepted Spingarn's invitation to become a member of the legal committee. White, encouraged by his success, soon recommended two more black attorneys, Jesse S. Heslip of Toledo, president of the National Bar Association, which was the formal organization of black lawyers, and Charles Houston, vice dean of Howard University Law School. White described both men as good lawyers, Harvard graduates, and young men that the Association could "tie up . . . in such a way as to have great returns in the future."[9] The next two black lawyers that White recommended to Spingarn were Louis Redding of Delaware and N. J. Frederick of Columbia, South Carolina. Heslip, Houston, Redding, and Frederick accepted the invitations and were listed as the new additions to the NAACP National Legal Committee in the Association's *23rd Annual Report for 1932*.[10] For the

People," delivered at the 23d Annual Convention, May 10, 1932, NAACP Papers, Box B-5; Jerold S. Auerbach, *Unequal Justice: Lawyers and Social Change in Modern America* (New York: Oxford University Press, 1976), 211–15.

8. Walter White to Arthur Spingarn, October 30, 1929, A. B. Spingarn Papers, Box 4.

9. White to Spingarn, October 17, 1931, A. B. Spingarn Papers, Box 5.

10. White to Spingarn, June 3, 1932, A. B. Spingarn Papers, Box 5; *23d Annual Report* (New York: NAACP, 1932).

first time the legal committee was composed of an almost equal number of black (six) and white (eight) attorneys.

White counted on the publicity surrounding the addition of four black lawyers to the Association's legal department to raise the prestige of the organization in certain black circles.[11] Predictably, the black press responded favorably. Wesley, for one, praised the National Association for its forward action in taking on black lawyers who could now obtain the experience of arguing before the Supreme Court: "*The Informer* and *Texas Freeman* commends and endorses the new policy of the NAACP regarding building up their legal staff." Wesley noted further, "These men are well trained . . . they have every requisite to make fine constitutional lawyers." He applauded the Association's actions because "it will give Negroes their own constitutional lawyers."[12]

The favorable reaction of the black press, black lawyers, and blacks in general encouraged White to make an increased effort. In 1933 the secretary was instrumental in arranging the first case in which the NAACP used all black lawyers—Charles Houston and his associates from the Howard University Law School, Edward P. Lovett, Leon Ransom, and James Tyson.[13] The case involved the question whether an accused murderer, George Crawford, could be extradited to Virginia for trial where black people were systematically denied the right to serve on grand and petit juries. When a federal judge accepted their reasoning, White proudly declared, "In all my years with the Association, nothing has given me greater pleasure than to help in the arrangements to have Crawford defended by an all-Negro Counsel." He observed that members "of a minority group" could work most effectively to better their own lot when, as in the Crawford case, conditions were in a state of flux: "It is due in part to these conditions and to the increasing number of trained, unselfish younger men and women which has enabled the Association to contend successfully for the Negro."[14]

11. Memorandum to Herbert Seligman from Walter White, June 25, 1932, NAACP Papers, Box A-27.

12. Houston *Informer,* July 16, 1932.

13. This unique strategy of questioning the racial composition of juries was employed in two other major cases dealing with blacks and southern justice during the early 1930s. The defense attorneys in the Angelo Herndon case (1932) involving a black communist accused of treason against the state of Georgia and the second and third trials of the Scottsboro boys (in which nine black youths ranging in ages from 13 to 20 were charged with raping two white girls) employed precisely the same tactics. In the 1935 *Norris* v. *Alabama* decision, the United States Supreme Court declared unconstitutional the systematic exclusion of blacks from juries. Charles H. Martin, *The Angelo Herndon Case and Southern Justice* (Baton Rouge: Louisiana State University Press, 1976), 40–41; Dan T. Carter, *Scottsboro: A Tragedy of the American South* (New York: Oxford University Press, 1969), 322–24.

14. White to Elewyza Dingind, president of NAACP College Chapter at Virginia Union, November 15, 1933, NAACP Papers, Box G-210.

Blacks regarded the Crawford case as the watershed in the developing prominence and significance of black lawyers. One black attorney remarked that the case "established in the minds and hearts of the people of the South respect for and belief in the ability and integrity of the Negro lawyers and more particularly in the younger ones." He further ranked the Crawford case as "the greatest permanent contemporary achievement which any Association has won for the Negro. Such an achievement will inevitably produce a slow but permanent innovation in the attitude of the Courts of our country."[15] Actually, the *Nixon v. Condon* decision and the NAACP's efforts to involve more black lawyers in the Association's work interested only a small proportion of blacks. By 1932 the majority of black Americans were reeling from the ravages of the Great Depression.

Everybody suffered during the Depression. Some, however, suffered more than others. Dire poverty, starvation, homelessness, unemployment, and untold agony were the lot of most black Americans. Already on the bottom rail of the economic ladder, they were the first to lose the menial, unskilled, domestic service jobs that whites had allowed blacks to have. Many middle-class blacks quickly depleted meager savings, lost homes and businesses, and joined the ranks of the poor.[16]

Under these circumstances economic and political needs were paramount. Career aspirations of a few black lawyers occupied a low priority for the majority of blacks. Their attention focused on national politics and the presidential election of 1932. Democrats were convinced that the presidency would be theirs while Republicans were stuck with Hoover and tainted with responsibility for the Depression. At the Democratic National Convention in Chicago, former New York governor Franklin Delano Roosevelt won nomination.[17]

The majority of black Americans did not vote for Roosevelt in his first presidential bid. Traditional allegiance to the Republican party coupled with the fact that as governor Roosevelt had not exhibited concern for blacks in appointments or legislation kept blacks mired in the party of Lincoln. Moreover, national Democratic party leadership had never made meaningful overtures toward black voters and had remained mum on the subject of the southern

15. J. Bryon Hopkins, attorney from Alexandria, Virginia, to White, January 3, 1934, NAACP Papers, Box G-206; see also Meier and Rudwick, "Attorneys Black and White," 938–40.

16. W. E. B. Du Bois, *The Autobiography of W. E. B. Du Bois* (New York: International, 1968), 303.

17. Frank Freidel, "Election of 1932," in *The Coming to Power: Critical Presidential Elections in American History,* ed. Arthur M. Schlesinger (New York: Chelsea House Publishers, 1971, 1972), 322–54.

Democratic white primaries. Black voters in 1932 still identified their political troubles with the Democrats.[18]

To be sure, Hoover's southern strategy and support of "lily whiteism" after 1928 gave blacks little reason to expect Republicans to be more favorably disposed to their needs than Democrats. Hoover's presidential record in regard to blacks was insulting, and a tremendous disappointment. He had appointed almost no blacks to first-class positions. Under his tenure blacks had been denied admittance to government cafeterias in federal buildings. Black Gold Star mothers had been provided with segregated and inferior accommodations when the administration sent them to visit their sons' graves in France. Lynchings of blacks had continued with no presidential admonition. In 1930 the NAACP, under Walter White's leadership, had engaged in an intense and costly struggle to block Hoover's nomination of Judge John J. Parker of North Carolina to the Supreme Court. Judge Parker had been quoted ten years earlier as saying that the participation of the Negro in politics was "a source of evil and danger."[19]

Despite Hoover's record, it required a difficult psychological adjustment for the black voter to have supported Democrats in 1932. Nevertheless, some key black leaders announced support for Roosevelt. Robert Vann, the influential publisher of the black newspaper the Pittsburgh *Courier,* advised blacks in 1932 to "go home and turn Lincoln's picture to the wall. The debt has been paid in full."[20] In Texas, black editor C. F. Richardson, a firm believer in political independence, became convinced that the Democratic party offered the best hope for the future of the black man.[21] This swing towards Roosevelt in 1932 was essentially, however, "a defection from the top."[22]

Roosevelt won the election by a wide majority. His strongest support came

18. Rita Werner Gordon, "The Change in the Political Alignment of Chicago's Negroes during the New Deal," *Journal of American History* 56 (December 1969): 592; Ralph J. Bunche, *The Political Status of the Negro in the Age of FDR,* 36, 608–10.

19. Arthur M. Schlesinger, Jr., *The Politics of Upheaval: The Age of Roosevelt* (Boston: Houghton Mifflin, 1960), 427–31; Darlene Clark Hine, "The NAACP and the Supreme Court: Walter F. White and the Defeat of Judge John J. Parker, 1930," *Negro History Bulletin* 40 (September–October 1977): 753–57.

20. Quoted in Arthur M. Schlesinger, *The Politics of Upheaval,* 430; James H. Brewer, "Robert Lee Vann, Democrat or Republican: An Exponent of Loose-Leaf Politics," in *The Negro in Depression and War: Prelude to Revolution, 1930–1945,* ed. Bernard Sternsher (Chicago: Quadrangle, 1969), 224–33.

21. Melvin James Banks, "The Pursuit of Equality: The Movement for First Class Citizenship among Negroes in Texas, 1920–1950" (Ph.D. diss., Syracuse University, 1962), 219–20.

22. Schlesinger, *The Politics of Upheaval,* 430.

from the South and West.[23] With an energy and verve unknown in modern presidents, Roosevelt inaugurated imaginative programs and established emergency agencies to alleviate widespread suffering and to restore economic prosperity. While he did not specifically speak to the problems and needs of black Americans, he gave them the impression that their interests would be considered. For the first time since Lincoln, no longer would blacks be the "forgotten men" in American society. Midway through his first term, FDR had captured the admiration and affection of most black Americans. In 1936 their votes would be his.[24]

In calculable terms, Roosevelt's efforts to assist blacks bore little fruit. Major pieces of legislation which, if fairly administered, would have aided black workers were the Agricultural Adjustment Administration (AAA) and the National Industrial Recovery Administration (NIRA). The effect of the AAA program was, however, especially disastrous on black tenants and sharecroppers, partly because the government paid farmers to plow under crops and reduce acreage. (Forty percent of black American workers were employed as farm tenants and laborers.) Benefit payments, unfortunately, were inequitably distributed and black sharecroppers received very little of the money allocated. The program eventually served to exacerbate their plight as more than 100,000 black and white sharecroppers were evicted from the land by planters.[25]

In the urban areas, black unemployment averaged from 30 to 60 percent greater than for whites. The proportion of blacks on relief was three times higher than whites. The National Industrial Recovery Administration aimed to increase production, raise wages, minimize hours, and encourage spending. Blacks rallied to support NIRA programs, but quickly discovered that employers generally ignored wage and hour regulations. When pressured to comply, they dismissed their black workers and hired whites in their places. Furthermore, the codes did not extend protection to the domestic service, agricultural labor, and service jobs held by the majority of black workers. Moreover, they recognized a wage differential that penalized the South, where the great majority of black workers lived.[26]

Blacks benefited most from the public spending programs. The Public Works Administration (PWA), Federal Emergency Relief Administration

23. Freidel, "Election of 1932," 353.

24. Leslie H. Fishel, Jr., "The Negro in the New Deal Era," in Sternsher, *The Negro in Depression and War*, 9.

25. Raymond Wolters, *Negroes and the Great Depression: The Problem of Economic Recovery* (Westport, Conn.: Greenwood Publishing, 1970), 3–79.

26. Ibid., 91, 214; Bunche, *The Political Status of the Negro in the Age of FDR*, 608.

(FERA), and the Works Progress Administration (WPA) provided low-rent housing, monetary relief, and employment for hundreds of thousands of blacks. Black unemployed youths also benefited from the National Youth Administration and the Civilian Conservation Corps (CCC). Yet, as Raymond Wolters observed, "It was not an adequate program for a time when the needy were numbered in the millions."[27] One of the primary difficulties in obtaining maximum benefits from New Deal legislation derived from the customs and racist attitudes of white officials towards blacks on the local level.[28]

Blacks' greatest benefits from Roosevelt and the New Deal were psychological. For the first time since Reconstruction, black participation in federal governmental affairs increased. Prominent blacks such as William H. Hastie, Robert Weaver, Ira De A. Reid, and Mary McCleod Bethune worked in various agencies and advised the president on Negro affairs. They were part of an informal group sometimes referred to as Roosevelt's "Black Cabinet." Black colleges and universities received increased federal funding and there were more professional opportunities in government. And, undoubtedly, the warmth and genuine human concern of Eleanor Roosevelt strengthened black affection and support for FDR.[29]

While black Texans were dealing with the problems of economic distress, white Texans, in 1932, were devoting considerable attention to maintaining the racial purity of Democratic primaries. Events on the national horizon did not alter the commitment of state level politicians to the white primary. After *Nixon v. Condon,* white Texans went back to the drawing boards and what they felt to be the perfect scheme to preserve the white primary.

Chairman of the Harris County Democratic Executive Committee and editor of the Houston *Chronicle,* Judge W. O. Huggins, presented the new disfranchisement plan on May 24, 1932, at the annual meeting of the state Democratic convention. The Huggins Plan, as it became known, called for the repeal of the resolution of the state Democratic executive committee and the adoption by the state convention of a new restrictive measure. He convinced his fellow Democrats that the Supreme Court would not rule that the state convention was an agency of the state of Texas and therefore that any resolution adopted would not be viewed as "originating in the mandate of the law." The convention, persuaded, adopted the following resolution: "Be it resolved that all white

27. Wolters, *Negroes and the Great Depression,* 215.
28. Fishel, "Negro in the New Deal Era," 9–11.
29. Ibid., 12–13.

citizens of the State, who are qualified to vote be eligible for participation in the primary."[30]

Black leaders of the Harris County Negro Democratic Club attorney James Nabrit and Carter Wesley, attempted to appear before the resolutions committee before the convention adjourned.[31] They were repeatedly repulsed because, as Huggins, chairman of the resolution's committee, claimed, the vote had already been taken. Incensed over what they considered to be a flagrant disregard of the two *Nixon* decisions, black Texans filed numerous suits requesting injunctions against local Democratic leaders and organizations in Bexar, Grayson, Tarrant, and Jefferson counties. Black lawyers spearheaded the legal attacks. R. D. Evans, W. J. Durham of Sherman, James Nabrit, and Carter Wesley quickly prepared individual cases to prohibit white Democratic officials from interfering with black voting in the primaries. All the petitions were defeated in local courts.[32]

C. A. Booker of San Antonio employed a white attorney, Carl Wright Johnson, to handle his suit. Booker sought an injunction to compel the Bexar County Democratic Executive Committee (specifically John K. Weber, chairman; C. O. Wolfe, secretary; and Adolph Lassner, presiding officer of Precinct 73) to permit him and other qualified black voters to exercise their franchise rights in the Democratic primaries. Judge T. M. Kennerly ruled against Booker but suggested that there was a possibility that the Democratic convention's adoption of the resolution had been illegal. For, he reasoned, if the state could not enact such a restrictive law, perhaps the same applied to the convention.[33]

Booker appealed the ruling and Johnson presented the case before the Forty-fifth Federal District Court in San Antonio. On July 22, 1932, the day before the first Democratic primary, the court granted Booker's request for an injunction. The district court based its decision to a large degree on the sec-

30. Nathan Margold to Felix Frankfurter, May 5, 1932; Wesley to Knollenberg, May 30, 1932, NAACP Papers, Box D-63; W. R. Smith, District Attorney General for the Western District at San Antonio, Texas, to the United States Attorney General, c/o Joseph Keenan, Washington, D.C.; Conrey Bryson, *Dr. Lawrence A. Nixon and the White Primary* (El Paso: Texas Western Press and University of Texas at El Paso, 1974), 72; "Nixon v. Condon," *Yale Law Journal* 4, no. 8 (June 1932).

31. Interview with James M. Nabrit, April 6, 1974.

32. Wesley to Knollenberg, May 30, 1932, NAACP Papers, Box D-63; Robert Wendell Hainsworth, "The Negro and the Texas Primaries," *Journal of Negro History* 18 (October 1933): 426–50; *White* v. *Harris County Democratic Executive Committee*, 60F (2d) 973 (S. D. Texas, 1932); Houston *Informer*, July 30, 1932.

33. Knollenberg to White, August 31, 1932, Nixon Papers, Box 3; O. Douglas Weeks, "The White Primary," *Mississippi Law Journal* 8 (December 1935): 135–53; Hainsworth, "The Negro and the Texas Primary," 426–50; Houston *Informer*, July 30, 1932.

ond *Nixon* case. Booker was delighted with the ruling and with the prospect of voting. His pleasure, however, lasted only hours. Bexar County white Democrats quickly protested the decision. Later in the same day, the Fourth Circuit Court of Appeals set aside the injunction. The circuit court of appeals held that a political party was a voluntary organization and possessed the power to determine its membership. Booker subsequently appealed to the Texas Supreme Court which dismissed the case and allowed the appellate court's decision to stand. Attorney Knollenberg wrote Walter White that the Supreme Court of Texas had "rendered a decision . . . which virtually denied the right to participate, on account of the fact that they [Booker and Johnson] had not included all of the persons who may have been responsible for passing the resolution that all white citizens are entitled to participate" in Democratic party primaries.[34]

In the meantime, El Paso blacks informed the NAACP national office of their desire to file another case, but were advised to wait. The national officers had closely observed the various proceedings and had decided to refrain from entering the fray against the convention's resolutions until all local litigation decisions had been handed down. Their caution, in part, stemmed from legal considerations, but was due also to a reluctance to work again with Knollenberg. Not only did the national officers judge Knollenberg to be less than competent, they were then in such a precarious financial situation that they could ill afford to pay Knollenberg's $1,500 fee.[35] Spingarn confided to White, "We must seriously consider what position we are to take concerning the retention of Knollenberg for any new action that we may institute." White, in turn, suggested to Nixon and El Paso branch president Washington that they should attempt to obtain the services of a different attorney, "as every step of the previous case has had to be prepared or amended or rewritten here."[36]

The branch, however, was adamant. It would entertain no thought of initiating a case without Knollenberg. As Washington explained, "He [Knollenberg] has entered the cases for us when we could not find anyone else to do so; and he has never refused us in any of our local legal work without compensation . . . he has withstood the jeers of some because of his legal assistance to

34. *County Democratic Executive Committee* v. *Booker,* 53 S.W. (2d) 123 (Texas, 1932); *County Democratic Committee in and for Bexar County et al.* v. *C. A. Booker,* 52 S.W. (2d) 908 (Texas, 1932); Knollenberg to White, August 31, 1932, Nixon Papers, Box 3.

35. Nixon to Robert Bagnall, August 3, 1932; White to Nixon, August 8, 1932, NAACP Papers, Box D-63.

36. Spingarn to White, October 19, 1932; White to Washington, White to Nixon, November 11, 1932, NAACP Papers, Box D-63.

our cause." Washington promised that he and his associates would do everything "possible to contact every person and organization who and which in our opinion can and will assist" in raising funds to pay the fee and expenses in this case, but they wanted Knollenberg to handle it. White reluctantly accepted their views and was relieved when Knollenberg reduced his fee to $750. Nevertheless, White reiterated his suggestion that a black lawyer, Carter Wesley in this instance, be asked to join in the fight as junior counsel. This, he asserted, would have "an excellent psychological effect upon colored people."[37]

As had been their experience in the previous *Nixon* case, the members of the legal committee were soon disagreeing with Knollenberg on procedural matters. Knollenberg, to Marshall's exasperation, suggested that they proceed as if the old Article 3107 which had been declared unconstitutional in *Nixon v. Condon,* was still the justification for the Democratic state convention's actions. Marshall felt that "Knollenberg was really proceeding on an entirely erroneous theory." He explained to the El Paso attorney that if there was to be a chance of victory the case had squarely to meet the proposition raised by the resolution of the Democratic state convention.[38]

Spingarn, with assistance from Margold and Marshall, eventually decided to ignore Knollenberg. The election officials who had denied Nixon the right to vote in the July and August primaries would be sued. Marshall outlined the three arguments that the Association utilized in this third case, *Nixon v. McCann.* First, the statutes of Texas had originally set forth the qualifications of voters in primary elections and had created and organized the structure of the state convention. Therefore, when the state permitted the state convention to modify the qualifications for participation in primaries in such a way as to create a distinction between voters on the grounds of race and color, it was acting unconstitutionally. Second, the state had created, in the state convention, a quasi-public body to perform a quasi-governmental function, thus making illegal any discrimination arising from the state convention on the grounds of race or color. Thus, regardless of whether there were state regulations as to participation in primary elections, any discriminatory resolution passed by this quasi-governmental body (the Democratic state convention) was unconstitutional. Finally, the election judges acting as election officials were vested with their authority by the state and they did not have the power to deprive Nixon

37. Washington to White, November 22, 1932; White to Knollenberg, December 20, 1932; White to Spingarn, January 4, 1933, NAACP Papers, Box D-G3.
38. James Marshall to White, April 18, 1933, NAACP Papers, Box D-63.

of his right to vote. Therefore, when they had denied Nixon his ballot because of his color, they had violated the Fourteenth Amendment.[39]

Fifteen months later, federal district court judge Charles Boynton held Cardozo's decision in *Nixon* v. *Condon* binding and ruled that the resolution of the state Democratic convention unconstitutionally deprived Nixon of his right to vote in the primaries. Boynton decided that the resolution passed by the convention did not exclude blacks from voting but merely established that white persons who were qualified voters could participate in the primaries. Thus, the judge continued, when the executive committee instructed the El Paso County chairman to exclude blacks, it was an action of the executive committee and not the convention. This decision constituted the first victory of the NAACP in a Texas white primary case in a federal tribunal lower than the Supreme Court. Ben Howell, attorney for the election officials and the Democratic Executive Committee of El Paso, decided not to appeal the decision. Nixon was awarded five dollars for damages. The national office was obviously relieved that the case required no further litigation because its financial problems had become even more acute. Knollenberg "generously reduced his fee from $750 to $500," yet the national office was still unable to pay all of it. White instructed Washington to organize a special campaign in El Paso to raise as large a part as possible of the $400 due Knollenberg.[40]

The decision in *Nixon* v. *McCann* had almost no effect on the political status of blacks in Texas. Due to the lack of unanimity among white Texans, some blacks were allowed to vote in certain counties even before the *Nixon* v. *Condon* decision and in spite of the Democratic party's resolution.[41] But for the majority of black Texans, voting in Democratic primaries remained only a hope. The constant reminder of their political impotence goaded Texas blacks into developing community-based political organizations through which they persisted in attempts to gain entry into the political process. Working from the outside was never satisfactory, and blacks in Dallas, Houston, and San Antonio continued agitating for their political rights. Because Texas blacks refused to let the question of their voting in primary elections die, it became a peren-

39. Marshall to Knollenberg, April 18, 1933, NAACP Papers, Box D-63.

40. White to Washington, March 3, 1934, NAACP Papers, Box D-63; El Paso *Herald Post*, February 7, 1934; NAACP Press Release: "Third Texas Primary Case Won in Federal Court," February 9, 1934, NAACP Papers, Box D-63.

41. NAACP Press Release: "Outcome of Attempts of Negroes to Vote at Democratic Primaries in Texas on July 25, 1932," August 11, 1932, NAACP Papers, Box D-63; Houston *Informer*, September 2, 9, 1932.

nial issue.[42] All white Democratic aspirants to political office confronted this issue and had to deal with it at one level or another during their election campaigns.

The gubernatorial election year 1934 was another setback for black Texans, adding to defeats in the local courts in 1932. There were seven contenders for the Texas gubernatorial office in the 1934 primaries. One candidate, however, occupied a unique position so far as the issue of black voting in the primaries was concerned.

James V. Allred, born March 29, 1899, in Bowie, Texas, had become the Texas attorney general in 1930. Allred had earned an impressive reputation as an attorney general who was not afraid to challenge big business.[43] In 1934, having served two terms as attorney general, Allred entered the governor's race and was promptly besieged with demands for some definite statement of his position on black voting in that year's Democratic primaries.

Allred found himself confronted with a dilemma. As a gubernatorial candidate, he knew that many blacks supported one of his opponents, C. C. McDonald, and that any decision or statement he rendered could affect the outcome of the election. His campaign advisers and organizers warned him that the black vote was going against him. For example, the chairman of the Allred-for-Governor Club in Houston, Judge C. A. Teagle, insinuated that one of his opponents was going to buy the black vote: "I know from experience what the negro vote means and that a little money will go a long way with them."[44] Another principal Allred organizer in Beaumont County, Jack Todd, warned the attorney general of the probable adverse consequences of the black vote. The white primary was a hot issue in Beaumont and some blacks had openly endorsed one of his opponents. Todd suggested that if Allred would wire him an endorsement of the white primary, it would "make lots of votes" in Beaumont.[45] In both of these counties blacks comprised a sizable proportion of the total population.

Finally, as a result of the advice from his supporters and his belief that the

42. Melvin James Banks, "The Pursuit of Equality: The Movement for First Class Citizenship among Negroes in Texas, 1920–1950" (Ph.D. diss., Syracuse University, 1962), 221–35.

43. Knollenberg to Allred, attorney general of Texas, January 26, 1932, Nixon Papers, Box 3; Walter B. Moore, *Governors of Texas* (Dallas: Dallas *Morning News,* 1963), 31; Walter Prescott Webb, H. Baily Carroll, and Eldon S. Branda, eds., *The Handbook of Texas,* 3 vols. (Austin: Texas State Historical Association, 1952, 1976), 3:21–22.

44. C. A. Teagle to Sidney Benhow, assistant attorney general, May 17, 1934, James V. Allred Papers, University of Houston, Container 84.

45. Jack Todd to Dick Watters, July 12, 1934, Allred Papers, Container 85.

opposition was using the black vote to his disadvantage, the attorney general and gubernatorial candidate issued an official declaration. In his opinion Allred maintained that blacks were prohibited from the Democratic primaries under the resolution adopted in the Houston Convention of 1932:

> In view of the resolution passed by the State Convention of the Democratic Party on May 24, 1932 you are respectfully advised that, in our opinion, negroes are not entitled to participate in the primary elections of the Democratic Party. . . .

Furthermore, he added that the legitimacy of the current resolution passed by the state Democratic convention was based on the *Nixon* v. *Condon* decision. He found additional support for his "Opinion" in the ruling of the Texas Supreme Court in *County Democratic Executive Committee in and for Bexar County* v. *C. A. Booker.*[46]

The factionalism within the Texas Democratic party was apparent in the divided and heated reactions of county chairmen and the white press to Allred's "Opinion." Many Democratic county chairmen heartily approved Allred's decree, particularly those who were involved in local power struggles. In Jefferson County, the county Democratic chairman, J. R. Edmunds, unsuccessfully attempted to restrict Jefferson County balloting to white Democrats. His actions created divisions within the county's Democratic party leadership. Allred's ruling, according to newspaper accounts, came just in time to unify Jefferson County's party organization.[47] A few county chairmen and editors of major white dailies disagreed with Allred's "Opinion." Will A. Morriss, Jr., chairman of the Bexar County Democratic Executive Committee, decided that he would permit the approximately 4,000 to 5,000 Bexar County blacks to vote. Morriss openly stated that the attorney general had acted "without full knowledge" and that he would not adhere to the ruling.[48] The Dallas *Journal's* editor reportedly criticized the "Opinion" as "mighty poor law." The editor contended that it was "manifestly absurd" for the attorney general to argue both that the party was not the creature of the state and at the same time insist that the attorney general, as the servant of the state, had the right to tell the party who may and may not vote at the primary.[49] These responses indi-

46. James V. Allred to D. B. Wood, Williamson County attorney, June 9, 1934, NAACP Papers, Box D-63.
47. Bay City *Tribune*, July 14, 1934; Fort Worth *Star*, July 8, 1934.
48. Ibid.
49. Houston *Informer*, July 21, 1934.

cated that the efforts to bar blacks were not unanimously supported by all white Democrats in Texas.

Two black men from Jefferson County responded to this latest assault on their franchise rights. W. H. Bell and E. L. Jones, without NAACP assistance, filed a petition for a writ of mandamus against the Governor of Texas, the attorney general, the state Democratic executive committee, the members of the Jefferson County Democratic Executive Committee, and the various election officers in Jefferson County. To prevent the Court from ruling against them on grounds of faulty pleadings and failure to name the right parties in the suit, Bell and Jones named approximately 200 individuals as defendants. The object of the suit was to invoke the jurisdiction of the Court to require the election officials to permit them to vote in the Democratic primaries on July 28, 1934.

Eight days before the July primary, the Texas Supreme Court denied Bell and Jones the writ of mandamus. It held that since no other Democratic convention had revoked the resolution of 1932, it was still valid and constituted the official policy of the Democratic party of the state. The Court drew upon the decision in the case of *Bexar County et al.* v. *Booker* to support its ruling. In that case, Special Associate Justice Searcy had proclaimed that "the Democratic Party [was] a voluntary political association," and that its convention possessed "the power to determine who shall be eligible for membership in the party, and, as such, eligible for participation in the primaries. A study of the election laws of Texas and their history can lead to no other conclusion." The Supreme Court of Texas concluded, "The Attorney General of this state, in a recent able opinion, has likewise sustained the validity of the resolution passed by the Houston Convention. With the opinion of the Court of Civil Appeals at San Antonio and with that of the Attorney General we are in accord."[50]

An elated Allred immediately issued a statement to every candidate for governor to request all election officials to follow the opinion of the Court. In a speech before a cheering crowd of 700 in Longview, Texas, Allred pointed out that when he first released his "Opinion" the campaign manager of one of the candidates had taken issue with it and two of the "big city newspapers" had attacked it. He added emphatically, "I now call upon the newspapers and all the candidates to follow the Supreme Court's opinion and keep the Democratic Party of Texas a white man's party."[51] His timely delivery of the "Opinion" proved to be the right political strategy. It won him the white vote and elimi-

50. Tyler *Telegram,* July 21, 1934; *Bell et al.* v. *Hill, County Clerk et al.* 74 S.W. (2d) 113– 22 (Texas, 1934).
51. Tyler *Telegram,* July 21, 1934.

nated the black vote. The Texas Supreme Court's decision in *Bell* v. *Hill* unquestionably strengthened his candidacy.[52] (Predictably, Allred won the gubernatorial election.)

Ironically, Nixon and his business associate in El Paso were the only two blacks allowed to vote in the July and August primaries. White Democrats chose not to risk involvement in another court action, so they provided Nixon with a ballot marked "colored," which Knollenberg thought a very "smart trick." The El Paso attorney theorized that this allowed election officials to ignore the ballot once cast and yet give the impression of compliance with the federal law as interpreted by the Supreme Court.[53]

Allred's "Opinion" and the *Bell* v. *Hill* decision seemingly closed another door on the possibility of blacks voting in Texas Democratic primaries. R. D. Evans of the National Bar Association, the organization of black lawyers, and Walter White of the NAACP were not at all satisfied with the turn of events in Texas. Leaders of both organizations, acting independently, filed complaints with the United States attorney general's office and requested investigations of election practices in Texas. The National Bar Association's president, E. Washington Rhodes, expressed concern about the *Bell* v. *Hill* decision while White questioned the legality of Allred's "Opinion."[54] Assistant Attorney General Joseph Keenan promised to give careful consideration to the matter to determine if any federal criminal laws had been violated. He also suggested to White that he contact Rhodes and assist him in furnishing affidavits from black Texans who were denied ballots in the most recent primaries.[55]

From his office in Waco, Texas, attorney R. D. Evans alerted black lawyers across the state to the urgency of sending as many affidavits as possible to the attorney general's office. Scores of affidavits from Waco, Beaumont, El Paso, Harris, Travis, Jefferson, and McLennan Counties were forwarded to White to send to Keenan.[56] Rhodes and White then met to work out other strategies to

52. John Speer to Allred, July 30, 1934, Allred Papers, Container 83.

53. Nixon to White, September 8, 1934, Knollenberg to White, September 21, 1934, NAACP Papers, Box D-63.

54. E. Washington Rhodes to Attorney General Homer S. Cummings, July 24, 1934; Joseph B. Keenan to E. Washington Rhodes, July 26, 1934; Walter White to Homer S. Cummings, July 27, 1934; Keenan to White, July 28, 1934; White to Keenan, July 30, 1934, Department of Justice Files, Folder 72-100-5 (all references are to this folder).

55. Joseph B. Keenan to Walter White, July 28, 1934, Department of Justice Files; White to Spingarn, summary of all of the developments concerning the Justice Department and the NAACP, August 7, 1934, NAACP Papers, Box D-63.

56. White to Keenan, August 3, 6, 1934, Department of Justice Files; White to Rhodes, August 9, 1934, NAACP Papers, Box D-63.

complement the weight of the affidavits and to increase the pressure on the department of justice in general. To dramatize the role of the black attorneys in the struggle, Rhodes proposed the appointment of a delegation of leading black lawyers who would go to Washington, D.C., to discuss the matter of the white primary directly with the attorney general. Evans enthusiastically supported Rhodes's ideas of a delegation but White vetoed it. White recommended instead that the National Bar Association and the NAACP jointly draft a memorandum brief for the attorney general, setting forth not only the legal grounds on "which the Attorney General may act, but citing the grounds on which he must act if the law so indicated."[57]

Keenan forwarded the affidavits and related material to Attorneys General S. D. Bennett of the Eastern District at Beaumont, Douglas W. McGregor of the Southern District at Houston, and W. R. Smith of the Western District at San Antonio. He ordered them to conduct a special investigation to review the allegations of voting discrimination and illegalities in violation of the United States Supreme Court decisions in the *Nixon* cases. They were further asked to determine whether or not criminal prosecution of election officials was warranted under the Civil Rights Statute of Sections 19 and 20 of the Criminal Code.[58] Black lawyers in Texas exerted continuous pressure on the district attorneys general and carefully monitored the progress of the investigations. Smith became defensive and refused to give out any voting information whereupon blacks suggested to the U.S. attorney general that Smith was failing in his responsibilities.[59]

The efforts of the NBA and the NAACP accomplished very little. The district attorneys general all agreed that prosecution of election officials who refused ballots to blacks was inadvisable. McGregor's staff concluded that "no grand jury in Texas would indict these officials, nor would a jury convict them."[60] S. D. Bennett wrote, "I am of the opinion that criminal prosecution under the provisions of the statutes referred to could not be successfully main-

57. Rhodes to White, August 1, 1934; R. D. Evans to Rhodes, August 15, 1934; White to Rhodes, August 9, 21, 1934, NAACP Papers, Box D-63.

58. Keenan to S. D. Bennett, U.S. attorney, Beaumont, Texas, August 11, 1934; Keenan to Douglas W. McGregor, U.S. attorney, Houston, Texas, August 11, 1934; Keenan to William R. Smith, Jr., U.S. attorney, San Antonio, Texas, August 18, 1934; Keenan to White, August 10, 1934; Smith to Keenan, August 21, 1934; Bennett to Keenan, August 16, 1934; McGregor to Keenan, August 16, 1934, Department of Justice Files.

59. Keenan to Smith, September 6, 1934; Smith to Keenan, September 13, 1934; White to Keenan, September 4, 1934, Department of Justice Files.

60. Carlos G. Watson, assistant to District Attorney General Douglas W. McGregor to the United States Attorney General, October 6, 1934, Department of Justice Files.

tained."[61] Smith, perhaps because of close attention blacks focused on him, filed a rather detailed report based upon James V. Allred's "Opinion" and the two cases adjudicated in Texas: *Bexar County* v. *Booker* and *Bell* v. *Hill.*

Smith argued that the Texas Court of Civil Appeals in the Booker case had upheld the resolution adopted by the Democratic party convention on May 24, 1932. In that opinion the court had ruled that the convention's resolution was in keeping with *Nixon* v. *Condon,* which had "strongly indicated that the Convention of the party itself could restrict its membership and determine the qualifications thereof in any way determined upon by the Convention." He concluded that the election officials who refused to allow blacks to cast their ballots were acting in good faith and without any criminal intent in following the decision of the court in the Booker case and in adhering to the "Opinion" of the Texas attorney general. Furthermore, he added, the Supreme Court of Texas had sustained the Allred "Opinion" in the *Bell* v. *Hill* litigation.[62]

Shortly before these reports were filed, J. Edgar Hoover, director of the Justice Department's Division of Investigation (which later became the Federal Bureau of Investigation), assigned a special agent from the San Antonio division office to look into the issue of voting irregularities. The agent arrived at the same conclusion later expressed by Smith. Agent Gus T. Jones informed Hoover that on the basis of preliminary study, no investigation was warranted because "the denial of the negro the right to vote was not a matter of fact but a matter of law." That is, the Texas Supreme Court's decision in *Bell* v. *Hill* and the resolution of the Democratic convention provided the legal justification for the disfranchisement of blacks.[63]

Keenan reviewed the reports and informed White that the Justice Department would not institute criminal proceedings and that the case was closed. He summarized the findings and advised White that it would be difficult, if not impossible, to prove that the election officials had any criminal intent to break the law or that they had not acted in apparent good faith pursuant to a state statute and its interpretation by the Texas Supreme Court. Keenan added that *Nixon* v. *Condon* had not determined that white Democrats violated the constitutional rights of blacks by excluding them from participation in the

61. S. D. Bennett to the United States Attorney General, January 17, 1935, Department of Justice Files.

62. Smith to the Attorney General, September 18, 1934, Department of Justice Files.

63. J. Edgar Hoover, director of the Division of Investigation, to Attorney General Keenan, October 17, 1934, File 72-100-5; Gus T. Jones, Special Agent in Charge of the San Antonio Division Office to J. Edgar Hoover, director of Division of Investigation, October 8, 1934; Douglas W. McGregor to Gus T. Jones, October 6, 1934; H. A. Fisher, attorney, to Keenan, November 16, 1934, Department of Justice Files.

party's primaries. That, according to Keenan, would have to be decided in the United States Supreme Court. Until then, the present practice in Texas was constitutional.[64]

By the end of 1934, the NAACP, black lawyers, and local black leaders in Texas seemed to have reached a dead end. After a decade of obstinate legal maneuvering, white Texas Democrats who favored black disfranchisement had apparently achieved their objective. The Allred "Opinion," the *Bell* v. *Hill* decision, and the Justice Department's decision not to intercede left blacks virtually defenseless and voteless. This disheartening situation was to become even more bleak in the following year.

64. Joseph Keenan to White, December 28, 1934, NAACP Papers, Box C-285; Keenan to Director J. Edgar Hoover, January 9, 1935, Department of Justice Files.

# 8

# *Grovey v. Townsend*, 1935

While the majority of Americans sought relief from the miseries of the Depression and riveted their hopes for a better future on Roosevelt and the New Deal, black Texans viewed with increasing dismay the seemingly endless disfranchisement schemes white Democrats devised to render them politically impotent. By employing a variety of techniques, Texas white politicians were able to nullify the U.S. Supreme Court's 1927 and 1932 decisions, which had seemed to benefit the cause of the black voters. In response to, and in spite of, a black frontal assault on the political system, by 1935 the Texas white primary had received the sanction of the United States Department of Justice and the Division of Investigation. On the state level, the Texas Attorney General defended, and the Texas Supreme Court upheld, the white primary against the frequent attacks of black lawyers, citizens, and the NAACP.

For black Texans the "thirties" represented no political New Deal. Efforts to gain access to, and influence the course of, Texas politics resulted in increased frustration. The political ostracism of black Texans was, in the larger view, however, but one example of the second-class status of black southerners. The overall legal and social oppression of blacks throughout the South during the 1930s was further illuminated in the noted Scottsboro and Angelo Herndon cases. The continued existence of the white primary remained the most glaring symbol of black powerlessness.

Although certain white Texas Democrats continued to allow blacks to vote in local primaries in spite of the party's resolution and the Allred "Opinion" of 1934, others rigorously enforced the restriction. White opposition to black participation in Democratic primaries was strongest and most determined in those counties where the black population was significant.[1] The large, politi-

1. R. D. Evans to Walter White, September 1, 1934, NAACP Papers, Box C-285; Ralph J. Bunche, *The Political Status of the Negro in the Age of F.D.R.,* ed. Dewey W. Grantham (Chicago: University of Chicago Press, 1973), 464–66, 567.

cally conscious black population of Houston in Harris County under the leadership of Wesley, Atkins, Love, White, and Grovey resolved to continue the fight against the white primary. The NAACP victories had not significantly altered their political situation, and the prospect of another costly series of lawsuits increased their frustration. By 1935, black Houstonians were convinced that they possessed the expertise and knew how to attack the white primary.

They first initiated a state-wide campaign to garner massive support and won the backing of social, fraternal, and religious organizations. The Colored Knights of Pythias, Dr. A. S. Jackson of the A.M.E. Church, the Houston alumni chapter of Kappa Alpha Psi, the black press, and the Houston Negro Chamber of Commerce provided funds, moral support, and publicity.[2]

Wesley, Atkins, and Grovey ignored protestations from the national office of the NAACP, Nixon, and black attorney R. D. Evans of Waco, and proceeded with plans to take their own case, *Grovey* v. *Townsend,* to the U.S. Supreme Court.[3] Attorney Evans "advised and even begged" them to drop their plans. Evans warned the Houstonians of the increasing conservatism of the Supreme Court and reminded them of the NAACP's "great services . . . rendered . . . before the Department of Justice at Washington" and of its efforts to have the federal election law enforced. He stressed that the Association should be allowed to continue the fight against the white primary with their support. But his pleas went unheeded, and so the Waco attorney moved to the sidelines, with Nixon and the NAACP, and waited "until this case from Houston could tell the story."[4]

The Grovey movement began in earnest in late 1934. The charismatic, articulate Houston barber Richard Randolph Grovey became the champion of the white primary fight and a symbol of hope in the face of political oppression.[5] Wesley and Atkins provided legal expertise; the Houston *Informer* kept Grovey's cause before the public and aroused black support throughout the state. Grovey was perhaps the ideal person for the new suit. He possessed a cer-

---

2. R. D. Evans to Walter White, April 28, 1935, NAACP Papers, Box D-92; Houston *Informer,* September 29, 1934, January 16, 1935, January 18, 1941.

3. Interview with James M. Nabrit, April 6, 1974; Thurgood Marshall, "The Rise and Collapse of the 'White Democratic Primary,'" in *The Making of Black America,* vol. 2, ed. August Meier and Elliott Rudwick (New York: Atheneum, 1969), 274–79; Walter White, *A Man Called White: The Autobiography of Walter White* (Bloomington: Indiana University Press, 1970), 87–89.

4. Evans to White, April 28, 1935, NAACP Papers, Box D-92.

5. Houston *Informer,* December 23, 1934; A. W. Jackson, *A Sure Foundation and A Sketch of Negro Life in Texas* (Houston: Yates Publishing, 1940), 681–82; Alwyn Barr, *Black Texans: A History of Negroes in Texas, 1528–1971* (Austin: Jenkins Publishing, 1973), 136.

tain instinct for politics; his identification with common men, coupled with his ability to write searing political articles that the black community could understand, made him an important spokesman.[6] He traveled the lecture circuit with ease and confidence, crisscrossing the state. At every stop, his message was the same: "The fight to win the right to vote should not be merely a skirmish every two years in courts clearly unfriendly to our cause ... we should make the fight an all year round fight with the Supreme Court of the United States always as the goal." Grovey and his colleagues stressed that "the fight to win the right to vote is essentially a fight which concerns all of the million Negroes of the State of Texas, and not merely the 70,000 of Harris County." Wesley and Atkins, through the *Informer,* urged "the cooperation of *Negro leaders* and lawyers from all parts of the state in waging war upon a common ground against the greatest enemy of Negro life and Negro progress."[7]

At times, the thrust of the Grovey movement seemingly obscured the white primary issue. Wesley, Atkins, and Grovey were as determined to create a politically unified black community as they were committed to overthrowing the white primary. Numerous articles and editorials in the *Informer* emphasized that the outcome of the *Grovey* case would affect blacks in Texas and throughout the South. They pointed out the need for close cooperation among all facets of the black population, regardless of class, education, or economic standing. Between January and March of 1935 the *Informer* sponsored a propaganda campaign that created a great deal of enthusiasm. Dr. William M. Drake, the financial director of the Grovey Primary Fund, posted the first $50 and announced in early January that $1,500 had been raised. The Houston alumni chapter of the Kappa Alpha Psi fraternity sponsored a Grovey Benefit Ball to raise even more money and to foster black solidarity.[8]

In March 1935, Wesley jubilantly declared: "Never before since Negroes were disfranchised by the Terrell Election Law has there been such widespread interest on the part of Negroes all over the state in a common point of view and common objective." The *Informer* editor posited, "Whether the Grovey case is won or lost, if the new spirit which it is bringing to the fore can be main-

6. Walter Lindsey, "Black Houstonians Fight against the Texas White Primary" (master's thesis, University of Houston, 1971), 26–71; Houston *Informer,* August 24, 1935.

7. Houston *Informer,* September 29, 1934.

8. Houston *Informer,* January 16, 1935, January 18, 1941; Dallas *Express,* January 18, 1941. Dr. Drake, a ten-year resident of the city of Houston was "one of the most respected leaders in the city." He became involved in the white primary fight in 1933 when he filed the case of *Drake* v. *Executive Committee of the Democratic Party for the City of Houston,* 2F. Supp. 486 (S. D. Texas, 1933). He was treasurer of the Houston NAACP and director of the Houston Negro Chamber of Commerce. A. W. Jackson, *A Sure Foundation,* 171–72.

tained and increased from year to year, not only the ballot, but every good thing must in due course of time come our way." Some of those "good things" Wesley alluded to were elaborated upon in subsequent editorials: "We need a tubercular hospital, a delinquent home for our destitute girls; we need fair pay for our teachers throughout the state." In many areas of Texas, the social, recreational, and medical facilities for blacks were abominable. Black physicians in Beaumont could not practice in the city hospitals. The streets in black neighborhoods in Houston were generally unpaved, without sidewalks or street lights, and, on rainy days, were virtually impassable. Some black areas had no garbage removal or at best intermittent collections. Even at the height of the Depression little was done to establish unemployment relief.[9] Only political power could redress these grievances.

The *Grovey* case differed significantly from others filed previously concerning the white primary. Grovey's attorneys, Atkins and Wesley, in a bold and novel move, took advantage of a Texas law which did not permit appeals to the higher state courts when the amount sued for damages did not exceed twenty dollars, because they desired to proceed as quickly as possible to the United States Supreme Court for a decision. They, accordingly, filed suit for ten dollars in damages against an election judge, Albert Townsend, in a justice of the peace court in Houston. In the event of any adverse judgment, the next court to review the decision, according to the law, would be the United States Supreme Court if the case dealt with a federal question.[10] The *Nixon* cases had all asked for $5,000 in damages and had been filed in district courts initially, then appealed to the circuit court before going on to the Supreme Court of the United States.

As expected, the justice of the peace court ruled against Grovey. His lawyers quickly filed an application for a writ of certiorari before the U.S. Supreme Court. In early January 1935, the Court agreed to hear the application of Texas blacks for a review of the method by which they were disfranchised in Texas's "statutory" Democratic primaries.[11]

Before the Court, Grovey's attorney argued that Texas, in its statutes, prescribed the behavior of all party officials and required them to issue a ballot to all voters except Negroes. Atkins and Wesley claimed that Texas law speci-

9. Houston *Informer,* March 2, 30, 1935; Bunche, *The Political Status of the Negro in the Age of FDR,* 561–67.

10. Houston *Informer,* September 19, 1934, October 13, 1934; Conrey Bryson, *Dr. Lawrence A. Nixon and the Democratic White Primary* (El Paso: Texas Western Press and University of Texas at El Paso, 1974), 74–75.

11. Houston *Informer,* January 19, 1935.

fied the same qualifications for voting in the primaries that it did in the general elections and that the state itself determined the number of ballots and required their use in the primary. These facts, they argued, were ample proof that primaries were regulated by state law and constituted state action within the meaning of the Fourteenth and Fifteenth Amendments. They maintained that the Democratic state convention's lily-white primary resolution could no more impose such restrictions than the state itself. Furthermore, the fact that candidates for senator and representatives in Congress were to be nominated in the same primary involved discrimination and violated the Fifteenth Amendment. The primary was an election in the constitutional sense. "Whenever in substantial relation to the selection of persons to fill offices of government, voting is going on under either the mandate or authority of the state, there the Fifteenth Amendment is present to strike down . . . any barriers of race and color." Last they asserted that the Democratic organization in Texas was only a small part of the national party, which had never declared or adopted a resolution to exclude Negroes.[12] This last assertion created trouble for black Houstonians, as it was interpreted as meaning that the national Democratic convention had the right to bar Negroes, but the state convention did not. Their contentions, in other words, did not raise the basic constitutional question of whether any quasi-public body could disfranchise others on the basis of race.

On April 1, 1935, Justice Owen Roberts delivered the Court's unanimous opinion, based to a considerable degree on the Texas Supreme Court's opinion in *Bell* v. *Hill,* which had held that political parties were not "creatures of the State of Texas" but were private voluntary associations possessing the right to limit their membership. Roberts concluded that in light of the principles announced by the Supreme Court of Texas, "we are unable to characterize the managers of the primary election as state officials in such a sense that any action taken by them in obedience to the mandate of the state convention respecting eligibility to participate in the Organization's deliberation is state action." In response to the charge that the Democratic party had never declared a purpose to exclude Negroes nationally, the Court observed that this conclusion drawn by Atkins and Wesley rested upon the premise that the party was not a state body but a national organization whose representative was the national Democratic convention. The Court refused to determine the correctness of the position but stated that "even if true it does not tend to prove that the petitioner was discriminated against or denied any right to vote by the

12. Ibid.

State of Texas." The Court pointed out the contradictions inherent in the argument: "Indeed the contention contradicts any such conclusion, for it assumes merely that a state association, has usurped the rightful authority of a national convention which represents a larger and superior country-wide association."[13]

The Supreme Court's adverse decision stunned blacks across the country. Banner headlines in the *Informer* declared: "In 1935 the Supreme Court of the United States in *Grovey* v. *Townsend* Makes Political Slavery in Texas and the South Constitutional just as the Dred Scott Decision Made Slavery Constitutional 78 Years Ago."[14] When the Associated Negro Press asked William J. Thompkins in the Recorder of Deeds Office in Washington, D.C., to comment on the decision, he stated: "I regard this decision as being infinitely worse than the Dred Scott decision." He elaborated: "The Dred Scott decision dealt with the slave whose feet had touched free soil and comprehended only the rights of a small handful of fugitive slaves who had been placed in a similar position." This decision of the Supreme Court, however, "affects directly every colored person in the State of Texas and might eventually affect every adult man and woman in every state in the Union."[15] E. Washington Rhodes, editor of the Philadelphia *Tribune,* lamented that if the Democratic party in Texas could legally exclude blacks from membership, the Republican party could do the same in Pennsylvania. Rhodes concluded his editorial by asking questions that were on the minds of many citizens, black and white: "We wonder where Justices Cardozo, Brandeis and Stone were when the decision was reached? What happened to the theory of 'against public policy' upon which recent decisions have been based? Is it not against public policy, even assuming that it is not contrary to the Fifteenth Amendment, to permit a dominant group to effectively disfranchise a minority group?"[16]

Black Texans who had opposed the suit from the beginning lashed out bitterly at Grovey supporters. R. D. Evans ruefully concluded, "Their Fido pack went bear hunting and treed a skunk."[17] Nixon angrily accused black East Tex-

---

13. *Grovey* v. *Townsend,* 295 U.S. 45 (1935); Marshall, "The Rise and Collapse of the 'White Democratic Primary,'" *Columbia Law Review* 43, no. 7 (November–December 1943): 1027ff.

14. Houston *Informer,* April 6, 1935.

15. William J. Thompkins to Marvin Hunter McIntyre, assistant secretary to President Roosevelt, April 23, 1935, in the Franklin Delano Roosevelt Library, Hyde Park, New York. A copy of Thompkins's statement was sent to McIntyre asking whether or not it met with his approval.

16. Philadelphia *Tribune,* April 4, 1935.

17. Evans to White, April 28, 1935, NAACP Papers, Box D-92.

ans of having "succeeded most admirably in tearing down everything that had been built" for them. He wrote C. F. Richardson, president of the Houston NAACP branch, reminding him of his previous plea for help "to convince our people of East Texas that we had received two favorable Supreme Court decisions against the Texas Democratic primary practices not because of any individual effort but because a great National Organization—the NAACP—had prosecuted those cases."[18] Editor Richardson called the decision "The darkest hour before the dawn."

NAACP executives were even more disturbed with the *Grovey* decision. Secretary Walter White noted in his autobiography, "It should not be difficult to imagine the gloom we all felt. Years of hard work and heavy expense appeared to have gone for naught."[19] White publicly emphasized that the Association had not been involved in the case. The editor of *The Crisis,* Roy Wilkins, observed that the decision would be a great weapon for those sections of the Democratic party that desired to remain white. He privately stated that the decision was doubly regrettable because in many places in and out of Texas the indecision had resulted in more and more local communities granting the ballot to the Negro. Attorney James Marshall felt that the *Grovey* case was "badly handled" from beginning to end. Important points which, in Marshall's opinion, should have been stressed had either been omitted, or had not been presented clearly enough. One of the black Houstonians who subsequently worked closely with the Association, James Nabrit, conceded that the *Grovey* case had been a "hasty law suit" inadequately prepared.[20]

These criticisms were unjustified. Granted, Wesley and Atkins had failed to elaborate certain points. For example, they had not considered it necessary to prove that election judge Townsend had acted on behalf of the state. In their opinion, this had been readily apparent. It is likely that had the NAACP handled the case it would have fared no better, however.

In marked contrast to the disappointment voiced by blacks over the decision, Texas white Democrats were jubilant. The *Texas Weekly* conceded that the Supreme Court had disfranchised black Texans and had effectively blocked

18. L. A. Nixon to C. F. Richardson, April 15, 1935, NAACP Papers, Box D-92.

19. White, *A Man Called White,* 88.

20. Memorandum: Walter White to Roy Wilkins, April 11, 1935; White to Prof. Albert Barnett, Scarrit College, April 11, 1935, NAACP Papers, Box C-392; NAACP Press Release: "NAACP Lawyers Study Latest Texas Vote Case," April 11, 1935; Roy Wilkins to P. L. Prattis, feature editor, Associated Negro Press, April 4, 1935, NAACP Papers, Box D-92; Marshall, "The Rise and Collapse of the 'White Democratic Primary,'" 277; James Marshall to White, April 15, 1935, NAACP Papers, Box D-92; James Nabrit to Thurgood Marshall, December 1, 1938, NAACP Papers, Box D-92.

their entrance into the "white man's political domain." The paper acknowledged, "The general election in which the Negro is allowed to participate, is
merely a routine formality which never controverts the nomination of the primary." It continued, "So the Negro is endowed by law with the privilege of exercising the ballot, and deprived by political considerations of exercising it
with anything but consummate futility."[21]

The *Grovey* decision aroused much speculation among observers of the
judicial process. To be sure, it was not the first time the Supreme Court had
ruled against blacks; e.g., the Civil Rights decisions of 1883, *Plessy* v. *Ferguson,*
and the Berea College and restrictive covenant cases. However, in the area of
the franchise—the grandfather clause decision, the two *Nixon* opinions—the
Supreme Court had served as defender of black rights. But with Grovey, the
Court appeared to have abandoned its more modern substantive interpretation and reverted to its former custom of deciding on form. Had the justices
found "the private" discrimination of the Democratic party too sophisticated
to nullify?[22]

The *Grovey* decision cannot be considered in isolation. The Supreme Court
justices who rendered it on the same day handed down a decision in a case
originating from the famous Scottsboro trials. Nine black youths were accused
of raping two white girls in Alabama. After a hasty trial, amidst an atmosphere
of intense racial hostility, the boys were summarily convicted and sentenced
to death. The Communist Party became involved in the case after the initial
trials and appealed the convictions to the United States Supreme Court on two
occasions. In 1932, in *Powell* v. *Alabama* the Supreme Court pointed out that
it was "perfectly apparent that the proceedings from beginning to end, took
place in an atmosphere of intense hostile and excited public sentiment." Furthermore, it was clear that the defendants "were not accorded the right of
counsel in any substantial sense." Consequently, the Court held that the defendants' constitutional rights to due process had been violated.[23] With this
decision, the Court entered the field of state criminal justice.

The Scottsboro "boys" were retried in state courts and again convicted, and
were sentenced to death or life imprisonment. The International Labor De-

21. Houston *Post,* April 28, 1935; *Texas Weekly* (Dallas), April 6, 1935; Melvin James
Banks, "The Pursuit of Equality: The Movement for First Class Citizenship among Negroes
in Texas" (Ph.D. diss., Syracuse University, 1962), 230–32.
22. Ward E. Y. Elliott, *The Rise of Guardian Democracy: The Supreme Court in Voting
Rights Disputes* (Cambridge: Harvard University Press, 1974), 76; Henry J. Abraham, *Freedom and the Court: Civil Rights and Liberties in the United States,* 2d ed. (New York: Oxford University Press, 1972), 331.
23. *Powell* v. *Alabama,* 287 U.S. 45, 51, 58 (1932).

fense returned to the United States Supreme Court on appeal. Chief Justice Charles Evans Hughes, on April 1, 1935, delivered the Court's unanimous decision in *Norris* v. *Alabama* invalidating the conviction on the grounds that the systematic exclusion of blacks from jury duty had deprived the black defendant of the equal protection of the law under the Fourteenth Amendment.[24]

While the *Norris* decision reflected an increasingly sympathetic attitude on the part of the Court towards civil rights, and strengthened the Fourteenth Amendment, the *Grovey* decision, delivered that same day, continued the emasculation of the Fifteenth Amendment. The *Norris* decision gave blacks back their right to serve on state court juries, which might mediate the excesses of southern "justice" as meted out to blacks. However, in most southern states, jurors were selected from the pool of property-owning, poll-tax-paying voters. Blacks who could not afford to vote could, therefore, still not serve on juries. NAACP field secretary William Pickens commented on the coincidence of the *Norris* and *Grovey* opinions being handed down the same day. "If one were suspicious of the Court's motives," he said, "it would look as if they [*sic*] made a trade."[25]

In another decision handed down the following month, the Supreme Court retreated from ruling positively on other fundamental civil liberties, such as freedom of speech. On May 20, 1935, the Supreme Court in a six to three decision dismissed Angelo Herndon's appeal. A young black Communist, Herndon earlier had been convicted, and the conviction had been upheld by the Georgia Supreme Court, for attempting to incite an insurrection, or conspiracy, against Georgia. Before the federal Supreme Court, Herndon's defense attorneys presented an eloquent plea for the protection of free speech and other civil liberties and argued that Georgia's insurrection law violated the due process clause of the Fourteenth Amendment. The majority opinion offered by Justice George Sutherland declared that Herndon had failed to raise the correct constitutional questions at the appropriate time and, thus, that the Court lacked jurisdiction. The dissenting opinion, by Justice Cardozo, with Brandeis

24. *Norris* v. *Alabama,* 294 U.S. 587 (1935); Dan T. Carter, *Scottsboro: A Tragedy of the American South* (Baton Rouge: Louisiana State University Press, 1969), 319–24.

25. Henry J. Abraham, *Freedom and the Court: Civil Rights and Liberties in the United States,* 331; Bunche, *The Political Status of the Negro in the Age of FDR,* 2; Pickens, quoted in Marshall, "The Rise and Collapse of the 'White Democratic Primary,'" 277; one could argue that the Supreme Court ruled favorably in the Scottsboro case because it was so controversial and the Court desired to redirect attention away from its deliberations. The white primary, on the other hand, was not as controversial, and had elicited little concern in the larger society; see G. Edward White, *The American Judicial Tradition: Profiles of Leading American Judges* (New York: Oxford University Press, 1976), 213–14.

and Stone concurring, asserted that the Court had jurisdiction and was essentially side-stepping the intrinsic complicated constitutional issues.[26]

The Court's vacillation can be attributed, in part, to the times. By 1935, its prestige stood at its lowest ebb in sixty years. The Supreme Court's posture towards social change, as proposed in New Deal measures such as the NRA and AAA, evoked angry attacks from Roosevelt and his liberal supporters. As it warded off these attacks, the Court, by 1936, became even more conservative and invalidated additional federal programs.

In an unprecedented and audacious move, Roosevelt, on February 5, 1937, submitted to Congress the famous Court reorganization, or "court-packing" scheme, as it became known. Opposition to the President's plan came quickly from all quarters—the press, the bar, Congress, etc. Overnight, the Supreme Court justices were pictured as "demigods" who abstractly weighted public policy on the delicate scales of law. After 168 days of furious controversy, the embattled President withdrew his proposal.[27]

Future changes in the Court's personnel would undoubtedly benefit blacks. But in the summer of 1935, black Texans and the national officers of the NAACP were concerned with more immediate problems. The shock of the *Grovey* decision chastened the Houston black leadership. Wesley and Atkins recognized the necessity of reestablishing a working relationship with the NAACP if they were to maintain their credibility. The national officers realized that the grievances of black Houstonians would have to be resolved before the Association could regain and sustain its hegemony in the white primary fight.

In the ensuing weeks, Atkins and Wesley for the first time openly and definitively discussed the problems they and other black Texans had with the NAACP. Once again, the issue of the retention of black legal counsel emerged as a major concern. Black Texas lawyers continued to resent the NAACP for its reliance on white attorneys.[28] Atkins, especially, expressed heartfelt dissatis-

26. Charles Martin, *The Angelo Herndon Case and Southern Justice* (Baton Rouge: Louisiana State University Press, 1976), 108, 149–50; *Herndon v. Georgia*, 295 U.S. 446–55 (1935).

27. James MacGregor Burns, *Roosevelt: The Lion and the Fox* (New York: Harcourt, Brace and World, 1956), 229–34, 291–315; William E. Leuchtenburg, *Franklin D. Roosevelt and the New Deal* (New York: Harper and Row, 1963), 231–38; Joseph Alsop and Turner Catledge, *The 168 Days* (Garden City, N.Y.: Doubleday, Doran, 1938), 1–21; Alpheus Thomas Mason, *The Supreme Court from Taft to Warren*, rev. ed. (Baton Rouge: Louisiana State University Press, 1968), 102–6.

28. August Meier and Elliott Rudwick, "Attorneys Black and White," *Journal of Ameri-*

faction with the NAACP's failure to develop the white primary campaign around black leaders such as R. D. Evans and C. N. Love, who had initiated the struggle. Nor had the NAACP, Atkins charged, attempted to include individuals—Wesley, Nabrit, Julius White, and himself—who had joined the fight in the early thirties. Had the Association approached the interested and committed black leadership at the outset, Atkins argued, the NAACP would have been much stronger "instead of being practically a nonentity in Texas today." While R. D. Evans had been the first to indicate the possibilities of a fight against the statutory Democratic white primary, "when the NAACP came to file its first Nixon case, it ignored Evans, ignored the lay leadership in *Love* v. *Griffith*, paid its money to white lawyers and went its merry way." Because Association headquarters was thousands of miles away, Atkins asserted, its leaders had made a tactical error in not establishing strong links with interested and respected local leaders. Consequently, a feeling of "absentee landlordship" existed towards the Association among certain influential black Texans. Atkins pointed out that DeWalt's death had removed from the Houston branch a very forceful and active leader "willing to make some sacrifices in the fight for the civic rights of the Negro."[29] Apparently C. F. Richardson, the present president of the branch, lacked strengths DeWalt had exhibited, and his unharmonious relations with Carter Wesley lessened the branch's effectiveness.

The national officers pondered these criticisms of its operations. Wilkins, editor of *The Crisis,* personally believed that Atkins, in particular, had been motivated to take the *Grovey* case to the Supreme Court out of a desire to become famous more than anything else.[30] White, in the meantime, searched for ways to prevent a recurrence of this "nightmare." White stepped up his already vigorous campaign to secure the appointment as special counsel of the NAACP for Charles Houston. Houston, vice dean of Howard University Law School since 1929, had established close relationships with black lawyers across the country. White successfully impressed upon other Association leaders (Spingarn, Marshall, Margold, and the members of the board of directors) the strategic importance of having a black lawyer in the national office. He argued that Houston could conduct the programs against educational discrimination and political disfranchisement in the South better than anyone else and would cost less to hire.[31] White asserted that southerners would "expect a

*can History* 62, no. 4 (March 1976): 270–79; J. Alston Atkins to Charles Houston, May 12, 1935, NAACP Papers, Box D-92.

29. Atkins to Houston, May 12, 1935, November 11, 1935, NAACP Papers, Box D-92.
30. Interview with Roy Wilkins, April 19, 1972.
31. White to Spingarn, July 8, 1933, A. B. Spingarn Papers, Box 6; White to Roger Bald-

colored man to be interested in his people," and if he was "a tactful person like Charlie," he could overcome, through his knowledge of the South," whatever difficulties may arise better than a northern man who is unfamiliar with the southern situation."[32]

White obviously favored Houston's appointment because he was a brilliant lawyer. Nevertheless, his race was expected to have a salutary effect in silencing some of the Association's more vocal critics, e.g., Atkins and Wesley. White explained to Spingarn that "the choice of a colored man as highly regarded as Charlie would have a most favorable effect on our branches." In October 1934, the committee representing the Garland Fund (which had contributed a sizable sum to further the execution of the Association's work) and the NAACP voted to ask Houston to direct the NAACP's legal campaigns.[33] Houston's appointment coincided with the disillusionment of blacks in the wake of the *Grovey* decision.

The value of Houston's appointment to disgruntled Houstonians became evident almost immediately. Atkins interpreted Houston's appointment as special counsel and a high-level NAACP salaried executive as being a real "victory for Negro lawyers." He wrote that since "the NAACP has had a Negro lawyer for the first time in its history to handle one of its important cases before the Supreme Court [referring to Houston's involvement in the Oklahoma Jess Hollins Case], I trust that this will be the beginning of a new policy, under which no case in the future will be presented in that tribunal without a Negro lawyer at the counsel table." Both Atkins and Wesley desired to see the black lawyer elevated to a position of prominence and power. They felt that a black lawyer had to be concerned with the advancement of black people, for the progress of the race was intimately tied to his own development. His entire practice, at that time, was almost totally dependent upon the black community—a community which often lacked confidence in the black lawyer's abilities. Many blacks also felt that given the nature of the judicial system, they would obtain better service and more favorable results by retaining white counsel. Black lawyers, as a result, often found it impossible to earn an adequate living from legal work alone.[34]

---

win, July 8, 1933; White to Margold, May 22, 1934, NAACP Papers, Box C-107; White, *A Man Called White,* 143ff.

32. White to Spingarn, May 22, 1934, A. B. Spingarn Papers, Box 7.

33. Ibid.; memorandum from the secretary to the board of directors, October 6, 1934, A. B. Spingarn Papers, Box 7.

34. Atkins to Houston, May 12, 1935, NAACP Papers, Box D-92; interview with Roy Wilkins, April 19, 1972; Carter G. Woodson, *The Negro Professional Man and the Commu-*

The chastening effect that the *Grovey* decision had upon Atkins and his colleagues, and Charles Houston's timely appointment, led Atkins to suggest a reconciliation between the NAACP and the Houston black leadership. Atkins shared with Charles Houston his desire to develop a new case in collaboration with the National Association again to challenge the white primary. He persuasively argued that "through such an alliance the National Association for the Advancement of Colored People could catch and hold the imagination of Texas Negroes more firmly than through any other approach, and lay a firm foundation . . . of progress for the Association in Texas." Atkins recommended that Houston secure an appropriation of $500 from the National Legal Committee to add to the funds Grovey and his committee had on reserve to begin a new case. He contended that "the interest stimulated in the NAACP through such a movement would, through increased membership and other contributions, more than reimburse any appropriations thus advanced." Furthermore, "Under the leadership of able Negro counsel like yourself," which he thought was "the most fundamental thing in the whole equation," the Houston attorney added, "it is my belief that Negro Texas can be led to go forward with the NAACP."[35]

Thus, Atkins presented the ironic possibility of turning the *Grovey* defeat into a victory for both the NAACP and the black Houston leadership. Charles Houston's assumption of control of the Association's legal affairs softened the blow Atkins and his group had suffered in the *Grovey* case. Atkins and the others could now work with Houston and the Association and benefit from their skills without giving the impression that black attorneys could not effectively handle matters affecting black people without the aid of whites. Reflecting a complete reversal of his earlier attitude toward the Association, Atkins announced, "The more I think of the matter the more I think that . . . the best way to handle this case would be for you to direct it from New York with such local assistance as you might find necessary; rather than that the matter be handled from this end with your help there." Later, he added, "I am more and more convinced that grave legal questions like this one need expert direction

---

*nity: With Special Emphasis on the Physician and the Lawyer* (Washington, D.C.; Association for the Study of Negro Life and History, 1934), 221–39; Jess Hollins was an Oklahoma black accused and found guilty of criminally assaulting a white girl. He was sentenced to death. In appeal to the United States Supreme Court, Charles Houston persuasively argued that the conviction was unconstitutional because blacks were excluded from the jury. In May 1935, the Supreme Court overturned the conviction; see NAACP Press Release, May 17, 1935, NAACP Papers, Box D-60; *Hollins* v. *State of Oklahoma*, 295. U.S. 394 (1935).

35. Atkins to Houston, September 26, 1935, November 11, 1935, NAACP Papers, Box D-92.

from Negro Counsel occupying some such position as that which you now hold with the NAACP."[36]

Association leaders were mindful of the new opportunity to strengthen the organization's position in Texas. They moved quickly to organize a drive to bring Texas into the NAACP fold and effectively silence opposition. As Wilkins observed, the *Grovey* decision, paradoxically, "added to our prestige, to the regard they held for the Association, and it did add to our membership."[37]

To coordinate the plan to organize Texas, White found a leader outside of Texas. Roscoe Dungee, editor of the Oklahoma *Black Dispatch* and president of the Oklahoma State Conference of Branches, had displayed his organizing ability in that state. Born at Harpers Ferry, West Virginia, in 1883, Dungee was the son of a former slave. His father escaped to Canada along the Underground Railroad and later became a prominent minister and educator after attending Oberlin College. Mainly self-educated, Dungee attended public schools and Langston University for a short period. His *Black Dispatch,* founded in 1915, was recognized as one of the nation's most outspoken newspapers.[38] White selected Dungee to help organize a Texas state conference of NAACP branches because he had been successful in accomplishing the same goal in Oklahoma.

Dungee and NAACP field worker William Pickens planned a tour of key Texas cities. Dungee immediately contacted all the black newspaper editors in the state and extracted promises from them for widespread publicity to help facilitate the organization of Texas. They urged Wesley, as owner and founder of the *Informer* chain of newspapers and as perhaps the most influential editor in Texas, to endorse the Dungee-Pickens visit so that they could secure speaking engagements and move into the local communities without difficulty. Atkins notified Charles Houston that "the *Informer* is already cooperating and will continue to cooperate with the Tour of Texas planned by Mr. Pickens and Mr. Dungee." Other black newspapers in Dallas, Austin, Waco, and San Antonio agreed to publish Association news releases, to emphasize the need for new branches, and to publicize all of the plans to organize a state conference of Texas NAACP branches.[39]

The national office, perhaps in order to ensure success for Dungee and Pickens, elected R. D. Evans to the NAACP board of directors. Dungee advised

36. Atkins to Houston, October 8, 1938, NAACP Papers, Box D-92.
37. Interview with Wilkins, April 19, 1972.
38. Biographical sketch of Roscoe Dungee in the Savannah *Tribune,* June 14, 1942.
39. Roscoe Dungee to William Pickens, September 26, 1938, August 29, 1935; Dungee to Wesley, August 29, 1935; Atkins to Houston, September 26, 1935, NAACP Papers, Box G-171 and D-92.

White to release the news of this honor while he and Pickens were in Texas, "to get the full effect of Evans' selection before every Texas audience." Dungee encouraged all Texas black newspapers to publish stories sketching Evans's life for "Texas consumption."[40] Atkins's criticism about the Association's failure to recognize and to organize its white primary campaign around local leadership apparently had impressed Walter White.

This campaign was successful. The Texas State Conference of Branches of the NAACP was established on October 14, 1936. At its first meeting in Dallas, the members elected R. D. Evans president. A few years later, the Houston *Informer* proclaimed: "The NAACP has the respect of white and colored citizens and is accepted as the Champion of all causes of action involving the civil rights of Texas Negroes."[41]

White, however, remained plagued by the *Grovey* setback. The NAACP secretary personally pursued another strategy to counteract the *Grovey* decision. A paragraph in the April 1935 issue of the *International Juridical Association Monthly Bulletin* gave White the idea of having Congress pass federal legislation to protect blacks' right to vote in primary elections. The *Bulletin* pointed out that the campaign for the enactment of federal legislation and "afterwards for its enforcement" would be important "as an agitational measure in the basic struggle for enfranchisement." The article convinced White that such a bill should be introduced in the Congress by a prominent Democratic senator from a southern or border state. He was aware of the slim chance of the bill passing in the 1935 session of Congress. Nevertheless, White hoped that the bill's mere introduction would have a pronounced moral effect on the country and would enable the Association to build support for passage in the next session. Both Marshall and Margold encouraged White to pursue this approach and Margold agreed to draft the bill.[42]

Actually, Hastie, with some assistance from Margold, drafted two separate bills. Hastie and Margold felt it "better from the point of view of logical treatment to introduce the two bills separately." The first bill regulated the manner of holding elections for senators and representatives in Congress. It provided that no person could be a candidate for senator or representative if he or she represented or was selected by a political party which denied the vote to otherwise qualified persons on account of race or color. The second bill followed

40. Dungee to White, November 14, 1935, NAACP Papers, Box G-171.
41. Houston *Informer*, January 18, 1941; Banks, "The Pursuit of Equality," 188–92.
42. Copy of *International Juridical Association Monthly Bulletin* 3, no. 11 (April 1935), in NAACP Papers; White to Spingarn, Marshall, and Nathan Margold, May 16, 1935, NAACP Papers, Box D-92.

a course allowed by the Fourteenth Amendment. It concerned the apportionment of representatives in Congress. It proposed that Congress reduce the basis of representation in proportion to the number of people who were denied the right to vote.[43] Both bills were sent to various members of the NAACP National Legal Committee, including Frankfurter, for comments.

One member of the national legal committee, attorney Louis Redding of Wilmington, Delaware, expressed reservations about the proposed legislation. Redding maintained that even if Congress passed both bills, the discriminatory restrictions against the participation of Negroes in local elections endured. Moreover, he continued, the field was still wide open for disfranchisement of blacks through the discriminatory application of the poll tax, educational, and property qualifications. He was pessimistic about the future of the bills in Congress as long as the Senate permitted filibustering. Redding agreed, however, that the propaganda and agitational value of the bills would be beneficial.[44]

In spite of this reservation, White contacted a southern senator, Mathew M. Neely of West Virginia, to introduce the proposed legislation. Neely refused to introduce any bill, pleading that he could not do so unless it originated in his state.[45] Undeterred, White failed to get the Republican national convention, in July 1936, to include a plank recommending the reduction of representation in Congress of those states which denied the ballot to Negro Americans because of race. An attempt to persuade Roosevelt to issue a statement denouncing the white primary proved to be fruitless. The President was either unmoved by the fact that 75.2 percent of Negroes polled supported his administration[46] or was unwilling to risk alienating southern white supporters.

White eventually abandoned the idea of the anti-disfranchising bills. Probably the United States Supreme Court would soon have declared both measures, had they been enacted, unconstitutional. Bill No. 1 was based upon Article 1, Section 4 of the United States Constitution, which declared, "The Times,

43. Margold to White, June 12, 1935, NAACP Papers, Box D-92. White noted that William Hastie was "in large part responsible for the drafting of the . . . two disfranchisement bills," in White to Spingarn Medal Award Committee, Re: William H. Hastie, April 19, 1937, NAACP Papers, Box C-108.
44. Louis Redding to White, June 21, 1935, NAACP Papers, Box A-27.
45. Secretary memorandum, July 13, 1935, NAACP Papers, Box D-92; White to Senator Mathew M. Neely, August 14, 1935, Box C- 39; Board of Directors of NAACP, Monthly Report, August 1935, Box A-18.
46. NAACP Plank to the Republican National Convention, Cleveland, Ohio, June 9, 1936, NAACP Papers, Box C-392; memorandum from Walter White to President Franklin D. Roosevelt, January 2, 1936, Roosevelt Papers.

Places and Manner of holding Elections for Senators and Representatives, shall be prescribed in each State by the Legislature thereof, but the Congress may at any time by Law make or alter such Regulations, except as to the Places of chusing Senators." However, the Court had ruled in effect in *Grovey* that a political party was a private organization of like-minded citizens who associated to nominate their choice for political office. Bill No. 1 obscured the Court's distinction between the nomination of candidates (in primaries) and the actual selection of officeholders (general elections). The Congress, it could be argued, had no authority to disqualify candidates of a political party because the party denied the vote in its (primary) elections to otherwise qualified persons on account of race or color.

Bill No. 2, concerning reapportionment of representatives to Congress in proportion to the number of people denied the right to vote, was based upon the provision of the hitherto unapplied Section 2 of the Fourteenth Amendment. Nevertheless, as drafted, Bill No. 2 was also unconstitutional. The Supreme Court had held in its major voting rights decisions that the Fourteenth and Fifteenth Amendments prohibited states from discriminating against state citizens. The southern states, Texas now included, had long skillfully avoided denying by statute the right to vote to state citizens on account of race or color. Blacks were free to participate in the general elections, once they paid poll taxes, passed literacy exams, and met other qualifications purportedly applied fairly to all citizens. In sum, until the primary, which was the underlying concern behind White's consideration of the disfranchising bills, had been judged to be part of the election process, legislation of this kind would be bound to be declared unconstitutional.

These futile efforts to have Congress enact the anti-disfranchising bills succeeded in generating press publicity. The national office, White in particular, felt an urgent need to do something to recover the ground lost in *Grovey v. Townsend*, if not in actuality then psychologically. The drafting of the bills and the meetings with various senators gave the impression that the NAACP was doing something. By 1935, the Association leaders were still worrying about the organization's survival and felt the need to re-emphasize its importance to black people. During the next few years, while white Texans relaxed secure in the knowledge that they had preserved the purity of the white primary, the NAACP built a strong base among Texas blacks. With a new sense of unity and direction, the national office joined hands with local leaders and prepared for the final battle against the white primary.

# 9

# Coming Together

## Black Lawyers, Black Texans, and the NAACP, 1936–1941

In the years between 1936 and 1941 notable modifications developed in the operational relationships between the NAACP and its branches. Significant changes occurred also in the personnel of the United States Supreme Court. The Court became much more aware of a need for judicial protection of fundamental civil liberties. The realignment of the majority of black voters from their traditional adherence to the Republican party to the Democrats, the party of Franklin Delano Roosevelt and the New Deal, heralded in 1936 the beginning of a new political era. The continuing struggle against the Democratic white primary helped to form the new politics.

NAACP executives recognized that the successful resolution of the white primary fight and continued survival and growth of the NAACP depended, in part, upon the establishment of strong and mutually supporting ties with local black leaders in Texas. Lessons learned from the *Grovey* disaster were applicable to the Association's relations with most of its branches. The case and the series of events surrounding it illuminated the dangers inherent in an oligarchic organizational structure.

Young, talented, ambitious black local leaders, such as J. Alston Atkins and Carter Wesley, had to be drawn into the Association and made an integral part of its operations. They were, by 1935, no longer content merely to receive directives and orders from above. What incensed them was the feeling of being left out or ignored. They expected to have their advice solicited, and they desired some indication from the national office that their opinions and services were important to the decision makers within the Association.[1]

1. J. Alston Atkins to Charles Houston, May 12, 1934, NAACP Papers, Box D-92; Walter

The New Deal years witnessed the coming of age of a small coterie of black lawyers, many of whom had been educated in Ivy League schools such as Harvard and Yale. Outspoken representatives of this group, e.g., Charles Hamilton Houston and William Henry Hastie, were committed to the protection and extension of black civil rights. It was natural for these black lawyers to view the NAACP as the major organization through which they could gain invaluable legal experience and effectively challenge segregation, discrimination, and inequality in American life. Addressing the 23rd Annual NAACP Convention in 1932, Charles Houston declared, "With the NAACP as the crystallizing force, the National Bar Association hopes to cooperate by directing that force, so far as it may be directed and applied through legal channels."

Perhaps more than any other group of black professionals, black lawyers were aware of connections between their advancement as professionals, the improvement of the lot of black people, and the success or failure of the NAACP. Black lawyers struggled long and arduously to win respect from their white peers, who excluded them from membership in the American Bar Association, and from blacks, who traditionally sought their services only in cases dealing with domestic and minor criminal affairs. By 1939, however, the National Bar Association leadership could assert with increased confidence; "We are cognizant of the fact that the lawyers constituting the National Bar Association are essential to the success of the NAACP . . . we are also cognizant of the fact that the NAACP is essential to the success of the lawyers."[2]

As black lawyers became more confident, NAACP executives, particularly Secretary Walter White, developed tremendous appreciation of the value of black lawyers to the Association. In 1935, chiefly as a consequence of White's machinations, the NAACP retained Houston as special counsel. Houston had been the vice dean of the Howard University Law School since 1929. During his tenure, he had converted Howard's law school into an accredited and high-

---

White to Arthur Spingarn, May 7, 1935, NAACP Papers, Box A-27; B. Joyce Ross, *J. E. Spingarn and the Rise of the NAACP* (New York: Atheneum, 1972), 204.

2. Charles Houston, "Cooperation between the National Bar Association and the NAACP," speech delivered before the 23d Annual NAACP Convention, May 10, 1932, NAACP Papers, Box D-8; National Bar Association to Thurgood Marshall, September 7, 1939, NAACP Papers, Box C-382. For a detailed analysis of some of the problems black lawyers confronted in attempting to establish their professional identity, see Carter G. Woodson, *The Negro Professional Man and the Community: With Special Emphasis on the Physician and the Lawyer* (Washington, D.C.: Association for the Study of Negro Life and History, 1934), 191–96; Jerold S. Auerbach, *Unequal Justice: Lawyers and Social Change in Modern America* (New York: Oxford University Press, 1976), 212–15; August Meier and Elliott Rudwick, "Attorneys Black and White: A Case Study of Race Relations within the NAACP," *Journal of American History* 62, no. 4 (March 1976): 913–46.

ly respected institution. Houston helped to establish the first and most fully developed civil rights course taught in any American law school. His role in the development of the black legal profession was critical, and his impact on civil rights law was incalculable. Using his classes at Howard as legal laboratories, Houston trained a generation of talented, dedicated black lawyers as "social engineers" and "legal architects" who would restructure American civil rights law.[3] He impressed upon them the necessity of commitment to social change.

Houston once referred to himself as being "not only lawyer but evangelist and stump speaker." The latter two "callings" were "quite necessary in order to back up . . . legal efforts with the required public support." Those closest to him shared his views. Hastie, the first black to be appointed to the Third Circuit Court of Appeals, said of Houston, "He was the Moses of that journey," and elaborated, "I think all who worked along that period would agree his was the guiding genius and the tremendous genius that helped to motivate all of us and give leadership to the entire drive for equal rights." Hastie observed that "without him [Houston] developments of the '40s and '50s might have come twenty years later." Attorney James Nabrit, who later served as president of Howard University, described Houston as "one of the ablest lawyers, the most assiduous worker and one of the most dedicated people to the whole area of legal rights of blacks I have been associated with or know."[4]

Immediately following his appointment as special counsel, Houston moved to balance the racial composition of the NAACP National Legal Committee. He recommended the establishment of a large national legal advisory committee, on which the Association could place black lawyers who were "somewhat peeved" because they had not been named members of the National Legal Committee. Houston thought it unwise to alienate black lawyers "who have some contribution . . . to make" regardless of how small.[5] He compiled a list

3. William H. Hastie, "Charles Hamilton Houston, 1895–1950," *Journal of Negro History* 35 (July 1950): 356; William H. Hastie, "Towards an Equalitarian Legal Order, 1930–1950," *Annals in the American Academy of Political and Social Science* 407 (May 1973): 21–33; Walter White, *A Man Called White: The Autobiography of Walter White* (Bloomington: University of Indiana Press, 1947), 153–55; Clement Vose, *Caucasians Only: The Supreme Court, the NAACP, and the Restrictive Covenant Cases* (Berkeley: University of California Press, 1967), 43–46; Richard Kluger, *Simple Justice: A History of Brown v. Board of Education* (New York: Alfred A. Knopf, 1976), 221.

4. Charles H. Houston to Thurgood Marshall, September 17, 1936, A. B. Spingarn Papers, Box 8; interview with Judge William H. Hastie, November 27, 1973; interview with James M. Nabrit, April 6, 1974.

5. Walter White to Arthur Spingarn, May 7, 1935; memorandum from Houston to White and Spingarn, September 19, 1936, NAACP Papers, Box A-27.

of black lawyers, noted their qualifications, and submitted it to White and Spingarn with a request that each be placed on the National Legal Committee when possible.

Among his nominees were A. Alexander Looby of Nashville, "the best trained and most outstanding lawyer in Tennessee"; George Johnson of California, "one of the best trained and best connected young lawyers on the Pacific Coast"; Walter R. Gordon of Oakland, California; Alexander P. Tureaud of New Orleans, "a leader of the fight against disfranchisement in Louisiana, president of a strong Catholic organization, and strong influence with younger elements in New Orleans"; Chester C. Gillespie, Cleveland branch president, acknowledged as "one of the most faithful workers in the Association"; Earl Dickerson, Chicago, assistant attorney general of Illinois, active in the Chicago branch legal committee, and "one of the best lawyers in the Middle West"; Raymond Pace Alexander of Philadelphia, an ex-president of the National Bar Association and an "outstanding trial lawyer of the East"; M. Hugh Thompson of Durham, North Carolina, "very steady, deeply interested in Association work, good lawyer, now pushing campaign against discrimination in the University of North Carolina." He offered special praise for one attorney, Leon A. Ransom of Washington, D.C. Ransom, according to Houston, was one "of the best legal minds in the Negro race" and had done "more than anyone else upon the Howard University faculty to inspire young law students with social purpose."[6]

Walter White agreed with the special counsel about the importance of giving black lawyers more representation on the National Legal Committee. Nevertheless, he proceeded cautiously, and hesitated to accept all of Houston's recommendations. White protested; "We ought to put on more white lawyers and not make it too heavily a Negro staff, though I can see your reasons for wanting to add so many colored lawyers." Houston responded, "I agree about some good white lawyers, but what I want to do is get the local works strengthened in the field."[7]

White's objections were merely perfunctory. The deaths of Louis Marshall and Moorfield Storey in 1929, coupled with the aging of other eminent white attorneys—who, at best, maintained only infrequent contact with the Association—had seriously depleted the reserve of legal talent upon which the Association had always depended. White admitted in his autobiography that, due

6. Ibid.; Charles Houston to Arthur Spingarn, November 5, 1937, A. B. Spingarn Papers, Box 8.

7. White to Houston, September 22, 1936, NAACP Papers, Box C-107; Houston to White, September 25, 1936, NAACP Papers, Box C-108.

to the nature of some of the cases the Association handled (e.g., the George Crawford case), it often experienced "difficulty in obtaining the services of top white lawyers." Black lawyers were, however, no longer an organizational liability, but were essential to the effective execution of the Association's work. "They were younger, more physically active and willing to travel around and undergo the inconveniences and hardships, tensions and physical dangers involved in going to try cases in southern communities."[8]

The black lawyers trained at Howard by Houston, Hastie, Ransom, and Nabrit were in basic accord with the objectives and procedures of the NAACP, which undoubtedly pleased White. Moreover, because of their shared educational background, they maintained a high degree of contact with one another through business, social, fraternal, and professional organizations. The NAACP could capitalize on this closeness, for it helped to create an informal nationwide network of dependable legal talent. Houston enlarged this network and brought more and more black lawyers into the NAACP's fold. Roy Wilkins, former executive director of the NAACP, lauded Houston's ability to involve "all kinds of people who had respect for him and his abilities" in the Association's work. "He was able to get black lawyers interested in civil rights cases because he talked it wherever he went." Wilkins added, "I don't think there can be an exaggeration of the good that he did, not only for the NAACP, not only for legal action as such, but for the general spread of the social gospel and correction of injustices." According to Nabrit, "When Houston selected a person to work with him, it was as if the mantle of the Lord had dropped on them and they would do anything for him."[9]

One young black lawyer attracted both White's and Houston's attention and interest. Thurgood Marshall, born in Baltimore, Maryland, in 1908, graduated from Lincoln University and, in 1930, entered Howard Law School where he studied under Houston, Hastie, and others. White described Marshall as a "lank," "brash," young law student who amazed him with his "assertiveness." Houston took a special interest in Marshall, insisted that the NAACP place him on the National Legal Committee, and lobbied to have Marshall offered a job in the national office. In a confidential memorandum to White, Houston argued, "Thurgood has lost a lot giving his time to the Association. . . . You would not be able to find a more faithful person than Thurgood or a more de-

8. White, *A Man Called White,* 153; interview with William Hastie, November 27, 1973.
9. Vose, *Caucasians Only,* 46–47; Auerbach, *Unequal Justice,* 214–17; Woodson, *Negro Professional Man,* 191–96; Hastie, "Towards an Equalitarian Legal Order," 21–22; interview with Roy Wilkins, April 19, 1972; interview with James Nabrit, April 6, 1974.

pendable office man. . . . You can generally depend on his judgement . . . and you can absolutely depend on his research."[10] When Houston resigned in 1938, Marshall was named special counsel for the NAACP.

By 1939, more than half of the attorneys on the National Legal Committee were black. In that year, the Association separated its legal work from its propagandizing, lobbying, and pressure group activities and created the NAACP Legal Defense and Education Fund with Marshall in virtual control. The incorporation of the fund allowed contributors the right to deduct donations from their income taxes. In the following year, the National Bar Association and the NAACP became almost inextricably wedded. In 1940, Arthur Spingarn became president of the NAACP and William Hastie accepted the chairmanship of the National Legal Committee.[11]

Strengthening the role of the black lawyer in the Association was only one of Houston's many objectives. The *Grovey* decision impressed upon him the necessity of continuing the white primary fight. J. Alston Atkins had suggested that they commence a new attack on the Texas white primary. The suit would be based on "the proposition that, if the purpose is private, the tax money and public machinery may not be used to sustain it." Atkins desired to force the primary to become in reality a private function of the Democratic party by making the party responsible for the financial costs of the election. He optimistically concluded, "For if they are made private in fact as well as in law they will fall of their own weight."[12] Houston weighed Atkins's recommendations while he laid the groundwork for a new attack on the white primary.

Houston, like Atkins, was convinced that the *Grovey* decision would not be the last word on the white primary. He maintained that the United States Supreme Court could "be induced to look through the subterfuge of private party regulations" if the NAACP compiled "a very factual record . . . showing in detail just how the primaries are run and how, in fact, the state actually has control. . . ." In an attempt to show his willingness to work with the local black leaders, Houston asked C. F. Richardson, president of the Houston branch, and A. Maceo Smith of Dallas, secretary of the Texas State Conference of Branches, to send him copies of the Texas law governing registration and information con-

10. Houston to White, April 17, 1936, A. B. Spingarn Papers, Box 8; White, *A Man Called White*, 154.

11. *29th NAACP Annual Report* (New York: NAACP, 1938); *30th NAACP Annual Report* (New York: NAACP, 1939); Meier and Rudwick, "Attorneys Black and White," 944; Vose, *Caucasians Only*, 46–47.

12. J. Alston Atkins to Charles Houston, October 8, 1935, NAACP Papers, Box D-92.

cerning appeals procedures when one had been denied the right to vote. Characteristically, he offered to travel to Texas to discuss the matter with them.[13]

Houston recognized the value of a close working relationship with local black leaders and used the Texas Conference of Branches as the "legal spearhead" of his efforts to break down political and educational discrimination in the state. His approach tapped a significant, but previously unexploited reservoir of talent and financial support. Texas blacks were perhaps the best organized Negro group in any southern state. A number of statewide associations, alliances, and committees had been formed in the late twenties and early thirties to foster black equality. The organizations employed different strategies and tactics, but their goals of equality and first-class citizenship remained a constant.

The Texas Negro Chamber of Commerce worked to advance the economic position of blacks and emphasized self-improvement and cooperation with the state business and industrial interests. The state Progressive Voters Leagues initiated massive programs of civic education and stressed the importance of participation in political affairs on the city, county, state, and national levels. The Interdenominational Ministerial Alliance approached the "power structure" directly. Representatives of the Ministerial Alliance went directly to city and county officials to discuss the grievances of the black community. The Texas Council of Negro Organizations served as a coordinating agency and represented a synthesis of black opinion. It aided in developing long-range strategies for full equality and integration, using a combination of legal redress and moral persuasion. The leaders of the Texas State Conference of NAACP Branches frequently occupied leading positions in the above organizations. Because of its national focus, the NAACP had the potential of becoming the most important black organization in Texas. Its strategies were comprehensive and its victories benefited all blacks, not just Texans.[14]

Several individuals soon offered their services to Houston without waiting to be asked. One in particular, attorney Fred C. Knollenberg, contacted the national office and volunteered his aid. He lamented, "I feel very much aggrieved over the fact that the *Grovey* case overturned our *Nixon* case and by virtue of that fact our *Nixon* cases are not effective, and this I regret very much." Houston thanked Knollenberg for his concern and asked the El Paso attorney to find

13. Houston to Arthur B. Spingarn, July 6, 1937, A. B. Spingarn Papers, Box 8; Houston to R. D. Evans, A. Maceo Smith, C. F. Richardson, March 9, 1938, NAACP Papers, Box D-60; Melvin James Banks, "The Pursuit of Equality: The Movement for First Class Citizenship among Negroes in Texas, 1920–1950" (Ph.D. diss., Syracuse University, 1962), 188.
14. Banks, "The Pursuit of Equality," 245–47.

out whether candidates paid the actual expenses for primary elections. Houston was still in search of the best strategy to pursue in a new attack on the white primary. He had been toying with the notion that the state contributed the major portion of the primary expenses, as well as all of the primary machinery. Knollenberg's research, however, gave the special counsel a different slant on the Texas primary situation, and forced him to abandon that strategy. According to Knollenberg, when Texas passed its primary election law, it had established every step of the proceedings: "The only thing they did not do was provide for the payment of the costs, and this was placed upon the candidates." Knollenberg confirmed that the candidates were assessed sufficient funds to carry on the election.[15]

An acute shortage of funds prevented Charles Houston and the NAACP from developing a case before the 1938 elections, but this did not restrain the local Houston branch. After deciding to sue the Democratic party of Houston, in October 1938, C. F. Richardson, Julius White, and Dr. William M. Drake filed the case of *C. F. Richardson et al.* v. *Executive Committee of the Democratic Party for the City of Houston, Harris County, et al.* Richardson asked for damages for deprivation of the right to vote, and for an injunction to prevent further interference with black voting. Their brief asked whether blacks could be prohibited from voting in municipal primary elections. Although black Houstonians were obviously aware that the United States Supreme Court had ruled in 1935 that the state Democratic party's convention could bar blacks from state primaries, the litigants nevertheless questioned whether the same ruling applied to city primaries. Richardson argued that the Houston City Charter contained no provision for a city Democratic convention and consequently possessed no legal authority to bar blacks. Indeed, he claimed the City Charter of Houston stated that "*all* qualified voters in the City *shall* vote in *all* primary elections."[16]

Shortly after the hearings, Judge T. M. Kennerly denied the requests for a preliminary injunction and refused to consider any of the other contentions of the plaintiffs. Kennerly maintained that there was no substantial difference between this case and the one that had been brought to the court in 1933 in

15. Fred C. Knollenberg, May 5, 1938; Houston to Knollenberg, June 9, 1938, July 12, 1938; Knollenberg to Houston, July 2, 1938, NAACP Papers, Box D-92.

16. Houston to Knollenberg, July 12, 1938; C. F. Richardson to Houston, June 25, 1938, NAACP Papers, Box D-92; Houston *Informer,* October 22, 1938; *C. F. Richardson et al.* v. *Executive Committee of Democratic Party of Houston,* Civil Action Number 20, United States District Court for the Southern District of Texas; attorneys Mandell and Combs to Thurgood Marshall, October 25, 1938, NAACP Papers, Box D-92.

*Drake* v. *Executive Committee of the Democratic Party for the City of Houston.* In both cases the plaintiffs had requested an injunction against the Democratic party of the city. The decision in the Drake case and the Texas Supreme Court's decision in *Bell* v. *Hill,* Kennerly stated, had fully discussed and settled the laws involved in the whole primary issue. Moreover, he added impatiently, the United States Supreme Court had delivered the final words in *Grovey* v. *Townsend* and underscored the decisions in the cases in the lower courts.[17]

Richardson forwarded copies of the petition and judgment to the national office and asked if it was interested in using this case to challenge the *Grovey* decision. He suggested they pursue the same strategy Grovey's attorneys had used—file a damage suit for $10 in a justice of the peace court and, in the event of an adverse decision, appeal directly to the United States Supreme Court. Thurgood Marshall's reply was cautious and noncommittal. The new special counsel and James Nabrit wanted to be sure that this case was not a replica of the *Grovey* disaster. Nabrit warned; "It is quite easy to make these primary cases a racket and I think the National Association for the Advancement of Colored People should be careful in this instance, especially in view of the setback suffered in the primary fight as a result of the unfortunate case of *Grovey* v. *Townsend.*" Nabrit was studying election laws in the South and predicted that he would complete the project by mid-1939. He, accordingly, recommended that they wait until he could outline the strategy under which they should proceed.[18] The *Richardson* case generated renewed interest in the white primary fight, but many of the internal problems of the Houston NAACP branch drew attention away from the suit.

For quite some time, there had been an undercurrent of tension and discontent there. During the summer of 1939, Richardson, though branch president, broke a long-standing NAACP rule against publicly endorsing national political candidates and exacerbated the branch's problems. Richardson attended the NAACP annual convention in Richmond, Virginia, and circulated reprints of an article by Dr. Kelly Miller endorsing the candidacy of John Nance Garner, vice president of the United States, for the presidency. The Houston branch repudiated Richardson's action in a resolution sent to the national office.[19] And, in a long *Informer* editorial, "Free the NAACP of Taint,"

17. Memorandum and copy of Judge T. M. Kennerly's decision in NAACP Legal Files, November 2, 1938, NAACP Papers, Box D-92.
18. Richardson to Thurgood Marshall, October 31, 1938; Marshall to Richardson, December 7, 1938; James Nabrit to Marshall, November 3, 1938, NAACP Papers, Box D-92.
19. Houston *Informer,* August 19, 1939; Secretary Report to Meeting of the Board of Directors, September 1939, NAACP Papers, Box A-18. For a detailed description of the prob-

Carter Wesley further criticized Richardson: "When C. F. Richardson was elected president of the Houston branch of the National Association for the Advancement of Colored People there were those who were for organizing a fight against his leadership of that body on the grounds that he was not the proper person. This writer took the position that Mr. Richardson was elected in a fair meeting for that purpose and was entitled to achieve active support of all until he proved unfit. . . ." Now, Wesley continued, "we believe that in the absence of threats [meaning an ouster movement] Mr. Richardson will relieve the NAACP of the embarrassment and avoid injuring an organization that has labored to advance . . . and part company, if the NAACP is to be freed of taint."[20]

Other problems weakened the effectiveness of the branch and created internal dissension. The most serious issue centered around an alleged misappropriation of funds, and this too erupted after the Richmond episode. Richardson and Edwin L. Snyder, the promotional secretary of the Texas State Conference of Branches, reportedly mishandled some of the "nearly $500.00" collected for delegates' expenses to Richmond. Portions of the funds were never adequately accounted for and this "irregularity" created distrust for the branch officers.[21]

Walter White sent NAACP field worker Daisy Lampkin, a former Pittsburgh newspaperwoman, to investigate the charges and help reorganize the branch. Lampkin found the situation "unbelievable" and confirmed the reports that the Houston NAACP branch was being used "as a political football by unscrupulous men." Without being specific, Lampkin informed White: "The branch and Chamber of Commerce [Negro] have the same men as officers, and there has been so much stealing and so many irregularities that each man is forced to support the others. There have even been threats of murder from one to another." According to Lampkin, this also accounted for the small amount of money reaching the national office from Houston. She concluded: "Many who have money are gingerly giving one dollar as they want to have the right to vote but do not trust the handling of their money to the present administration."[22]

In spite of the corruption Lampkin found several honest and supportive in-

---

lems and issues affecting the NAACP in Texas and the personalities involved, see Michael L Gillette, "The Rise of the NAACP in Texas," *Southwestern Historical Association* 81 (April 1978): 393–416.

20. Houston *Informer,* August 19, 1939.
21. Daisy Lampkin to Walter White, November 6, 1939, NAACP Papers, Box G-204.
22. Ibid.

dividuals, including A. Maceo Smith, secretary of the Western Mutual Life In-surance Company; Dr. William Drake, a Houston physician; Mrs. Lulu White, wife of Julius White and a former schoolteacher (who, incidentally, became the first full-time salaried executive secretary of the Houston branch in 1943); and Carter Wesley. These individuals felt it necessary to force a new election. Lampkin agreed that this was the only way to save the Houston branch, but added: "Unless we can get honorable men elected, I shall recommend to our Board that we recall the charter."[23]

The confirmation of corruption within the Houston branch led an enraged White to exclaim vehemently: "It is utterly contemptible that grafters and crooks like these should prostitute the good name of the Association and jeop-ardize it." White agreed with Lampkin that if the situation did not improve, the charter of the Houston branch should be cancelled. For the meantime, however, he suggested that "a more effective step than immediate cancellation would be to recommend to the Board that any office to which Snyder is elect-ed be declared vacant and the same thing done with anybody else who is guilty of practices such as he has been pulling."[24]

Shortly before these issues were resolved, C. F. Richardson died. By the fall of 1939 many changes had occurred which affected the local organization of the NAACP in Texas. R. D. Evans, president of the Texas Conference of NAACP Branches, had died on June 26, 1938. Attorneys J. Alston Atkins and James Nabrit had left Houston to pursue other goals. The "veteran warrior," C. N. Love, had aged considerably. It was obvious to all that the Houston branch needed a complete reorganization under new leadership.[25]

By mid-November 1939, the members of the Houston branch had selected a whole new slate of officers. The Reverend Albert A. Lucas, the dynamic min-ister of one of the largest black Baptist churches in Houston, was elected pres-ident of the branch. Lucas was born July 17, 1886, in the Dabney Hill Com-munity, a settlement named in honor of his grandfather, who owned a vast area of land in Burleson County, Texas. Lucas completed his theological train-ing at Conroe College in Conroe, Texas. He became an ordained minister and pastored Baptist churches in Hammond, Rockdale, Waco, Wichita Falls, and Galveston. In December 1934, the membership of Good Hope Baptist Church in Houston voted unanimously to offer Lucas the pastorate. He possessed su-perb organizational leadership and fund-raising talents. Within two years af-

23. Ibid.
24. White to Lampkin, November 15, 1938, NAACP Papers, Box G-204.
25. Houston *Informer,* September 2, 1939, August 19, 1938.

ter he had accepted the Good Hope pastorate he had raised enough money to pay an $8,000 church debt, purchased an adjoining lot worth $2,500, and laid plans to construct a larger church to accommodate overflowing crowds.[26]

Two individuals destined to play a prominent role in the latter years of the white primary battle were also elected to key positions within the Houston branch. Dr. Lonnie Smith, a Houston dentist, and Sidney Hasgett, a hod carrier, were elected second and third vice-presidents respectively. According to Carter Wesley, "the new deal group was elected without opposition." A well-coordinated membership campaign attracted 1,484 new members to the Houston branch, Wesley reported. By February 1940, the new leaders and some older ones such as R. R. Grovey, head of the Legal Redress Committee, had struck a new note of solidarity and increased cooperation between the NAACP national office and the Texas black community. Gradually, other groups, such as the Phi Beta Sigma fraternity, the Interdenominational Ministerial Alliance, and the state Progressive Voters League, resolved to work closely with the Association in various fund-raising drives. In addition to fund-raising activities, all three groups worked diligently to raise the political consciousness of black Texans, while the Houston *Informer*'s staff unanimously voted to take out an institutional membership in the NAACP.[27]

Lucas generated a kind of infectious confidence and enthusiasm. Within a very short time, observers noted "a substantial increase on the membership roll of the local branch." Not a man to rest on his laurels, Lucas quickly moved to unify his congregation and members of the branch behind an all-out attack on the white primary. In March 1940, he called a citywide mass meeting to discuss and formulate plans to secure full political rights for blacks. During this meeting and the others that followed, NAACP local leaders evolved a strategy. They would issue a call to blacks from all parts of the state to attend the annual conference of branches in May 1940, in Corpus Christi, Texas. An invitation went also to national officers in the NAACP.

At the Corpus Christi meeting, the members of various NAACP branches met with Thurgood Marshall who assisted them in drawing up a ten-year program. Its chief goal was the elimination of the white primary. Other objectives were the achievement of complete educational equality and an all-out attack on all Jim Crow segregation laws. For the time being, however, the conference proposed a very simple program, and executed it immediately. The conference decided, first, to select a local attorney to coordinate the fight against the white

26. Jackson, *A Sure Foundation,* 45–47; Houston *Informer,* November 18, 1939.
27. Houston *Informer,* November 18, 1939, February 3, 1940, March 23, 1940.

primary on the local level; second, to appeal to all blacks to contribute more money and appoint a director for the fund-raising efforts; and third, after much discussion, to select a plaintiff.[28]

After the conference agreed upon the program, Marshall met with several black lawyers and leaders from various sections of Texas. They included attorneys H. D. Davis, R. Q. Mason, and Carter Wesley, and two prominent leaders from Dallas, A. Maceo Smith and Charles Thomas Brackins. Smith was "possibly the most publicized [black] man in Texas." He had moved to Dallas in 1933, "at once got into the civic life of the community, and by his push and iron determination . . . made enough friends and enemies to become well known." Born in Texarkana, Texas, Smith had graduated from Fisk University and received a master's degree in business administration from New York University in 1928. Almost single-handedly, Smith reorganized the Dallas Negro Chamber of Commerce and served as its executive secretary up to the time of his appointment as Regional Racial Relations Adviser of the United States Housing Authority, covering six states.[29] The equally prominent Dallasite Charles Brackins reportedly possessed more than a quarter million dollars and was described as "one of the best types of the self-made man." The Dallas *Express* noted that Brackins owned much real estate in the city and enjoyed large additional income from his bonding and insurance business. The *Express* continued: "Politically nothing goes in Negro Dallas without the key of Charlie Brackins. . . . His contributions to the NAACP, the YMCA, and the Negro Chamber of Commerce and the Progressive Voters League of this city will aggregate several thousand dollars." He was generally regarded "as one of the most powerful Negroes financially and politically in the South."[30]

After discussion, Marshall and the others agreed that the National Legal Committee of the NAACP would have general control over the legal phases of the case. On the state level, one lawyer appointed as local counsel would coordinate local preparations in the case. Attorney W. J. Durham of Sherman, Texas, became the Texas Resident Counsel, with Wesley and Henry S. Davis as his assistants. Born on a farm near Sulphur Springs in 1896, Durham attended briefly Emporia State College in Kansas. He read law in the office of a white attorney in Sherman and after several unsuccessful attempts passed the Texas bar exam in 1926. Durham's practice as legal counsel to an insurance compa-

28. Houston *Informer,* April 3, 1940, March 23, 1940, May 11, 1940; Banks, "The Pursuit of Equality," 192, 233.

29. Dallas *Express,* October 30, 1941, May 17, 1941; Banks, "The Pursuit of Equality," 157–59.

30. Dallas *Express,* February 1, 1941, April 12, 1941.

ny provided sufficient economic resources to permit his involvement in numerous unprofitable civil rights cases. One scholar described Durham as the leading black lawyer in Texas who by 1940 was virtually indispensable to the civil rights movement in Texas. At Marshall's urging, the conference issued a blanket invitation asking all black lawyers in Texas to become part of the state legal committee and aid the effort in any way they could.[31]

In a move to solicit and to secure the participation of the black masses in the effort, the convention created a statewide Democratic Primary Defense Fund. The *Informer* reported that the convention had voted to ask all black citizens of Texas to contribute to the suit. The paper later proclaimed "at last Negroes will work together instead of separately in a lot of weak cases." The convention appointed Dr. C. A. Whittier of San Antonio chairman of the Primary Defense Fund. Whittier was charged with the responsibility of raising the $8,000 needed to finance the suit through the Supreme Court. Brackins of Dallas was named treasurer. Together, Whittier and Brackins established the following apportionment of the amount to be raised:[32]

| Houston | $1,500 | Tyler | $600 |
|---|---|---|---|
| Dallas | $1,250 | Ft. Worth | $750 |
| San Antonio | $1,000 | Kingsville | $150 |

Other small amounts were assigned to towns on the basis of population.

The selection of a plaintiff temporarily disrupted the conference. Maceo Smith and others supported Clifton F. Richardson, Jr., who had taken over *The Defender* after his father's death. Wesley adamantly objected to the choice proclaiming that he would not give "large blotches of publicity to a competitor." To preserve harmony, Reverend Lucas recommended two willing members of his congregation—Lonnie E. Smith and Sidney Hasgett; both men were quite active in the Houston NAACP branch. Although Hasgett was finally selected to be the plaintiff, both men attempted to vote in the July 1940 primary and were refused ballots. Lonnie Smith went to the county clerk's office on July 15 and requested an absentee ballot for the Democratic primary election on July 27. Hasgett went to the polls on July 27 and requested a ballot. The local legal committee first delayed filing suit in order to include the denial of another ballot to Hasgett who, accompanied by Grovey, Wesley, and White, attempted to

31. Houston *Informer,* May 11, 1940; Thurgood Marshall to Belford V. Larson, Jr., February 9, 1942, NAACP Papers, Box 285; Gillette, "NAACP in Texas," 402–4.
32. Houston *Informer,* May 18, 1940.

vote in the August 24 runoff primary. Then additional delay occurred because of Thurgood Marshall's involvement in the Maryland Teachers Equalization Salary case.[33]

Finally, on January 14, 1941, attorney Davis and Reverend Lucas filed suit, in the United States Court for the Southern District of Texas, on behalf of Hasgett, against election judges Theodore Werner and John H. Blackburn. They sought $5,000 in damages for the refusal to permit Hasgett to vote in the Democratic runoff primary on August 24, 1940. Defense counsel Charles Kamp immediately moved to dismiss the case.[34]

District Court Justice T. M. Kennerly set an early March date for a preliminary hearing. After the preliminary hearing he denied the motion to dismiss, and set the trial date for April 25, 1941. *The Informer* observed, "Negroes have passed the first hurdle and will be able to make a complete fight." Marshall, in a speech before a mass meeting of blacks in Texas, declared, "This is the first time in the history of the primary cases that a Federal Court has ordered the hearing on its merits."[35]

When the hearings opened, Hasgett's attorneys contended that the Democratic primary in Texas was state action within the meaning of the Fifteenth Amendment. They maintained that the right to vote comprised three steps: first, qualifying to vote; second, selecting a candidate; and third, the actual election. The United States Supreme Court had ruled that blacks could not be prevented from taking part in steps one and three. The NAACP lawyers intended to prove now that the selection of candidates by a primary election (step two) was as much a part of the election process as the actual general election. Further, Marshall and Durham sought to establish that the primary elections were held in accordance with statutes and that the Democratic party was an organization with no rules or regulations except the state's statutes. They produced statistics to substantiate that, since 1859, all Democratic nominees had been elected in Texas, with two exceptions, and that the Democrats had used the county clerks and other state officers in these elections.[36]

33. Houston *Informer*, August 10, 1940; Walter Lindsey, "Black Houstonians Fight against the Texas White Primary" (master's thesis, University of Houston, 1971), 56; Gillette, "NAACP in Texas," 405.

34. Ibid., 59; Memorandum from Legal Department to Members of the National Legal Committee, Re: Activities and Developments during January and February 1941; Texas primary case, *Hasgett* v. *Werner*, NAACP Papers, Box 222; Houston *Informer*, February 8, 1941.

35. Houston *Informer*, March 8, 1941, April 26, 1941; Gillette, "NAACP in Texas," 406.

36. Savannah *Tribune*, April 24, 1941; quoted from W. J. Durham to Thurgood Marshall, October 12, 1940; correspondence between Texas and National NAACP, October 8, 1940,

While this litigation was underway, another case, *United States* v. *Classic,* concerning fraudulent primary election officials in Louisiana, was making its way to the Supreme Court of the United States. The case was not concerned with blacks or with the white primary. Justice Department officials of the Civil Liberties Section, created in 1939 by Attorney General Frank Murphy, had charged Patrick B. Classic and four other election commissioners with fraud. Classic and his cohorts, overzealous in their attempt to undermine the Huey Long machine in Louisiana, had allegedly altered 83 ballots cast for one candidate and 14 cast for another, and had marked and counted them as votes for a third candidate. They subsequently certified them falsely as votes cast for the respective candidates before the chairman of the Second Congressional District Committee.[37]

Herbert Wechsler, assistant attorney general, presented the government's case in *United States* v. *Classic* before the Supreme Court. Wechsler based his arguments on Section 19 of the Criminal Code, derived from the Enforcement Act of 1870. This section made it a criminal offense to conspire to injure a citizen in the exercise of any right or privilege secured to him by the Constitution. The government brief raised additional questions of critical importance to black onlookers. Editor Wesley predicted that, as far as *Hasgett* v. *Werner* was concerned, "Whatever the court says in the case from New Orleans will be used either by the Negroes or by the defendants representing the Democratic Party, in their arguments as the case proceeds up."[38]

For black lawyers and the NAACP, the critical questions focused on the constitutional status of primary elections. Wechsler argued that the right of a voter in a Louisiana congressional primary election to have his ballot counted as cast was a right secured by Article I, Section 2 of the United States Constitution. Article I, Section 2 provided that members of the House of Representatives be chosen by the people of the several states. Section 4 of the same article gave Congress the power to make or alter any state regulations as to the times, places, and manner of holding elections for senators and representatives. Wechsler asserted that congressional power and the voter's rights extended to primary elections. He differentiated between Article I and the Fourteenth and Fifteenth Amendments, arguing that, unlike the rights secured by the latter two, the right to choose members of Congress was secured against

Smith Papers, in Banks, "The Pursuit of Equality," 320–22; Houston *Informer,* April 26, 1941.

37. *United States* v. *Classic,* 313 U.S. 299 (1941).

38. Houston *Informer,* May 12, 1941.

interference by private individuals as well as against interference by action of the state. The defendant attorneys maintained that the voters had not been deprived of their freedom to express their will at the general election. Furthermore, they argued that no prohibition against a candidate defeated in the primaries prevented his winning in a general election.[39]

The United States Supreme Court that heard the arguments in *Classic* was composed of virtually all new justices. Chief Justice Harlan Fiske Stone and Justice Owen Roberts were now the only non-Roosevelt appointees remaining on the bench.[40] Chief Justice Stone delivered the majority opinion of the Court. On the eve of his own retirement, Justice Charles Evans Hughes disqualified himself for having been counsel to Senator Newberry in *Newberry* v. *United States.* Justices Black, Douglas, and Murphy dissented. Surprisingly, Roberts, who had authored *Grovey,* went with the "new" majority.

In rendering the *Classic* decision, Stone was obviously aware that *Grovey* was a potentially troublesome precedent. He sought to distinguish *Classic* from *Grovey.* Essentially, however, Stone adopted the arguments the Court had rejected in *Grovey,* and based his opinion on Article I, Section 2. He pointed out that the right of qualified state voters to cast their ballots and have them fairly counted at congressional elections was secured by the Constitution by a command without restriction. Furthermore, Article I, Section 2, unlike the rights guaranteed by the Fourteenth and Fifteenth Amendments, protected the rights of state citizens against the actions of individuals, as well as of states, as Wechsler had argued. Referring to Section 4 of Article I, Stone elaborated, "We think the authority of Congress . . . includes the authority to regulate primary elections when, as in this case, they are a step in the exercise by the

39. *United States* v. *Classic,* 313 U.S. 299 (1941); Steven A. Lawson, *Black Ballots: Voting Rights in the South, 1944–1969* (New York: Columbia University Press, 1976), 39–41.

40. G. Edward White, *The American Judicial Tradition: Profiles of Leading American Judges* (New York: Oxford University Press, 1976), 220–21; Vose, *Caucasians Only,* 177. Although President Roosevelt had soon abandoned his "court-packing" scheme of 1937, by the early forties the Court's personnel had undergone marked changes. Due to resignations and deaths the President was able to appoint several new justices who closely identified with the sentiments and objectives of his administration. Three of Roosevelt's appointees were academics: Felix Frankfurter, appointed in 1939, had been a professor of law at Harvard; William O. Douglas, 1939, professor of law at Yale; Wiley B. Rutledge, 1943, former dean of the State University of Iowa Law School. Two had been legal practitioners and government officials: Stanley Reed, 1938, and Robert H. Jackson, 1941, both of whom had served as solicitor general under Roosevelt. Frank Murphy, 1940, former governor of Michigan, had also served as attorney general under Roosevelt. Two others, Hugo Black, 1937, and James Byrnes, 1941, were former senators from Alabama and South Carolina, respectively. Byrnes resigned from the Court after a year and went to work with Roosevelt in the White House.

people of their choice of representatives in Congress." Looking beyond form to substance and effect, the Court then rendered its most significant constitutional interpretation of the primary: "Moreover, we cannot close our eyes to the fact already mentioned that the practical influence of the choice of candidate at the primary may be so great as to affect profoundly the choice at the general election even though there is no effective legal prohibition upon the rejection at the election of the choice made at the primary and may thus operate to deprive the voter of his constitutional right of choice." Stone also found that Classic and the other dishonest state officials could be prosecuted under the Enforcement Act of 1870, even though primaries had not been in existence when the act had been passed.[41]

By merging the concept of "primaries" with "elections," the Supreme Court, without a single reference to *Grovey,* practically overruled it and paved the way for congressional regulation of primaries. The implications of *Classic* appear to have eluded Justice Roberts. Why he supported the decisions remains unclear. It is possible that Roberts was simply confident that congressional jurisdiction over primaries under Article I, Section 4 (which is not expressly limited to state action) could be distinguished from jurisdiction over primaries under the Fourteenth or Fifteenth Amendments. Alternatively, Roberts may have been swayed by Wechsler's arguments, which painstakingly distinguished *Classic* from *Grovey.* Wechsler had argued that Texas had not made the primary an integral part of the electoral system. He had concluded in his brief, "[The] implicit premise of the Grovey decision is that Negroes excluded from the Democratic primary were legally free to record their choice by joining an opposition party or by organizing themselves." In Louisiana, however, the voters had expressed their preference, only to have their ballots nullified.[42]

Justices Douglas, Black, and Murphy, in a strong dissent, objected to Stone's finding that dishonest state election officials could be prosecuted under the Enforcement Act of 1870. "The important consideration is that the Constitution should be interpreted broadly so as to give to the representatives of a free people abundant power to deal with all the exigencies of the electoral process," Douglas conceded. He continued, "To hold that Congress is powerless to control these primaries would indeed be a narrow construction of the Constitution inconsistent with the view that that instrument of government was designed not only for contemporary needs but for the vicissitudes of time." Douglas insisted that he was in basic accord with the views expressed in the

41. *United States* v. *Classic,* 313 U.S. 299 (1941).
42. Lawson, *Black Ballots,* 40.

opinion of the Court and added, "It is with diffidence that I dissent from the result there reached."

The dissenters disagreed with the Court's interpretations of Section 19 of the Criminal Code. Douglas argued, "If a person is to be convicted of a crime, the offense must be clearly and plainly embraced within the statute." He continued, "It is one thing to allow wide and generous scope to be the express and implied powers of Congress; it is distinctly another to read into the vague general language of an act of Congress specifications of crimes. . . . It is not enough for us to find in the vague penumbra of a statute some offenses about which Congress could have legislated and then to particularize it, as a crime because it is highly 'offensive.'"[43]

The *Classic* decision came at a very propitious moment for the Association. The Supreme Court had established two criteria to determine whether a primary was regulatable by federal authority under the Constitution. If a state law made the primary an integral part of the election machinery and if the primary effectively controlled the choice of elected officials, then Congress had the power to regulate and control such primaries. These were the arguments Marshall and Durham were advancing in the *Hasgett* v. *Werner* white primary case. The initial hearings in Hasgett were held shortly before the Supreme Court's ruling in the *Classic* litigation. Marshall was encouraged by the *Classic* decision to believe that the Court was now ready to render a favorable decision on the white primary. The NAACP special counsel was confident that both Roberts, who had authored the *Grovey* opinion, and Stone were cognizant of the fact that *Classic* jeopardized the Court's traditional opinion that voting in a primary was a privilege of party membership rather than a constitutional right.[44] Roberts, in fact, was actually not at all aware of this, as Marshall would later discover.

Marshall termed the *Classic* decision "striking and far reaching." Of particular importance was the Court's statement that primary elections involving the selection of members of Congress came under the same federal constitutional prohibitions against interference with a man's right to vote in general elections. Texas attorney W. J. Durham was equally pleased with *Classic*: "With this decision of the United States Supreme Court's now on our side of the question, we must press forward with new hope and determination."[45]

43. *United States* v. *Classic,* 313 U.S. 299 (1941).
44. *United States* v. *Classic,* 313 U.S. 299 (1941); Robert E. Cushman, "The Texas 'White Primary' Case: *Smith* v. *Allwright,*" *Cornell Law Quarterly* 30, no. 1 (September 1944), 66–76; Marshall to Attorney Belford V. Larson, December 19, 1941, NAACP Papers, Box 285.
45. Marshall to Larson, December 19, 1941, NAACP Papers, Box 285; quoted from

After much discussion and debate, the NAACP attorneys decided that *Hasgett* v. *Werner* was not the proper case to present before the Supreme Court. They concluded that the only course of action left for them to pursue was to drop the case and file a new one embodying the same cause of action that had been adjudicated in the *Classic* case.[46] The lawyers had many reasons for believing that the Hasgett case should be dropped. First and most important, the case had not involved the election of senators or representatives; therefore, Marshall was prohibited from broadening the legal basis of the case and would have had to depend exclusively upon the Fourteenth and Fifteenth Amendments. Second, according to Judge Hastie, the Hasgett case had already received an adverse decision, and they could not go back into the lower court requesting it to deal again with the same questions. Hastie explained, "from the technical point of view we have a doctrine called *res judicata;* it literally means the thing has been decided."[47]

Once it had agreed upon the decision, according to Hastie, the NAACP national office had to sell "the . . . citizens of the local NAACP in Texas on the abandonment of maybe a couple of years of effort and the money that was spent on the then pending case." Walter White and Marshall undertook to persuade black Texans that "it was a part of wisdom and that it would increase our chances of success just to write off the time and effort and money that was gone in the first pending case and to start it again." Some disgruntled black Texans were not easily persuaded and accused Marshall of "messing up the case." On his next visit to Houston, the truculent Julius White allegedly warned Marshall that he "had better win the next case or not return to Texas."[48]

Their feelings were understandable. Black Texans had supported the Hasgett case enthusiastically; black churches, fraternities, women's leagues, voting leagues, and business organizations had contributed generously to the campaign. For example, A. A. Brasswell of Dallas, manager of the Crawford Funeral Home and chairman of the Inter-Fraternity Council, had launched a drive to raise $1,000 to support the Texas primary fight. Brasswell had asked all clubs to cooperate with the fraternities and sororities and contribute not less than ten dollars to the drive. All donors were to be listed on the Scroll of Honor, which had been placed on exhibit at the NAACP annual meeting in Houston, June 24–29, 1941. Another Dallasite, the editor of the Dallas *Express,*

---

Durham to A. Maceo Smith, May 27, 1941, Smith Papers, in Banks, "Pursuit of Equality," 322.

46. Marshall to Larson, December 19, 1941, NAACP Papers, Box 285.
47. Interview with Judge William H. Hastie, November 27, 1973.
48. Ibid.; Gillette, "NAACP in Texas," 408–9.

L. I. Brockenbury, had used his newspaper to solicit funds with editorials and slogans such as "Brother have you spared that dime for your liberation and freedom." The editor and the local NAACP had established a month-long joint fund-raising drive, called the Dallas *Express*–NAACP Defense Fund. The drive had its beginning at the State Theater in Dallas when, "after a brief appeal by the Chairman of the Committee [Brockenbury] the members of the audience responded with $28.37 in pennies, nickels, dimes, quarters, halves and bills." This type of activity was reported to have occurred throughout black Texas during late 1940 and 1941. White Texans were also reported to have contributed to the white primary fight: "White friends of Charles Brackins gave up to $40.00, but anonymously," announced the Dallas *Express*.[49]

In spite of all they had invested in the Hasgett case, Wesley was convinced that the NAACP counsel had done the right thing and tried to explain the new developments to his readers. He wrote: "One thing is certain as a result of the *Classic* case in Louisiana—the tables are turned; and whereas the Democratic Party has had all of the protection . . . now the Negroes are on top of the world."[50] Wesley's optimism, and that of NAACP officials, would soon prove to be justified. With renewed vigor and determination, Thurgood Marshall now began preparation for what he hoped would be the last of the white primary cases.

49. Dallas *Express,* June 14, 1941; August 2, 1941; September 6, 1941; November 1, 1941.
50. Houston *Informer,* November 22, 1941.

# 10

# Smith v. Allwright and the Fall
# of the White Primary, 1944–1952

The *Classic* decision impressed upon some Americans the serious implications of restrictions on voting rights. America's entry into World War II and the rise of Nazism in Germany with its emphasis on theories of racial superiority forced many Americans to come to grips with the need to balance national security with representative government. The hypocrisy of fighting a war against totalitarianism and for the freedom of peoples external to America while blacks were unable to be first-class citizens at home proved too much to bear for most black Americans. With renewed vigor, blacks, during the war years, took advantage of the new questioning mood in this country and pushed forward their demands to be treated as equals, particularly in the political arena.

One scholar has labeled the period between 1939 and 1945 the "forgotten years" of the black revolution.[1] By 1940 blacks were not only disproportionately represented among the unemployed but encountered widespread discrimination in the United States armed forces. The latter factor undercut black morale even more than employment discrimination. Blacks were, initially, ambivalent towards the war effort. Many felt the "Hitlers" at home were a greater threat to them than the "Hitlers" abroad. Following the attack on Pearl Harbor, black opinion shifted decidedly. The dominant attitude became the "two-pronged struggle" approach. Blacks felt the necessity to fight for democracy on both fronts—at home as well as abroad.

The NAACP and *The Crisis* employed every opportunity to connect the

1. Richard M. Dalfiume, "The 'Forgotten Years' of the Negro Revolution," in *The Negro in Depression and War: Prelude to Revolution,* ed. Bernard Sternsher (Chicago: Quadrangle Books, 1969), 299.

struggle for racial equality and first-class citizenship at home to the democratic ideology espoused by the Allied powers. Black newspapers took advantage of the war emergency "to persuade, embarrass, compel and shame our government and our nation . . . into a more enlightened attitude toward a tenth of its people."[2]

In 1941, A. Philip Randolph, president of the International Brotherhood of Sleeping Car Porters, consolidated black protest organizations and masses into the powerful March on Washington Movement (MOWM). He used the tactic of mass demonstrations to threaten Roosevelt with the specter of 100,000 blacks marching on Washington if the President did not end employment discrimination in defense industries. Roosevelt's timely issuance of Executive Order 8802, and the creation of the Committee on Fair Employment Practices, led Randolph and other black leaders to cancel the march.[3] The MOWM symbolized the deep dissatisfaction of black Americans and their growing militancy. Unlike the NAACP, with its traditional adherence to legalism and carefully orchestrated court battles, the MOWM reached deeply into the black lower classes across the nation, stirred them, and gave direction to their desire for immediate, direct action.

While the NAACP supported the MOWM and paid increasing attention to economic issues, the fight against the Democratic white primary continued throughout the war years. Black Texans and the NAACP were perhaps more aware of the significance of the *Classic* case than white Texans. *Classic* provided the NAACP with a new legal strategy to attack the white primary. The *Nixon* cases had been decided under the equal protection clause of the Fourteenth Amendment without a determination of the status of the primary as a part of the electoral process. When the United States Supreme Court upheld the conviction of Patrick Classic for falsifying primary election returns, Thurgood Marshall surmised that the Court and the United States Justice Department could now be persuaded to investigate and indict election officials in Texas who refused to permit Negroes to vote in the primary. The Court had held that corrupt acts of election officers were subject to congressional sanctions because that body had the power to protect federal suffrage rights secured by Article I, Sections 2 and 4 of the Constitution, in primary as well as general elections. The fusing, in the *Classic* case, of the primary and general elections into a single process for choice of officers bore directly upon the permissibility un-

2. Pittsburgh *Courier,* January 10, August 8, 1942, quoted in Dalfiume, "The 'Forgotten Years,'" 303–4.
3. Herbert Garfinkel, *When Negroes March: The March on Washington Movement in the Organizational Politics for FEPC* (New York: Atheneum, 1969), 7–96.

der the Constitution of excluding blacks from primaries. Marshall interpreted the Court's decision to mean that the justices could now be persuaded to rule against the exclusion of black voters from primaries as a violation of the Fifteenth Amendment.[4]

Marshall planned to pursue this argument in the new *Smith* v. *Allwright* primary case, but he wanted first to test this position on the Justice Department. He approached Assistant Attorney General Wechsler, who had presented the government's position in the *Classic* case. For political and legal reasons, Wechsler declined to join Marshall and the NAACP in the new litigation, however. Wechsler felt that the *Classic* decision had not dealt with the scope of the Democratic party's freedom to select its members, and he desired also to avoid possible conflict with the southern-dominated Senate Judiciary Committee.

Wechsler's refusal led Marshall to attempt to involve the Justice Department in another way. The special counsel instructed the Texas NAACP branches to request all black citizens to make an effort to vote in the August runoff primaries in 1942. The branch leaders were also urged to notify all sailors and soldiers to apply for absentee ballots. Once denied ballots, all blacks were to send affidavits to the national office, which would forward them to the United States Justice Department. A sufficient number of affidavits would, Marshall reckoned, pressure the Justice Department to investigate the complaint.[5]

Blacks in Dallas, Galveston, and Houston heeded Marshall's directives. Blacks sent several affidavits to the Department of Justice swearing that, though they had paid their poll taxes, they had been refused ballots. On September 25, 1942, a federal grand jury met in Dallas to investigate "the violation of the ruling in the *Classic* case with reference to voting in primary elections in Texas for Congressional Representatives." The grand jury subpoenaed only four witnesses for the hearing: Charles Brackins, A. Maceo Smith, Reverend T. M. Chambers, and L. Virgil Williams, executive secretary of the Dallas Negro Chamber of Commerce.

The hearings were an exercise in futility. Smith informed Marshall, "Despite our vigorous attempts to show that the violation warranted prosecution, it is evident that nothing will be done." He was convinced that the federal district

4. Dallas *Express,* August 22, 1942; Richard Claude, *The Supreme Court and the Electoral Process* (Baltimore: Johns Hopkins University Press, 1970), 31–36; Ward E. Y. Elliott, *The Rise of Guardian Democracy: The Supreme Court and Voting Rights Disputes, 1845–1969* (Cambridge: Harvard University Press, 1974), 76–77.
5. Dallas *Express,* September 12, 1942; Herbert Wechsler, "Toward Neutral Principles of Constitutional Law," *Harvard Law Review* 73, no. 1 (November 1959): 1–35; Richard Kluger, *Simple Justice: A History of* Brown *v.* Board of Education (New York: Alfred A. Knopf, 1976), 234.

attorney Clyde Eustus "has his mind made up on the fact that the facts set out in our affidavits do not constitute a violation of the Supreme Court ruling in the *Classic* case." Smith added that Eustus felt that the Texas primary differed from the Louisiana primary "in that the state pays the expenses of primary elections in Louisiana while the candidates for office cover the expenses in Texas."[6]

White hostility to the interference of the U.S. Justice Department in "local matters" was understandably high. Texas white Democrats believed that the *Classic* decision had not overruled *Grovey* and that continued investigation was, therefore, unwarranted. Given the local hostility, and the Justice Department's reluctance to become involved in the issue of the white primary, it came as no surprise to black Texans when no indictments were returned. The black-owned Dallas *Express* noted that the whole disappointing episode marked "another step in the Association's long fight against the Democratic white primary."[7]

Undaunted by the Justice Department's failure to assist him, Marshall went to work on the briefs for the new white primary case. The special counsel and the local attorney, W. J. Durham, of Sherman, Texas, in the new brief emphasized that Dr. Lonnie Smith, who had attempted to vote in the same elections as Sidney Hasgett, had been denied a ballot in the July 1940 primary and the August 1940 runoff primary. In these primaries, candidates for both the U.S. Senate and the U.S. House of Representatives had run for election.[8]

On April 20, 1942, Durham and Marshall presented the new *Smith* v. *Allwright* case before the United States District Court for the Southern District of Texas. Attorneys for Smith and for the defendant, S. E. Allwright, mutually consented to use most of the testimony that had been taken during the hearings in the *Hasgett* case. In order to expedite the proceedings, they agreed on several stipulations of fact: Smith was a qualified elector, who believed in the tenets of the Democratic party. When the primary was held, both prospective representatives and senators had been candidates. All nominees in the Democratic primary had been elected in the general elections since 1859, with two

6. A. Maceo Smith to Thurgood Marshall, September 26, 1942, NAACP Papers, Box 267; Dallas *Express,* September 12, 1942, October 10, 1942.

7. Ibid.; Dallas *Morning News,* October 5, 1942.

8. Savannah *Tribune,* May 7, 1943; transcript of testimony filed June 6, 1942, in the District Court of the United States for the Southern District of Texas, Houston Division; case of Lonnie E. Smith on behalf of himself and other similarly qualified Negro voters *v.* W. D. Miller, county clerk of Harris County, Texas, and S. E. Allwright, E. George, and James Liuzza, associate election judges, 48 Precinct, Harris County, Civil Action 645, NAACP Papers, Box 267.

exceptions. Lists of electors were prepared by the clerk without charge or expense to the Democratic party or candidates. Generally, the elected precinct committee chairmen were appointed as presiding judges and, generally, the same men were appointed later by the commissioners' court as election judges. The last fact showed that the appointees from the Democratic party were actually the same appointees of the state for the general election, and that there was, thus, a connection. The attorneys further agreed upon a fact that maintained that the Democratic party's resolution barring blacks had never been annulled or repealed. They concurred similarly that nominees of the Democratic primary became candidates in the general election and that the defendants had not deprived blacks of the right to vote in those contests in the general election.[9]

In presenting his arguments before the district court, Marshall stressed that the Democratic party in Texas possessed few characteristics of a closed organization. Contrary to the defense attorney's allegation, Marshall argued that the Texas Democratic party had no constitution, no by-laws, no rules save statutes of Texas, no membership rolls, and no method of becoming a member, except by an individual considering himself one. He asserted that in facts and laws, the case was almost identical to *Classic* in which the Supreme Court had held that the primary election in Louisiana was an integral part of the election machinery of the state, and was, therefore, subject to federal control.[10]

On May 11, 1942, Judge T. M. Kennerly decided in favor of Allwright. Kennerly ruled that the election judge, by enforcing the policy of denying blacks the right to vote in primaries had not abridged their right to vote within the meaning of the Fourteenth, Fifteenth, and Seventeenth (direct election of senators) Amendments. He was not completely persuaded that the Supreme Court had intended to overrule *Grovey* v. *Townsend*. Therefore, he followed that case in rendering his decision. The judge also ordered that all costs and other expenditures in the case be levied against the plaintiff.[11]

This ruling came as no surprise. Marshall and Durham immediately appealed it to the Fifth Circuit Court of Appeals. On the day of the appeal hearing, a large crowd, mostly black, was present to hear Marshall's arguments and the counterarguments by Glen A. Perry of Houston, attorney for the white

9. Ibid.; Houston *Informer,* April 21, 1942; Dallas *Express,* May 2, 1942.

10. Transcript of testimony filed June 6, 1942, *Smith* v. *Allwright,* Civil Action 645, NAACP Papers, Box 267.

11. Findings of Fact and Conclusion of Law Prepared and Filed by the Trial Judge Under Rule 52 of the Federal Rules of Civil Procedure, Judge T. M. Kennerly, NAACP Papers, Box 267; Savannah *Tribune,* May 21, 1942.

Democrats. Marshall again argued that the Democratic party was a "loose-joined organization with no constitution or by-laws." He added, "The only resolution we've been able to find that they've ever passed . . . is this one against the Negro." The special counsel reiterated his charges that the Democrats permitted every white citizen to vote in the Democratic primaries, whether Democrat, Republican, Socialist, or Communist. The Democrats' refusal to permit the Negro vote in the primary cut the Negro out of voting entirely, because winning the primary was tantamount to winning the election. To support Marshall's arguments, attorneys for the American Civil Liberties Union introduced a brief *amicus curiae*. It asserted that "any arbitrary and discriminating restriction on the use of the ballot, particularly where it is based on race, creed or color, is viewed as an impediment to the democratic process." They asked the circuit court to reverse the decision of the lower court. The National Lawyers Guild also entered the case as a friend of the court and made the same request.[12]

The circuit court judges Samuel Sibley, Joseph C. Hutcheson, and Edward R. Holmes were unmoved by these arguments. Judge Hutcheson did most of the questioning, and at one point exclaimed: "If everybody can vote in the Democratic primary, they would probably have to abolish the primary." The judges affirmed the district court's decision and ruled that the primaries were party affairs, not elections in the constitutional sense. Smith's lawyer, W. J. Durham, was not surprised by the decision, particularly because seated on the circuit court of appeals bench was "Joseph Hutcheson, who had held against Negroes repeatedly when he was on the District Court in Houston." Following this decision, the NAACP attorneys filed a petition for a writ of certiorari in the United States Supreme Court, which granted it on June 7, 1943.[13]

Marshall and the chairman of the NAACP National Legal Committee, William H. Hastie, prepared the brief, which was also signed by a cross section of black attorneys from all parts of the country: W. J. Durham, Sherman, Texas; W. Robert Ming, Jr., Chicago, Illinois; George M. Johnson, Berkeley, California; Leon A. Ranson, Washington, D.C.; and Carter Wesley, Houston, Texas.[14] Arthur Garfield Hayes of the American Civil Liberties Union, the National

12. Transcript of Record: United States Circuit Court of Appeals, Fifth Circuit No. 10382; *Lonnie E. Smith* v. *S. E. Allwright*, NAACP Papers, Box 267; Savannah *Tribune*, November 19, 1942.

13. Dallas *Express*, November 14, 1942, December 5, 1942; Savannah *Tribune*, December 10, 1942; NAACP Press Release: "Background on Texas Primary Case," March 20, 1944, NAACP Papers, Box 285; *Smith* v. *Allwright*, 131 F. (2d) 593 (C.C.A. 5th, 1942).

14. Copy of Brief for Petitioner, Supreme Court of the United States, October Term, 1943, No. 51 in the case of *Lonnie E. Smith* v. *S. E. Allwright*, NAACP Papers, Box 267.

Lawyers' Guild, and the Workers Defense League filed other briefs *amicus curiae.* The Democratic party and the accused precinct judges were represented by George W. Barcus of Austin, Texas. Wright Morrow, Democratic national committeeman for Texas, also filed a brief.[15]

Months later, on November 12, 1943, blacks from across the United States filled the Supreme Court to hear Marshall, Hastie, and Durham argue the last of the Texas white primary cases. There was an air of anticipation and excitement among the spectators who included Mrs. Mary McLeod Bethune of the National Council of Negro Women, Major Harriet West of the WACs, Hastie's mother, Mrs. Roberta Hastie, Miss Thomasina Johnson of the Alpha Kappa Alpha sorority, and attorneys Arthur Shores of Birmingham and Carter Wesley of Houston. Marshall's opening statement described the nature of the primary and its effect on black voting, while Hastie followed with a head-on attack on the *Grovey* v. *Townsend* decision. Durham was prepared to answer any claims of fairness in the Texas primary but, according to the Houston *Informer* reporter, did not get a chance to speak, since the opposition neither filed a brief nor appeared before the Court. The participants and onlookers expected a barrage of questions from the Court, but, as Wesley recalled, "they were surprised and baffled when the justices sat on the edge of their seats to listen but asked no questions." There was some anticipation that Hastie's attack on the *Grovey* decision would elicit sharp reactions from Justice Roberts, who authored the opinion, "but at every blow he grimly closed his lips closer." In spite of the Court's silence, the black lawyers remained optimistic about the outcome.[16]

Unexpected developments delayed the Supreme Court's delivery of an opinion. As had occurred in both *Nixon* cases, the attorney general of Texas belatedly requested permission to file a brief *amicus curiae* shortly before the Court was to issue its decision. Wesley speculated that Texas Democrats in Washington had become alarmed at the possibility that the Supreme Court would decide against them. Pressure had apparently been exerted on Texas attorney general Gerald Mann at least to make an attempt to preserve the status quo. The Supreme Court granted the request and scheduled the case for reargument January 12, 1944.[17]

During the reargument, Mann put forth the same arguments that All-

15. NAACP Press Release: "Background on Texas," March 20, 1944, NAACP Papers, Box 285; Conrey Bryson, *Dr. Lawrence A. Nixon and the Democratic White Primary* (El Paso: Texas Western Press and University of Texas at El Paso, 1974), 77.
16. Houston *Informer,* November 20, 1943.
17. Ibid., December 4, 1943; NAACP Press Release: "Background on Texas," March 20, 1944.

wright's lawyer had advanced in the district court and in the circuit court of appeals. He asserted that the Democratic party of Texas was a voluntary organization with members "banded together for the purpose of selecting individuals of the group representing the common political beliefs as candidates in the general election." As a voluntary organization, he claimed, the Democratic party was free to select its members and limit to whites participation in the party primary: "Such action . . . does not violate the Fourteenth, Fifteenth or Seventeenth Amendments as officers of the government cannot be chosen at primaries and the Amendments are applicable only to general elections where governmental officers are actually elected." The NAACP attorneys used the same line of argument they had presented earlier.[18]

After the hearings, Chief Justice Stone appointed Justice Frankfurter to write the Court's opinion declaring the white primary unconstitutional. Other justices expressed misgivings. Justice Jackson summarized their apprehensions: "It seems to me very important that the strength which an all but unanimous decision would have, may be greatly weakened if the voice that utters it is one that may grate on Southern sensibilities." Jackson candidly pointed out that Frankfurter "in the First place, is a Jew. In the second place, he is from New England, the seat of the abolition movement. In the third place, he has not been thought of as a person particularly sympathetic with the Democratic party in the past." Jackson suggested that because the decision was bound to arouse bitter resentment it would "be much less apt to stir ugly reactions if the news that the primary is dead, is broken to it, if possible, by a Southerner who has been a Democrat and is not a member of one of the minorities which stir prejudices kindred to those against the Negro." Stone quickly withdrew Frankfurter from writing the decision in the case and reassigned it to Justice Reed.[19]

Justice Reed, a border state Democrat from Kentucky, in delivering the eight-to-one opinion remarked, "When *Grovey* v. *Townsend* was written, the Court looked upon the denial of a vote in a primary as a mere refusal by a party of party membership." The *Classic* case, however, undermined the rationale of *Grovey* v. *Townsend* because the Court then decided that "recognition of the place of the primary in the electoral scheme makes clear that state delegation to a party of the power to fix the qualifications of primary elections is delegation of a state function that makes the party's action the action of the state."[20]

18. *Smith* v. *Allwright,* 321 U.S. 657, 64 Supreme Court 757 (1944).
19. Alpheus Thomas Mason, *Harlan Fiske Stone: Pillar of the Law* (New York: Viking Press, 1956), 614–16.
20. Ibid.; *Smith* v. *Allwright,* 321 U.S. 660, 661, 64 Supreme Court 757 (1944).

After reviewing the constitutional and statutory provision relating to political parties and primaries in Texas, the Court reached this conclusion:

> We think that this statutory system for the selection of party nominees for inclusion on the general election ballot makes the party which is required to follow these legislative directions an agency of the state so far as it determines the participants in a primary election. The party takes its character as a state agency from the duties imposed upon it by state statutes; the duties do not become matters of private law because they are performed by a political party. . . . If the state requires a certain election procedure, prescribes a general election ballot made up of party nominees so chosen and limits the choice of the electorate in general elections for state officers, practically speaking, to those whose names appear on such a ballot, it endorses, adopts and enforces the discrimination against Negroes practiced by a party entrusted by Texas law with the determination of the qualifications of participants in the primary. This is state action within the meaning of the Fifteenth Amendment.[21]

The Court, had, in effect, applied to the *Smith* case the two tests or criteria it had established in the *Classic* case concluding that the primaries were part of the election process and effectively controlled the choice of the officials elected. Consequently, the Court decided that the Democratic party's refusal to permit Smith to vote in the Democratic primaries had been state action and violated the Fifteenth Amendment. This decision also answered the two questions to which the Supreme Court had avoided addressing itself in the *Nixon v. Condon* case: Did a political party in Texas have the inherent power to determine its membership? Did the Texas legislation transform the concept of a political party as a voluntary association?[22] The *Smith* decision implicitly answered "no" to the first question and "yes" to the second. Texas's statutes had affected the political party in such a way that it was neither a voluntary association nor a private organization but served a quasi-governmental function as a quasi-public body. Thus, it could not be said to possess any inherent power to determine its membership or the qualifications for voting in the primaries. Justice Reed found much firmer footing for attacking the white primary under the Fifteenth Amendment than Holmes and Cardozo had found under the Fourteenth.

---

21. Ibid., 663–64.
22. *Nixon v. Condon,* 286 U.S. 73–106 (1932); Mason, *Harlan Fiske Stone,* 617.

Not surprisingly, Justice Roberts, author of the *Grovey* opinion, bitterly objected to the *Smith* decision. The lone dissenter exploded: "Not a fact differentiates [the *Grovey* case] from this except the names of the parties." He traced the history of white primary litigation in the Supreme Court and said that *Grovey* had received the attention and consideration that the questions involved demanded, and the opinion in that case represented all of the justices. Roberts declared that the present decision "tends to bring adjudications of this tribunal into the same class as a restricted railroad ticket, good for this day and train only. I have no assurance, in view of current decisions, that the opinions announced today may not shortly be repudiated and overruled by justices who deem they have new light on the subject."[23]

Roberts insisted that there were sharp differences between the election laws of Louisiana, which had been considered in the *Classic* case, and those of Texas. The Louisiana statutes required the primary to be conducted by state officials and made the primary a state election, while under Texas statutes the primary was a party election conducted at the expense of members of the party and by officials chosen by the party. Roberts continued, "It is suggested that *Grovey* v. *Townsend* was overruled sub silentio in *United States* v. *Classic.* . . . If so, the situation is even worse than that exhibited by the outright repudiation of an earlier decision, for it is the fact that, in the *Classic* case, *Grovey* v. *Townsend* was distinguished in brief and argument by the Government without suggestion that it was wrongly decided, and was relied on by the appellees, not by way of analogy. The Case is not mentioned in either of the opinions in the *Classic* Case." Justice Roberts concluded that the *Classic* case had not overruled *Grovey* v. *Townsend* and added that "if it was the intention of the Court to accomplish this result it should have adopted the open and frank way of saying what it was doing rather than state that that was done after the event."[24] It is evident that Roberts had been duped, intentionally or unintentionally. Without his vote there would have been no *Classic* precedent.

As elated as he was with the case's outcome, Marshall expressed concern about the practical effects of the Court's decision. He pointed out that there was precise and imprecise language in Justice Reed's opinion. On the one hand, Reed implied that barring a person from a primary election on account of color or race was a deprivation of a constitutional right, regardless of how that result was achieved. On the other, Marshall observed, Reed also stated that

23. *Smith* v. *Allwright*, 321 U.S. 669, 64 Supreme Court (1944).

24. Ibid., 669–70; Robert Cushman, "The Texas 'White Primary' Case: *Smith* v. *Allwright*," *Cornell Law Quarterly* 30, no. 1 (September 1944): 66–76.

the statutory system for the selection of party nominees which the party was required to follow made it an agency of the state. In other words, the party took its character as a state agency from the duties imposed upon it by the state statutes; that the state made the privilege of membership in a party the essential qualification for voting in the primary, thus constituting state action. Marshall warned that "this language concerning the statutory scheme in Texas and what is and what is not action may open the door for the invention of new contrivances to bar Negroes from voting in primary elections."[25]

As preparation for this eventuality, the special counsel sent a memorandum to all NAACP branches in areas affected by the Texas primary decision. He warned, "There is no doubt that in some instances Negroes will be denied the right to vote despite this ruling by the United States Supreme Court." He urged them, therefore, to encourage qualified black electors to present themselves at the polls in the coming primaries. If denied the ballots, they were to follow established procedures: fill out affidavits and send them to the national office. He added, "Unless we correlate all of the activities along these lines, there is a possibility of one case injuring another."[26] Marshall also sent a letter to U.S. attorney general Francis Biddle. In it, he asked Biddle to direct the Justice Department to ensure that United States attorneys informed Democratic party officials throughout the South that exclusion of black voters from the primaries was now a distinct and definite federal crime.[27]

Texas blacks were overjoyed at the conclusion of the case and conceded that the Association had done a magnificent job. Dr. Smith thanked the National Association on behalf of the Negroes of the South "and the whites of the south for the fortitude and perseverance applied to making this great achievement."[28] Carter Wesley reported that the decision granting the blacks the right to vote, "being the fruits of the relentless effort on the part of the National Association for the Advancement of Colored People has acted as a stimulant to the local branch's 20,000 membership campaign. The latest report . . . reveals that the membership has reached more than 4,000 netting over $5,000." While J. Alston Atkins described the history of the primary fight as "one of baffled hopes, sickening disappointments and grim deathless courage," he also proclaimed that the struggle showed "the patience, and endurance, and character

25. Memorandum to Board of Directors from the Legal Department, April 5, 1944, NAACP Papers, Box 285.

26. Marshall to branches in areas affected by Texas primary decision, May 8, 1944, NAACP Papers, Box 285.

27. Washington *Post,* April 4, 1944.

28. Houston *Informer,* April 8, 1944.

of the Negro race at its best." The leadership of the Texas Conference of Branches took pride in the victory because of the unity it occasioned within the black community. As one spokesman exulted, "We won this victory because we worked together with singleness of purpose and had faith and confidence in the final triumph of justice." All agreed that the more than $11,000 spent on the case "was well worth the price."[29] The NAACP experienced a tremendous growth in its membership. From a total of 355 branches and a membership of 50,556 in 1940, the NAACP grew to 1,073 branches and a membership of slightly less than 450,000 in 1946.[30]

All Association officials were jubilant over the outcome of the case but none more so than Hastie. Hastie later described his reaction: "I remember when I learned of the decision I was on a mission down to the West Indies. When I came back to Miami, the plane from Jamaica was a little late and as I was literally rushing through the airport I picked up the paper and on the plane I read the headlines reporting a reversal of *Grovey* v. *Townsend*. I am sure the people on the plane thought I was crazy because I just let out one whoop and had it not been for the seat belt I would have gone straight up in the air."[31]

The response of white southern Democrats to the *Smith* decision ranged from cautious evasiveness to stubborn announcements of undying determination to preserve the traditional white control of state election machinery. In Mississippi, chairman Herbert Holmes of the Democratic executive committee declared that "we still have a few State's rights left, and one of our rights is to have Democratic primaries and say who shall vote in them." He added, "The Supreme Court or no one else can control a Democratic primary in Mississippi." Florida's Democratic committee chairman, Tom Conely, declared, "We'll certainly resist, if possible, any attempt to have Negroes vote in our primaries." J. C. Barett, of the Arkansas Democratic Committee, said that he wished to study the ruling. In Virginia, E. R. Combs, national Democratic committeeman, reflected a short memory by asserting that the party had "never undertaken to bar Negroes from [Virginia] Democratic primaries if they claimed to be Democrats."[32]

Southern members of the U.S. Congress feared that the decision, while

29. J. Alston Atkins, *The Texas Negro and His Political Rights: A History of the Fight of Negroes to Enter the Democratic Primaries of Texas* (Houston: Webster Publishing, 1932), 6; memorandum, Texas Conference of Branches of NAACP, April 20, 1944, A. Maceo Smith Papers, quoted in Melvin J. Banks, "The Pursuit of Equality" (Ph.D. diss., Syracuse University, 1962), 332.

30. Dalfiume, "The 'Forgotten Years' of the Negro Revolution," 306.

31. Interview with Judge William H. Hastie, November 27, 1973.

32. All quotes from the *New York Times,* April 4, 1944.

specifically applicable only to Texas, might be extended to cover restrictions against blacks in other states where nomination in the Democratic primary was tantamount to election. Senator Burnet Maybank of South Carolina announced that his state would do what it could to "protect our white primary." Mississippi senator James O. Eastland declared that the ruling revealed "an alarming tendency to destroy State sovereignty" and amounted to Supreme Court usurpation of congressional functions. Senator Walter George of Georgia maintained that party primaries should not be subject to court control beyond punishment of fraud.[33] John H. Overton, senator from Louisiana, argued that the decision would tend to force the Negro vote upon the South. "We're not going to submit to Negro voting in our elections," he asserted, and added, "We don't need white primaries, or poll taxes. We can keep them out on educational qualifications."[34]

While the white northern press tended to be noncommittal about the decision, the southern editorial response split geographically. Editors in the Upper South, on the whole, hailed the decision, while some in the Deep South argued that it could and would be circumvented. The Greensboro, North Carolina, *News* remarked, "There will be a terrific protest from the deeper South. From this immediate part of the world we expect to hear little or no uproar." In Virginia, the editorial opinions of the two capital dailies, the Richmond *News Leader* and the *Times Dispatch,* were approbative. The *Times Dispatch* commented, "Since Negroes have been admitted to Democratic primaries in Virginia for many years, it is a little difficult to understand the tremendous amount of indignation and heat generated in the Deep South by the United States Supreme Court's decision that they have a right to enter such primaries everywhere. The skies haven't fallen in the Old Dominion because of participation by colored citizens in our primaries."

The reaction of the white press in Texas was mixed. The Dallas *Times Herald* deplored the decision of the Court, but asked Texans to do nothing about it "that might be construed as contempt of that august body." The editor appeasingly noted, however, that "a vote for the Negro in the Democratic primaries in Texas and other Southern states will not help" their situation. The San Antonio *Express* indignantly observed, "It did not require a Supreme Court decision to tell the people that . . . the Democratic primaries are, to all practical purposes, State elections, subject to State legal control." Nevertheless, the *Express* reassuringly added, the primary decision would not cause or "work

33. Ibid.
34. Washington *Post,* April 4, 1944.

a political revolution in the South." The Fort Worth *Star-Telegram*, on the other hand, refused to give in to the decision. The *Star-Telegram* calculated that it was "safe to presume that the Democratic party in the South will remain a 'white man's' party and that Texas, against which the newest and most formidable challenge is directed, will devise the pattern by which this status will be retained."[35]

The *Star-Telegram* was not alone in its desire to have the Democratic party remain a "white man's party." Many southern states soon attempted to preserve the white primary and nullify the *Smith* decision by removing all primary laws from the law books, and/or requiring loyalty oaths pledging to uphold the white supremacist principles of the Democratic party. The most determined effort to circumvent the Court's decision came from South Carolina. In 1938 the South Carolina General Assembly had empowered the state convention of political parties to define qualifications for party membership and for voting in county and municipal primary elections. This law had been designed to take advantage of the *Grovey* decision; the *Smith* ruling, of course, made such legislation unconstitutional. To circumvent the *Smith* decision, therefore, Governor Olin D. Johnston asked the legislature to repeal all of its 147 laws and the one constitutional provision relating to the conduct of primaries. In a speech delivered shortly after the *Smith* opinion, Johnston emphatically declared, "History has taught us that we must keep our white primaries pure and unadulterated so that we might protect the welfare and home of all people in our state." He vehemently proclaimed, "White Supremacy will be maintained in our primaries. Let the chips fall where they may!" The general assembly, accordingly, expunged all reference to primaries from the state constitution. The South Carolina Democratic State Convention also moved to preserve the purity of the white primary. The convention adopted a resolution requiring that membership in the Democratic club (and thus eligibility to vote in Democratic primaries) be limited to white Democrats who could read, write, and interpret the state constitution. Blacks were consequently to be barred from the upcoming primaries.[36]

35. "Southern Editorial Opinion on the Primary Decision," *The Crisis* 100 (June 1944): 186–87.

36. Ward E. Y. Elliott, *The Rise of Guardian Democracy*, 80; Walter White, *A Man Called White: The Autobiography of Walter White* (Bloomington: Indiana University Press, 1948), 89; Henry J. Abraham, *Freedom and the Court: Civil Rights and Liberties in the United States* (New York: Oxford University Press, 1972), 333; James O. Farmer, Jr., "The End of the White Primary in South Carolina: A Southern State's Fight to Keep Its Politics White" (master's thesis, University of South Carolina, 1969), 59.

One black South Carolinian decided to fight this restriction. George A. El-more, a black merchant in Columbia, South Carolina, contacted the NAACP and Marshall for assistance in initiating a suit against John D. Rice, Richland County Democratic Executive Committee chairman, to force the state to comply with the Supreme Court's *Smith* decision. Federal district judge J. Waties Waring, a tenth-generation member of the Charleston, South Carolina, aristocracy, heard pleadings in the case and ruled in Elmore's favor. Judge Waring branded the Democrats' attempted distinction between the situation before and after repeal of the primary laws as "pure sophistry." He rejected the assertion that the Democratic party was a private club not subject to federal control: "Private clubs and business organizations do not vote and elect a president of the United States ... Senators and ... members of our national Congress; and under the law of our land all citizens are entitled to a voice in such elections." He concluded: "It is time for South Carolina to rejoin the Union. It is time to fall in step with the other states and to adopt the American way of conducting elections."[37]

White South Carolina Democrats appealed the decision. On December 30, 1947, however, the Fourth Circuit Court of Appeals sitting in Richmond, Virginia, sustained Waring's ruling. Ironically, Chief Judge John J. Parker—the same individual who had been rejected as President Hoover's nominee to the United States Supreme Court in 1930 by a 41–39 vote, in part because of his alleged racial attitudes—wrote the opinion. Parker held that "Even though the election laws of South Carolina be fair on their face, yet if they be administered in such a way as to result in persons being denied any real voice in government because of race or color, it is idle to say that the power of the State is not being used in violating the Constitution." On April 19, 1948, the United States Supreme Court, apparently satisfied with Parker's reasoning, refused to review this ruling.[38]

The Supreme Court's refusal to review the Rice case for a time seemed to have administered the judicial *coup de grace* to the white primary. Yet white Texans were determined to make a last attempt to preserve, if not resurrect, the white primary. Since 1889, the white citizens of Fort Bend County had held preliminary elections under the auspices of the Jaybird Democratic Association. The Jaybirds conducted what amounted to "pre-primary" primaries early in May of each election year to endorse candidates for the Democratic nom-

37. *Elmore* v. *Rice*, 72 Fed. Supplement 516 (E.D.S.C., 1942); Farmer, "The End of the White Primary in South Carolina," 59; White, *A Man Called White*, 89–90.

38. *Elmore* v. *Rice*, 165 F. 2d, 387 (4th Circuit Court of Appeals, 1947); Cert. denied 333 U.S. 875 (1948); White, *A Man Called White*, 91; Abraham, *Freedom and the Court*, 333.

ination. The elections were independent of state law and were held at the expense of the members of the organization.[39]

Membership in the Jaybird organization was limited to white people. They were automatically members if their names appeared on the official list of county voters. The voting qualifications were identical to those of the state entitling electors to vote in county-operated primaries. The names of Jaybird nominees were put on the ballot in the Democratic primary without indication that they had been nominated by the organization. The sole purpose of the organization was to deny blacks any voice in the election of county officials.[40] Jaybird nominees invariably won in the Democratic primary, which as of 1944, was open to blacks and whites, and in the general elections that followed.

John Terry and Willie Melton, prosperous black farmers in Fort Bend County, and several black supporters pooled their resources and filed a class action suit against A. J. Adams and other officers of the Jaybird organization. The NAACP Legal Defense Fund declined to participate in the case. Marshall later explained that Terry "was well able to finance it himself."[41] Terry employed Houston attorney J. Edwin Smith to handle the litigation. The case was first argued in the district court before Judge Kennerly, who ruled that the Jaybird Democratic Association was a political party and not a private organization. The exclusion of blacks from Jaybird elections was therefore held to be unconstitutional in the light of *Smith* v. *Allwright*.

The Jaybird officers then took the case to the Fifth Circuit Court of Appeals, which reversed the district court's judgment. The appeals court declared that although the white voters in Fort Bend County were "vainly holding" to "outworn and outmoded" practices, the action of the association was not "action under color of State law" and was therefore, "not in violation of federal law."[42]

Terry, unwilling to accept this decision, appealed to the United States

39. *Terry* v. *Adams*, 345 U.S. 461 (1952); Pauline Yelderman, "The Jaybird Democratic Association of Fort Bend County" (master's thesis, University of Texas, 1938), 77–79; Nina Benware Margraves, "The Jaybird Democratic Association of Fort Bend County: A White Man's Union" (master's thesis, University of Houston, 1955), 45ff; Doris T. Asbury, "Negro Participation in the Primary and General Elections in Texas" (master's thesis, Boston University, 1951), 58–60; Millie R. Kochan, "The Jaybird-Woodpecker Feud: A Study in Social Conflict" (master's thesis, University of Texas, 1929), 48–63; Banks, "Pursuit of Equality," 341–43; Elliott, *The Rise of Guardian Democracy*, 81; Thurgood Marshall, "The Rise and Collapse of the 'White Democratic Primary,'" in *The Making of Black America*, vol. 2, ed. August Meier and Elliott Rudwick (New York: Atheneum, 1969), 274–79.

40. *Terry* v. *Adams*, 345 U.S. 461 (1952).

41. Marshall, quoted in Claude, *The Supreme Court*, 4.

42. Summarized in *Terry* v. *Adams*, 345 U.S. 461 (1952).

Supreme Court. And in 1952, the Court agreed to hear arguments in *Terry* v. *Adams,* the last of the white primary cases. James M. Nabrit joined attorney Smith in the oral arguments. The two lawyers asserted that the Jaybird party, "by engrafting its primaries onto the election processes of the state," had "become a de facto agency of the state subject to the Fourteenth and Fifteenth Amendments of the Constitution of the United States." They concluded their arguments with the contention that the Jaybird organization was "in actual fact the local Democratic Party."[43]

The defense attorneys, Edgar E. Townes, Jr., and Clarence I. McFarlance of Houston, argued that "the constitutional prohibition against abridgement or deprivation of civil rights applies only to state action." They maintained that the Jaybird Democratic Association was not a political party; it had been organized "in the sole interest of economic and honest county government and the election of honest and faithful county officials." They concluded: "The right to vote, protected by the Federal Constitution and statutes, is the right to vote in an official political election. These provisions do not cover voting in private organizations—fraternal, religious, labor, social, or even organizations political in character not exercising functions of the state nor participating in state electoral processes."[44]

Justice Black was joined by Douglas and Burton in announcing the opinion of the Court reversing the judgment of the court of appeals. Frankfurter, Clark, Vinson, Reed, and Jackson supported the opinion but for different reasons. Justice Sherman Minton dissented. Black, Douglas, and Burton based their opinion on the Fifteenth Amendment. They held that it prohibited a state from permitting any organization, private or not, to duplicate the state's election process, for the purpose and with the effect of stripping blacks of any influence in selecting county officials.

Frankfurter emphasized the fact that the county election officials participated in and condoned the continued effort effectively to exclude blacks from voting. He stressed the idea that the character of an act as state action was determined by its purpose and effect and that the failure of a state to condemn discriminatory practices touching on governmental functions constituted a denial of rights under the Fourteenth and Fifteenth Amendments. In his opinion, what the state permitted, happened.

Clark, Vinson, Reed, and Jackson rested their decision on the ground that the organization was a political party—operated as part and parcel of the

43. Ibid.
44. Ibid.

Democratic party—whose activities fell within the Fifteenth Amendment's self-executing ban. In sum, the Court saw the Jaybird party as much more than a private club. It was inseparable from the Democratic party, and its activities determined the final choice of candidates and their ultimate chances of election. Furthermore, the Court maintained that the characterization of an act as state action ought to be determined by its purpose and effect, and that the failure of a state to condemn discriminatory practices touching on governmental functions was clearly a denial of rights under the Fourteenth and Fifteenth Amendments.[45]

In a spirited dissent Justice Minton declared that while he was "not concerned in the least as to what happens to the Jaybirds or their unworthy scheme," he was concerned about how the Court defined state action within the meaning of the Fifteenth Amendment. He compared the Jaybirds to a pressure group. "It must be recognized that elections and other public business are influenced by all sorts of pressures from carefully organized groups. We have pressure from labor unions, from the National Association of Manufacturers, from the Silver Shirts, from the National Association for the Advancement of Colored People, from the Ku Klux Klan and others." He continued: "Far from the activities of these groups being properly labeled as state action under either the Fourteenth or Fifteenth Amendment, they are to be considered as attempts to influence or obtain state action." He argued that the organization's action was not forbidden by state law, and that the state's failure to prevent individuals from doing what they had the right as individuals to do did not amount to state action. Justice Minton found it difficult to comprehend the reasoning in the majority decision and attributed the opinion to other motivations. "Apparently it derives mainly from a dislike of the goals of the Jaybird Association. I share that dislike. I fail to see how it makes state action."[46]

The *Terry* v. *Adams* decision represented the last gasp of the Democratic white primary. The death of the white primary, unfortunately, did not signal the end of blacks' difficulties, in general, but it was a most significant victory in the black struggle for unfettered access to the political process. The major barrier between blacks and the ballot was now overcome, and with its destruction the black political revolution could be said to be well underway. The ballot, lost since Reconstruction, had now been retrieved, and the ongoing battle to destroy white supremacy would now be fought by blacks armed with "the most potent weapon in the democratic arsenal"—the vote.

45. Ibid.
46. Ibid.

# Afterword

## The Second Reconstruction

The *Smith* v. *Allwright* decision had a profound impact on constitutional jurisprudence and American politics. The implications of the decision likewise had far-reaching effects on race relations in the South. *Smith* was the watershed in the struggle for black rights. It signaled the beginning of the so-called Second Reconstruction and the modern civil rights movement. The political and social advances of blacks could not have occurred without the changes that came in the wake of the overthrow of the Democratic white primary.

The first Reconstruction, in many respects, was a political draw. It was successful in that the Fourteenth and Fifteenth Amendments were added to the United States Constitution. These amendments clearly were designed to grant and provide protection for black citizenship and voting rights. After 1877, however, southern whites, with the aid of the Supreme Court's restrictive interpretation of these amendments, particularly the Fifteenth, were able to devise quasi-constitutional subterfuges to strip the black man of the vote. Blacks were left defenseless against white supremacists. Their civil and economic position deteriorated proportionately to their political powerlessness.

The Democratic white primary, where enforced, was the most effective device adopted by southerners to disfranchise blacks. While the poll tax, literary requirements, and a variety of other measures significantly reduced black participation in the political process, they also worked in such a way as to restrict the suffrage of a large number of whites in the lower socioeconomic classes. The white primary, however, was in many ways a magnificent disfranchisement tool. It was a logical consequence of the development of the one-party South. By the turn of the century, the South was solidly Democratic and particular classes of whites reigned supreme.

Throughout the post–Civil War era, Democrats had struggled to solidify their hold on the South's political fortunes. The emergence of third parties, such as the Greenbackers in the 1870s and the Populists in the 1890s, formed from coalitions of dissidents in both major parties and blacks, posed a continuous threat to the hegemony of the Democratic party. Democratic leaders were concerned with three things. First, they had to buttress white supremacy with white solidarity. Second, they had to eliminate blacks completely from the political arena. Third, they had to remove the threat of third parties. These goals were achieved with the introduction and adoption of mandatory state-wide white primaries. No longer would blacks become political power brokers when whites divided to decide which group of whites would rule. With a vote-less black population and a restricted white electorate, white solidarity would be virtually assured. The factions within the Democratic party would replace the need for or stifle the impulse toward developing third parties.

The NAACP, as a black rights organization, was in a unique position to fight the white primary. It possessed a measure of financial resources and had access to eminent legal expertise unavailable to the individual black litigant. The Association leaders were determined that such a blatantly racist and discriminatory measure be declared unconstitutional by the United States Supreme Court. Blacks with improved educational and economic status could at least hope to overcome other obstacles such as the poll tax or literacy requirements. They would never, however, be able to overcome the obstacle of color.

The NAACP with its battery of top-flight constitutional lawyers (Moorfield Storey, Louis Marshall, etc.) initially decided to attack the white primary because the principle of exclusion based upon race affronted their constitutional sensibilities. The white primary laws, in their opinion, assaulted not only the Fourteenth and Fifteenth Amendments but went against their understanding of the total legal and judicial foundation upon which America was grounded. If white southern Democrats could get away with the white primary legislation, it only opened the door for the enactment of restrictive laws against other groups in the society.

After Storey's and Marshall's deaths, the NAACP continued its attack against the Democratic white primary under the leadership of James Marshall and Nathan Margold. By the mid-thirties, an increasing number of aroused Texas black citizens, most of whom were middle-class entrepreneurs and professionals, became caught up in the struggle against the white primary. These local leaders in Texas had the firm backing of blacks on the grassroots level who contributed their nickels and dimes to the fight. The attack on the white primary consequently took on additional significance.

The white primary struggle became more than one of principle. To the black Texans the white primary symbolized their powerlessness, their second-class citizenship, their caste-like position within the total society. Their efforts to acquire education, skills, and to improve their economic position amounted to very little if they could not vote. The lack of meaningful access to the ballot box undermined whatever gains that were made in other areas and only enhanced their vulnerability to the capriciousness of the whites. The ballot meant protection. With the vote blacks could defend themselves, their property, and their futures by electing those politicians most responsive to their needs.

One key group of black middle-class professionals was the small but growing collection of black lawyers. At the moment when the NAACP was searching for legal talent to replace the eminent white counsel who had died or had inadequate time and were no longer able to handle all of the Association's legal activities, young talented black lawyers, many of whom were trained and inspired by Charles Houston, needed the experience of arguing cases before the Supreme Court. They needed to build up esteem in the eyes of both blacks and whites. By the mid-thirties, the NAACP and black lawyers had come to recognize their interdependence and that cooperation was needed not only for the successful conclusion of the white primary fight but for their mutual advancement.

NAACP leaders, during the white primary campaign, also became aware of the essence of leadership. None of their programs and activities would succeed unless they were fundamentally linked to local leaders—men and women whom the black community in a given locale viewed or selected to be its representatives. As illustrated in the aftermath of *Grovey* v. *Townsend,* rank-and-file blacks and their representatives were no longer content to receive directives from afar. They demanded to be active participants in their liberation struggles. The NAACP was able to survive and grow stronger as an organization when it realized this and made certain concessions and alterations in its *modus operandi.* Walter White, Charles Houston, and Thurgood Marshall in preparing for the *Smith* case launched an all-out effort to involve local leaders. To be sure, this approach was nonrevolutionary. The fact remains, however, that it worked. By adopting the practice of national control with local-level consultation, the NAACP was able to turn the white primary into a virtual mass movement in Texas and gained even greater support. The white primary became a rallying cry for black Texans and assisted them in developing black solidarity. It is ironic that the white primary served both races so well. When initially conceived it was a basis for white solidarity, but the process of fighting to overturn it led to the unity of blacks.

The black victory against the white primary could not have been achieved without a responsive Supreme Court. By 1944 the Supreme Court reflected more determination to end the white primary–black disfranchisement charade than at any time previously. This new attitude can perhaps be attributed to the influence of President Roosevelt and the ideology underlying his New Deal programs. Seven of the nine Supreme Court judges ruling in *Smith* were Roosevelt appointees. Most of them were favorably disposed towards the black cause. Moreover, these men continually reflected deep concern with practical and sophisticated infringements on the rights of all American citizens.

The liberal outlook of the new Roosevelt appointees to the Supreme Court was, in part, influenced by the crises of war. World War II aroused antipathy towards racism within the American population. Hitler's Nazism and the extermination of large numbers of Jews shocked Americans into a deeper awareness of the consequences of excessive racial hatred and bigotry. America's entry into the war also underscored the necessity of pulling together to fight a common foe. Black fighting men and blacks in general resolved that in the aftermath of this war, second-class citizenship and "business [racism] as usual" would not continue. The black community developed both a sense of urgency and a new level of militancy. The hypocrisy of fighting for liberty abroad and oppression at home became too glaring for any segment of the country to ignore. The white primary was one of the casualties of World War II. Its death gave rise to a new era in American constitutional, political, and civil life.

The Supreme Court in *Smith* answered questions that had haunted it since the late nineteenth century. It now demolished existing legal and constitutional doctrines. The Court conceded that the Fifteenth Amendment could protect voting rights from private as well as state infringement. Article I, Section 4 empowered Congress to control private and state action when a case involved federal elections. The Fourteenth Amendment had nothing to do with voting rights. Both amendments definitely prohibited state action. In a sense, just as the Supreme Court had provided the constitutional basis for the construction of the edifice of white supremacy, after *Smith* it set in motion judicial shock waves which would undermine the entire structure. The logic of the decision eventually led the Court to rule against restrictive covenants and educational segregation and to reassess state apportionment practices.

As a consequence of expanding the "state-action" theory in *Smith*, the Court in 1948 was able unanimously to declare restrictive covenants unconstitutional. Restrictive covenants were agreements among private individuals adopted to prohibit the selling or leasing of property in a given neighborhood "to any one of any race other than the Caucasian."[1] In *Shelley* v. *Kraemer*, the

---

1. Clement Vose, *Caucasians Only: The Supreme Court, the NAACP, and the Restrictive Covenant Cases* (Berkeley: University of California Press, 1967), vi.

Court observed that while the formation of restrictive covenants was by private action, their purposes "were secured only by judicial enforcement by state courts." The Court held that judicial enforcement of covenants restricting the use or occupancy of real property to Caucasians violated the equal protection clause of the Fourteenth Amendment. The Court conceded that the Fourteenth Amendment was directed against state action only and did not apply to private conduct. However, the Court reasoned that judicial action, even for the enforcement of private agreements, was state action and within the Fourteenth Amendment's field of operation.[2]

With similar clarity the Supreme Court rendered white supremacy another blow in the 1954 *Brown* v. *Board of Education* case.[3] In *Brown,* the Court ruled that separate educational facilities for white and black children were inherently unequal. Segregated schools deprived black children of the equal protection of the laws guaranteed by the Fourteenth Amendment. The *Brown* ruling was subsequently extended to prohibit racial segregation in remaining areas of public life.

The Supreme Court's progress toward a broader reading of the equal protection of the laws clause of the Fourteenth Amendment led it to decide on the decency of state apportionment. Malapportionment essentially reduced city-dwellers to second-class citizens. In the 1962 *Baker* v. *Carr*[4] case, the Court found that territorial divisions could and did discriminate against the urban areas of a state in both legislative representation and the distribution of state revenue. The Court held malapportionment to violate the equal protection of the laws clause. The "one man, one vote" standard voiced by the Court commenced the reapportionment revolution in which every district of a state had to be equal in its population. The *Baker* v. *Carr* decision, followed by the 1964 *Reynolds* v. *Sims* opinion, "marked a revolutionary shift of political power to the metropolitan areas which would redirect the course of American politics and change state political patterns that in some instances had existed for half a century," according to one scholar.[5]

It would be difficult to exaggerate the political significance of the white primary cases. In 1940, 5 percent of voting age blacks were registered in the South;

2. Ibid., 205–7; *Shelley* v. *Kraemer,* 334 U.S. 1 (1948).
3. *Brown* v. *Board of Education,* 347 U.S. 483 (1954); Richard Kluger, *Simple Justice: The History of* Brown *v.* Board of Education *and Black America's Struggle for Equality* (New York: Vintage Books, 1975), 707.
4. *Baker* v. *Carr,* 369 U.S. 186 (1962).
5. Richard C. Cortnet, *The Apportionment Cases* (Knoxville: University of Tennessee Press, 1970), 155, 228, 251.

after *Smith,* black registration increased to 12 percent. By 1956, 25 percent of southern blacks were registered.[6] The Texas figures illustrate even more the political impact of *Smith.* In 1940, only 30,000 black Texans were registered. By 1947 the number more than tripled to 100,000. The total number of registered Texas blacks was exceeded only by Georgia. In that state the figures increased from 20,000 in 1940 to 125,000 in 1947. Twelve years after *Smith,* the 214,000 black Texans registered to vote far exceeded that of any southern state. Georgia ranked second with 163,389 blacks registered to vote, followed by Louisiana with 152,378.[7]

This increase in black registration and voting did not proceed without white opposition. The immediate reaction of white Democrats in Georgia is illuminating. In 1944 Georgia repealed her constitutional poll-tax requirement for voting and liberalized her suffrage provisions. At the same time, however, the state legislature deleted all constitutional provisions pertaining to primaries in an attempt to remove them from state control. The Democratic committee then adopted a resolution that "all white electors who are Democrats and qualified to vote in the general election, and who in good faith pledge themselves to support the Democratic candidates for all the offices to be voted on this year, are hereby qualified to vote in such primary." Consequently blacks were generally refused primary ballots.[8]

A black challenge to this restrictive resolution was sustained by the federal district court and the Fifth United States Circuit Court of Appeals. The U.S. Supreme Court refused to review the decision by denying certiorari. The state Democratic executive committee as a result opened the 1946 primaries to blacks. It is estimated that approximately 100,000 of the 125,000 registered blacks voted. In 1947 in a feeble attempt to preserve "white supremacy," the state Democratic rules committee adopted a "white primary" under which blacks were required to vote in separate buildings from white voters.[9]

The national Democratic and Republican parties were affected by reenfranchisement of hundreds of thousands of black voters. Neither party had ever seriously attacked the white primary. Even President Roosevelt had remained silent on the issue, possibly from understandable fear. Republicans

---

6. Ward E. Y. Elliott, *The Rise of Guardian Democracy: The Supreme Court and Voting Rights Disputes, 1845–1969* (Cambridge: Harvard University Press, 1974), 85–86.

7. Steven F. Lawson, *Black Ballots: Voting Rights in the South, 1944–1969* (New York: Columbia University Press, 1976), 134.

8. O. Douglas Weeks, "The White Primary: 1944–1948," *American Political Science Review* 42, no. 3 (June 1948): 500–510.

9. Ibid., 506–7.

feared, perhaps, that if the white primaries were overthrown even more blacks would embrace the Democratic party. After all, the majority of blacks had voted for Roosevelt in 1936. Moreover, the Republican party, particularly under Hoover, had done little to solicit or maintain black allegiance.

The Democratic party's national leaders feared that an attack on the white primary from their quarters would, perhaps, split their own regional factions by alienating white southerners.[10] Their apprehensions were justified as Texas events following *Smith* illustrate. O. Douglas Weeks observed that in May 1944, the Democratic convention, dominated by "regular" Democrats, denounced the *Smith* decision and selected a national convention delegation and an electoral slate opposed to President Roosevelt. A bolting convention at the same time selected pro-Roosevelt delegates and electoral candidates. Later in 1944, the September state Democratic convention nominated a pro-Roosevelt electoral ticket. The Texas Supreme Court upheld the latter as the official Democratic electoral list. The "regular" Democrats became the "Texas Regulars" and intra-party antagonisms continued into 1946.[11] In spite of these protestations it was clearly evident that a new political day was dawning and that the black vote would soon become a force in American politics with which both parties would have to reckon.

The rise of rights-consciousness in the Supreme Court encouraged the development of the same in both the legislative and executive branches of government. Every president since Roosevelt has paid at least lip service to black rights. Their actions and utterances have often left much to be desired. Nevertheless, the new consciousness is an improvement over the neglect and indifference of presidents in the early twentieth century.

The Congress also, influenced by the spirit of the modern Supreme Court, became more amenable to protecting black rights. In August 1957, the Senate voted on, and on September 9th Eisenhower signed into law, the first Civil Rights Act of the twentieth century. The act was regarded as a victory for black enfranchisement. It established a Civil Rights Commission to protect against interference with constitutional rights by private persons. Three years later the U.S. Congress passed the Civil Rights Act of 1960. This legislation empowered the attorney general to examine voting records and provided for court-appointed federal referees to register voters in areas where the courts found discrimination.[12]

The Voting Rights Act of 1965 was the most important legislation protect-

10. Elliott, *The Rise of Guardian Democracy,* 87–88.
11. Weeks, "The White Primary," 502–3.
12. Elliott, *The Rise of Guardian Democracy,* 82; Lawson, *Black Ballots,* 199, 290, 405.

ing the franchise rights of blacks. It signaled the coalescence of federal legislative and executive commitment to the free ballot. This act was to remain in effect for five years and applied to those states and districts (mostly southern)
where less than 50 percent of adult blacks were registered for the 1964 elections. The act authorized suspension of state tests and substitution of federal
examiners to register blacks where discrimination was evidenced. The act also
established a sixth-grade education as proof of literacy. President Johnson declared on August 6, 1965, "[W]e will not delay or we will not hesitate, or will
not turn aside until Americans of every race and color and origin in this country have the same rights as all others to share in the progress of democracy."[13]
The Justice Department moved quickly into action.

Federal examiners were deployed to selected counties in the five southern
states (Alabama, Mississippi, Georgia, Louisiana, and South Carolina). The
immediate results were noteworthy. One scholar observes that "on the first an-
niversary of the passage of the Voting Rights Act, an average of 46 percent of
adult blacks in the five Deep South states to which examiners had been assigned could vote, thereby doubling the percentage from the year before."[14]

The cumulative effects of the political and constitutional developments
since *Smith* can be seen in the fact that by 1973 blacks held 2,627 elected offices nationwide. Approximately half of these black elected officials were in the
South. To be sure, these figures constitute far less than 1 percent of the estimated 500,000 elective offices in the nation. Moreover, the figure would have
to increase to 12 percent to make black officeholders proportional to the numbers of blacks in the total population.[15] Nevertheless, the increase in the number of black officeholders represented an enormous advance from pre-*Smith*
and pre-reapportionment days.

The Supreme Court's "modern" position as guardian of democracy served
black rights well. Its broadening interpretation of the applicability of the Fourteenth and Fifteenth Amendments has, however, created problems with which
the Court is still grappling. In recent litigation, such as the 1972 *O'Brien* v.
*Brown*[16] and *Cousins* v. *Wigoda*,[17] and the 1977 *Elrod* v. *Burns* cases,[18] the
Court has encountered difficulties which raise questions of the continued
desirability of its "modern" viewpoint.

Both the O'Brien and Cousins cases asked the Supreme Court to settle dis-

13. *Public Papers of the Presidents, Lyndon B. Johnson,* 1965, 2: 843, quoted in Lawson,
*Black Ballots,* 329.
14. Lawson, *Black Ballots,* 330.
15. Elliott, *The Rise of Guardian Democracy,* 221.
16. *O'Brien* v. *Brown,* 409 U.S. 1 (1972).
17. *Cousins* v. *Wigoda,* 409 U.S. 1201 (1972).
18. *Elrod* v. *Burns,* 427 U.S. 347 (1977).

putes arising from the Democratic National Convention's Credential Committee's refusal to seat certain delegates from Illinois and California. On the eve of the 1972 convention, the Court was reluctant to engage in a hasty consideration of the delegate dispute. Furthermore, the justices could not agree on whether it was a political or judicial question. In the O'Brien case the Court evidenced marked unwillingness to undertake final resolution of the important constitutional questions presented concerning "justiciability, due process, and rights of association."[19] To have made a definite decision would have involved the Court in adjudicating the internal deliberations of a national political party.

In *Elrod* v. *Burns*, a badly divided Court, in separate opinions, affirmed a Seventh Circuit Court's decision that political patronage dismissal of non–civil service employees violated the First and Fourteenth Amendments. Justices Brennan, Marshall, and White decided that "the practice of patronage, especially patronage dismissal, placed severe restrictions on First Amendment freedoms of political belief and association." Justices Blackmun and Stewart concurred. They emphasized that "nonpolicymaking, nonconfidential government employees could not be discharged from a job on sole ground of his political beliefs, it being unnecessary in the instant case to consider the broad contours of the patronage system or the constitutionality of confining the hiring of some governmental employees to those of a particular political party."[20]

Chief Justice Burger dissented. He argued that the Court's decision represented an improper intrusion into the area of legislative and policy concerns. Justices Powell and Rehnquist wrote a dissenting opinion in which Burger concurred. They voiced the view that "even assuming that beneficiaries of the patronage system could challenge the system when their turn came to be replaced, nevertheless the burdens imposed on First Amendment interests of employees by patronage hiring were justified by the state's interest in stimulating political activity and strengthening parties, particularly at the local level, thereby helping to make government and political parties accountable to the voters." The dissenters cautioned: "If a thing has been practiced for two hundred years it will need a strong case for the Fourteenth Amendment to affect it." They concluded, "The judgement today unnecessarily constitutionalizes another element of American life."[21] Justice Stevens did not participate.

How the Court will ultimately resolve the questions raised by *Smith* v. *Allwright*, which it did not answer at the time, remains to be seen.

---

19. *O'Brien* v. *Brown*, 409 U.S. 1 (1972).
20. *Elrod* v. *Burns*, 427 U.S. 347 (1977).
21. Ibid.

# Bibliography

## Manuscripts

Allred, James V. Papers. University of Houston. Houston, Texas.

Department of Justice Files. National Archives. Washington, D.C.

Frankfurter, Felix. Papers. Manuscript Division, Library of Congress. Washington, D.C.

Marshall, Louis. Papers. Jewish Union Theological Seminary. Cincinnati, Ohio.

Moody, Dan. Papers. Archives Division, Texas State Library. Austin, Texas.

National Association for the Advancement of Colored People Archives. Manuscript Division, Library of Congress. Washington, D.C.

Nixon, L. A. Papers. Lyndon Baines Johnson Library. University of Texas. Austin, Texas.

Spingarn, Arthur Barnett. Papers. Library of Congress. Washington, D.C.

## NAACP Documents

*Annual Report of the NAACP,* 1911–1944.

*The Crisis,* 1910–1944.

*The Mobbing of John R. Shillady, Secretary of the NAACP, Austin, Texas, August 22, 1919.* New York: NAACP, 1919.

## Public Documents

General Laws of Texas. *38th Legislature Journal,* 2d Called Session (Austin, 1923).

House Journal. *38 Legislature,* 2d Called Session (Austin, 1923), April 25, 1923, p. 1295.

Journal of the House of Representatives of Texas. *40th Legislature,* 1st Called Session (Austin, 1927).

The Revised Civil Statutes of Texas, 1925.

Senate Journal. *38th Legislature,* 2d Called Session (Austin, 1923).
U.S. Bureau of the Census. *Negroes in the United States, 1920–1932.* Washington, D.C.: U.S. Government Printing Office, 1935.

## Court Decisions

*Baker* v. *Carr,* 369 U.S. 186 (1962).
*Bell et al.* v. *Hill, County Clerk et al.,* 74 Southwestern Reporter (2d), 8, pp. 113–22 (Texas, 1934).
*Brown* v. *Board of Education,* 347 U.S. 483 (1954).
*C. F. Richardson et al.* v. *Executive Committee of Democratic Party of Houston,* Civil Action No. 20, United States District Court for the Southern District of Texas.
*Chandler* v. *Neff,* 298 Fed. 515 (W.D. Texas, 1924).
*Civil Rights Cases,* 109 U.S. 3, Ct. 18 (1883).
*County Democratic Committee in and for Bexar County et al.* v. *C. A. Booker,* 52 W.W. 52 S.W. (2d) 908 (Texas, 1932).
*County Democratic Executive Committee* v. *Booker,* 53 S.W. (2d) 123 (Texas, 1932).
*Cousins* v. *Wigoda,* 409 U.S. 1201 (1972).
*Drake* v. *Executive Committee of the Democratic Party for the City of Houston,* 2F Supp. 486 (S.D. Texas, 1933).
*Elmore* v. *Rice,* 72 Fed. Supp. 516 (E.D.S.C., 1942).
*Elmore* v. *Rice,* 165 F. 2d 387 (4th Circuit Court of Appeals, 1947).
*Elmore* v. *Rice,* 333 U.S. 875 (1948).
*Elrod* v. *Burns,* 427 U.S. 347 (1977).
*Giles* v. *Harris,* 189 U.S. 475 (1903).
*Grovey* v. *Townsend,* 295 U.S. 45 (1935).
*Guinn* v. *United States,* 238 U.S. 347 (1915).
*Herndon* v. *Georgia,* 295 U.S. 446 (1935).
*Hollins* v. *State of Oklahoma,* 295 U.S. 394 (1935).
*Kay* v. *Schneider,* 218 S.W. 479 (1920).
*Love* v. *Griffith,* 236 S.W. 239 (Texas Civ. Appl. 1922).
*Love* v. *Griffith,* 266 U.S. 32 (1924).
*Newberry* v. *United States,* 256 U.S. 232 (1921).
*Nixon* v. *Condon,* 34F (2d) 464 (W.D. Texas, 1929).
*Nixon* v. *Condon,* 49F (2d) 1012 (C.C.A. 5th, 1931).
*Nixon* v. *Condon,* 286 U.S. 73 (1932).
*Nixon* v. *Herndon,* 273 U.S. 538 (1927).

*Nixon* v. *Herndon,* 994 Law, U.S. District Court, Western District of Texas.

*Norris* v. *Alabama,* 294 U.S. 587 (1935).

*O'Brien* v. *Brown,* 409 U.S. 1 (1972).

*Plessy* v. *Ferguson,* 163 U.S. 537 (1896).

*Powell* v. *Alabama,* 287 U.S. 45 (1932).

*Reynolds* v. *Sims,* 377 U.S. 533 (1964).

*Robinson* v. *Holman,* 282 U.S. 804 (1930).

*Shelley* v. *Kraemer,* 334 U.S. 1 (1948).

*Slaughterhouse Cases,* 16 Wall 36 (1873).

*Smith* v. *Allwright,* 321 U.S. 657 (1944).

*Terry* v. *Adams,* 345 U.S. 461 (1952).

*United States* v. *Classic,* 313 U.S. 299 (1941).

*United States* v. *Cruikshank,* 92 U.S. 542 (1876).

*United States* v. *Harris,* 106 U.S. 629 (1883).

*United States* v. *Reese,* 92 U.S. 214 (1976).

*Waples* v. *Marrast,* 184 S.W. 180 (1916).

*West* v. *Bliley,* 33f (2d) 177 (E.D. Va. 1929).

*West* v. *Bliley,* 42f (2d) 101 (1930).

*White* v. *Harris County Democratic Executive Committee,* 60F (2d) 973 (S.D. Texas, 1932).

*Williams* v. *Mississippi,* 170 U.S. 213 (1898).

## Newspapers

*Arkansas Gazette,* 1928.

Austin *Statesman,* 1927.

Bay City *Tribune,* 1934.

Dallas *Daily Times Herald,* 1892.

Dallas *Express,* 1927, 1941, 1942.

Dallas *Morning News,* 1891, 1892, 1916, 1927, 1930, 1942.

El Paso *Herald,* 1927.

El Paso *Herald-Post,* 1934.

El Paso *Post,* 1928.

Fort Worth *Star,* 1934.

Galveston *Daily News,* 1916.

Houston *Informer,* 1927, 1930, 1931, 1932, 1934, 1935, 1938, 1944.

Houston *Post,* 1934, 1935.

Houston *Post-Dispatch,* 1927.

New York *Age,* 1927.

New York *Herald-Tribune*, 1927.
*New York Times,* 1944.
New York *World,* 1927.
Philadelphia *Tribune,* 1935.
Pittsburgh *Courier,* 1942.
Richmond *Planet,* 1927.
San Antonio *Express,* 1922, 1923.
Savannah *Tribune,* 1928, 1941, 1942, 1943.
*The Texas Weekly* (Dallas), 1935.
Tyler *Telegram,* 1934.
Washington *Post,* 1944.

## Interviews

Hastie, William H. Judge, Third Circuit Court of Appeals, Philadelphia, Pennsylvania. Interview, November 27, 1973.
Nabrit, Dr. James M. Former President of Howard University, Washington, D.C. Interview, April 6, 1974.
Wilkins, Roy. Executive Director, NAACP, New York, New York. Interview, April 19, 1972.

## Unpublished Materials

Asbury, Doris. "Negro Participation in the Primary and General Elections in Texas." Master's thesis, Boston University, 1951.
Banks, Melvin James. "The Pursuit of Equality: The Movement for First Class Citizenship among Negroes in Texas, 1920–1950." Ph.D. diss., Syracuse University, 1962.
Chamberlain, Charles Kincheloe. "Alexander Watkins Terrell, Citizen, Statesman." Ph.D. diss., University of Texas, 1956.
Duke, Escal Franklin. "The Political Career of Morris Sheppard, 1875–1941." Ph.D. diss., University of Texas, 1958.
Farmer, James O., Jr. "The End of the White Primary in South Carolina: A Southern State's Fight to Keep Its Politics White." Master's thesis, University of South Carolina, 1969.
Garner, W. T. "The Primaries in Texas." Master's thesis, University of Texas, 1920.
Goldman, Robert Michael. "A Free Ballot and a Fair Count: The Enforcement

of Voting Rights in the South, 1877–1893." Ph.D. diss., Michigan State University, 1976.

Goodwyn, Lawrence Corbett, "The Origins and Development of American Populism." Ph.D. diss., University of Texas, 1941.

Greene, Howard Mell. "Legal Regulation of Political Parties in Texas." Master's thesis, University of Texas, 1923.

Grose, Charles William. "Black Newspapers in Texas, 1868–1970." Ph.D. diss., University of Texas, 1972.

Hinze, Virginia Neal. "Norris Wright Cuney." Master's thesis, Rice University, 1965.

Kochan, Millie L. "The Jaybird-Woodpecker Feud." Master's thesis, University of Texas, 1929.

Lindsey, Walter. "Black Houstonians Fight against the Texas White Primary." Master's thesis, University of Houston, 1971.

Margreaves, Nina Benware. "The Jaybird Democratic Association of Fort Bend County: A White Man's Union." Master's thesis, University of Houston, 1955.

Moore, Sue E. Winston. "Thomas B. Love, Texas Democrat, 1901–1949." Master's thesis, University of Texas, 1971.

Perry, Douglass Geraldyne. "Black Populism: The Negro in the People's Party in Texas." Master's thesis, Prairie View University, 1945.

Stroud, Roy Wallace. "The Run-off Primary." Master's thesis, University of Texas, 1941.

Tarver, Harold M. "The Whiteman's Primary." (An Open Letter to D. A. McAskill, 1922.) Texas State Historical Library, Austin, Texas.

Tillman, Nathaniel Patrick. "Walter Francis White: A Study in Interest Group Leadership." Ph.D. diss., University of Wisconsin, 1961.

Watt, Donley E., Jr. "The Presidential Election of 1928 in Texas." Master's thesis, University of Texas, 1970.

Wood, Dale Brown. "The Poll Tax as a Voting Requirement." Master's thesis, University of Texas, 1942.

Yelderman, Pauline. "The Jaybird Democratic Association of Fort Bend County." Master's thesis, University of Texas, 1938.

## Books

Abraham, Henry J. *Freedom and the Court: Civil Rights and Liberties in the United States.* 2d ed. New York: Oxford University Press, 1972.

Alexander, Charles C. *The Crusade for Conformity: The Ku Klux Klan in Tex-*

*as, 1920–1930.* Houston: Texas Gulf Coast Historical Association, 1962.

———. *The Ku Klux Klan in the Southwest.* Lexington: University of Kentucky Press, 1966.

Alsop, Joseph, and Turner Catledge. *The 168 Days.* Garden City, N.Y.: Doubleday, Doran, 1938.

Argersinger, Peter H. *Populism and Politics: William Alfred Peffer and the People's Party.* Lexington: University of Kentucky Press, 1974.

Atkins, J. Alston. *The Texas Negro and His Political Rights: A History of the Fight of Negroes to Enter the Democratic Primaries of Texas.* Houston: Webster Publishing, 1932.

Auerbach, Jerold S. *Unequal Justice: Lawyers and Social Change in Modern America.* New York: Oxford University Press, 1976.

Bardolph, Richard, ed. *The Civil Rights Record: Black Americans and the Law, 1849–1970.* New York: Crowell, 1970.

Barr, Alwyn. *Black Texans: A History of Negroes in Texas, 1528–1971.* Austin: Jenkins Publishing, 1973.

———. *Reconstruction to Reform: Texas Politics, 1896–1906.* Austin: University of Texas Press, 1971.

Berger, Raoul. *Government by Judiciary: The Transformation of the Fourteenth Amendment.* Cambridge: Harvard University Press, 1977.

Brisbane, Robert H. *The Black Vanguard: Origins of the Negro Social Revolution, 1900–1960.* Valley Forge, Pa.: Judson Press, 1970.

Bryson, Conrey. *Dr. Lawrence A. Nixon and the White Primary.* El Paso: Texas Western Press and University of Texas at El Paso, 1974.

Bunche, Ralph J. *The Political Status of the Negro in the Age of FDR.* Ed. Dewey W. Grantham. Chicago: University of Chicago Press, 1973.

Buni, Andrew. *The Negro in Virginia Politics, 1902–1965.* Charlottesville: University Press of Virginia, 1967.

Burns, James MacGregor. *Roosevelt: The Lion and the Fox.* New York: Harcourt, Brace and World, 1956.

Carter, Dan T. *Scottsboro: A Tragedy of the American South.* New York: Oxford University Press, 1969.

Claude, Richard. *The Supreme Court and the Electoral Process.* Baltimore: Johns Hopkins Press, 1970.

Corner, Richard C. *The Apportionment Cases.* Knoxville: University of Tennessee Press, 1970.

Curtis, James C., and Lewis L. Gould, eds. *The Black Experience in America.* Austin: University of Texas Press, 1970.

Davidson, Chandler. *Biracial Politics: Conflict and Coalition in the Metropolitan South.* Baton Rouge: Louisiana State University Press, 1972.

Du Bois, W. E. B. *The Autobiography of W. E. B. Du Bois.* New York: International Publishers, 1968.

Elliott, Ward E. Y. *The Rise of Guardian Democracy: The Supreme Court's Role in Voting Rights Disputes, 1845–1969.* Cambridge: Harvard University Press, 1974.

Fishel, Leslie H., Jr., and Benjamin Quarles, eds. *The Black American: A Documentary History.* Glenview, Ill.: Scott, Foresman, 1970.

Fox, Stephen R. *The Guardian of Boston, William Monroe Trotter.* New York: Atheneum, 1971.

Franklin, John Hope. *Reconstruction: After the Civil War.* Chicago: University of Chicago Press, 1961.

Frazier, E. Franklin. *Black Bourgeoisie.* New York: Collier Books, 1962.

Garfinkel, Herbert. *When Negroes March: The March on Washington Movement in the Organizational Politics for FEPC.* New York: Atheneum, 1969.

Gillette, William. *The Right to Vote: Politics and the Passage of the Fifteenth Amendment.* Baltimore: Johns Hopkins University Press, 1965.

Gould, Lewis. *Progressives and Prohibitionists: Texas Democrats in the Age of Wilson.* Austin: University of Texas Press, 1975.

Grimes, Alan P. *The Puritan Ethic and Woman Suffrage.* New York: Oxford University Press, 1967.

Hare, Maud Cuney. *Norris Wright Cuney: A Tribute of the Black People.* 1913. Reprint, Austin: Steck-Vaughn, 1968.

Harlan, Louis. *Booker T. Washington: The Making of a Black Leader, 1856–1901.* New York: Oxford University Press, 1972.

Haynes, Robert V. *A Night of Violence: The Houston Riot of 1917.* Baton Rouge: Louisiana State University Press, 1976.

Hirshson, Stanley P. *Farewell to the Bloody Shirt: Northern Republicans and the Southern Negro, 1877–1893.* Bloomington: Indiana University Press, 1962.

Hixson, William B., Jr. *Moorfield Storey and the Abolitionist Tradition.* New York: Oxford University Press, 1972.

Hofstadter, Richard. *The Age of Reform: From Bryan to F.D.R.* New York: Vantage Books, 1960.

Hyman, Harold M. *A More Perfect Union: The Impact of the Civil War and Reconstruction on the Constitution.* New York: Alfred A. Knopf, 1973.

Jackson, A. W. *A Sure Foundation and a Sketch of Negro Life in Texas.* Houston: Yates Publishing, 1940.

Jackson, Kenneth T. *The Ku Klux Klan in the City, 1915–1930.* New York: Oxford University Press, 1967.

Johnson, James Weldon. *Along This Way: The Autobiography of James Weldon Johnson.* New York: Viking Press, 1933.

Kellogg, Charles Flint. *NAACP: A History of the Association for the Advancement of Colored People.* Baltimore: Johns Hopkins University Press, 1967.

Kelly, Alfred H., and Winfred A. Harbison. *The American Constitution: Its Origins and Development.* 3d ed. New York: Norton, 1963.

Key, V. O., Jr. *Southern Politics in State and Nation.* New York: Alfred A. Knopf, 1949.

Kluger, Richard. *Simple Justice: The History of Brown v. Board of Education and Black America's Struggle for Equality.* New York: Alfred A. Knopf, 1976.

Konvitz, Milton R. *The Constitution and Civil Rights.* New York: Columbia University Press, 1947.

Kousser, J. Morgan. *The Shaping of Southern Politics: Suffrage Restrictions and the Establishment of the One-Party South, 1880–1910.* New Haven: Yale University Press, 1974.

Kraditor, Aileen S. *The Ideas of the Woman Suffrage Movement, 1890–1920.* New York: Columbia University Press, 1965.

Kutler, Stanley I. *Judicial Power and Reconstruction Politics.* Chicago: University of Chicago Press, 1968.

Lawson, Steven A. *Black Ballots: Voting Rights in the South, 1949–1969.* New York: Columbia University Press, 1976.

Leuchtenburg, William E. *Franklin D. Roosevelt and the New Deal.* New York: Harper and Row, 1963.

Lewinson, Paul. *Race, Class, and Party: A History of Negro Suffrage and White Politics in the South.* New York: Oxford University Press, 1932.

Martin, Charles H. *The Angelo Herndon Case and Southern Justice.* Baton Rouge: Louisiana State University Press, 1976.

Mason, Alpheus Thomas. *Harlan Fiske Stone: Pillar of the Law.* New York: Viking Press, 1956.

———. *The Supreme Court from Taft to Warren.* Revised ed. Baton Rouge: Louisiana State University Press, 1968.

Matthews, Donald R., and James W. Prothro. *Negroes and the New Southern Politics.* New York: Harcourt, Brace and World, 1966.

Meier, August. *Negro Thought in America, 1880–1915.* Ann Arbor: University of Michigan Press, 1963.

Meier, August, and Elliott Rudwick, eds. *The Making of Black America.* Vol. 2. New York: Atheneum, 1969.

Merriam, Charles Edward, and Louise Overacker. *Primary Elections.* Chicago: University of Chicago Press, 1928.

Miller, Loren. *The Petitioners: The Story of the Supreme Court of the United States and the Negro.* New York: Pantheon Books, 1966.

Moore, Walter B. *Governors of Texas.* Dallas: Dallas *Morning News,* 1973.

*The Negro Problem: A Series of Articles by Representative American Negroes of Today.* 1903. Reprint, Miami, Fla.: Mnemosyne Publishing, 1969.

Ovington, Mary White. *The Walls Came Tumbling Down.* 1947. Reprint, New York: Harcourt, Brace and World, 1970.

Parker, Richard Denny. *Historical Recollections of Robertson County, Texas.* Ed. Nona Clement Parker. Salada, Tex.: Anson Jones Press, 1955.

Parsons, Stanley B. *The Populist Context: Rural versus Urban Power on a Great Plains Frontier.* Westport, Conn.: Greenwood Press, 1971.

Price, Hugh Douglas. *The Negro and Southern Politics: A Chapter in Florida History.* New York: New York University Press, 1957.

Ramsdell, Charles William. *Reconstruction in Texas.* 1910. Reprint, Austin: University of Texas Press, 1969.

Redkey, Edwin S. *Black Exodus: Black Nationalist and Back-to-Africa Movements, 1890–1910.* New Haven: Yale University Press, 1969.

Rice, Arnold S. *The Ku Klux Klan in American Politics.* Washington, D.C.: Public Affairs Press, 1962.

Rice, Lawrence D. *The Negro in Texas, 1874–1900.* Baton Rouge: Louisiana State University Press, 1971.

Richardson, Rupert Norval. *Texas: The Lone Star State.* New York: Prentice Hall, 1943.

Rosenstock, Morton. *Louis Marshall, Defender of Jewish Rights.* Detroit: Wayne State University Press, 1965.

Ross, B. Joyce. *J. E. Spingarn and the Rise of the NAACP.* New York: Atheneum, 1972.

Schlesinger, Arthur M., Jr., ed. *The Coming of Power: Critical Presidential Elections in American History.* New York: Chelsea House Publishers, 1971, 1972.

———. *The Politics of Upheaval: The Age of Roosevelt.* Boston: Houghton Mifflin, 1960.

Schwartz, Bernard, ed. *The Fourteenth Amendment: A Centennial Volume.* New York: New York University Press, 1970.

Shadgett, Olive Hall. *The Republican Party in Georgia: From Reconstruction through 1900.* Athens: University of Georgia Press, 1964.

Sternsher, Bernard, ed. *The Negro in Depression and War: Prelude to Revolution, 1930–1945.* Chicago: Quadrangle Books, 1969.

Styles, Fitzhugh Lee. *Negroes and the Law in the Race's Battle for Liberty, Equality, and Justice under the Constitution of the United States.* Boston: Christopher Publishing House, 1937.

Thornbrough, Emma Lou. *T. Thomas Fortune: Militant Journalist.* Chicago: University of Chicago Press, 1972.

Vose, Clement. *Caucasians Only: The Supreme Court, the NAACP, and the Restrictive Covenant Cases.* Berkeley: University of California Press, 1967.

Washington, E. Davidson, ed. *Selected Speeches of Booker T. Washington.* Garden City, N.Y.: Doubleday, 1932.

Waskow, Arthur I. *From Race Riot to Sit-In, 1919 and the 1960's: A Study in the Connections between Conflict and Violence.* Garden City, N.Y.: Doubleday, 1967.

Webb, Walter Prescott, H. Baily Carroll, and Eldon S. Branda, eds. *The Handbook of Texas.* 3 vols. Austin: Texas State Historical Association, 1952, 1976.

Wells, Ida B. *Crusade for Justice: The Autobiography of Ida B. Wells.* Ed. Alfreda M. Duster. Chicago: University of Chicago Press, 1970.

Wharton, Clarence R. *History of Fort Bend County.* San Antonio: Naylor, 1939.

White, Dabney, ed. *East Texas: Its History and Its Makers.* New York: Lewis Historical Publishing, 1940.

White, G. Edward. *The American Judicial Tradition: Profiles of Leading American Judges.* New York: Oxford University Press, 1976.

White, Walter. *A Man Called White: The Autobiography of Walter White.* Bloomington: Indiana University Press, 1970.

Williams, Annie Lee. *A History of Wharton County, 1846–1961.* Austin: Von Voeckman-Jones, 1964.

Wolseley, Roland E. *The Black Press in the United States of America.* Ames: Iowa State University, 1971.

Wolters, Raymond. *Negroes and the Great Depression: The Problem of Economic Recovery.* Westport, Conn.: Greenwood Publishing, 1970.

Woodson, Carter G. *The Negro Professional Man and the Community: With Special Emphasis on the Physician and the Lawyer.* Washington, D.C.: Association for the Study of Negro Life and History, 1934.

Woodward, C. Vann. *Origins of the New South, 1877–1913.* Baton Rouge: Louisiana State University Press, 1951.

———. *Reunion and Reaction: The Compromise of 1877 and the End of Reconstruction.* 1st ed. Boston: Little, Brown, 1951.
———. *The Strange Career of Jim Crow.* 2d rev. ed. New York: Oxford University Press, 1957.


## Articles

Abramowitz, Jack. "The Negro in the Populist Movement." *Journal of Negro History* 38, no. 3 (July 1953): 257–89.
———. "Origins of the NAACP." *Social Education* 15, no. 1 (January 1951): 21–23.
Alexander, Charles. "The Crusade for Conformity: The Ku Klux Klan in Texas, 1920–1930." *Texas Gulf Coast Historical Association* 6, no. 1 (August 1962): 1–88.
Cushman, Robert E. "The Texas 'White Primary' Case: *Smith* v. *Allwright.*" *Cornell Law Quarterly* 30, no. 1 (September 1944): 66–76.
Evans, Luther Harris. "Primary Elections and the Constitution." *Michigan Law Review* 32 (February 1934): 451–56.
Frank, John P., and Robert F. Munro. "The Original Understanding of 'Equal Protection of the Laws.'" *Columbia Law Review* 50, no. 2 (February 1950): 131–69.
Frantz, Laurent B. "Congressional Power to Enforce the Fourteenth Amendment against Private Acts." *Yale Law Journal* 73, no. 8 (July 1964): 1353–84.
Gillette, Michael L. "The Rise of the NAACP in Texas." *Southwestern Historical Quarterly* 81 (April 1978): 393–416.
Goodwyn, Lawrence C. "Populist Dreams and Negro Rights: East Texas as a Case Study." *American Historical Review* 76, no. 5 (December 1971): 1435–56.
Gordon, Rita Werner. "The Change in the Political Alignment of Chicago's Negroes during the New Deal." *Journal of American History* 61, no. 3 (December 1969): 584–603.
Grave, John William. "Negro Disfranchisement in Arkansas." *Arkansas Historical Quarterly* 26, no. 3 (autumn 1967): 199–225.
Hainsworth, Robert Wendell. "The Negro and the Texas Primaries." *Journal of Negro History* 18, no. 4 (October 1933): 426–50.
Harlan, Louis R. "The Secret Life of Booker T. Washington." *Journal of Southern History* 37, no. 3 (August 1971): 393–416.

Hastie, William H. "Charles Hamilton Houston, 1895–1950." *Journal of Negro History* 35, no. 3 (July 1950): 355–58.

———. "Towards an Equalitarian Legal Order, 1930–1950." *Annals of the American Academy of Political and Social Science* 407 (May 1973): 18–31.

Haynes, Robert V. "The Houston Mutiny and Riot of 1917." *Southwestern Historical Quarterly* 76, no. 4 (April 1973): 418–39.

Hine, Darlene Clark. "The NAACP and the Supreme Court: Walter F. White and the Defeat of Judge John J. Parker, 1930." *Negro History Bulletin* 40, no. 5 (September–October 1977): 753–57.

Isaac, Paul E. "Municipal Reform in Beaumont, Texas, 1902–1909." *Southwestern Historical Quarterly* 78, no. 4 (April 1975): 409–30.

Jarmon, Le Marquis de. "Voting: One Hundred Years to the Beginning." In *Legal Aspects of the Civil Rights Movement,* ed. Donald B. King and Charles W. Quick. Detroit: Wayne State University Press, 1965.

*The Law Reporter* 41, no. 9 (March 24, 1930): 713.

Lynch, John R. "Some Historical Errors of James Ford Rhodes." *Journal of Negro History* 2, no. 4 (October 1917): 345–68.

Meier, August, and Elliott Rudwick. "Attorneys Black and White: A Case Study of Race Relations within the NAACP." *Journal of American History* 62, no. 4 (March 1976): 913–46.

*Michigan Law Review* 28 (1930): 613.

"The Riot at Longview, Texas." *The Crisis* 18, no. 6 (October 1919): 297–98.

Rudwick, Elliott M. "The Niagara Movement." *Journal of Negro History* 42, no. 3 (July 1957): 177–200.

Silard, John. "A Constitutional Forecast: Demise of the 'State Action' Limit on the Equal Protection Guarantee." *Columbia Law Review* 66, no. 5 (May 1966): 855–72.

"Southern Editorial Opinion on the Primary Decision." *The Crisis* 100 (June 1944): 186–87.

Van Alstyne, William W. "The Fourteenth Amendment, the 'Right' to Vote, and the Understanding of the Thirty-Ninth Congress." *Supreme Court Review* (1965): 33–86.

"The Waco Horror." *The Crisis* 12, no. 3 (July 1916, supplement): 18.

Wechsler, Herbert. "Toward Neutral Principles of Constitutional Law." *Harvard Law Review* 73, no. 1 (November 1959): 1–35.

Weeks, O. Douglas. "The White Primary." *Mississippi Law Journal* 8 (December 1935): 135–53.

———. "The White Primary, 1944–1948." *American Political Science Review* 42, no. 3 (June 1948): 500–510.

Wood, Forrest G. "On Revising Reconstruction History: Negro Suffrage, White Disfranchisement, and Common Sense." *Journal of Negro History* 51, no. 2 (April 1966): 98–113.

*Yale Law Journal* 41 (1932).

# *Index*